EDUCATION AND CULTURAL DIFFERE
LC 213 E37 1992

DATE DUE

JE 29 '93	AP 30 '98		
NO 28 '94	DE 18 '98		
AP 7 '95	OC 25 '99		
MY 2 '95	NV 6 '00		
JE 1 '95	NV 30 '00		
NO 2 '95	OC 12 '00		
DE 22 '95	NO 28 '00		
DE 12 '96	DE 19 '00		
AP 7 '97	JE 11 '01		
NV 29 '97	NO 17 '01		
JY 2 '97	DE 19 '01		
NO 20 '97	AP 5 '02		
RENEW	JE 10 '02		
DE 19 '97			
DE 19 '97	JE 3 '04		
	FE 9 '06		

EDUCATION AND
CULTURAL DIFFERENCES

REFERENCE BOOKS IN
INTERNATIONAL EDUCATION
(General Editor: Edward R. Beauchamp)
VOL. 15

GARLAND REFERENCE LIBRARY
OF SOCIAL SCIENCE
VOL. 594

Reference Books in International Education

Edward R. Beauchamp
General Editor

EDUCATION AND CULTURAL DIFFERENCES
New Perspectives

edited by
Douglas Ray and
Deo H. Poonwassie

GARLAND PUBLISHING, INC. • NEW YORK & LONDON
1992

Library of Congress Cataloging-in-Publication Data

Education and cultural differences : new perspectives / edited by
Douglas Ray, Deo H. Poonwassie.
    p.   cm. — (Garland reference library of social science ; vol.
594. Reference books in international education ; vol. 15)
    Includes index.
    ISBN 0-8240-6047-4
    1. Educational equalization. 2. Educational anthropology.
3. Indigenous peoples—Education—Case studies. 4. Minorities—
Education—Case studies. 5. Discrimination in education—Case
studies. 6. Intercultural education—Case studies. I. Ray,
Douglas. II. Poonwassie, Deo H. III. Series: Garland reference
library of social science ; v. 594. IV. Series: Garland reference
library of social science. Reference books in international
education ; vol. 15.
LC213.E37 1992
370.19—dc20   91-45117
                                                   CIP

Printed on acid-free, 250-year-life paper
Manufactured in the United States of America

These studies of cultural differences, and of the ways that education can make a difference to the lives of minorities, are dedicated to our students and readers, in hopes of a better tomorrow.

Acknowledgements

The development of this collection would have been impossible without the support of the Deans of Education at The University of Manitoba and The University of Western Ontario: John Stapleton and B. B. Kumlicka. Their financial contributions for support services were unstinting and substantial.

Insightful commentaries and suggestions for extension and revision were regularly available from colleagues, and Professor Romulo Magsino of The University of Manitoba and Drs. Jud Purdy and Aniko Varpalotai of the University of Western Ontario were particularly important.

The transformation of submissions into the finished product is always a time consuming and little rewarded task. Initial work was done by Cheryl Ann Beals-MacAulay, and after her departure the task was capably shared by Carol Mills, a wizard with complex computer presentations, and my Associate Beatriz Franco, who did the translations, consolidations, checking, and word processing.

SERIES EDITOR'S FOREWORD

This series of scholarly works in comparative and international education has grown well beyond the initial conception of a collection of reference books. Although retaining its original purpose of providing a resource to scholars, students, and a variety of other professionals who need to understand the role played by education in various societies or regions of the world, it also strives to provide up-to-date information on a wide variety of selected educational issues, problems and experiments within an international context.

Contributors to this series are well-known scholars who have devoted their professional lives to the study of their specialization. Without exception these men and women possess an intimate understanding of the subject of their research and writing. Without exception they have not only studied their subject in dusty archives, but they have also lived and travelled widely in their quest for knowledge. In short, they are "experts" in the best sense of that often overused word.

In our increasingly interdependent world, it is now widely understood that it is a matter of survival that we not only understand better what makes other societies tick, but that we also make a serious effort to understand how others, be they Japanese, German or Chilean, attempt to solve the same kinds of educational problems that we face in North America. As the late George Z.F. Bereday wrote: "[E]ducation is a mirror held against the face of a people. Nations may put on blustering shows of strength to conceal public weakness, erect grand facades to conceal shabby backyards, and profess peace while secretly arming for conquest, but how they take care of their children tells unerringly who they are" (*Comparative Method in Education*, New York: Holt, Rinehart & Winston, 1964, p. 5).

Perhaps equally important, however, is the valuable perspective that studying another education system (or its problems) provides us in understanding our own system (or its problems). To step outside of our own limited experience and our commonly held assumptions about schools and learning in order to look back at our system in contrast to another places it in a very different light. To learn, for example, how the Soviet Union or Belgium handle the education of a multilingual society; how the French provide for the funding of public education; or how the Japanese control admissions into their universities enables us to understand that there are alternatives to our own familiar way of doing things. Not that we can often "borrow" directly from other societies; indeed, educational arrangements are inevitably a reflection of deeply rooted political, economic and cultural factors that are unique to a society. But a conscious recognition that there are other ways of doing things can serve to open our minds and provoke our imaginations in ways that can result in new approaches that we would not have otherwise considered.

Since this series is intended to be a useful research tool, the editor and contributors welcome suggestions for future volumes as well as ways in which this series can be improved.

Edward R. Beauchamp
University of Hawaii

TABLE OF CONTENTS

Contents

III. Long Established Stigmas

IV. Integration of Recent Immigrants

Contents

V. Conclusion: Schooling and Teacher Education

SECTION I

INTRODUCTION:

IDEALS AND RESEARCH

MODERN INEQUALITY AND
THE ROLE OF EDUCATION

Douglas Ray

Inequality

Because it pervades human society, inequality has preoccupied some of the greatest minds of many civilizations. Even when advocating political or social reforms that reflect the best ideas of their times and cultures, thinkers and planners often disagree about many details, ignore some injustices close to them, fail to execute the designs they advocate, or otherwise stumble in their attempts to create a society that is equal. "Man is born Free and Equal, but everywhere he is in chains," proclaimed Rousseau, and the French Revolution was but one of the many famous experiments that tried, but failed, to bring equality into existence.

This book is about the interaction between ideals and reality, with the focus upon social inequality and education in modern society, and the possibilities for education to lessen the related problems. The contributors examine three forms of inequality that are widespread in current global society: 1) aboriginal societies in modern industrial states, 2) long-established communities that have been denied full status, and 3) differences arising from recent population migrations. Although the contributions emphasize western societies, they include several non-western civilizations.

Economic inequality may provide incentive by rewarding initiative. It also introduces problems--notably poverty (Bowen 1970). Throughout the world, most of the population lives in

3

depressed conditions, a depression that may not be so severe as to threaten life or create misery of the worst kind, but which galls its victims because they realize that others have much more wealth and opportunity, and that they can do little. Some of these poor persons are spurred to actions intended to promote greater justice by removing the inequality through working harder, smarter, longer, or (more directly still) by begging, theft, murder, war, or revolution.

One major problem for these programs of "self-improvement" is that such actions of the poor are easily offset by responses by the wealthy (Laszlo et al. 1980) who can manage to create a degree of security for themselves. Security can come from various forms of property (land, factories, etc.), strength, skills, ideas, beauty or wisdom--which are quite widely distributed in the population and can be stimulated through various social programs like education, health care, cultural and recreational improvement. In short, there is some potential for simultaneously increasing both the equality and the total wealth of society. It is the tragedy of many societies that wealth is counted so completely in the realm of land, bricks, and factory output rather than in social good.

There are exceptions. Japan was an inherently impoverished nation that has become rich through initiative that results mainly in high quality material products. Switzerland, Stratford, and Disneyland have won similar recognition for their excellence in personal services, artistic creativity and entertainment. All of these forms of material and intellectual contributions have aided their societies, partly by distributing wealth to regions that would otherwise have little. Would such solutions lose their effectiveness if they were created to serve *peoples* such as language or ethnic groups that are obviously in great need? What part would education play in creating conditions for the success of such social policy?

Political inequality, although less endemic, is also widespread. It refers to several possible conditions. Part of the population may be denied fundamental rights like the vote, the right to seek political office, or equal treatment by the courts. More commonly, some groups face constrained access to the courts or reduced chances of being heard on political questions.

They may be oppressed by laws that may have the support of the majority and are therefore strictly legal, but which are unequal, unjust and partial (Berger 1981). As numerous reports by Amnesty International (1962-1975) and United Nations (1981) report, some states fail to protect such disadvantaged groups from persecution by other citizens, and sometimes the state itself may be the abuser (Weeramantry, 1982).

One of the groups likely to be affected is women--who may be further identified and perhaps further disadvantaged politically by such other status indicators as "married" or "mothers." Other groups likely to be disadvantaged include the mentally or physically disabled. Some nations contain large groups of disadvantaged that are identified by language, religion, ethnicity, birthplace, citizenship, or status of political recognition. The obvious examples are the majority of South Africans, the millions of refugees in various nations, and the temporary residents of many lands. In some cases their political disadvantage extends over many generations, and may be accompanied by economic and social penalties. As Ghosh (1981) points out, there may be double burdens for some groups, for example, the female members of the disadvantaged ethnic or religious groups.

Social inequality exists even where neither economic nor political disadvantage accompanies it, but usually it reinforces the other forms of inequality. It reflects differences in the way that society acknowledges the interests of the particular group, ignoring their history, taboos, obligations, and aspirations. The consequences for the disadvantaged may be complex to remedy, for change of status (citizenship, religion, language, name, educational status or professional standing, occupation, etc.) may be denied by the rulers or unwanted by the minority.

Inequality in Modern Society

Three types of inequality are dealt with in this book, and each of them has several potential sub-groups. The first discusses *aboriginal peoples* in virtually all parts of the world, who in all cases are disadvantaged (in varying degrees) socially and politically, and usually economically. The justification for their survival, not merely as a collection of individuals but as a *separate and sometimes unique civilization*, assumes that they should have a choice of maintaining and developing their cultures, drawing as they wish from the societies around them, so long as there are no pressing arguments to the contrary (Cumming and Cumming 1972). It is the denial of this right to the majority of South Africans to participate in the benefits theoretically available in their society that makes Apartheid so repugnant. The most extreme forms of repression have been even more violent: genocide. This has occurred in several parts of the world in recent history. There are no more Beothucks in Newfoundland (Howley 1915), no more Tasmanians of Tasmania (Hughes 1987). Nearly the same has recently been accomplished in the Marshall Islands by dislocation (Caldicott 1984), and in the Brazilian jungle by settlement of the coastal peasants. Cultural dislocation may not be so obvious a form of genocide, but it may be equally disastrous.

Aborigines are peoples whose ancestors dominated continents and created great civilizations, but who may now be diminished, impoverished, and forlorn beggars in the lands of their ancestors (Jensen 1984). In the worst situations, they are still hunted as wild animals. The arguments for respecting aboriginal rights are therefore explored in a number of countries: Australia, New Zealand, The United States, Canada and Sweden.

Persistent Inequality, the second classification used in this book, refers to a condition that has been traditionally accepted or even justified. Although it has often included aborigines in the underclass, it does not necessarily victimize them. In fact, some aborigines may well be among the oppressors, either of newcomers or of other aborigines. Inequality--ranging up to slavery of various types--exists in many lands.

The societies studied here have "justified" their inequality by various excuses, which are often identified externally as racism, religious bigotry, feuds and conquests of long ago, even though nationals may excuse their practices with idealism. One famous example of traditional inequality is found in India, where for centuries the caste system held sway.

Although castes were officially discarded as bases for discrimination two generations ago, with the former "untouchables" (together with other disadvantaged castes or tribes renamed "scheduled castes") entitled to affirmative action programs (Zachariah 1982), the traditional social attitudes have not given way to a greater measure of acceptance. This official solution has not diminished the advantages of the higher castes. Not even the creation of India as a secular state has removed the pervasive and divisive influence of religion.

In the Nazi regime there was the brutal discrimination of the Holocaust, which has become a synonym for inhumanity. In some current societies, the oppressed try to call attention to their fates by calling upon the images of either Holocaust or Apartheid, even though the details may be different. The contributors to this volume examine widely diversified examples of traditional inequality in The Soviet Union (where a complex of religions, languages, races, and nationalities compete for status), China (where the Han family effectively predominates in a form of caste system in which the "national minorities" form a small part of the total population), the United States (racism), Northern Ireland and Bahrain (religion), and Britain (traditional class system). In Spain, there is a curious inversion of late, for the Basques who were so oppressed by Franco have become among the most prosperous and progressive workers in Spain, and they now have educational, cultural, and political rights that they were recently denied. But the divisions and resentment remain as deep as before.

The third type of inequality identified in this book may be the initial stages of the formation of a permanent and obdurate system of privilege and underclass (Wirt 1982). In many nations there have been recent population movements, and the newcomers (defined for our purposes as foreign born) may be grievously disadvantaged. Some newcomers have much higher status than others, and perhaps even higher status than some of those long established within the society. Japanese in Canada, Brazil or Australia, Chinese in Malaysia, Indians in Thailand or Germans in Paraguay may serve as examples.

Goal of Equal Status

The contributors to this book accept that equal rights should be extended if possible to all members of society, and education (not necessarily schooling, at least not exclusively) might support the efforts of all members of society to pursue this goal.

There are two basic approaches to the removal of social barriers in these modern situations. One of these is conscious assimilation--like the legendary "melting pot" of American society, which attempts to replace the older identity with a new one, in which little or nothing of the old survives (Glazer and Moynihan 1970). The second is the attempt to create a society that accepts or even celebrates cultural differences, and enables each community to develop its own sense of identity while contributing to and enjoying the collective system of the larger society (Mallea and Young 1984). Many nations have employed one or both of these models in their recent policies. Examples include The United States, Canada, Australia, Brazil, Israel, West Germany, France, The Soviet Union, and several Caribbean nations. However, these case studies will demonstrate that statements of policy are rarely perfectly reflected in society.

Education as a Solution to Inequality

No education system can create a society of equals--not even with a great deal of assistance from other institutions. Conversely, educational efforts are essential for changing the nature of society, and appropriate efforts may be directed through the schools and/or some other institution (such as the pioneer movement of the Soviet Union, the church, mosque or synogogue, the labor unions, the army, or the media). Usually reforms are coordinated, with various institutions selected for their prospect of success in reaching a particular part of the population and thereby effecting changes in attitudes and ultimately behavior. Usually youth are priority targets.

The key starting point for such programs is probably the identification of appropriate goals that might be embraced by most of the members of society. Often these will be found in the words of a prophet or political leader (Nehru for example), who may draw upon the roots of the society but demonstrate new social possibilities. Sometimes (as in the case of the American dream of the "melting pot") the words are formed by a playwright and spoken by an actor. New ideas may be proclaimed in songs or even jocularly introduced in popular publications like a comic strip or novel. Whatever the device, it must affect the ordinary person and the message must be convincing, penetrating, and inspiring. The authority of the author or messenger, or perhaps the situation, may give special impact. Jefferson, Bolivar, Lenin, Kenyatta, Gandhi, and Mao made their impact because they seized the moment, achieved the critical mass of supporters, and institutionalized their power. Even their "legendary wisdom" may be partly the creation of admiring journalists like John Reed[1] and subsequent historians.

Social and Technical Functions of Education

Education may be seen partly as a transmission of techniques that are useful for survival, but it is also the creation and perpetuation of social identity, of myths selected from the facts or even fabricated to enable people to endure and to create outstanding civilizations (Piddington 1951). Technical and social education are both present in language instruction and history, music and even in cooking. The purely technical requirements could be satisfied with a computer and various programs, but social education requires emotional considerations, including interaction, so that even filmed presentations which present data with a high degree of fidelity may prove to be inadequate.

The "social educational" claims are sometimes thought to be silly and idealistic, romantic and impractical. Why would Chief Smallboy ask Indian youth of Alberta to accompany him into the bush, to abandon their cars and comfortable homes, to live through the winter in tents, to eat game and berries in the

---

[1] John Reed was present during the Bolshevik Revolution. His *Ten Days That Shook the World* influenced public opinion and was generally flattering to Lenin.

manner of their ancestors? Why did Bishop Gruntvig assert that the Danes must create new folk high schools that glorified the past and defined a new future, thereby distinguishing themselves from their German-speaking neighbors who were following the Prussians into a new and great empire? (Stabler 1987). Why would Latvians aspire to a renewal of a tiny nation tied by history to the Hanseatic League when they could be a part of the Soviet Union with aspirations for the twenty-first century? (Pennar et al. 1971). Why would the Iranians turn away from the modernization of the Shah and return to the rigid clericalism of the Ayotollah? These examples deal with forty people to forty million people. To outsiders, some of these social objectives are incomprehensible. But to the convinced members of the group, they identify minimum objectives for maintaining their identity.

Values in Education

No research program and no educational reform has ever succeeded in removing all the social content from its curriculum (Myrdal 1967). Despite the educational excesses of a few infamous regimes like that of the Nazis (Mann 1939, Kneller 1941), no worthwhile educational system would emerge if we tried to eliminate the passion from subjects like history (Sewall 1987).

A strong case can be made for putting more passion into schooling, and that passion need not divide the population.

Measures of Equality

This book is concerned with the interaction between social equality and education (Lessard 1991). Three important measures which will be considered by the authors of case studies are *access, curriculum* and *the special case of teacher recruitment and training*.

Access

The simplest form of educational opportunity is the right to education: free basic schooling, secondary schooling which is diversified and available on the basis of merit, and access to higher education on the basis of merit. These objectives are affirmed in *The Universal Declaration of Human Rights* (1948) and subsequently by many other treaties (Ray and Tarrow 1987). *The International Convention on the Rights of the Child* (1989) is the latest United Nations standard.

Since many nations do not yet offer all their youth such opportunities, the means for extending the rights to schooling give one index of the equality of opportunity for that society (Farrell 1982; Rideout 1987). For example, the best education in South Africa is available only to whites; in Saudi Arabia to Muslims (Ghosh and Attieh 1987); in the Philippines to English speakers (Foley 1984). In all nations there are disadvantages, even though the accessibility problem shifts progressively in richer nations to the more sophisticated forms of education.

Curriculum

A second aspect of education is the quality of education, and particularly of the social education, that is available to minorities. Together with teaching other children about *their* responsibilities to minorities (Masemann and Iram 1987), such curricula may determine whether minority youth will persist and overcome.

In most cases, the ideal is claimed to be an educational system that 1) reflects something of the ideals of the minorities, 2) is controlled or strongly influenced by them, and 3) is taught by teachers who know and respect their interests. There will be differences of design, for some nations believe in a single school system with a curriculum designed to deal fairly with all the population, and beyond the immediate nation to a more complex world view (Haavelsrud 1976). Other states have divided the school system so that at least the initial stages of schooling can focus more completely upon the social values of the parents, even responding to distinctive ethnic groups, religions or sects, or languages.

Teacher education

An important contribution to equal opportunity among complex populations may come from teacher education. The most basic approach would examine the extent to which recruitment attracts teachers who would be acceptable--even inspirational--to the minority communities. Some of their own members would be ideal. In many nations it is difficult for the best qualified persons from minority communities to become interested in teaching, for other professions usually confer more wealth and prestige. In still others, there are severe problems (perhaps because of a history of neglect and abuse in schooling) in finding sufficient numbers with competitive academic backgrounds, and there are often bitter arguments about which persons would be best qualified for teaching in any schools-- including those of minorities. The remedies may lie in revising entrance requirements which are culturally biased, improving publicity, preparing students before they start professional training, providing scholarships or bursaries for candidates from minority communities. Because some graduates may have personal experiences that drive them away from any association with schools, reforms are doubly difficult.

Teacher education must also address a curriculum challenge. It should contribute to an understanding (shared by the whole profession) of the importance of and means of achieving equal opportunity despite complex population problems. For example, the curriculum for teachers of any school would include courses providing a comprehensive notion of human society, with no sub-humans, no sub-species, no superior breeds (Kallen 1982). It would affirm that no human beings were to be treated in a way that diminished their status. Conversely, no group would be denied their right to develop their culture, provided only that their teachings never infringed unduly on the rights of others. It would provide for linguistic and cultural background or enrichment as necessary, either for teachers who would deal with specific cultural groups or for those who would be expected to provide accurate and sympathetic interpretations to children of other cultures. Most scholarly associations and journals provide many studies that would be suitable for these purposes (Branson and Torney-Purta 1982, The Special Issue on Human Rights Education of *The Canadian Journal of Education 1986*, are examples).

The existence of the expected topics within teacher education may not be enough, for unless students are given the correct orientation, the lessons may be quite counterproductive. Omissions, or words and illustrations that convey biased and mistaken impressions, and actual factual errors may exist in the school books (McDiarmid and Pratt 1971). These researchers charged that the official books *taught prejudice* against certain Canadian cultural groups, so they recommended means by which the system should be reformed. Similar assessments of school materials are often made by members of various communities, probably with the interests of their own cultural group in mind. Because all aspects of education could be similarly scrutinized and reformed, this volume provides an initial step by considering educational policy (including curriculum) and teacher education.

References

Amnesty International. 1962-1975. *Annual Reports.* London: Amnesty International.

Berger, T. R. 1981. *Fragile Freedoms: Human Rights and Dissent in Canada.* Toronto: Clarke Irwin.

Bowen, I. 1970. *Acceptable Inequalities.* Montreal: McGill-Queen's University Press.

Branson, M. S., and J. Torney-Purta, eds. 1982. *International Human Rights, Society and the Schools.* Washington, D.C.: National Council for the Social Studies.

Caldicott, H. 1984. *Missile Envy: The Arms Race and Nuclear War.* New York: William Morrow.

Canadian Journal of Education. 1986. 11:3 (A special issue on Human Rights in Education).

Cumming, P. A., and N. H. Cumming. 1972. *Native Rights in Canada.* Toronto: General Publishing.

Farrell, J. P. 1982. Educational expansion and the drive for social equality. In P. G. Altbach, R. F. Arnove, and G. P. Kelly, eds. *Comparative Education.* New York: Macmillan.

Foley, D. 1984. Colonialism and schooling in the Philippines, 1898-1970. In P. G. Altbach, and G. P. Kelly, eds. *Education and the Colonial Experience.* 2nd ed. London: Transaction Books.

Ghosh, R. 1981. The double minority. In George Kurian and Ratna Ghosh, ed. *Women in the Family and the Economy: An International Comparative Survey.* Westport, Connecticut: Greenwood Press.

Ghosh, R., and A. Attieh. 1987. The right to education free from discrimination: The cases of India and Saudi Arabia. In N. B. Tarrow, ed. *Human Rights and Education*. London: Pergamon.

Glazer, N., and D. P. Moynihan. 1970. *Beyond the Melting Pot*. Cambridge, Mass.: Harvard University Press.

Haavelsrud, M., ed. 1976. *Education for Peace: Reflection and Action*. Guildford, Surrey, U.K.: IPC Science and Technology Press.

Howley, J. P. [1915] 1980. *The Beothucks or Red Indians: The Aboriginal Inhabitants of Newfoundland*. Toronto: Coles Reprint Series.

Hughes, R. 1987. *The Fatal Shore*. New York: Alfred A. Knopf.

Jensen, K. 1984. Civilization and assimilation in the colonized schooling of Native Americans. In P. G. Altbach, and G. P. Kelly, eds. *Education and Colonial Experience*. 2nd ed. London: Transaction Books.

Kallen, E. 1982. *Ethnicity and Human Rights in Canada*. Toronto: Gage.

Kneller, G. F. 1941. *The Educational Philosophy of National Socialism*. New Haven: Yale University Press.

Laszlo, E., J. Lozoya, A. K. Bhattacharya, J. Estevez, R. Green, and V. Raman. 1980. *The Obstacles to the New International Economic Order*. New York: Pergamon.

Lessard, C. 1991. Equality and inequality in Canadian education. In R. Ghosh and D. Ray, eds. *Social Change and Education in Canada*. Revised ed. Toronto: Harcourt Brace Jovanovich.

Mallea, J. R., and J. C. Young. 1984. *Cultural Diversity and Canadian Education: Issues and Innovations.* Ottawa: Carleton University Press.

Mann, E. 1939. *School for Barbarians: Education Under the Nazis.* London: Lindsay Drummond.

Masemann, V., and Y. Iram. 1987. The right to education for multicultural development: Canada and Israel.

McDiarmid, G., and Pratt, D. 1971. *Teaching Prejudice.* Toronto: OISE.

Myrdal, G. 1967. *Objectivity in Social Research.* New York: Pantheon.

Pennar, J., I. Bakalo, and G. Z. F. Bereday. 1971. *Modernization and Diversity in Soviet Education.* New York: Praeger.

Piddington, R. 1951. An anthropologist's viewpoint. In J. A. Lauwerys, and N. Hans, eds. *The Yearbook of Education.* London: Evans Brothers.

Ray, D., and N. B. Tarrow. 1987. Human rights and education: An overview. In N. B. Tarrow, ed. *Human Rights and Education.* London: Pergamon.

Reed, J. 1967. *Ten Days That Shook the World.* New York: Vintage (Republication of a 1917 journalist's account of the Bolshevik Revolution).

Rideout, W. M. 1987. Rights of access and equal opportunity: focus on Sub-Sahara Africa. In N. B. Tarrow, ed. *Human Rights and Education.* London: Pergamon.

Sewall, G. T. 1987. *American History Textbooks: An Assessment of Quality.* New York: Educational Excellence Network, Columbia University.

Stabler, E. 1987. *Founders: Innovators in Education, 1830–1980.* Edmonton: University of Alberta Press.

United Nations. 1981. *Yearbook on Human Rights for 1975–1976.* New York: United Nations.

Weeramantry, G. G. 1982. *An Invitation to the Law.* Sydney: Butterworth.

Wirt, F. M. 1982. The stranger within my gate: ethnic minorities and school policies in Europe. In P. G. Altbach, R. F. Arnove, and G. P. Kelly, eds. *Comparative Education.* New York: Macmillan.

Zachariah, M. 1982. Education for status development: the use of positive discrimination for scheduled castes in India. In P. G. Altbach, R. F. Arnove, and G. P. Kelly, eds. *Comparative Education.* New York: Macmillan.

PERSPECTIVES ON EQUALITY OF OPPORTUNITY IN EDUCATION

Deo H. Poonwassie

This chapter examines some concepts that may be used to analyze issues which arise from the case studies contained in this book. The broad spectrum of differences in human beings based on race, culture, class, sex, ideology and geographic location cannot be adequately covered in any one volume, far less a single chapter. The many factors that affect life chances are interrelated and complex; however, regardless of national, group, or individual distinctiveness there are certain concepts that are used for the analysis of the human condition. This chapter will discuss 1) social justice, 2) equality of educational opportunity, 3) equality of results, 4) equity and affirmative action, and will conclude with 5) an international perspective on the relations between rich and poor nations. Unless otherwise stated, the context is Western Nations with all their internal contradictions, dilemmas, and differences.

Social Justice

John Rawls (1971) proposed that the structure of society is the proper subject of social justice; he posed two principles of justice, namely:

> . . . each person is to have an equal right to the most extensive basic liberty compatible with a similar liberty for others . . . social and economic inequalities are to be

arranged so that they are both (a) reasonably expected to be to everyone's advantage, and (b) attached to positions and offices open to all. (P. 60)

Rawls goes on to explain the first principle by stating that people determine rights and liberties in their institutions by the creation of laws and regulations based on equal consideration for others; he is also aware that these rights and liberties prescribed by law are often in conflict. In expanding on the second principle he considers several fundamental precepts such as the system of natural liberty, liberal equality, and democratic equality.

Rawls' main aim was to propose a theory of justice based on fairness and different from "classical utilitarianism and intuitionist conceptions of justice." He proposed that the idea of justice or fairness be seen as original agreements among equals for their own interests. The principles of these original agreements are to govern all subsequent rights, duties, claims and liberties so that social benefits may be allotted through cooperation for the benefit of all persons. This Rawls regarded as "justice as fairness"; ". . . it conveys the idea that the principles of justice are agreed to in an initial situation that is fair" (p. 12).

This conception of justice assumes that circumstances are such that persons are equal and free to determine the criteria of fairness. But this is highly unlikely in a practical sense, hence the creation of hypothetical situations in which all conditions are ideal so that Rawls could begin the discussion of a theory of justice.

Another feature of this conception assumed that persons are "rational and mutually disinterested." Rawls was aware that the many caveats and conditions of his theory of justice were problematic and questionable. However, his determination to provide principles of justice as an example of contract theory different from utilitarianism and perfectionism provided approaches for considering the bases of social justice, chief among these being ". . . the basic structure of society, or more exactly, the way in which the major social institutions distribute fundamental rights and duties and determine the division of advantages from social cooperation" (p. 7).

Writers from Lenin to Rescher (1966) have argued that social justice is a prized ideal, involving both the political and economic aspects of people's activities. Distributive justice concerns "the whole economic dimension of social justice, the entire question of the proper distribution of goods and services within the society" (p. 5). The task of distributive justice is to determine a principle by which various ways of allocating the resources of society can be assessed. All too often society's allocation of goods and services are based on criteria determined by status: social status, level of employment, and inheritance. Thus in all societies there are people who are homeless, destitute, and starving. For western societies, Rescher (1966) proposed a *utility floor* below which no individual should be forced to exist. Hence the purpose of justice is to keep to a bare minimum (if not eliminate) the number of persons who live in a state of deprivation.

Although social justice is a prized value in western society, promoting a sense of fairness becomes problematic because the existence of injustice and inequality make a mockery of genuine efforts by a few to move forwards the achievement of this ideal. One of the major beliefs in western society is that education can assist in establishing social justice through the improvement of conditions for identifying and developing abilities. However, the attempts to equalize life chances through equality of educational opportunities pose real dilemmas and contradictions.

Equality of Educational Opportunity

With the publication of the *Equality of Educational Opportunity* report in the U.S. in July 1966 came a series of articles, books and conferences (for example: *Harvard Educational Review* 1968, Mosteller and Moynihan 1972, Jencks et al. 1972). The study was undertaken by the U.S. Office of Education because of a concern about "the lack of availability of equal educational opportunities for individuals by reason of race, color, religion, or national origin in public educational institutions at all levels in the United States . . ." (Quoted in Mosteller and Moynihan 1972, 4-5). This section will not deal with this report but will concentrate on a discussion of the concept: equality of educational opportunity.

James Coleman (1968) traced the shifts in interpretation of the concept of equality of educational opportunity. He began by examining the role of the child in pre-industrial Europe when the entire family was involved in production to the industrial revolution when families began to employ labor from other units. Then public schooling of the early nineteenth century started providing skilled manpower for the labor market. In the U.S.A. public schools were available for all except some poor, Blacks and Indians; thus as early as 1870 the effects of social structure could be seen as having an impact on the availability and distribution of educational opportunity. The meaning of educational opportunity always focussed on notions of equality and included the elements of free education up to a point, a common curriculum, attendance at the same school regardless of background, and equality within taxation geographic boundaries. The assumptions were that free schools would eliminate economic sources of inequality and that a common curriculum would ensure equality in educational opportunity. The responsibility for achievement was now shifted to the individual since the school would have provided an "opportunity," the role of the school now became passive.

There were (and still are) several challenges for this notion of equality of provision. For whom was the common curriculum designed? What was meant to be an "equalizer" was seen as unfair because the curriculum served the status quo; the students from economically poor homes were unable to cope with subject content designed for middle class children. This is still the case today in many countries where the system of public education produces inequality of educational opportunity because of a common curriculum. Yet a true dilemma is created when specialized curricula are designed for different groups because the child's future is pre-determined! Thus Coleman (1968) notes a shift in focus for the concept of equality of educational opportunity from *inputs* into the school system (e.g.

curricula, qualified teachers, facilities) to *outputs* or effects of schooling (e.g. achievement, job prospects).

Another issue raised in the consideration of this concept is "individual vs. group" dichotomy. On the one hand the individual is seen as having attributes that may be different from others (even within a particular ethnic/racial group) and therefore may wish to develop these talents or pursue a particular orientation. But laws reflecting human rights (e.g. in Canada the recognition of Native peoples as a group) emphasize the group rather than the individual. In practice western society still holds the value of rugged individualism high in a competitive, meritocratic social system. Usually criteria for special recognition of groups are not clear, creating animosity towards groups of people such as religious, linguistic, and visible minority groups, and, even when the basis for special treatment is fully explained, tensions and disagreements still arise because certain privileged groups prefer to keep their hegemonic advantage by exploiting the less fortunate in society.

In democratic societies freedom of choice is seen as a basic right; this liberty to choose appears to be antithetical to equality in education. "Equality may be promoted only at the expense of liberty and conversely liberty may be safeguarded only at the expense of equality" (Holmes 1985, 7). In the case of an urban-rural dichotomy there are problems in freedom of choice; in rural areas there are fewer choices in education than in urban areas. Larger concentrations of population in urban areas provide for more options and choices, and thus a greater degree of equality of educational opportunity. The potential for society compensating for such differences led Holmes (1985) to conclude "that decentralized control produces inequality in terms of provision" (p. 11). Centralization of education systems, on the other hand, has been a response to the provision of greater equality (Clignet 1974).

Husén (1979) recognizes the dilemmas in implementing and achieving equality in education: ". . . the educational system is there to impart competencies and therefore almost by necessity creates differences" (p. 89). Because people have different abilities, a uniform educational provision will allow some to take greater advantage of what is available. Hence the school system, in a meritocratic and competitive society, recognizes differences and reinforces them. The school which is expected to serve as an equalizer in fact becomes a perpetrater of inequality.

The second dilemma is seen in the equality--meritocracy relationship. Husén (1979) sees an increased emphasis on progressively intense competitive society. The influence on the lives of people based on meritocratic achievement provides unequal distribution of privileges in western societies; and further, these privileges tend to be passed on to the next generation and serve as "a substitute for the inherited privileges in the ascriptive society" (p. 90).

Equality of educational opportunity is seen according to the filter through which it is viewed. The educationist sees contradictions and dilemmas which undermine it as an analytic tool. From the political angle, equality of educational opportunity is a convenient principle to uphold because of the particular ring of democracy and freedom of choice. False as these may be, these ideas are generally acceptable to upholders of the status quo who obviously take advantage of this from a privileged position. To the economically poor in society, equality of educational opportunity is a myth and a convenient slogan of the powerful to maintain the hierarchical arrangements of society. Jencks et al. (1972) concluded that educational opportunity in schools would not produce equality in society; more fundamental changes in the structure of society and in the economic conditions of the poor must be effected before we see movement towards equality. While recognizing the limitations of school's influence, equality of educational opportunity serves the interests of particular individuals who can compete successfully in a meritocratic society. It is a passive and mythical conception to those who are not advantageously placed in a highly technocratic and industrialized society.

Equality of Results

The provision of physical requirements for schooling such as buildings, books, and school personnel does not ensure or produce equal achievement (Jencks et al. 1972, Mosteller and Moynihan 1972). Equality of educational opportunity, with all its contradictions and dilemmas, maintains that the individual will achieve according to his/her ability if provided with the opportunity to do so. What constitutes "opportunity" in this narrow sense is the physical requirements for education. This individualistic approach to educational opportunity satisfies the functionalist elite in western society whose ideology prescribes that meritocracy and competition are the bedrocks of progress and success. Psacharopoulos and Woodhall (1985) regard this approach as passive and merely concerned with inputs into the system of education. The equality of results approach is seen as active and considers output as a measure of achievement (Anisef et al. 1982a); in other words, for several groups of people (e.g. aboriginals, blacks in the U.S., and recent immigrants) the provision of basic requirements such as buildings and books is not enough for success. Other factors such as educational background, cultural values, family life, and family income determine whether students will be able to benefit from the public provision of educational opportunities (Anisef et al. 1982a). The schools therefore have to go beyond the provision of facilities.

Equality of condition suggests that an equal distribution of needed goods and services be provided for all members of society so that the biologically inherited characteristics (such as color, race, sex) do not influence the equal allocation of resources and neither socio-economic differences nor the existing hierarchical power structure in society should affect the allocation of requirements for living. The school cannot be called upon to *equalize* the persistent inequalities based upon economic and social position; in fact the school transmits and perpetuates these inequalities (Tawney 1964). An equality-of-results approach seeks to diminish these unfair advantages which appear to preserve the advantages of the status quo.

In a comprehensive study dealing with the pursuit of equality of opportunity in post-secondary education in Ontario, Canada, Anisef et al. (1982b) confirmed that inequality of educational opportunity reflected differences in social class, ethnicity, gender, geographical region, and financial position. These inequalities were manifested in poor living conditions, low self-esteem and a feeling of powerlessness; so while the educational institutions were "open to all residents," individuals and groups were unable to take advantage of these "opportunities" because they did not meet the criteria for entry. Suggestions for correcting these inequalities fall into three basic patterns.

First, the education system must be restructured to meet the needs of all members of society. Providing equal opportunity for participation in education does not mean the availability of *the same* or the *identical* conditions for learning, nor does it mean that there should be separate school systems based on race, class, gender, or neighborhood mainly because *separate* does not mean or imply *equal* (Blair 1990). The school system must be reformed to consider the abilities of students, the cultural values, the home background and the initial exposure to education.

Second, the school system must implement measures of early intervention. These will include a careful analysis of needs in the home that deal with education of the parents, employment income, and psychological factors such as self-esteem, personal power, and social acceptance. The provision of adequate day care (a western phenomenon) and early childhood education must be seen as necessities if the socially disadvantaged are to receive initial parity at the educational gates. Curricula must be designed so as to include the values and language of the people being served.

Third, compensatory and remedial education must be available in the educational system (Anisef et al. 1982b). Because of the lack of formal initial education many people and groups tend to be left out of mainstream education. Evidence of this can be seen in most countries today; for example, the recent immigrants and their children in Western Europe (West Indians in Britain, Turks in West Germany), aboriginal peoples (Canada, U.S.A., Australia, New Zealand, Norway) and peoples of lower castes (India) are often educationally disadvantaged. The phenomenon of elitism in education militates against this approach; social Darwinism in education (i.e. the survival of the best and the brightest in a meritocratic, competitive society) is upheld and actively promoted by the powerful in society.

Equity and Affirmative Action

If we subscribe to the concept of equality of results, that is, we are concerned about what comes out of the educational system, then we must be prepared to repair some of the imbalances by providing extra resources to parts of the system where it is required. In other words the responsibility for success or failure in education must be shifted from the individual alone to the educational system (Husén 1979). Groups within society (ethnic, religious, immigrant) are treated differently based on a multitude of criteria (such as skin colour, political affiliation); members of certain groups enjoy greater privileges and a larger share of society's resources without concern for the plight of other groups (such as aboriginal peoples in Australia or New Zealand). There needs to be an *equity principle* (Rescher 1966) by which a redistribution of resources can take place; surpluses can be shared without hardship to the privileged but with considerable advantage to those who are in need.

At first, this principle appears to support the unequal distribution of resources in any given society; and it is clearly so. However, if we subscribe to a principle of social justice then it is imperative that all members of society be given a fair chance to contribute to the general good and also be provided with conditions conducive to developing their abilities. This means less of the surplus (tax dollars) to those who "have" and more to those who do "not have." An equity principle that involves fairness and social justice requires a redistribution of resources; this redistribution manifests itself in the form of affirmative action programs (an example of which is compensatory education discussed above).

One of the major issues of the 1990's will be accessibility to education--which form depends on where you are in the world. In poor countries the loudest cry will be for access to elementary school and literacy training; in rich countries the emphasis will be on accessibility to post-secondary education. The demands will be made by groups that are under-represented in institutions at various levels; for example, racial minorities, aboriginal peoples, the physically and mentally handicapped, and women will be demanding their fair share of places and resources available for education and training. Minority groups in the United States of America, Canada, England and Australia, and in several other countries, have been on the rocky road to fair treatment in education for several decades but the results have been questionable. The best examples have been documented in the United States of America.

The Civil Rights Act of 1964 in the U.S., Section 402, deplored the unavailability of equal educational opportunities for individuals by reason of race, colour, religion or national origin. The explicit purpose of this act was that no individual should be identified, yet Monteller and Moynihan (1972) noted that the act was really concerned about blacks. Programs of compensatory education of various types (e.g. Head Start and Upward Bound) mushroomed all across the country. Affirmative action, that is, preferential treatment of racial minorities in education and employment, was encouraged by federal departments. This was the great effort by the U.S. to provide equal opportunities, especially for blacks, Indians and Hispanics.

In June 1978 a Supreme Court decision was handed down on one of the most controversial cases dealing with affirmative action: *Allan Bakke v. Regents of the University of California*. Very simply, Allan Bakke, a white student, was denied entry to medical school; he took his case to court on a charge of reverse discrimination. He won the case and was admitted to medical school. But the ruling was not clear about the legality of affirmative action--it ruled that quotas based on minority group membership were illegal, yet race can be used as a "factor in admissions procedures designed to foster educational diversity" (Fields 1988, A14). In 1978 this was regarded as a blow to the civil rights movement (and especially to affirmative action) in the U.S.A. Ten years later the arguments for and against preferential treatment of minority groups in education are just as controversial.

The arguments against affirmative action are essentially based on the principles of competition and meritocracy: it is a free market and only the best should be chosen. Another argument is that blacks in the U.S. do *not* perform as well as whites in higher education, and this puts black students at a double disadvantage: in addition to lower achievement, they realize their grades may have been inflated because of their race, still further undermining their self-esteem. It should be clear that selecting unqualified or underqualified students to compete with well qualified peers will end in disaster regardless of race, color, or gender. It is a recipe for perpetuating failure. The answer is intervention at all levels of schooling starting with pre-kindergarten. But it costs money to correct imbalances in all the related deficit areas of minority peoples--employment, housing, education, drug abuse, and health. The school cannot correct these compounded problems. Affirmative action programs, when practised according to the principles of equality-of-results, provide a glimmer of hope for minority peoples. Whereas the entry point may differ for educational programs, standards at the exit point should be the same as for anyone else regardless of race, color, or gender. The crucial and important factor is the quality, quantity, and variety of support that the minority student receives along the way between entry and exit; this is what makes the difference between equity and equality in educational opportunity.

International Perspectives

The concepts discussed so far can be used for analysis of situations within nations and communities; they are also applicable to international circumstances, but the scope of interpretation of variables becomes wider and even more complex. In considering an overview of the world order we observe dichotomies such as rich and poor nations, developed and less developed countries, first and third worlds, industrial and agrarian economies, east and west, north and south, capitalist and communist. Then there are the international organizations such as the United Nations, World Bank, European Economic Community, and Council for Mutual Economic Assistance. And probably the most influential organizations in the world are the multi-national (trans-national) corporations that control every aspect of our beings directly or indirectly; for example, controlling the sources of energy (Exxon, Shell, Texaco); controlling food and its distribution (Carghill Grain Company); controlling communications (ITT, Reuters), and controlling finances (Citibank, Lloyds).

World view is shaped by information and influence (among other things); the theories and actors listed above provide us with approaches for assessing quality of life that exist in different parts of the world. A closer look will reveal such extremes as surplus food versus starvation; high levels of education or training versus illiteracy and ignorance; high versus low life expectancy. In analyzing the roles of multi-nationals we find mechanisms for assisting economically less fortunate countries, but these very organizations exercise considerable power and control over other nations (Meier 1984, Sen 1984, Torrie 1983). The domination of trade and development by industrial countries (who primarily trade among themselves and develop each others' economy) has contributed a great deal to the economic inequality that exists among nations today. The spheres of influence of the USSR and the USA embrace or affect every third world country on this planet to the extent that if a particular ideology is not embraced, these less developed countries can choose from the apocalyptic list of armed invasion, trade exchange, denial of food supplies, and denial of loans on the international market (Afghanistan, Cuba, Nicaragua).

In 1969 a Commission on International Development chaired by Lester B. Pearson submitted its report entitled *Partners in Development* (called the Pearson report). This commission was sponsored by a major financial institution, the World Bank. (Considering the role of the World Bank in the underdevelopment of third world countries, e.g. Brazil and The Sudan, one can be very skeptical about the unstated purposes of this commission report or, worse, the use made of information gathered by a very high-powered group under the impeccable international reputation of Lester B. Pearson!). The industrialized nations recognized the growing gap between developed and developing countries and were interested in finding ways to "reduce disparities and reduce inequalities" through cooperation in international development--the report labelled it "A Question of Will." In a summary of the report there were ten objectives listed for strengthening international development:

1. To create a framework for free and equitable international trade . . .
2. To promote mutually beneficial flows of foreign private investment . . .
3. To establish a better partnership, a clearer purpose and a greater coherence in development aid . . .
4. To increase the volume of aid . . .
5. To meet the problem of mounting debts . . .
6. To make aid administration more effective . . .
7. To redirect technical assistance . . .
8. To slow the growth of population . . .
9. To revitalize aid to education and research . . .
10. To strengthen the multilateral aid system . . .
    (Pearson 1969, 14-21)

The gap between rich and poor countries is greater than in 1969; the financial debt of third world countries has grown to such large proportions that a few, including Brazil, Chile, Peru, and Nigeria, cannot afford to pay the interest on their loans. The unequal distribution of resources, technology, and capital has contributed to global social and economic injustices. It is most noteworthy that the social scientists are gradually beginning to analyze and explain the courses of misery and backwardness in less fortunate countries (Torrie 1983, Oxaal et al. 1975, Roxborough 1979, Chilcote 1984).

In 1980 a report entitled *North-South: A Program for Survival* was published (Brandt 1980), it contained the findings of an independent commission on international development issues under the chairmanship of Willy Brandt. (In this report, called the Brandt report, North denotes the developed countries including Australia and New Zealand, while South includes all developing countries which are mainly situated in the South. Although these terms "North" and "South" are not clearly defined, they are associated with a large gap in quality of life).

This report was submitted to the United Nations. Whereas the Pearson report was concerned about creating partnerships for strengthening international development to provide some form of equality and justice on the international scene, the Brandt report had the same concerns but chose to focus on creating a new international economic order (NIEO). The emphasis was not only on survival but on peace and "how to overcome world hunger, mass misery and alarming disparities between the living conditions of rich and poor" (p. 13).

The Brandt (1980) report contained major elements of a program to redress some of the causes of poverty in developing nations, which are summarized as follows:

1.   A large-scale transfer of resources to developing countries.
2.   An international energy strategy.
3.   A global food program.
4.   A start on some major reforms in the international economic system. (p. 276)

A summary of recommendations contained in this report included: a consideration of measures to alleviate the misery in the poorest countries first; attention to removing hunger and malnutrition; developing programs to deal with population--growth, movement and environment, disarmament; assault on major problems from within the poor countries; trade; industrialization; the role of transnational corporations, investment and sharing technology; reforming the world monetary order; developing a new (more equitable) approach to development finance and better coordination and use of resources within international organizations. The role of education in implementing any of these is crucial and complex.

Coombs (1985) provides us with a global perspective on education and maintains that the most significant dimension is a "crisis of confidence in education itself." Studies in the sixties and seventies (for example Coleman 1968, in the USA) have already suggested that education alone cannot solve the problems of inequality and social injustice. Coombs notes that although the educational environment has changed on a world-wide scale the problems for education have not been solved but are compounded. He lists four major environmental factors that affect education: economic changes, political instability and eruptions, demographic changes, and changes in educational thought itself.

Using cross-national data, Fry (1981) reports that the expansion of schooling shows little relationship with inequality while economic dependency has the strongest association. On the international level, from the data collected, Fry concludes that

> . . . those societies most dependent on foreign capital have the greatest degree of inequality . . . it appears that greater equality does not result from the expansion of schooling, but rather from fundamental structural changes that reduce dependency on foreign capital. (p. 115)

Education can theoretically promote equity in this environment of international differences and tension; this sentiment has been echoed by world leaders and cross-national organizations.

The Fry (1981) research is reflected in recent international studies like *Education for All* (Unesco et al. 1990) and *Investing in the Future: Setting Educational Priorities in the Developing World* (Hallak 1990). These international perspectives renew the thrust of the Pearson arguments, calling for an international partnership dedicated to dramatic improvements of the world's poorest schools.

Conclusion

This chapter brings together some basic concepts and issues that are germane to each of the ensuing sections. In analyzing the case studies contained in this book, the issues raised by social justice, equality of educational opportunity, equality of results, equity and affirmative action at both the local and international levels should create considerable debate and discussion. These are not new issues, but the context in which they are provided allows for easy comparison and critical thought.

It is clear from the overviews presented in the introductions to sections II, III, and IV that issues pertaining to social justice are complex, convergent and sometimes contradictory. Justifiable positions are often held, depending on one's situation in the social structure, one's ethnicity and above all one's ideology. While the principle of fairness is basic to all topics considered in this book, cases have been discussed elsewhere in equality (Brown 1988).

Schooling and education are seen as pre-requisites for the achievement of a better quality of life; but this is not supported by research cited in this chapter; indeed Tawney (1964) sees the public school and inherited wealth as the twin pillars of inequality. The social structures of nations must be reformed to accommodate the needs of all based on an equitable distribution of goods, services and resources.

References

Anisef, P., N. R. Okihiro, and C. James. 1982a. *Losers and Winners*. Toronto: Butterworths.

_____. 1982b. *The Pursuit of Equality: Evaluating and Monitoring Accessibility to Post-Secondary Education in Ontario*. Toronto: Ontario Ministry of Education.

Blair, S. 1990. Congress should reject "separate but equal" aid programs. *The Chronicle of Higher Education*, March 7, A52.

Brandt, W. 1980. *North-South: A Program for Survival*. Cambridge, Mass.: The MIT Press.

Brown, H. P. 1988. *Egalitarianism and the Generation of Inequality*. Oxford: Clarendon.

Chilcote, R. H. 1984. *Theories of Development and Underdevelopment*. Boulder, Colorado: Westview.

Clignet, R. 1974. *Liberty and Equality in the Educational Process*. Toronto: John Wiley & Sons.

Coleman, J. 1968. The concept of equality of educational opportunity. *Harvard Educational Review* 38(1): 7-22.

Coombs, P. H. 1985. *The World Crisis in Education. The View from the Eighties*. Oxford: Oxford University Press.

Fields, C. M. 1988. 10 years after Bakke ruling, opinions on affirmative action still polarized. *The Chronicle of Higher Education*, June 29, A14.

Fry, G. W. 1981. Schooling, development and inequality: Old myths and new realities. *Harvard Educational Review* 51(1): 107-115.

Hallak, J. 1990. *Investing in the Future: Setting Educational Priorities in the Developing World*. Paris: UNESCO, International Institute for Educational Planning.

Harvard Educational Review. 1968. Vol. 38, No. 1.

Holmes, B., ed. 1985. *Equality and Freedom in Education. A Comparative Study*. London: George Allen and Unwin.

Husén, T. 1979. *The School in Question*. Oxford: Oxford University Press.

Jencks, C., M. Smith, H. Acland, M. J. Bane, D. Cohen, H. Gintis, B. Heyns, and S. Michelson. 1972. *Inequality. A Reassessment of the Effect of Family and Schooling in America*. New York: Basic Books.

Meier, G. M., ed. 1984. *Leading Issues in Economic Development*. 4th ed. Oxford: Oxford University Press.

Mosteller, F., and D. P. Moynihan. 1972. *On Equality of Educational Opportunity*. New York: Random House.

Oxaal, I., T. Barnett, and D. Booth, eds. 1975. *Beyond the Sociology of Development*. London: Routledge and Kegan Paul.

Pearson, L. B. 1969. *Partners in Development*. New York: Praeger.

Psacharopoulos, G., and M. Woodhall. 19185. *Education for Development. An Analysis of Investment Choices*. New York: Oxford University Press, published for the World Bank.

Rawls, J. 1971. *A Theory of Justice*. Cambridge, Mass.: Belknap.

Rescher, N. 1966. *Distributive Justice.* New York: Bobbs-Merrill.

Roxborough, I. 1979. *Theories of Underdevelopment.* London: Macmillan.

Sen, A. 1984. *Resources, Values and Development.* Oxford: Basil Blackwell.

Tawney, R. H. 1964. *Equality.* (With an introduction by R. M. Titmus). London: George Allen and Unwin.

Torrie, J., ed. 1983. *Banking on Poverty. The Global Impact of the IMF and World Bank.* Toronto: Between the Lines.

UNESCO, World Bank, UNICEF and UNDP. (1990). *Education for All.* Washington, D. C.: World Bank.

SECTION II

ABORIGINAL PEOPLES

ABORIGINAL POPULATIONS AND EQUAL RIGHTS IN EDUCATION: AN INTRODUCTION

Deo H. Poonwassie

Aboriginal peoples[1] of the world have suffered from the oppression of colonialism, albeit delivered in different systems. This section deals with several examples of these circumstances in both northern and southern nations, where there have been both significant successes and crashing failures to recognize the special conditions of Aboriginal claims in education.

Attempts by missionaries and government agencies to "civilize" and "educate" aborigines have taken many forms, with the most obnoxious being residential schools which created lasting scars on the psyches of many aboriginal students. Some of these individuals, now adults, are telling stories of abuse, regimentation, and neglect. These schools attempted to eliminate languages, religions, and other aspects of aboriginal culture.

Schools have assisted various nations in controlling the development of aboriginal peoples: curricula imbued with alien values have devastated the self-confidence of their youth. The effects of this are seen in high drop-out rates in schools, personal disorientation, and consequent social problems. While

---

[1] *Peoples* in international law refers to a group of persons who are entitled to be treated as one group for cultural, economic and political programs. Sometimes the word will be employed as a claim without being widely recognized. Some governments will deny any justification for using the term "people" (or the more inflammatory claim of nation) because of its challenge to their authority.

schools have thwarted the progress of aboriginal peoples, it must be made clear that bad living conditions such as poor housing and sanitation, high unemployment, and the lack of political power have all added to the many injuries suffered by aboriginal peoples.

Recently these peoples are recognizing the problems they face and are beginning to confront their situation and then develop the powers that can initiate and sustain change. First, aboriginal peoples are analyzing their own internal strengths, potentials, and institutions. Second, they are using political (and sometimes violent) means to convince governments that their situation is intolerable and needs immediate attention. They are proposing ways to improve the essentials. Aboriginal peoples in the developed countries are no longer sitting back and accepting the evils of history; they are on the march to improve their socio-economic conditions for better living, self-determination, and a renewed pride.

Deirdre Jordan shows that the history of the Australian Aborigine included attempted genocide: they were not regarded as human beings in the early days of European settlement. As Jordan addresses the current issues of schooling and teacher training, she makes it clear that the schools still perpetuate elements of racism. In an attempt to resist this menacing discrimination, aboriginal youngsters adopted a negative self-image as a form of resistance, and over time internalized these values. The institution of schooling that was once used to destroy aboriginal culture is now being used to preserve and promote it. Jordan describes a system of "two days" schooling to include "white knowledge" within aboriginal culture.

Teacher training for the Australian Aborigine appears to be quite inadequate for the needs of this population. Initiatives such as the *Enclave Support Program* provide only a very feeble attempt to provide teachers trained from the Aboriginal population of Australia.

Deo H. Poonwassie hypothesizes that the imposition of a foreign schooling system on the aboriginal populations of Canada (traditionally called Indians, Eskimos and Métis, but now often First Nations) has resulted in alienation, cultural destruction, and consequent poverty. Education is seen as a crucial element in the development of the aboriginals of Canada. He goes on to analyze a successful model for teacher training in Manitoba, where First Nations are both a significant part of the population and widely distributed. The features of this program include: 1) community involvement, 2) support systems and finances, 3) cooperation between agencies, 4) strong commitment of the aboriginal peoples and the students, and 5) a goal of self-determination.

Poonwassie points out that further education/training and economic development must be planned and executed simultaneously; the growth of one does not benefit the community without the other. While the comparisons of aboriginal living conditions with those of the third world are clear and the analysis is helpful, it remains a limited conceptual tool: political autonomy remains a more accessible solution within the third world than for the First Nations of Canada because the latter are so widely dispersed and insignificant in total numbers.

Graham Smith addresses the problems of assimilation experienced by the Maori people of New Zealand and postulated an approach of educational resistance through *Kura Kaupapa Maori* (total immersion in Maori language and culture schooling). The dominant *Pakeha* (white) influences are described and placed historically from a revised Maori perspective.

The struggle to resist Pakeha domination and assimilation is evident in the Maori recognition of the importance of the Maori language. The proposal of an alternative--*Te Kohanga Reo* (the language of the nursery)--involves an immersion of pre-schoolers in the Maori language and cultural environment. The continuation of schooling at the upper levels becomes a problem because there are few teachers who are trained in the Maori langauge. The Kaupapa schooling is important because its graduates can participate fully in New Zealand society while maintaining their language and culture.

The challenge is clear: to provide appropriate schooling for Maori children within the educational system. Smith believes that the Maori are politicised to this end for pursuing the goals of cultural and social survival.

While Tom Svensson recognizes the complexities of claims to aboriginal status by the *Sámi* people (formerly called the Lapps), he advocates a strategy of adaptation through improved educational opportunities. His chapter draws from anthropology and history and comments on the impact of missionary intervention through segregated schools based on ethnic origin and occupation. The folk high school, the boarding school and the Nordic Sámi Institute are all evidence of schooling and education as instruments of adaptation (and assimilation!).

The notion of developing cultural competence by establishing knowledge bases rooted in educational, political, and social institutions constitutes an on-going struggle by the Sámi people. The development of language, crafts, and employment skills are crucial for survival, but equal importance may be attached to the promotion of the arts: poetry, drama, novels, and the traditional ceremonies. The restoration of Sami autonomy can only be achieved by pursing ethno-political and educational goals. Svennson postulates that for minorities, this can be achieved best through bi-cultural competence. In the formulation of a contemporary Sámi ideology--a basis for policy formation--education as an instrument for implementing policy is decisive in the road to self-government.

Linda Lippitt and Mary Romero provide an example of excellence in aboriginal education from the United States. Their case study examines the Santa Fe Indian School in New Mexico, which stands out as a beacon in Indian-controlled education. They sketch historical inequities suffered by the Pueblo people through government policies in land ownership, housing, employment, and education. While they document the assimilationist policies of the off-reserve boarding school, Lippitt and Romero show how the Indian people were able to redirect these policies into actions for self-government, pride, and dignity by re-establishing the Santa Fe Indian School in 1981. The Pueblo Governors of this school were able to use public policies for establishing a residential school according to the wishes and needs of their people. This Indian School stands out as an example of local control that works.

EDUCATION AND THE STRUGGLE FOR ADEQUATE CULTURAL COMPETENCE IN THE MODERN WORLD: THE SÁMI CASE

Tom G. Svensson

To ethnic minorities claiming aboriginal status, cultural difference remains complicated, both in terms of formal training from the existing school system and from informal socialization. Since the minority groups in question usually are weak, both in actual power and in numbers, their strategy for coping with this dilemma of inequality is the ability to adapt to life in a culturally plural situation. In the following presentation the process toward improving educational opportunities will be explored. The perspective is anthropological, laying stress on education as a cultural-political process.

Before presenting my case, let me offer some facts concerning the Sámi minority situation. The *Sámi* are an indigenous minority people living in Norway, Sweden, Finland, and the Soviet Union. The total population is estimated to be 60,000; most are in Norway. The 2,000 Sámi of the Kola peninsula in the USSR will not be treated in the following paper, mainly because on vital points their minority situation is not comparable to the situation prevailing in the three Nordic countries. Originally the Sámi were autonomous in terms of politics as well as culture.

Sámi adaptation to marginalization and life in rather small dispersed groups resulted in their gradual encapsulation within the increasing domains of established nation-states. By the sixteenth century this process was consolidated by formal taxation to the respective Crown and the beginning of missionary activities, both of which led to increased controls and claims of national sovereignty over the marginal regions mainly inhabited and utilized by the Sámi. Throughout the centuries that followed, the grip on the Sámi as a people was tightened further, and the ecological niche necessary for their traditional resource development was gradually encroached upon, in particular after the advent of the industrial revolution which began in Scandinavia about 1880. This revoking of Sámi autonomy has continued into our own time, with the only real difference being that during the last forty years, an ethnopolitical mobilization has occurred. The Sámi school system is part of this loss of autonomy, and with the above background in mind we examine various aspects of the system of education and socialization toward career opportunities available to the Sámi.

Historical Background

Among the Sámi, formal education dates back to the early part of the seventeenth century, when schools were established in Sámi land through missionary policy initiated by the state. It was the expressed interest of the nation-states to have all their subjects converted to the official state religion (Lutheranism), which required incorporating the Sámi with their pagan beliefs. This policy coincided with the Reformation and transition from Catholicism to Protestantism, which endorsed state superiority *vis-à-vis* the church in matters of property and power. Erecting churches with specifically defined parishes in Lapland and Finnmark, together with educating some Sámi as clergymen to serve in the area, was considered the most effective means to achieve this end. Basic literacy, ability to read and write, in addition to substantial knowledge of the Lutheran faith, were the subjects to be taught in these schools. There was no intention of offering a general education. Moreover, it was decreed that priests should act as travelling teachers, moving from one place to another to cover the Sámi areas distant from the few permanent schools. The explicit task of these travelling teachers, called "*katekets*," was to improve the level of education among the Sámi and to carry on and speed up the Christianization process. The gradual development of schools in Sámi districts went on, and as early as 1723 seven schools (one for each parish in Swedish Lapland) were established. This was more than one hundred years before the passage of the 1842 statute requiring education on the primary school level for Swedish citizens. Even if bilingualism was considered an important factor at this early stage of the Sámi school system, competence in Sámi and one of the Scandinavian tongues was constrained to clerical and missionary activities. The focus laid on certain school subjects was heavily influenced by an assimilationist policy, the aim of which was to reduce Sámi cultural distinctiveness in favor of conformity to the life style and ideology of the larger society.

In terms of education the assimilationist policy aimed at cultural conformity. The Sámi way of life, with its special use of land and reindeer pastoralism, gained some exemptions. However, when the clash of interests between the Sámi and the dominant society, with its growing engagements in the industrial development of resources in the Sámi land, started to be more severely felt (during the later part of the nineteenth century), the emphasis on non-Sámi training and the neglect of Sámi culture in the school system led to their inferiorization. The opportunity to acquire appropriate knowledge and skills for coping with inter-ethnic conflicts was virtually unavailable to the Sámi. In facing the demands of modern times, with their ever increasing pressure on the Sámi and their land, the Sámi school system appeared both irrelevant and insufficient.

This inadequate and deficient schooling was reinforced in the beginning of the twentieth century with the institution of a nomad school system, mainly reserved and designed for children belonging to reindeer herding families. In order to give the Sámi school system more consistency and uniformity, the nomad schools were meant to offer as good as possible an education for children with a nomadic life style which in no way would make them break away from the nomadic way of life (Sameutredningen 1975). At the turn of the century there were no less than five different forms of schools available to Sámi children, which maintained diversity in quality and standard of formal schooling. After several years of parliamentary inquiry this school reform was inaugurated in Sweden in 1913, a very significant date in contemporary Sámi political activities. The purpose of this school reform was segregation, influenced by the social-Darwinistic ideas of the leading circles of politicians and authorities in Scandinavia from the 1880s. Special laws and regulations like the Reindeer Pasture Act had been instituted in 1886 in order to regulate reindeer pastoralism and make it easier to administer and control. Even this act was inspired by the same evolutionary reasoning, by which nomads were graded particularly low and characterized as having a less promising future. At about the same time similar processes bureaucratized the reindeer pastoralist economy and unified the Sámi schools in Norway and Finland.

In Sweden the nomad school system reconfirmed occupational differentiation, already established by means of the Reindeer Pasture Act; only children belonging to reindeer herding families were entitled to enter these schools for very long. Other Sámi children were assigned to the common Swedish primary schools, thus cutting them off from the study of their own culture. Consequently the segregation was based on ethnic origin and occupational background. Sámi children were thus separated from one another, undermining ethnic unity. Such an internally segregated school system impaired the Sámi minority even further, a negative process which had its origin in the Reindeer Pasture Act, which for the first time differentiated Sámi with certain rights *qua* Sámi, i.e. reindeer herding rights, and rights to fish, hunt and trap, etc. which all relate to a reindeer pastoralist adaptation, from other Sámi who were denied such rights.

The philosophy behind this school policy was that "Lapp shall be Lapp" in a conservative non-evolutionary sense, assuming that the children of reindeer herding families should be content with an educational program inferior to the rest of the population. Since their way of life was considered rather primitive, the formal training of children could be also. This protective attitude is the most flagrant example of paternalism experienced by the Sámi. Through a special school system the authorities decided how the Sámi culture should be defined, mainly as the reindeer pastoralist subculture which ought to retain most of its nomadic features. Furthermore they determined that everyone else claiming Sámi origin should be excluded from their schools and consequently assimilated by Swedenization--life in the industrial society. The schools qualified a child for a life as a reindeer herder or for a life in urban centres of the majority society. Only to a limited degree did they qualify the graduate for an adequate career choice in local centres of the minority society (Hoem 1971). More than one generation of Sámi have suffered tremendously from a school system stressing the idea of Finnicization, Norwegianization or Swedenization, gradually reducing the number of Sámi who actively show cultural awareness regardless of livelihood.

In Norway the differentiation between different categories of Sámi took place within the same school, where classes separated children from reindeer herding households and those living a sedentary way of life in the semi-urban townships in Finnmark. This differentiation probably came closer to the actual needs of the pupils than the Swedish variant, but the impact of Norwegianization was equally felt.

Sámi Efforts to Improve Training

In order to face contemporary challenges emerging from continuous and closer contact with the larger society, a return to cultural and political autonomy is absolutely indispensable to indigenous minorities. The paternalistic school system designed for the Sámi did not meet these requirements. Therefore, adequate training on different levels of education to develop appropriate and versatile competence has been one of the most important issues on the Sámi political agenda for many years.

The establishment of a Sámi folk high school, or county college, in Jokkmokk in 1942 represents the first important step towards changing the premises needed for an improvement of formal training. This boarding school for adult education, run originally by the Swedish Missionary Society but eventually by a school board dominated by Sámi members, has served as a vital cultural centre, gathering young aspiring Sámi from all over Sámi land. In this school the significant revival of Sámi arts and crafts occurred, and one of its main objectives has always been to offer appropriate training in the various traditional Sámi crafts, both from a practical and a theoretical (cultural-historical) point of view. Thereby a sense of quality, as well as a feeling for traditional values, has been secured and is transferred to ever wider circles of Sámi. Advanced courses in the Sámi language, in cultural history and in resource management related to the traditional environment give this folk high school its special profile. Basic training in organizational work and general courses in social science and civic affairs provide cultural competence in typical schools of this type.

The purpose of the Sámi folk high school was to support, maintain, and develop Sámi culture, traditions, ways of thinking, and basic values. The emphasis was on subjects such as Sámi language, Sámi crafts, and ecology in the sub-arctic zone. This school filled a gap occasioned by the inferior level of the nomad schools and prepared the Sámi for an ethnopolitical movement, where improvement of the educational sector, including the language question, emerged as one of the most urgent problems the Sámi minority has to resolve. In the late 1960s this school went through a severe recruitment crisis: the number of students declined considerably, so that to preserve the school for the future it was opened to non-Sámi students. The programs are differentiated, with part of the curriculum exclusively for Sámi and the rest offered to all. This change meant that the number of students enrolled on a full time basis in a few years rose from the bottom low of twelve to ninety, half of whom were Sámi. From 1976, university-level courses authorized by the department of linguistics at Umea University are offered regularly at the Sámi folk school. Later on other academic courses were added to the program.

The impact of this school has been very far-reaching: many of the Sámi political leadership and intellectual elite were given their first appropriate training there, as were several of the consultants and instructors of Sámi handicraft. An important responsibility resting on the Sámi folk high school has always been to communicate insight and knowledge about the Sámi, their culture and basic life conditions, to broader circles of the dominant society. Transforming the school to a polytechnic folk high school, although retaining its Sámi identity, emphasized this special purpose even more (for more details on the Sámi folk high school see Sameutredningen 1975).

The second step in improving Sámi education had to do with the nomad school system. Although the Sámi had objected for years to the inferior standard of the nomad school, not until 1959 did they obtain their first goal of having the nomad schools placed on the same level with the primary school system in general. This meant that Sámi children were offered the same number of weeks in school as the rest of the school-age population. However, Swedish and Norwegian respectively, not their mother tongue, were still prescribed as the basic languages of education, leaving Sámi as a minor language to be taught for an average of two hours a week. This policy constrained the Sámi children in their effort to develop full competence in their own culture.

The Sámi were deeply concerned about these incongruities and continued to press for improvements to better meet their needs. After a new parliamentary inquiry, the nomad school system went through a noticeable change in 1962. The derogatory and obsolete name "nomad school" was abandoned in favor of "the Sámi school," which was opened to all children whose parents defined themselves as Sámi--irrespective of occupation. Sámi cultural diversity was thereby recognized and this strengthened the feeling of community among the Sámi as a distinct people. Until this time, the nomad school had been mandatory to all reindeer herding families; now the individual had a right to choose. This choice, which had appeared as a Sámi cultural political request for years, was introduced in connection with the 1962 school reform. The leading idea behind the improvement was that the level of education in the Sámi school system should be equal to regular schools in terms of quality and quantity, without necessarily being *identical*.

A Sámi boarding secondary school, located in the town *Gällivare* in northern Lapland, with grades seven to nine was instituted in 1964, offering Sámi youth education beyond the primary school level. Sámi culture and craft were to be emphasized. A special vocational training focusing on reindeer management, both from a theoretical, managerial point of view and from a practical perspective, formed the entire last year of compulsory schooling, with the students taking part in various seasonal herding activities in nearby Sámi local communities.

The Norwegian Sámi were the first to define the issue of education and its improvement as a political strategy related to the future conditions of the Sámi minority. One reason for this is probably that the majority of Sámi live in Norway, and that the vast majority of them are sedentary with a mixed economy based on inshore fishing and small scale dairy farming, not reindeer pastoralism. In Finnmark there are also some townships with a clear predominance of Sámi inhabitants, which helps to explain dissimilarity in the importance granted to the schooling (Hoem 1971).

As early as 1963 Sámi children were entitled to learn how to read and write in their mother tongue; and the training in Norwegian takes into consideration their unfamiliarity with this language, and modifies the teaching accordingly. The ultimate goal was to have Sámi children reach a level of competence in Norwegian similar to Norwegian pupils at grade six by the time they finished grade seven.

In the secondary schools and the newly established senior high schools for Sámi, a new language policy was launched in the 1970s which met with Sámi demands and requirements. By the new curriculum provisions, Sámi students were exempted from the national requirements of having to take two different official Norwegian languages (*bokmål* and *nynorsk*) and instead were allowed to chose Sámi and one of the Norwegian languages. Learning an extra Norwegian language with its peculiar grammar and vocabulary was replaced by a more thorough training in their own language for every young Sámi who wished it.

This change called for production of accurate textbooks and adequate training of teaching personnel. A teacher's training college was founded in Alta in 1973 with the explicit objective of qualifying teachers in linguistically-mixed regions, with the greatest concern directed toward the Sámi minority. The recruitment to the teacher profession of young Sámi from all over Sámi land increased.

Other elements which contributed to Sámi cultural competence and the elevation of formal schooling are the creation of a chair in Sámi language and accompanying expansion of Sámi studies in the northern universities in all the three Nordic countries, that is, Tromso, Umeå, and Uleåborg. This extended and diversified professional training and academic career opportunities among the Sámi. Special entrance or scholarship quotas in particularly needed fields, such as in medicine, dentistry, and social work, have also been introduced.

Another landmark in the strengthening of Sámi cultural competence is the establishment in 1973 of the Nordic Sámi Institute, *Sámi Instituhtta*, in the most viable Sámi township (Kautokeino) in Finnmark. This institute brought an old Sámi aspiration into being. It is staffed entirely by highly qualified Sámi personnel, of whom fourteen presently are based in Kautokeino with several more (and some non-Sámi) engaged on separate projects elsewhere. The institute is funded on a proportionate basis by the five Nordic countries through the Nordic Council. (Denmark and Iceland are included although they do not have any Sámi living within their boundaries). The board of the Sámi Institute is also set up according to the same norms with the addition of a Sámi representation appointed by the Nordic Sámi Council.

The Sámi Institute aims to engage actively in relevant Sámi research, to define urgent problems for inquiry, and to build up versatile Sámi expertise. These fields of activity become instrumental in the arduous task of reinforcing Sámi identity and culture. Externally they contribute to the communication of a more accurate and thorough insight about the Sámi culture, and crucial circumstances connected to its minority situation, all addressed to the majority society and its authorities. The institute is supposed to collaborate closely with the universities considered especially active in Sámi organizations at both the national and inter-Nordic level. Three fields of activity are specified: one dealing with Sámi language and cultural life in a broad sense; one focusing on economic, legal, and environmental issues; and finally one having to do with problems concerning education, vocational training, and information. Most research reports under the auspices of the Sámi Institute are published bilingually, and their publication *Diedut* has published thirty separate issues.

Present and Future Prospects in Education

The Sámi reactions and initiatives outlined above gradually have improved the level of education, making it possible for the Sámi to develop adequate bi-cultural competence. *Integration* of the Sámi school system into its community appears to be a key concept in this transformation. To achieve this end, active parent participation should be encouraged and strengthened. The assistance and support from interested parents brings problems from their poor command of Sámi due to the deficient linguistic training offered in the old nomad schools. Special adult education could remedy this, creating awareness of their own language and its usefulness. In addition to teaching reindeer management and basic ecology, parents can promote and transmit Sámi oral traditions. This transmission of mindset and values lays a foundation for the maintenance and extension of cultural awareness and self-respect. The schools depend on parent involvement. These goals of Sámi parent participation in education have come furthest in Norway.

Sámi schools should promote both general and special cultural competence and knowledge, for such an integrated orientation permits the Sámi culture and language to develop and change dynamically, while at the same time maintaining its cultural peculiarity. The Sámi program of the schools must therefore be given high priority rather than reduced to minor "curiosity" learning having little or no implication for general career choices (Saiton-Burman 1988). To stress integration, a special course called "To live in two cultures" has been designed for both teachers and other personnel, housemothers, porters, etc., in the schools in Swedish Lapland.

High schools for Sámi youth are found only at present in the Norwegian townships Karasjok and Kautokeino in the interior of Finnmark. Each has one Sámi senior high school focusing on reindeer management. In 1987-88 the students attending were: Karasjok, ninety-nine; Kautokeino, sixty-five; and the reindeer management school, ten. Most courses in the curriculum in these schools are offered in Sámi. There is one more Norwegian high school, located in Oslo, which offers courses in Sámi, in a recent response to the demands by the many Sámi living in Oslo (Sámisk Utdanningsråd 1987).

Culture-specific skill development has to start early; consequently the Sámi have tried for years to convince the authorities to establish Sámi nursery schools to prepare the children for entering the primary schools and to contribute to Sámi enculturation generally. They eventually succeeded, and now there are nursery schools in many townships with significant Sámi populations. Oslo was persuaded to support a nursery school run entirely by Sámi with about ten children. The language of communication in the nursery schools is predominantly Sámi, and play, games, and other daily activities relate intimately to Sámi conceptions and idioms.

The attempt to integrate the school into the local community is the latest standard plan for the Norwegian schools. This innovative proposition opens a new avenue to the Sámi, strengthening the specific curriculum in their schools. The standard plan also affirms that all teachers employed in the Sámi schools must master Sámi so that they are able to use it as their primary language of instruction. Hitherto these teachers were left to choose their teaching language. In addition teachers are to be conversant with the Sámi way of life.

A community-oriented school should be anchored in the local community without being cut off from the society at large. Teaching and textbooks are supposed to be community-oriented in terms of social factors, cultural circumstances, and natural conditions. The Sámi school accepts this focus as part of its educational policy. The experiment of community-oriented schools has so far worked particularly well in areas with numerous reindeer herding families, with a reindeer pastoralist school, the so-called "*fjellskole*," as the most successful. This school addresses itself to all Sámi children, meaning that even sedentary Sámi can get acquainted with Sámi reindeer pastoralism and its traditions, thereby reinforcing a feeling of community and cultural belonging within the entire ethnic category. Both parents and grandparents have been mobilized to realize the intended goals of the "fjellskole" with its explicit community orientation (Sara 1987).

The development of school autonomy continues. Instead of having to model their education according to Norwegian or Swedish standards, the Sámi now wish to develop their own plan. One important step of this process is the establishment of a teachers' training college (with the possible expansion into a Sámi University) operated and controlled exclusively by the Sámi. A college of this sort is meant to be inter-Nordic, preferably located in one of the Sámi cultural centers and incorporating academic studies and research in addition to training for the teaching profession (Sámisk Læererutdanning 1983).

Ethnopolitical Implications of Education

A crucial concept in the transformation described has been the perception of adequacy, of "cultural competence." Adequacy requires *bi-cultural competence* in contrast to *semi-cultural competence*. If successfully obtained, bi-cultural competence will serve as an adaptive force in a culturally plural situation. But what does it take to achieve this ultimate goal? Skill development is complex and requires either 1) that individuals be competitive in diverse facets of life related to the majority society but maintain ethnic distinctiveness, or 2) that individuals pursue traditional means of livelihood but develop sufficient qualifications in theoretical terms, so that economic viability can be secured when facing the challenge of the modern world. The appropriate ethnic educational system offers general socialization through which an indigenous ethnic minority can progress toward bicultural competence.

A *language protection* law illustrates successful restoration of autonomy (Samisk kultur 1985). This 1989 law indicates Norwegian and Sámi are equal languages in education and as official languages in all areas where there are significant numbers of Sámi. In Kautokeino township practice predated the legislation to ensure that:

1) all documents and communications are to be translated into Sámi,

2) Sámi is now considered a supplementary and real qualification in regional civil service employment,
3) all public meetings must be simultaneously interpreted,
4) the status of Sámi in the regional and municipal schools has been raised,
5) street signs are bi-lingual,
6) information technology, computer processing, must adapt to Sámi peculiarity (Kautokoino Kommune *[Guovdageainnu Suohkan]* 1988).

Another ethnopolitical implication has to do with the legal strategy. For those taking active part in the on-going legal struggle for the improvement of Sámi land rights, bi-cultural competence derived from education and training, which is more or less adequate for its purpose, has had a considerable impact. A number of young Sámi have begun to study law. Such broadening of competence development relies heavily on a form of education which combines general intellectual capability and fundamental knowledge with thorough culture-specific insight.

The increase in Sámi language proficiency has produced new poetry, novels, short stories, and drama. Activities in these fields have increased noticeably during the last twenty years, and in 1979 an association of Sámi writers was formed, *Sámi Girjecalliid Searvi*, in 1982 supplemented by a Sámi drama association, *Sámi Teahter Searvi*. These new organizations related to the field of expressive culture are inter-Nordic (for further information see Svensson 1987). Such literary developments enhance self-image and pride among the Sámi and reinforce cultural awareness, and develops their own idiom while seeking innovative verbal expression in the process of creative writing. By means of such versatile applicability of their language, the Sámi demonstrate vitality.

Conclusion

This chapter stresses the impact and meaning of education in realizing the important ethnopolitical goals leading to the restoration of Sámi autonomy. The continuous enhancement of education is not merely a matter of strategy to bring about more viable minorities in a world where aborigines are at odds with the rapid change of industrially-based nation-states. It is both a strategy and a prerequisite for ethnopolitical advances, because among relatively powerless minority groups politics can only be formulated and executed by people who have attained full bi-cultural competence. I perceive adequate bi-cultural competence to relate to prevailing conditions in any given situation; consequently it has to be revalued and reconfirmed constantly with changing external circumstances influencing the lives of Sámi.

Apparently education is a political issue as well as a crucial element in the general cultural process having to do with the continuous readjustment to the Sámi minority situation. The culture's political program of 1971 and the Sámi political program of 1980, both formulated and adopted by the Nordic Sámi Council, are clear indications of that (Samisk kultur 1985). These statements are highly decisive in the formulation of a contemporary Sámi ideology as a platform from which most current policy is derived.

> We are Sámi and we wish to continue being Sámi, without being either more or less than any other people in the world. We are a people with our own area of habitation, our own language and our own cultural and social structure. Throughout the time of history we have made our living and lived in *Sámiaetnam* (the Sámiland), and we have a culture we want to develop and preserve. (Hoem 1971, 23)

Following Jean-Guy Goulet (1988) I wish to summarize that the development of adequate competence through the manifold means of education appears to be an agent by means of which cultural vitality is reaffirmed and cultural survival reassured. Education then emerges as one of the most decisive factors leading to increased self-determination.

References

Goulet, J. G. 1988. Learning Tradition and Change in the North. In *Education in the North: Tradition, Process and Product*. Boreal Institute Conference "Knowing the North," Edmonton.

Hoem, A. 1971. *Nasjonale skoler og etniske minoriteter En sammenligning*. Tidskrift for Samfunnsforskning Bind 12, Oslo.

Kautokoino Kommune. 1988. PM Information. Kautokeino.

Saiton-Burman, E. 1988. Vår skola behöver hjälp av föräldrarna. *Samefolket*, 12.

Sameutredningen. 1975. *SOU*, 99. Stockholm.

Samisk kultur og utdanning. 1985. *NOU*, 14. Oslo.

Samisk Lærerutdanning. 1983. *Innstilling fra Hoem utvalget*. Alta.

Samisk Utdanningsråd. 1987. Årsmelding, Kirke- og undervisningsdept. Oslo.

Sara, J. I. 1987. *Skole - nærmilo i samiske miljöer*, Forsoksrådet for skoleverket. Oslo.

Svensson, T. G. 1987. Current Issues in Sámi Cultural Policy. In M. A. Stenbaek, ed. *Arctic Policy*. Montreal: Centre for Northern Studies and Research, McGill University.

AUSTRALIAN ABORIGINES: EDUCATION AND IDENTITY

Deirdre Jordan

Aboriginality, eh?
I don't care how hard it is. You *build* Aboriginality, boy, or you got nothing. There's no other choice to it. If our Aboriginal people cannot change how it is amongst themselves, then the Aboriginal people will never climb back out of hell. (Grandfather Koori in Gilbert 1977, 304-305)

Grandfather Koori's statement highlights the perception of Aboriginal people in Australia that their culture has been destroyed by white contact and white dominance. In their contemporary society, they are seizing on education to begin a cultural construction to reestablish and to maintain an Aboriginal identity.

Historical Background

There are six stages of evolution of policy towards Aboriginal people in Australia. First, the early policies *denied the existence* of a non-white people; a belief stemming "naturally" from a contemporary world view where Aboriginal people were considered to be a sub-species of humankind. *The Foundation Act of 1834* of South Australia for example, declared the land unoccupied. Second, by the 1860s, *segregation* became the official policy, legitimated later in the century by pseudoscientists who warped Darwin's theories to proclaim the Aboriginal people as the missing link between apes and men--a "theory" which exonerated those involved in shooting, massacring, exploiting, and banishing the Aborigines to reserves and then excluding them from interaction with the white world. Rowley (1971) saw segregation as growing from the conviction that there was no other way to avoid extermination.

Third, in the 1940s, in the belief that the Aborigines were a "dying race," the "problem" of part-Aborigines was dealt with by a policy of *dispersal*--the fore-runner of assimilation.

> It would appear that the more ready means of bringing about a process of physical and social assimilation of the Australian mixed bloods into the community would be by the simple device of ensuring that a maximum dispersal or spread of the minority group will take place. (Tindale 1941, 119)

Fourth, by the 1950s, *assimilation* had become official policy. Hasluck (1953) noted that assimilation was the objective of native welfare measures. Aborigines were eventually expected to live like white Australians. Ten years later the policy was reiterated (Commonwealth Parliamentary Papers 1963):

> The policy of assimilation means that all Aborigines and part Aborigines will attain the same manner of living as other Australians and live as members of a single Australian community enjoying the same rights and privileges, accepting the same responsibilities, observing the same customs and influenced by the same beliefs, hopes and loyalties as other Australians. (p. 651)

This policy blatantly contradicted the existing legislation referring to Aborigines. It noted the specific (restrictive) legislation for Aborigines and dismissed the "rather loose use of the term 'citizenship'" by saying that, ". . . such statutes can in no sense derogate from their citizenship in the sense of their status as Australian citizens" (Commonwealth 1963, 651). Thus, although Aborigines in 1963 in most states were not entitled to vote, this was not seen as derogating from their status as Australian citizens!

Fifth, in 1967 a nationwide referendum in Australia, supported by an overwhelming majority, placed Aboriginal affairs in the hands of the Commonwealth. Aboriginal people were given the vote, and became citizens in their own country. *Integration* was proposed by South Australia, following the election of a Labor government which turned its back on previous policy. King, the Minister for Aboriginal Affairs in the South Australian Labor government, issued a statement entitled *The Shaping of a New Aboriginal Policy in South Australia*, repudiating the official policies of assimilation held by previous governments. King (in Commonwealth Hansard 1972) maintained:

> The final wrong would be to attempt to destroy the Aborigine's racial and cultural identity and to turn him into a pseudo-white man. A most encouraging sign is the development among Aborigines of the desire to identify with their own people and to be proud of their race and its culture. This desire of educated Aborigines to be with their own people, rather than escape from their environment into the white community, is a most hopeful indication of the rapid recovery of self-respect of the Aboriginal people. (p. 756-757)

King defined the policy of integration as ". . . the right of the Aboriginal people to live in our community on fully equal terms but retaining, if they so desire, a separate and identifiable Aboriginal heritage and culture" (Commonwealth Hansard 1972, 756). King advocated active encouragement of a "sophisticated and articulate Aboriginal public opinion" through autonomous government on reserves and participation of Aborigines in the political community. The policy of integration put forward by King recognized an Aboriginal identity that was *alternative* to that of white society, but located *within* mainstream society. For the first time, there was a move away from legislation to control and contain the Aboriginal people and toward policies requiring consultation and negotiation.

The policy made a major impact on "official" theorizing about Aborigines: for the first time statements from mainstream society projected a positive world of meaning with which Aboriginal people could interact. They now had the possibility of locating themselves and being located by the white world within a positive Aboriginal identity.

Sixth, the 1973 platform statement of the federal Labor Party proposed legislation against all forms of discrimination and promoted the rights of Aborigines with regard to social services, land rights, and health. These were all new policies. Aboriginal people were to receive the standard rate of pay for employment and the same industrial protection as other Australians, a dramatic departure from practice. Educational opportunities were to be provided that were in no way inferior to those of the general community. Pre-school and adult education were to be provided where possible. Non-Aboriginal Australian children were to be taught the history and culture of Aboriginal Australians as an integral part of the history of Australia. Recognizing that Aborigines were not a monolithic group, options were left open so that people might choose and construct an identity within an Aboriginal world of meaning.

The philosophy underlying these programs was *self-determination*, and the Aborigines seized the concept and built a new, positive meaning for themselves. The tradition-oriented people expressed this by saying "The *marrngu* (the people) are the boss!" This has been used both as a rallying cry and as a firm basis for building a world of meaning in which Aboriginal people might exert autonomy. Aboriginal people at every level in society and in every sphere of action, health care, legal rights, and educational policy-making asserted "we will do it ourselves."

Autonomy and Educational Policy-Making

Education was important in the push for autonomy, despite the complex construction of modes of schooling/education. At the time of colonization, there were 250 Aboriginal languages, each for a separate, distinct people, and each had their own name: the Marrngu, the Yolngu, etc. Today, Aborigines do not form a homogeneous group. Those in the far north of Australia or in the centre had less contact with the white world than those in the south. In many areas, for older people, the vernacular remains the only tongue spoken. In schools and for mature students, English is both a second language and the *lingua franca* for communicating with others, both Aborigines and non-Aborigines. Education for these people has traditionally been part of the law, of initiation into religious beliefs, into the complex ordering of "skin" groups, into the rules governing every aspect of interaction in Aboriginal society. Figure 1 shows the distribution of tradition-oriented Aboriginal people in non-urban areas. In urban areas, different conditions exist. From 1939 onward, under an amendment to the Aboriginal Protection Act of 1911, some part-Aboriginal people were exempted from some of the restrictions affecting Aboriginal people.

> In any case where the Board is of the opinion that any Aborigine by reasons of his character and standard of intelligence and development should be exempted from the provisions of this Act, the Board may, by notice in writing, declare that the Aborigine shall cease to be an Aborigine for the purpose of this Act. (Aborigine Act 1934-1939, section IIA)

The "notice in writing" consisted of a dog-tag which had to be carried at all times to permit entry to or residence in a town. As a result of these exemptions, by the time of the Referendum, numerous part-Aboriginal people had been assimilated to varying degrees into white society. Depending upon their cultural and geographical location, their educational needs (and the mode of delivering these needs) differ in fundamental ways. The differences between urban and tradition-oriented people are shown clearly in their "theorizing" about schooling and teacher education. It is on these two areas that this chapter will focus.

Figure 1. Principal Aboriginal Reserves of Australia.

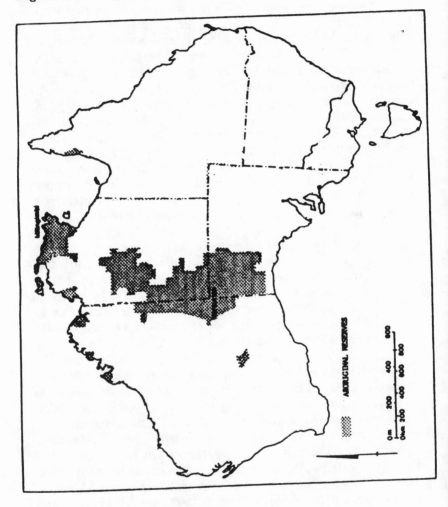

Schooling

On reserves, the highest level of education considered appropriate for Aborigines was fourth grade of primary school, often taught by untrained people. In the towns, Aboriginal children in New South Wales, for example, were not free to enter ordinary state schools until 1949 (Lippmann 1973). In some other areas accessibility to state schools took place even later. Even then Aboriginal children could be excluded on the slightest pretext.

> Well into the 1950's, each time there was a protest by white parents concerning Aboriginal children being admitted to a school the education authorities took heed of the complaints and sent the black children home. (Lippman 1981, 139)

In general, schooling has been seen by Aboriginal people as part of the white world, either irrelevant to their culture or actively destructive of it.

Researchers consistently found negative stereotyping of Aborigines by mainstream society and hence the offering of negative identity. Lippmann (1973) and Wundersitz (1979) found that non-Aboriginal people stereotyped Aborigines negatively. These stereotypes persist as part of what the white world holds as "knowledge" about Aborigines, and while anti-discrimination legislation was introduced in the seventies, the stereotypes persist in the white world. Turnbull (1972) related the following anecdote:

> People selling buttons in Melbourne streets for an Aborigine cause not long ago were astounded by the savagery of the answers given by some of those asked to buy--"I'd rub the lot out," "Give 'em a bait." (p. 233)

In Turnbull's judgment, these people "had probably never seen an Aborigine." Their "theorizing" could be explained as stemming from knowledge "sedimented" from the world of colonialism, when such actions against Aborigines were permitted by white society and indeed seen as providing a "solution" to the Aboriginal problem. A missionary gave the following account of events in Port Augusta in the late thirties:

> The Aboriginal children were neglected and not welcome at the Port Augusta school but public opinion was stirred and in 1937 a portable classroom was erected in the vicinity of the camp and a subsidised teacher was appointed . . . one councillor stood up and gave his opinion that the best thing to do was to turn a machine gun on the whole camp and wipe it right out, people and all. (Cantle 1978, 16)

Non-Aboriginal students at school still possess sedimented knowledge about Aborigines not gained from the theorizing of the school but at an early age from primary socialization. Palmer (1986, 81) reports the views of pre-school children at Port Augusta:

> Can some little Aboriginal boys or girls come to Kindy sometime?
> No, cause I kill 'em, all of 'em.

Thirty-two pre-school children were asked to analyze stories read to them. Palmer's (1986) findings were that twenty-nine showed a definite tendency to associate positive terms with the white characters and negative terms and feelings with Aboriginal characters. Some of the negative feelings expressed were disliking, hatred, contempt, and fear accompanied by a sense of danger.

Many subjects stated quite simply "I don't like black people" but others' feelings were much stronger (Palmer 1986, 77-79):

> Why don't you like Aborigines?
> 'Cause they're black and I hate black people.

Then, in a later session:

Would you like to have an Aboriginal friend?
Na.
Why not?
'Cause (pause) I reckon they're horrible. Aborigines.

Before students even meet Aboriginal children, their attitudes
have begun to form. The child from Port Augusta pre-school
who expressed the intent to kill, reflects the attitudes contained
in the statement of the Port Augusta councillor fifty years
earlier. The negative statements of the pre-school children are
coherent with their belief:

Ya gotta like white people and not Aboriginals.

The rudimentary theorizing is couched in language that is
derogatory--

Which one's a dirty boy?
(Child points to Aboriginal child in the illustration)
Why is he dirty?
Because he's a black boong.

Clearly the attitudes of white children are formed in the family
situation by parents repeating white views of the recent past
which theorized that Aborigines are not quite human, inferior
to white society and should be excluded from this society and its
schools.
        Jordan (1984a) found that aboriginal students also
typified "Aborigines" negatively; that is, they had internalized
for the aboriginal "world" the negative typifications of white
society. Negative typifications have been internalized also by
adult aboriginal people, sometimes because this is the only
reality offered, sometimes as a form of resistance. The
calculated *choice* of a negative identity as a means of resistance
is found in a response to Gilbert (1977) during interviews with
aboriginal people--"They think we're shit. So why not be shit?"
(p. 267). Mullard (1976) saw alcoholism as a form of resistance
on the part of Aborigines.

My own research (Jordan 1983) showed that aboriginal youth considered a "real" aboriginal male to be initiated into a world of alcoholism, petty theft, assault, breaking and entering, and sojourns in gaol. A "real" aboriginal female had passed through the rites of dropout and pregnancy. Peer pressure was exerted to make Aboriginal students drop out of school and become part of a delinquent sector of Aboriginal youth.

Low attendance rates at school or drop-outs may likewise be interpreted as resistance to a white world of meaning and to a particular Aboriginal identity being offered. "Formal education has sometimes served to divorce a child from his group, without substituting white acceptance in its stead. From the child's viewpoint, 'drop-out' is inimical to self-esteem and the development of personality" (Fitzgerald 1976, 185). Many problems are connected with such a response: in particular it locked the people back into a situation of disadvantage. Schooling became "white."

Jordan (1987) identifies the dramatic changes that have taken place in the late 1980s, giving rise to a new situation. The same students who dropped out in the early 1980s are returning to school as mature students determined to "have a future." Aboriginal youths who dropped out of school are urging students in school to persevere.

> It's horrible on the dole. There's no future in our lives. Stay at school. (p. 9)

These views are internalized by students (Jordan 1988),

> I have been hungry and cold and rejected all my life. I have been thrown out of home by my parents. One day, I will have children. They are not going to lead the life that I have lived. (p. 5)

To the slogan of the early 1980s impelling adults to new initiatives "We will do it ourselves," young school children have now added "We have to have a future!"

Urban schooling

Aborigines, determined to assert their autonomy, have founded alternatives to white schools. Instead of destroying their culture (Jordan 1987), schools are now being structured to maintain it. Aboriginal people in cities now promote *independent schools* which have always promoted the social/cultural/religious/economic welfare of particular sectors of society--usually the wealthy or a particular religious group.

Aboriginal people believe that control over their lives will come about largely through education. For them, control over their schools is an important facet of self-determination/self-management, of raising the level of education of their children and of structuring an Aboriginal identity. In these independent schools, they become the majority group. Their identity is a source of pride, not of shame.

The independent school permits control by Aborigines of policies, the curriculum and the structuring of identity. There are role models for Aborigines on staff who have succeeded in higher education without becoming part of the white world. They have maintained their Aboriginal identity.

One problem facing these independent schools is assimilationist pressure. Large sections of the white world would deny them a place in white structures with the spurious argument that they smack of apartheid policies. Nevertheless, this movement towards independence will persist.

In other urban situations, students attend *neighborhood schools*, which vary in their policies, in the leadership given by principals and deputies, and in the commitment of staff. Some schools do not meet the needs of non-Aboriginal students, still less of Aboriginal students. The latter tend, moreover, to be concentrated in low socio-economic areas, where the expectations of staff with regard to student achievement in general are often low and the aspiration and achievements of non-Aboriginal students are low. Aboriginal students with high aspirations often move to other schools, sometimes to white independent schools promoting the entry of Aboriginal students. In schools where they form a large proportion of the total numbers, determined efforts are being made to construct a positive identity among them.

Aboriginal Studies, the teaching of history and culture and sometimes language of Aboriginal people to both Aboriginal and non-Aboriginal students, has become part of the curriculum in some schools. In others, subject content has been revised to include Aboriginal perspectives in English, music, art, the social sciences. In many schools, a room is set aside for this purpose and becomes the home-room for Aboriginal students, where they feel secure, where they become at least temporarily the majority group, where they "have other Aboriginal faces around them." One or more Resource Teachers (occasionally Aboriginal) are appointed to plan curricula experiences which will heighten the self-esteem, confidence, and aspirations of students. In these situations, respected people are appointed as *Aboriginal Education Workers*, working with teachers, children and parents.

These efforts have met some success. In South Australia, for example, the number of Aboriginal students persevering to Year 12 has increased from zero in the early 1980s to twenty-eight in 1986, fifty-six in 1987, and one hundred and twelve in 1988 (Jordan 1986, 1987, 1988). Similar increases are to be found in other states. As a result of the efforts made by schools, and of the responses of parents and students, there is a conviction that *today* it is better to identify as an Aboriginal person and a surge of hope that "tomorrow will be better" with regard to achievement.

In the case of tradition-oriented people in the far north and center of Australia, there is a strong movement to persevere and maintain their culture, their language and their identity. The schooling of the white world is given high priority. But the form of schooling sought is not one that is the product of the imposition of an alien group. Rather, schooling, seen as a construct of the white world, is actively sought by the people and accommodated into their over-arching religious/social philosophy, the "Law."

Because Aboriginal people do not form a homogeneous group, the particular ways in which different groups seek to exercise autonomy vary greatly from one to another. While no one group can be seen as "typical," to illustrate the implementation of autonomy by tradition-oriented groups, a case study of one group will be examined, that of the *Strelley Mob*.

The Strelley Mob experienced prolonged contact with white people on cattle and sheep stations in this century. Their covert resistance to oppressive working conditions and to the destruction of their culture took on dramatic, overt form in the 1940s, when they went on strike for a just wage. Squatters and police reacted against this threat to the economy of the white world by branding the Aboriginal people as communists, to their considerable bewilderment.

> We talk about wages and place to stay, and squatters and police keep saying Communist. We say 'What's this Communist'? (Rowley 1971, 253)

The demanding of basic human rights by Aborigines could not be tolerated in a world that needed cheap labor; such demands had to be rejected. Clearly the branding as "communist" the Aboriginal request for basic needs, wages and housing reflected the dominant society's world of meaning.

The "mob" had to reject their location in a particular world by white people, whether it was the "world" of communism or the world of dependence on white men and their culture.

The group (about 600 people in all) still contains members of the 1940s strike--recent enough to preserve powerful memories of group suffering and group support. Membership in the Mob is not strictly according to tradition. There is a number of languages represented, the chief ones being *Nyangurmata* and *Manyjiljarra*. Nevertheless, the group is more than a mere agglomeration, for its bonds arise from the group's promotion of the "Law" as a way of life. All aspects of life are subjugated to the Law; within the marrngu world, the Law and religion are one. It is in keeping the Law that the marrngu see themselves surviving as a people and renewing themselves. This results in order, and builds a stable social structure. The Law today is adapted by the people, for the people; it is not merely a ritually preserved tradition, but a modern day interpretation of the past, giving meaning to the present.

> They told him that whitefellas should not mess about with Aboriginal law and change it just to suit the whitefella. They told him that the old group since 1946 and how they talk to people who are going against the marrngu way [sic]. They showed the Commission how strong the Law is in this place. How the marrngu way of dealing with such things as marriages, children's upbringing and deaths is still right for the people and should be left alone by the whitefella. They told him about how the people have changed the Aboriginal Law to help run the stations and develop their economic lives. How these changes are made by the people and not outsiders. (Mikurrunya 1982, 6)

The breakdown of the Law is seen by the Strelley Mob as based in two sources: 1) the Christian religion broke down authority structures and thus resulted in anomie, leaving individuals without a world view from within which identity was nurtured and strengthened, and 2) contact with government agencies and white culture.

The "world" in which the Law is pre-eminent and which is seen as protecting the people from the evils of the white world is poignantly described in an article by Jacob Oberdoo, Snowy Jitamurra, and Crow Youkarla, leaders in the group (Mikurrnya 1982). They condemn white men for introducing grog; they condemn missions for saying the "old way was rubbish, they left the old people on the woodheap"; they condemn the government for undermining the authority of the elders of the tribe, and "picking the marta-marta bloke (that is, the part-Aboriginal person) and putting him in the middle." To summarize their statement: "The law must be structured and restructured. The law must be obeyed (otherwise anomie will result). The law is articulated by the elders" (Mikurrnya 1982, 28).

At the same time, the community does not reject or ignore the white man's law. Despite the fact that state and Christian laws work against the interests of the Aborigines, the marrngu respect them. Aborigines interact with the white world to enforce its law, while at the same time upholding their right to punish in their own way. In the case of the Mob, punishment integrates individuals back into the group instead of destroying their ties with their people and destroying them as individuals.

Just as the tradition-oriented people have accommodated to the white man's law, so they expect their white employees to accommodate to their Law. Teachers contract not to bring alcohol to community property. For the white staff, the acceptance of a job depends upon the acceptance also of the aims and objectives of the group, and a loyalty to the group in its endeavours.

All members of staff and their children are integrated into the community in a flexible but clear way. They are given section membership so that the members of the community know the correct way to interact with them; white staff in turn are educated in the correct way to interact with the marrngu. This giving of kinship groupings is a means of contributing to the good order of the group. Avoidance relations can thus be observed by members, and more importantly, strangers (that is, the white teachers) are integrated into a group having responsibilities towards them.

The Strelley Mob exercises their autonomy in decision making in the school. Although "Schooling" was not part of their traditional "world," education was of pre-eminent importance. "Schooling" is an introduced element--a mystery of the white man's world that is important in the evolving Aboriginal structures contiguous to white society.

The aims of schooling for the Strelley Mob are precise-- the white teachers are responsible for numeracy and literacy in English, the marrngu are responsible for both education in its widest sense and for teaching the vernacular in its written form. Pre-schools are taught for the most part by marrngu teachers, bridging groups by white and marrngu, and older age children by white teachers, assisted by marrngu. Adult classes in the vernacular may be taught by either. The school children and teachers are divided in a way that reinforces the traditional classification system of the Western Desert.

Schooling is a specific, limited part of education, integrated within the station activities, with curriculum geared to specific ends relating to the economy. There is not the disjunction between ends and means that confronts the youth of the nearby town. Strelley Community School is what its name implies--an alternative independent school embedded in the total community structure and under the control of the people themselves. Education in its wider sense is the responsibility of the whole community. At times the whole community meets to discuss school issues at length. Problems of "discipline" are seen as community problems with one "important man" ultimately responsible for this area at each school.

Since schooling is on-going, it is not meaningful to talk of primary or secondary education. The skills needed for sewing programs, or for typing or sheepbreeding, might be classified as secondary or post-secondary: but gaining skills is directed towards specific ends rather than representing stages. Moreover, the ends of schooling, connected with running a cattle station, are subsumed under one generalized end: self-determination.

The direction of schooling is from the Strelley world view, so it becomes a real alternative to the western model of schooling and does not reflect the ideology or practice of other contemporary school systems, even where these are held to be "alternative." The problem for the people is one of finding fulfilling activities on cattle stations so that young people will not be lured away to the cities. The problem for the white world is one where they see Aboriginal people opting out of mainstream culture, and out of an "Australian" identity.

It is always difficult to identify who created names to describe new structures which are not contained in the aboriginal languages. The notion of *"two-way"* schooling was certainly embedded in the theorizing of the Strelley Mob from the late 1970s. Socialization into the group and education into the Law were the province of the marrngu. Schooling belonged to the white world, with the crucial difference that the white staff was employed by the marrngu under the latter's conditions, and the curriculum was controlled by the marrngu.

White social studies was not to be part of the curriculum, and the literate form of the vernacular (the product of white linguists) was taught first to Aboriginal adults who then communicated it to young people. The sociological truism *in the language is the culture* was clearly perceived by the marrngu. Nevertheless, the major problem is that *their culture is in the Aboriginal language*, and the culture of the western world is in theirs. Harris (1988) faces the major dilemma of how Aboriginal students can be successful in their (western) schooling without losing their Aboriginal ways of believing and thinking. His solution lies in domain separation, of a bi-culturalism that implies a retention of different identities through separation, boundary maintenance, compartmentalization, disengagement and parallel development. Harris maintains that "separation is rare, possible, and necessary for cultural survival" (p. 78).

Other writers see "both-ways" education as complementing each other. Aboriginal people in the Kimberleys, for example, celebrate Christian ceremonies, by incorporating dances growing out of an Aboriginal tradition. The integrity of Christian (in this case Catholic) teaching is preserved, but ceremonies are carried out in the Aboriginal cultural mode (Jordan 1986a).

Still other writers see "both ways" education as contributing to a new emerging culture. Traditional culture is changed, modified, adapted into a new composite form. McTaggart (1988) discusses the notion of "both ways" or "two ways" education in schools as a "sophisticated form of resistance to cultural colonization" (p. 12). He interprets both ways schooling not as boundary maintenance, but Aboriginal people appropriating white knowledge into their culture. An aboriginal teacher-trainee in a college project echoes this idea and, using an example from his own environment, speaks of clear water entering salt water with a resulting new creation of brackish water. In the numerous examples used by the Aboriginal people in tradition-oriented areas, *their* culture is seen as strong, taking and absorbing elements of white culture.

These competing conceptualizations constitute a major dilemma. Although it is unclear how they will be resolved by the different groups of Aboriginal people, they recognize that these are theoretical issues with practical implications of immense importance to schooling on the culture of tradition-oriented Aboriginal people, so they will try to realize the slogan "we will do it ourselves." Clearly urban-based schooling for

Aboriginal people in remote areas demands different modes of teacher education.

Teacher Education for Aboriginal People

The National Aboriginal Education Committee (NAEC) was set up in 1979 as a structure intended to promote Aboriginal control of their own education. One of its first acts was to respond to a National Inquiry into Teacher Education with a substantial report (NAEC 1980) which surveyed the opportunities then available to Aboriginal people for access to teacher-education programs.

Teacher education was considered to be important because Aboriginal teachers would provide models for students to persevere at school and continue with higher education, and teaching had always been the chief avenue to higher education for those from disadvantaged backgrounds, and often provided a springboard to other careers where individuals could exercise leadership.

The NAEC, using the proportion of Aboriginal to non-Aboriginal people, planned to graduate one thousand teachers by 1990. This is under-representation, for three thousand would be justified (NAEC 1984).

In 1979, four colleges of advanced education offered special entry procedures for Aboriginal people. The NAEC (1984) submission to the National Inquiry into Teacher Training describe these structures as *enclaves*--defined in the following way:

> An enclave support program is where Aboriginal students enrolled in standard courses within a tertiary institution are given additional support appropriate to their culture, life-styles and educational background.
> (p. 4)

In a study of these support systems, I identified the following functions (Jordan 1984b):

1. They are structured to provide *academic support*, which on the one hand acts to fill in gaps in past educational experiences, and, on the other hand, works toward consolidating the fruits of study currently being undertaken.
2. They provide personal support, introducing the student to social welfare networks and making available to the student the knowledge and insights needed to exercise a degree of control over those adverse circumstances in life which inhibit motivation and perseverance in study.
3. They provide a situation which promotes a positive sense of Aboriginal identity. (p. 6–7)

In general, policies of segregation and the adverse treatment of Aborigines by white society meant that very few adult Aboriginal people have reached the level of senior high school. Watts (1982), investigating the schooling level of parents of 900 Aboriginal children receiving Aboriginal study grants, found that five percent had no schooling, fifty-eight percent had some primary schooling, and twenty-one percent had junior secondary. Only two percent had reached senior secondary.

Particular problems militate against the success of Aboriginal students in higher education. Many of these are associated with family, schooling, social prejudice, identity crisis, isolation, and loneliness. All these issues relating to difficulties in the background and personal lives of Aboriginal students, prompted interventions in the late 1970s, aimed at increasing the participation of Aboriginal people in teacher education, and support the conclusion that such intervention required academic and personal support systems, and bridging courses to promote the entry of mature age students into teacher education institutions and to facilitate success in the courses undertaken.

These support systems have grown rapidly, from four in 1979 to nineteen in 1984 (Jordan 1984b), with an increase in Aboriginal participation from eighty-five to five hundred and fifty-one. Support systems have been extended beyond teacher education programs to encompass most faculties in universities and colleges of advanced education. On any measure used, the increase of participation of urban Aboriginal people in higher education has been dramatic, particularly given the educational and socio-economic disadvantages which they have suffered.

The Aboriginal population of Australia is one percent of the total. However, it forms a much larger percentage in remote areas where there has been less white contact--i.e. desire to seize their lands for agriculture. 22.4 percent of the Northern Territory population is Aboriginal. Ten percent of Northern Territory Aborigines live in outstations or Homeland centres, remote from white settlements and even from Aboriginal settlements with a large visibility of white staff.

For tradition-oriented people, teacher training programs have to take into account a particular cultural orientation with regard to their sites, mode of delivery of courses and curriculum structure. Leaving home and the security of one's family support system to study is an enormous problem even for non-tradition-oriented people in country situations. For tradition-oriented Aborigines, the problem is compounded because an outcome may be loss of culture and identity.

Both the elders of the group and potential teacher trainees rejected separation from their culture. The NAEC (1984) report quotes a senior member of a traditional community:

> We do not want our people going away for study. They become "broken people"; they think like whitefellas. Sometimes they do not come back to our community. We want our people to stay here and do their study. They are joined to our people. They are joined to our land. (p. 31)

Two efforts have been made to meet the needs of tradition-oriented people, one from South Australia in its early stages of development, the second in the Northern Territory, at Batchelor College, located some 100 kilometers away from the white influences of the nearest city, Darwin. Batchelor was established in the mid-1960s to provide formal training for teacher aides. By 1974 it was offering a three year certificate course which allowed those who graduated to be employed as Band I teachers-

-that is, permitting them to teach in a restricted form in beginning classes in Aboriginal schools. An Associate Diploma of Teaching (Aboriginal schools) was established in 1981. In 1986 this level of education was extended to a program allowing people to obtain a B.A. (Ed.), a degree equivalent to three years of higher education.

Several modes of delivery are employed to meet the needs of the people. Courses have always been offered by a "sandwich" arrangement of time. This structure, designed to prevent the distancing of students from their involvement in the community, alternates one year of study with a period back in the community. It also provides defined exit points to employment.

Currently the Associate Diploma is available in an on-campus model, but it and the final B. Ed. year are available in a mixed mode of delivery--that is, a combination of on-campus study with study and practicum experiences in the community. In addition, a model known as Remote Area Teacher Education (RATE) is now being piloted. In these programs some lecturers operate from the College, others live at one of the larger centres of tradition-oriented people and visit students at even more remote outstations.

A number of benefits result from this approach. Not only are the students located in their communities, as the elders and students themselves wish, but the communities also have come to "own" the program at Batchelor. The College sees this as one of its greatest successes.

> Perhaps the greatest achievement of Batchelor College in recent years and the one which is most propitious for future developments, is the identification of Aboriginal people in remote and traditionally-oriented communities with Batchelor College. This sense of identification has taken some time to develop, but it is a crucial factor in the success or failure of education programs for Aboriginal people. (Batchelor College 1988, 18)

This close link between theory and practice, with the wide experience of the students as a basis for theory, enables community aspirations and expectations to be more readily taken into account.

The notion of self-determination/self-management is encouraged by the college in a number of ways. All policy-making committees include Aboriginal representation. More importantly, since a large part of the program is sited within communities, it is possible to take account of the particular linguistic and cultural backgrounds of different communities. Students sometimes write sections of their assignments in their own language, then translate them into English. A trend of this sort makes it more likely that students will communicate their thinking and the content of their programs to the significant people in the community, so that the course does not become part of the mystery, the secrets of white man's learning. Participation in policy-making by each community becomes a possibility, and indeed is now being demanded by the people.

Complex and difficult issues remain to be faced and explored. A model permitting largely community-based study with one lecturer to eight students or less is costly. Though the cost is easily justified, financial support of the project by a government determined to cut back on funding for tertiary institutions cannot be counted upon. Second, there will be a varying ability of staff to withstand isolation and the lack of academic and social peers who read back to them an identity established in a city situation. Lecturers may not persevere in remote areas so there is the possibility of high staff turnover.

Aboriginal people want their culture to survive. Although they want their children to be educated into "white" learning, they practice two-way learning, where "Aboriginalization" of schools is intended eventually to replace many whites by Aborigines. This has implications for the evolution in theorizing about two-way schooling, which becomes one-way schooling if the Aboriginal culture, strong as it is in remote areas, absorbs elements of white culture and becomes the assimilating culture.

One latent problem in this situation is that few native English speakers are employed by the communities to teach English. This may work against the "empowerment" of Aborigines in their interactions with the white world, and "Aboriginalization" may become another form of assimilation in which Aboriginal people merely replace whites in their jobs, without bringing an Aboriginal philosophy to bear on policy-making. Furthermore, while by present consensus the schools have been the principal agents in destroying the culture of Aboriginal peoples, only two-way schooling will halt this. Even so, this new conceptualization means different things to different communities. It also means different things to academics who prepare teacher trainees for a model of schooling which is alternative to "white" schooling.

One dilemma inherent in this situation is that lecturers may impose their version of two-way schooling unintentionally, merely by posing the key questions for discussion. A second dilemma is that provoking student teachers to question the accepted modes of "western" schooling may also result in students questioning their own culture, and thereby breaking down community authority structures, repeating from a different motivation the practices of the white world during the period of colonialization.

It must be recognized that there are unintended consequences of teaching English, an element of schooling on which the communities place a high value. Despite policies of Aboriginalization of staffing, of curriculum, of methodology, it is inescapable that "the language is the culture," and the teaching of English brings ideas into a culture. The ambition to obtain a formal degree brings new interactions within a particular group. These are unintended consequences of the fulfillment of a desire by Aboriginal people to have power through English. The case is somewhat different when *academics* set out to be agents of change.

It is to be hoped that policies of Aboriginalization will work, that the interventions of academics will be in tune with the aspirations of Aboriginal people, and that the control exercised by Aboriginal people over their schools will not only have the potential to provide real alternatives to white schools but will ultimately provide insights for white educators to change white schools. If Aboriginal control is not real and is really influenced or guided by white people, then new "missionaries" will undermine real possibilities of self-determination.

Today looks promising for the education of Aboriginal people in Australia, with regard to their rate of participation both at the level of schooling and their rate of perseverance. Tomorrow can be still better when it is the Aboriginal people themselves who succeed in implementing their policies of Aboriginalization of education at all levels, and who succeed in establishing their autonomy in constructing their theorizing about the maintenance of their culture, the direction of evolution of their culture, the construction of identity, and ensuring that this theorizing is read back to them by the white world.

References

Aborigine Act. 1911. no. 1048, South Australia.

Anderson, D. S., and A. E. Vervoorn. 1983. *Access to Privilege- -Patterns of Participation in Australian Post-Secondary Education.* Canberra: ANU Press.

Batchelor College. 1988. *A Proposal to Develop Batchelor College as an Institute of Aboriginal Tertiary Education.* Northern Territories.

Cantle, M. 1978. The *Umeewarra* Story. Unpublished manuscript. Port Augusta.

Commonwealth Hansard. 1972. *Senate Budget-King Debate, 1971-72.* Canberra.

Commonwealth Parliamentary Papers. 1963. *Aboriginal Welfare.* Report of Conference of Commonwealth and State Ministers. Vol. III. Darwin: Australian Government Press.

Fitzgerald, R. T. 1976. *Poverty and Education in Australia.* Fifth Main report. Commission of enquiry in poverty. Canberra: AGDS.

Gilbert, K. 1977. *Living Black: Blacks Talk to Kevin Gilbert.* Melbourne: Allen Lane.

Harris, S. 1988. Culture maintenance in change, and two-way Aboriginal schools. *Curriculum Perspectives* 8(2): 76-83.

Hasluck, P. 1953. A report on the Native Welfare Conference. *Native Welfare in Australia,* September. Speeches and Addresses by the Hon. Paul Hasluck. Perth.

Jordan, D. F. 1983. Identity as a problem in the sociology of knowledge: the social construction of Aboriginal identity with special reference to the world of education. Ph.D thesis. University of London, England.

_____. 1984a. The social construction of identity: The Aboriginal problem. *The Australian Journal of Education* 28(3): 274-90.

_____. 1984b. Support systems for aboriginal students in higher education institutions. Report to CTEC and NAEC. Flinders University, South Australia.

_____. 1986, 87, 88. Career aspirations of Aboriginal students in Year 12 (mimeo). Flinders University.

_____. 1986a. The Balgo complex (mimeo). Flinders University.

Lippmann, L. 1973. *Words or Blows: Racial Attitudes in Australia*. Ringwood, Victoria: Pelican Books.

_____. 1981. *Generations of Resistance*. Melbourne: Longman Cheshire.

McTaggart, R. 1988. Aboriginal pedagogy versus colonization of the mind (mimeo). Canberra.

Mikurrunya. 1982. Strelley Community Newsletter. Vol. 2, no. 1. Strelley.

Mullard, C. 1976. A study of the roots and organization of Black resistance in Australia. Unpublished manuscript. Canberra.

NAEC. 1980. *Rationale, Aims and Objectives in Aboriginal Education*. Canberra: National Aboriginal Education Committee.

_____. 1984. *Aborigines and Education, a Framework for the 1985-87 Triennium.* Canberra: National Aboriginal Education Committee.

Palmer, G. 1986. Determining pre-school children's racial attitudes from their responses to books. Unpublished M.Ed. Thesis, Flinders University.

Rowley, C. D. 1971. *The Remote Aborigines. Aboriginal Police and Practice.* Vol. III. Aborigines in Australian Society, no. 7. Canberra: ANU Press.

Tindale, N. B. 1941. Survey of the half-caste problem in South Australia. *Proceedings, Royal Geography Society of South Australia* 42: 66-161.

Turnbll, C. 1972. Tasmania: Ultimate solution. In F. S. Stevens, ed. *Racism: The Australian Experience.* Vol. 2, Black versus White. Sydney: Australia and New Zealand Book Company.

Watts, B. H. 1982. *Aboriginal Futures.* A review of research and developments and related policies in the education of Aborigines, ERDC. Report no. 33, Vol. I-IV. Canberra: AGPS.

Western, J. S. 1973. Aborigines -some survey results. In Tugby, D., ed. *Aboriginal Identity in Contemporary Australian Society.* Brisbane: Jacaranda Press.

Wunderitz, J. 1979. A study of White attitudes toward Aborigines in the Maitland and Port Victoria District Central Yorke Peninsula. Master's thesis, University of Adelaide.

KURA KAUPAPA MAORI: CONTESTING AND RECLAIMING EDUCATION IN AOTEAROA

Graham H. Smith

This chapter examines educational resistance (Giroux 1983) by the indigenous *Maori* of New Zealand to the assimilating influences of dominant *Pakeha* (non-indigenous) culture. The education system in general and schooling in particular are major sites for Pakeha assimilationist practices and policies. The arguments present the contest between dominant Pakeha and subordinate Maori language and culture.

This chapter considers the wider social, political, economic, and cultural implications of the emergent *Kura Kaupapa Maori* (total immersion in Maori language and culture schooling) in response to the escalating crisis of Maori language and cultural erosion. Maori Language and cultural demise is viewed as being facilitated by conservative, traditional Pakeha ideologies of colonisation. Generally these policies and practices, no matter how well intentioned, have been influenced by the "hidden curriculum" (Apple 1979) of colonization: the overt and covert assimilation of Maori culture and language into the language and cultural norms of dominant Pakeha New Zealanders.

Kaupapa Maori relocates Maori and Pakeha inter-relations within a revised historical context which embraces a Maori perspective. This reinterpretation of history is followed by a description of Kaupapa Maori schooling and then by a critical assessment of its educational implications with particular reference to the wider social, political, economic and cultural relevance for Maori people located within a societal context of differential power relations.

A Revised History

Prior to the arrival of Europeans to New Zealand in the late eighteenth century, the Maori possessed and practised a sophisticated and functional system of education, which was supported by a rational and complex knowledge structure (Salmond 1987). This system was highly integrated through a cogent network of oral tradition, a legacy common to "related" cultures from the Pacific region. While many of these traditional forms of knowledge and cultural practice remain valid and functional within present day contexts, the continued decline in oral use of Maori language (Benton 1971, 1984, 1985) threatens the survival of traditional knowledge structures and cultural foundations, and by extension, Maori identity and cultural uniqueness.

For the most part, the "official" history of Maori and Pakeha interactions has been interpreted within a dominant Pakeha perspective. Pakeha have written the valid or "official" history of Maori and Pakeha interrelations. This control of knowledge (Young 1971) has sustained Pakeha interests. Pakeha domination in New Zealand society (Shuker 1987) has been facilitated through colonizing actions, policies, and practices which were sanctioned, justified, rationalized or redeemed within illusions of "piety," and maintained by a false consciousness of "justice," "fairness," or "equality." These false notions have helped perpetuate the interests of dominant Pakeha society. For example, Maori resistance to attempts to seize their land are often described in the Pakeha literature as the "Maori land wars" (Harrop 1937) with the Maori depicted as the aggressors; confiscations of thousands of acres of tribal lands have been recorded as "just" punishment measures taken against Maori tribes for fighting against the Crown (Mahuta and Ritchie 1988) and excessive rates of Maori underachievement within the State schooling system were regarded as the "failure" of Maori pupils inhibited by their social and cultural circumstances (Forster 1969). These are *victim blaming* interpretations which benefit the interests of dominant Pakeha society.

Maori have been effectively controlled and dominated by manipulating numerical strength within the egalitarian structures of democracy. A more effective and potent Pakeha dominance has been contrived through appropriate coercive ideologies, through "positively" upholding and reinforcing Pakeha actions, and undermining and attacking Maori opposition, for example, by trivializing the legitimacy and validity of Maori language and culture. Pakeha history has promoted the acceptance of Pakeha knowledge, language, and culture, and conversely the subversion of Maori knowledge, language, and culture.

Ideology undermines Maori cultural norms within the debate of what constitutes valid New Zealand history. Although Pakeha history recognizes "tangible," "observable," and the "written word" as acceptable forms of historical evidence, oral traditions, ritual ideology, and practice (Vansina 1965, Finnegan 1988) are often considered "inferior" evidence. Thus those elements which Maori consider important are often described in marginalizing terms as "mythologies," "superstitions," "folktales," and "legends" (Vansina 1965, Hopa 1988). Maori people did not originally have a written language in the European tradition, so early Maori "illiteracy" has been associated with notions of inferior knowledge structures, thinking modes, and cultural practices.

While undermining and demeaning Maori knowledge, language, and culture, Pakeha cultural norms were evaluated as "useful" and "superior." This enhanced the potential to assimilate Maori knowledge, language, and culture so colonization proceeded more quickly and easily. The acceptance of the superiority of Pakeha cultural norms and therefore the subsequent acceptance of the inferiority of Maori cultural norms has been promoted and practised since the arrival of the first Europeans. In many instances this hierarchical ordering of knowledge has become internalized by many Maori as well. Little credence has been attached to Maori interpretations of the omnipotent symbolism embodied in the traditional practices of carving, weaving, tattooing, mimeographics, or oral traditions such as genealogical recital (*whakapapa*). Collectively, these traditions performed for Maori what writing has done for

Pakeha and other western cultures. In this sense the Maori have always been a "literate" culture, and it has been mostly the Pakeha who have been unable and in many instances unwilling to "read" or to interpret these different literary traditions. Maori perceptions of valid history based upon oral tradition have been largely unacknowledged because history in New Zealand has both intentionally and unintentionally served the interests of dominant Pakeha society.

While Pakeha commentators have been able to identify, describe, and at times critically engage the actions of colonization, they have rarely been prepared to confront powerful ideologies which inform such practice. These shallow analyses have the eventual outcome of failing to interrupt meaningfully the processes of colonization.

The original subversive ideologies underpinning colonization survive relatively intact, effective, potent, and dangerous. These ideologies remain influential beneath the surface of New Zealand society and thoroughly imbue all social structures including the education system.

Two of the most effective ideologies curbing Maori interests are *the superiority of Pakeha knowledge and cultural norms* and *the liberating potential of Pakeha knowledge and learning*. These two ideologies cut at the heart of Maori knowledge, language, and culture, producing the belief that *Maori language and culture is inferior to that of the Pakeha* and that *it is of little practical use within the modern technocratic society* as defined by Pakeha.

These and similar ideologies which sustain Pakeha interests have become entrenched within State education. State schooling continues to propagate and reproduce them, and thereby undermines honest endeavours to deal with the overt symptoms of Maori educational crises. Policy attempts to alleviate Maori difficulties within education rarely acknowledge, confront, or deal with the influence of these forces. Until they are recognized and effectively controlled, the educational experience for most Maori will continue to be unequal despite the liberal attempts at reform based on egalitarian notions such as "equality."

Efforts to manage the difficulties created for the Maori have generally been temporary and cosmetic (Smith 1988b) and have failed to ameliorate significantly the educational crises faced by Maori pupils--such as disproportionate and high levels of underachievement, early leaving of school, excessive truancy and low enrollments.[1] Historically and currently, most reform initiatives in New Zealand education have failed to recognize, understand, and respond to the deeper forces involved (such as covert ideological influences) or the context of unequal power relations from which these ideologies have been derived.

Will the dominant Pakeha education system (and schooling in particular) be able to provide equitably, fairly, or justly for Maori perceived needs through its present structures? A growing number of the Maori recognize that present schooling structures are unable to provide complete support and security for their language and culture needs. Many Maori parents have begun consciously to resist Pakeha social and cultural reproduction processes imbued within State structures. They have moved to control the detrimental ideological forces

---

[1] *Labour Force*: In 1986 Maori were 7 percent of the total New Zealand labour force; yet they made up 20 percent of all unemployed people. 33 percent of Maori of working age were not seeking work because they believed they lacked the necessary skills or that no suitable work was available; non-Maori was 21 percent. *Education*: Of all Maori students leaving secondary school in 1984 about 65 percent of males and 60 percent of females had no formal qualifications, non-Maori percentages were male 32 percent and female 25 percent. In 1983, 8.7 percent of Maori males (school leavers) and 12.2 percent of Maori females intended to pursue a full-time education; non-Maori figures were 21.4 percent and 29.1 percent. *Welfare Dependency*: In the 1981 Census of Population and Dwellings 11 percent of Maori men and 47 percent of Maori women were totally dependent on Social Security Benefits for their incomes. The corresponding proportions for non-Maori were 6 percent for males and 25 percent for females (The Race Relations Office 1988).

of assimilation and colonization by exercising their power to withdraw. Kaupapa Maori schooling has enabled parents to determine *what* children should be taught, *how* it should be taught, by *whom*, *when* and so on. As Maori parents have moved to reject many of the inhibitions of State education, such as assimilation and colonization, they have also acted to set in place powerful, alternative structures which endorse the validity and legitimacy of Maori knowledge, language, and culture. These penetrate the Pakeha controls of education. The logic behind New Zealand State schooling is being demystified. The reproduction of dominant Pakeha ideology, knowledge, skills, and culture as a function of New Zealand schooling has been exposed and confronted.

The Maori Alternative Education

Te Kohanga Reo means "the language nursery" (or nest), where there is a natural immersion of pre-school children within the Maori language and cultural environment. A typical nest might consist of twenty pre-school children, from babies to six years, who learn their mother culture and language in a *total immersion* environment. Methods of organization vary according to facilities, resources, and the family management philosophy. Maori cultural values, practices and philosophies are "preferred" so the *kohanga* may be influenced by tribe and region. The many variations share some common organizational, management, pedagogical, and philosophical bases: support for Maori language revival and survival, support for the legitimacy and validity of Maori knowledge and culture, the use of *whanau* (extended family) management principles and community support networks, and increased Maori autonomy over key educational decision-making.

The concept of Te Kohanga Reo was formally proposed at a conference for Maori leaders in 1980 and the first one established in February 1982 in the Wellington region. The growth of Te Kohanga Reo has since been rapid and widespread (see table 1). Te Kohanga Reo have been established in private

Table 1. **Growth Rate of Kohanga Reo**

1982	December	50
1983	October	148
1984	August	240
1985	August	326
1986	August	428
1987	May	480
1988	August	520

Source: Smith 1988b, p. 38

houses, rented buildings, parts of schools and on traditional Maori meeting centres. They have been established in Singapore, Honolulu, Brisbane, Perth, Sydney and Salt Lake City.

The generic term which embraces the many different patterns of organization, pedagogy, and unifying principles is *Kaupapa Maori* (Maori philosophy and principles). Each year at the annual national conference, the Kaupapa of Kohanga Reo is reaffirmed. The reaffirmation of the core principles is also possible through a sophisticated communication network and administrative structure which has a national organizing committee and regional committees working with individual management.

The rapid development and success of Kohanga Reo owes part of its genesis to a 1971 Maori language survey conducted throughout New Zealand by a team of researchers led by Richard Benton (1971), which forecast the imminent death of the Maori language, statistically evident in a rapidly diminishing Maori speaking population. Maori alarm with this situation produced the radical innovation of Te Kohanga Reo, as a vehicle to regenerate, revive, and ensure the survival of Maori oral language.

The strength and vitality of Kohanga Reo have been successful in facilitating support for Maori language and culture because they are:

1) sustained by an almost universally shared agreement among Maori that urgent steps be taken to ensure the survival of spoken Maori language,

2) successful under Maori organizational and administrative autonomy,

3) politicizing: making Maori parents more aware of the education process, so they express their needs, and demand and question more of the functioning and practices of schooling,

4) successful in producing children with well developed fluency in Maori language.

The development and success of Te Kohanga Reo has made it the largest growth area within early childhood education since 1981, the fastest growing preschool service, with optimistic forecasts predicting that it will serve an estimated potential pool of 35,000 Maori children under the age of five (there were 8,000 children enrolled in December 1986). Each of the 520 Kohanga can be expected to produce two or three five-year-olds ready for primary school each year. This situation has created new difficulties for primary schools which for the most part are ill equipped to handle the fluently speaking Kohanga Reo graduates.

In New Zealand, children must attend school from the age of six, and almost all New Zealand children attend State primary schools. Most Maori children graduating from Kohanga Reo at present have little choice but to enter State schools where there are few Maori speaking staff, suitable language materials or appropriate language environments to maintain the impetus of Te Kohanga Reo. The observable trend is that they lose the language and cultural gains made within Te Kohanga (Peel 1988, Smith 1983, Sharples 1988). The emergence of the Kaupapa Maori schooling innovation, is an attempt to maintain the successful language and cultural gains begun in Te Kohanga Reo, and to provide a viable primary schooling option to do this.

Kaupapa Maori Schools

Kaupapa Maori Schooling is based on Maori philosophy and principles of education from Te Kohanga Reo. It takes for granted the validity of Maori knowledge, pedagogy, and cultural practice through total immersion in Maori language and cultural practices. Maori parents have moved to establish, independently, a frequently requested schooling option not provided by the State schooling structures (Smith 1988a).

Kaupapa Maori schooling asserts the right of *tangata whenua* (people of the land) and their culture to exist and continue to flourish in *Aotearoa* (New Zealand)--the land in which their language and culture are rooted. While the revival and survival of Maori language is central, Kaupapa Maori schooling is not a retrenchment in the traditional past, but an aid to enable Maori children to participate in and contribute fully to modern New Zealand society. The dominant influence of English language and Pakeha culture are so powerful outside of the school that Maori children learn to speak English anyway. Therefore Kaupapa Maori does not require a choice of Maori culture to the exclusion of Pakeha culture. The outcome of the total immersion experience for pupils is bilingualism and biculturalism and includes Maori parents assuming power to choose those aspects of Pakeha culture which are to be incorporated in the curriculum.

The inability of ordinary State primary schooling to provide adequately for the Maori language and cultural needs of Te Kohanga Reo graduates has precipitated the establishment of Kaupapa Maori schools outside the State system, without State funding, State teachers and typical material resources. Peter Sharples (Director of *Haoani Waititi Marae* and one of the principal founders of *Hoani Waititi Kura*--the first Kaupapa Maori School to be established, listed factors contributing to the founding of the school:

> Frustration with waiting for the system to move toward suitable programming for Te Kohanga Reo graduates; realization that the system did not have sufficient resources; the desire to ensure that *what* was taught and *how* it was taught was *tuturu* Maori (authentic Maori) based on the principles and practices already established in Te Kohanga Reo; to have the power to ensure that what was to be taught and how it was to be taught were decisions based on Maori principles. (Smith 1988b, 39)

Recent experience and small scale research (Peel 1988) has seen growing Maori parental dissatisfaction with State schooling. In 1983, when Te Kohanga Reo was born, this call was made to educators:

> The initial conception, implementation and maintenance of this program has been completely in Maori hands and under Maori control. The program has proved highly successful as far as it goes and the "ball" is now in the hands of the schools who are to receive these children . . . . It is to be hoped that the schools will fulfil their part of this challenge . . . and that these programs be accepted on the basis that these children are entitled to expect their needs to be met by New Zealand schools. (Smith 1983, 10)

The State has largely ignored the implied challenge and has not responded with appropriate programs that would satisfy Kohanga parents and allay their fears. Experience to date tends to show that children from Te Kohanga Reo place their Maori language fluency at risk by entering State schools. A curious contradiction is apparent: despite full rhetorical support by education officials and by government for Te Kohanga Reo and some funding support, there is not yet support for "total immersion" primary schooling as a natural progression from Te Kohanga Reo. While State funding is sought for Kaupapa Maori Schooling, there is growing scepticism (Sharples 1988) whether Maori decision-making autonomy would remain if these schools were to be eventually funded by the State. Increasing numbers of Maori parents doubt that present State structures fairly deliver Maori interests or aspirations. It is these experiences that make Maori people wary of hidden agendas. There were, in 1989, four Kaupapa Maori Schools in operation, established by the initiative and collected resources of the Maori parents and their communities. This is an endorsement of the view that present State structures are inadequate (and historically ineffective) in the delivery of education to Maori people.

Critical Analysis

Maori encounters with the New Zealand education system have been mostly disastrous. The evidence is seen in Maori schooling statistics: small numbers in tertiary institutions, under-representation within specific subject areas, and excessive absenteeism. The wider societal repercussions are reflected in higher mortality rates, excessive imprisonment rates, poorer health, greater welfare dependency, and higher unemployment statistics related to Maori people. Recent criticism of the system must cut through contrived ideologies which protect it. The education system and its various structural manifestations are now seen by Maori as "problematic" and no longer to be "taken for granted" as acting in the best interests of all its pupil clients.

The assimilation of Maori language and culture has continued since the arrival of Pakeha people to New Zealand and their intent to colonize the Maori through assimilation policies and practices. "Maori problems" within education have been periodically addressed, with policies loosely labelled and reflecting their themes of "accommodation," "assimilation," "integration," "biculturalism," and "multiculturalism." More direct intervention strategies within schooling have ranged from the use of "religion" to "civilize" the early Maori population to current "problem-solving" theories which address Maori "cultural deprivation" and "skills deficiencies." In spite of the good intentions implied within these initiatives, the crises facing Maori within education have remained.

Two important factors have been consistent: the difficulties faced by Maori within education have inevitably been perceived as the "Maori problem" (the failings of Maori people and the detrimental effects of their social and cultural baggage); and intervention strategies have been developed, organized, sanctioned, and implemented by dominant Pakeha interest groups.

Kaupapa Maori schooling is an intervention strategy entirely different from the unsuccessful strategies attempted by Pakeha in the past. It is clearly Maori in design, content and practice. Its establishment *outside of the system* questions the right of Pakeha to dominate education to the exclusion of Maori-preferred interests in education. Kura Kaupapa schooling asserts the right to overtly validate Maori knowledge, language, custom and practice. Implied is an analysis of (and a response to) the unequal power relations that led State schooling to serve only dominant Pakeha interests. Maori autonomy over key educational decision-making assures Maori interests through determining crucial educational questions such as those related to the control of knowledge, and thereby reasserting the validity and legitimacy of Maori language and culture. Kaupapa Maori schooling directly confronts ideologies of domination reflected in depositing myths like "Maori language won't get you a job," or "its a technocratic world we live in, Maori language can't cope with modern needs."[2]

Kaupapa Maori schooling asserts the right of Maori knowledge, language, custom and practice to continue to flourish in the land of its origin, as the *Tangata Whenua* culture.

Dominant groups influence, identify, maintain and protect "acceptable knowledge," using gate-keeping strategies such as culturally biased methods of evaluation which ensure that "success" is nearly always predetermined by the dominant group (Mitchell 1984). Gate-keepers also establish curriculum hierarchies which endorse the dominant culture and assign relatively low priority to those areas which do not conform to the norms, values, and expectations of dominant group decision makers (Gadd 1984). Gate-keepers also timetable schools so that "low status" subjects such as Maori studies and Maori language are often presented as options to more "academic" subjects such as maths, physics and chemistry.

The construction of the total school environment, including its "culture," is also questioned. To use Bourdieu's (1977) term, the *habitus* of State schooling connects more with middle-class Pakeha culture than with the backgrounds, homelife, day to day experiences, culture, customs, and

---

[2] These depositing myths are discussed in detail in the finding of the Waitangi Tribunal Relating to Te Reo Maori and a Claim Lodged (Wellington Government 1986).

practices of Maori pupils. The overwhelming domination of Pakeha within schooling ensures the maintenance of Pakeha "cultural capital" (Bordieu 1977). Schools actively protect privileged groups by creating and then upholding their dominance through overt actions such as policy creation or covert means such as ideological subversion. This may be assisted through gate-keeping measures such as the fostering of dominant ideologies (Simon 1982), the manipulation of resources (Douglas and Barrett-Douglas 1984), the imposition of economic sanctions (Bedggood 1980), the co-option, marginalization, and hegemonic influences on Maori individuals working for dominant Pakeha interests (Smith 1988c), or the deliberate manipulation of government policies, such as immigration policy (Simon 1988).

The State schooling structures in New Zealand are locked into a cycle of social and cultural reproduction of Pakeha cultural norms premised on imperialistic presumptions of the superiority of Pakeha defined cultural capital. Maori people are beginning to see through the veil of "myth and magic" that underpins the false promise of the Pakeha education system (Smith L. T. 1986).

Recent policy initiatives[3] in regard to Maori education replicate the errors of the past. However, the development of Kaupapa Maori schooling has signalled that Maori are now prepared to challenge the structural and ideological modes of domination in a more co-ordinated way. As Kaupapa Maori schooling resists the deterministic and reproductive role of State schooling, it directly confronts the cultural reproduction of Pakeha norms, the legitimizing ideologies underpinning Pakeha political dominance, and the social reproduction of Maori into predetermined labour categories by dominant Pakeha capitalist interests (Giroux 1983) in a way that no other intervention

---

[3] For example; current educational reviews in all sectors of New Zealand education; pre-school, primary, secondary and tertiary sectors, government policy documents; *Before Five* (1988), *Tomorrow's Schools* (1988a), and *Learning for Life* (1989) outline new reforms within these areas.

measure has been able to achieve in the past. In these and other ways Kura Kaupapa Maori provide meaningful and viable interventions to the existing schooling crisis.

Conclusion

Recently, major developments have been incorporated within New Zealand education, which demonstrate a strong link between education and "free market" economic philosophies. A greater emphasis upon the relationship between education and economic productivity has already created "new" ideologies which contain the "old" subversive agendas. Maori language and culture face increased pressures to demonstrate an economic "worth." This agenda continues ideologies of the inferiority of Maori language, culture, and knowledge and therefore also continues to question the value of such cultural items within a modern, economic, technocratic Pakeha world. Whereas the State has been traditionally indifferent towards meaningfully supporting Maori cultural norms (relying on the affectiveness of ideology to covertly undermine these norms) the new state bureaucracy openly attacks Maori language, culture, and knowledge using the weapons of discourse from the New Right, such as "accountability," "excellence," and "standards." Such policy works against the cultural aspirations of Maori people, thereby making them even more susceptible to assimilation by dominant Pakeha culture and interests.

Under the guise of "free market" philosophy, there is an illusion of devolution of the control of education to the consumers at the local level. The real outcome is the devolution of responsibility to the local level with a corresponding increase in the power of the State. Given the State's past record in relation to Maori education, language, and cultural interests, the outlook for Maori language and cultural survival is dismal. Maori people have always been wary of the assimilationist tendencies of Pakeha education, as a song, composed in 1950 by Tuini Ngawai (Tokomaru Bay), indicates:

Te Matauranga o te Pakeha
He mea whakato, hei tinanatanga
Mo wai ra? Mo Hatana?
Kia tupato i nga whakawai
Kai kaha ra! Kia kaha ra![4]

Maori people have resisted assimilation by Pakeha culture through both individual and collective actions. Within the existing schooling crisis, Maori resistance can be gauged through disproportionate levels of pupil absenteeism, truancy, early school leaving, disruptive school behaviour, underachievement, and at times overt cultural expression. Kura Kaupapa Maori has moved Maori resistance to another level and to another site. "Withdrawal" is a culturally appropriate strategy to be taken by Maori, particularly when considered within the cultural framework of *mana* (dignity), *whakaiti* (humility), and *whakama* (embarrassment). Maori people have been able to analyze critically and therefore respond more effectively than in previous futile attempts to transform the existing inhibiting structures.

While alternative schooling structures provide "relative autonomy" and are more able to emancipate Maori, other liberating structures still require development: notably curriculum initiatives such as the teaching of political literacy (Lankshear and Lawler 1988) to preserve the internal workings of these schools from the external pressures of Pakeha social power.

Kaupapa Maori schooling has decoded the ideological interests of Pakeha pedagogy, curriculum, and evaluation. Whereas State schooling has been sustained by covert ideological assumptions such as the superiority of Pakeha cultural norms; Kaupapa Maori schooling takes the validity and legitimacy of Maori knowledge for granted. It is this counter logic which underpins the radical pedagogy of such schools.

---

[4]   The knowledge of the Pakeha/Is propagated and nurtured/For whose benefit? For Satans!/Be careful of its temptations/Be strong! Be steadfast!

The reality of running a Kura Kaupapa Maori school reveals to Maori people what is a "fair" and "just" education. Through having to pay the state in order to rent rooms, to pay teachers' salaries, to produce material resources, to pay for the upkeep of buildings and to travel great distances to get to the school, Maori parents have become politicised. They recognize the enormous contradictions of their situation; unjust contradictions that go far beyond mere cultural difference explanations between Maori and Pakeha. These contradictions connect with broader oppositions between the State and the individual, the colonizers and the indigenous people, the powerful and the powerless, the oppressors and the oppressed.

References

Apple, M. W. 1979. *Ideology and Curriculum*. London: Routledge & Kegan Paul.

Bedggood, D. 1980. *Rich and Poor in New Zealand*. Auckland: Allen and Unwin.

Benton, R. A. 1971. *Results of Sociolinguistic Survey of Language Use in Maori Households*. Wellington: Maori Unit, N.Z. Council for Educational Research.

_____. 1984. Bilingual education and the survival of the Maori language. *Journal of the Polynesian Society* 93(3): 247-266.

_____. 1985. Maori as an official language: What this might mean and why is it desirable. *Waitangi Tribunal Submission*. Wellington: Government Print.

Bordieu, P. 1977. *Outline of a Theory of Practice*. Cambridge: University Press.

Douglas, T., and R. Barret-Douglas. 1984. *Nga Kohanga Reo*: A Salvage Programme for the Maori Language. Turangawaewae (March): MED Conference Papers.

Finnegan, R. H. 1988. *Literacy and Equality*. New York: Oxford.

Forster, J., and P. Ramsay. 1969. The Maori population 1936-66. In J. Forster, ed. *Social Process in N. Z.* Auckland: Longman Paul.

Gadd, B. 1984. Ethnic Bias in School Certificate. Turangawaewae (March): MED Conference Papers.

Giroux, H. A. 1983. Theories of reproduction and resistance in the new sociology of education: A critical analysis. *Harvard Educational Review* 53(3): 257–293.

Harrop, A. J. 1937. *England and the Maori Wars*. London: Whitcombe & Tomb.

Hopa, N. K. 1988. Ancient things are today. Auckland (August): NZASA Conference Papers.

Lankshear, C., and M. Lawler. 1987. *Literacy, Schooling and Revolution*. Wiltshire: Palmer Press.

Mahuta, R. T., and J. E. Ritchie. 1988. *Raupatu:* The confiscation of the Waikato and tribal attempts to seek redress. University of Waikato (August): NZASA Conference Papers.

Mitchell, I. 1984. Maori examination failure. Turangawaewae (March): MED Conference Papers.

New Zealand Department of Education. 1988. *Before Five*. Wellington: Government Press.

_____. 1988a. *Tomorrow's Schools*. Wellington: Government Press.

_____. 1989. *Learning for Life*. Wellington: Government Press.

Peel, N. 1988. *Te Kohanga Reo* pupils in primary schooling. Unpublished research paper. Education Department, University of Auckland.

Salmond, A. 1987. Maori epistemologies. In J. Overing, ed. *Reason and Morality*. London: Tavistock.

Sharples, P. 1988. *Kura Kaupapa Maori: Recommendations for Policy Access* (in press). Auckland: Education Department, University of Auckland.

Shuker, R. 1987. *The One Best System ? A Revisionist History of State Schooling in New Zealand*. Palmerson North: Ounmore Press.

Simon, J. A. 1982. Policy, ideology and practice--Implications of the views of primary school teachers of Maori children. Unpublished M.A. Thesis, University of Auckland.

_____. 1988. Cultural diversity in New Zealand: A cause for celebration. Auckland: NZASA Conference Papers.

Smith, L. T. 1986. Seeing through the magic: Maori strategies of resistance. *Delta* 37(June): 3-10. Palmerston North: Education Department, Massey University.

Smith, G. H. 1983. Te Kohanga Reo: Implications for primary school. Address, Primary School Principals Association.

_____. 1988a. Kaupapa Maori schooling: Implications for educational policy-making. *Towards Successful Schooling*, Royal Commission on Social Policy. Wellington: N.Z. Council for Educational Research.

_____. 1988b. The Picot Report: A cocktail for a cultural and social catastrophe? *NZPPTA Journal*(March): 34-44.

_____. 1988c. *Pikau: A Burden for One's Back in ACCESS*. Education Department, University of Auckland.

The Race Relations Office. 1988. *The Treaty of Waitangi and Social Policy*. 2nd ed. Wellington: Government Press.

Vansina, J. 1965. *Oral Tradition*. London: Routledge.

Wellington Government. 1986. *Finding of the Waitangi Tribunal Relating to Te Reo Maori and Claim Lodged.* Wellington: Government Press.

Young, M. F. D., ed. 1971. *Knowledge and Control: New Directions for the Sociology of Education.* London: Collier Mcmillan.

ABORIGINAL TEACHER TRAINING AND DEVELOPMENT IN CANADA: AN EXAMPLE FROM THE PROVINCE OF MANITOBA

Deo H. Poonwassie

Introduction

During 1990 many historic events heightened (or at least awakened) international consciousness concerning major issues affecting the well-being of Canada's aboriginal population. While these were local incidents, their effects were felt and followed throughout the country. Six examples of such events are given.

1) An inquiry was lauched into the judicial system of the province of Nova Scotia, prompted by the wrongful conviction and incarceration of Donald Marshall, an Indian, resulting in compensation for the victim and an inquiry into the circumstances leading to his conviction, where the legal system was found to be negligent.

2) The shooting of J. J. Harper by the Winnipeg police led to the Manitoba Native Justice Inquiry and to the re-opening of the Betty Osborne (a native person) murder case. Improprieties were alleged. The final report is due in 1991.

3) A major land claim was settled in the North-West Territories between the Dene people and the Canadian government.

4) The Oka crisis brought world-wide attention to how justice is meted out to aboriginal peoples in Canada. The Oka incident was prompted by a dispute concerning jurisdiction over land between the Mohawk people and other Canadians.

5) The Meech Lake constitutional proposal lapsed, partly because it failed to address outstanding grievances concerning Native persons.[1]

6) Physical and sexual abuse of native children in residential schools was alleged by Chief Phil Fontaine of the Manitoba Assembly of Chiefs, leading to an inquiry and numerous articles in Canadian newspapers and television. Although none of the above issues will be discussed in this chapter, they have intensified the quest for social justice, fulfillment of moral obligations, and legal claims in relation to the Native persons. Among legal questions, the education of the native child has been a major concern.

In 1988 the National Indian Brotherhood, Assembly of First Nations published *Tradition and Education: Towards a Vision of Our Future,* reviewing First Nations' education and declaring the First Nations' jurisdiction over education. These three volumes of research reported aboriginal jurisdiction over education, from a brief history of a failed Federal system to recommendations on the management and quality of education, and resourcing and implementation of programs. The report declares clearly that the future of aboriginal peoples in Canada is dependent on their jurisdiction over education, which is closely tied to aboriginal self-government.

This document is ideologically convincing: aboriginal people must control their own education if they are to progress as a people, as they have advocated for decades. Although change has been slow in coming, there are signs that First Nations and Tribal Councils are moving toward jurisdiction over their own education. In a country geographically as large as Canada, it is difficult to detail progress in each region. However, issues will be raised relating to education and teacher

---

[1] The aboriginal people requested that their rights be entrenched in the Constitution, but this was denied. Elijah Harper, a Cree Indian and an elected member of the Manitoba Legislative Assembly, effectively voted against the adoption of the Constitution by stalling the house beyond the deadline date set out by the Canadian government.

training in the context of third world development, with specific reference to a project in the province of Manitoba, illustrating one innovative attempt at training aboriginal peoples to become teachers. In addition, this chapter will discuss living conditions in native communities which affect schooling in a very direct way.

The terms *education* and *training* will be used interchangeably to mean learning through voluntary commitment what is deemed worthwhile by both the learner and the community. There is much confusion in the use of terms in referring to the first peoples of Canada. Such terms as Indian, native, aboriginal, First Nations people, and, in the legal sense, Status, Treaty, non-Status, non-Treaty, and Métis have all been used in the literature. For the purposes of this chapter, the terms *aboriginal* and *native* will be used to include any or all of these categories or terms. However, it must be noted that there are many differences in cultures, language, location, and economic status among the aboriginal population of Canada. Where the term *Indian* is used it will refer only to the aboriginal people with legal rights as defined by the *Indian Act* (p. 2).

The term *development* has been defined by many scholars (Goulet 1968, 1978, Roxborough 1979, Harrison 1988). Generally, this term will refer to the planned effort of a people to realize their potentials--human, environmental, and artificially created--in the quest for the "good life." Any comprehensive definition of this term raises several striking questions; for example, who does the planning, what are the roles of international organizations and dominant powers, what constitutes potential, and who defines the "good life"?

Operating Conditions

The aboriginal peoples of Canada live under conditions similar to those in the Third World: including massive unemployment, dependency on government welfare, and poor health care facilities (Lithwick et al. 1986). In addition, most reserves have an inert economic base and consequently little opportunity for the development of industries; the people have been colonized by the Federal Government under a system of trusteeship enshrined in treaties; and many urban natives suffer from blatant racism, anomie, and a personal sense of defeat. In northern Manitoba, these conditions are prevalent, and are reflected in the suicide rates--which are very high compared to the rest of the population (Hull 1987b). Education through schooling and special programs is seen as an answer to these problems.

The education on reserves consists of a system transplanted from the southern anglo or French society. In many ways this system is inappropriate and damaging to the traditional values of Indian peoples. Birch and Elliott (1987) state that:

> Education is, fundamentally, an intellectual and moral enterprise. It is concerned at root with introducing people to their intellectual heritage; . . . Education is concerned with enabling people to understand their world; to accept, respect, and rejoice in their world; and to interact with and control that world both effectively and responsively. (p. 484)

If this is correct, then the system of education imposed on the native people is irrelevant to their culture and ways of living. The traditional values, the intellectual heritage, and the world view of Indian people do not form the basis of the existing philosophy or practice of education on reserves. In addition to the imported system, many teachers are still trained in the tertiary institutions of southern Manitoba and, at one time, most teachers were of European descent. Indian values and languages have not been seen as significant in the development and training of these people: in fact, children were often punished for using their first language in schools (especially in residential schools), thus negating their own culture and identity.

Elders, leaders, chiefs, and the Indian people recognized these problems in education as devastating to their culture and way of life. They knew that education was important for their survival as a distinct people but they also knew that Euro-Canadian values were alien and dysfunctional in their way of life. They recognized that as long as their education was controlled from Ottawa or provincial capitals they had no chance of shaping and developing their future. Hence the intensive efforts to control their own schools and decide on curriculum inclusions and issues became a primary goal (Indian Tribes of Manitoba 1971, National Indian Brotherhood 1972). One way of executing effective control of Indian education was to train their own people as teachers and administrators.

Persistent Problems

People who live under Third World conditions have been subjected to colonization and oppression (Freire 1971). Education is regarded as a means to improve the economy and to promote social mobility. If the dropout rate of students in Indian schools is high, these young people will not achieve the skills to improve themselves and their community. One of the major reasons for the high dropout rate among Indian students is that they find school to be an alien environment. If this alienation is accompanied by a lack of support from the home and teachers who do not understand their students' culture, then schools on reserves serve merely as a front for the fulfilment of Federal *official* obligations. Indian leaders in Manitoba and Canada are painfully aware of these conditions arising from colonization, economic dependency, and political impotence. They realize that if they are to forge ahead in their own development, they must achieve local (and eventually total) control of their education as well as the right to self-determination.

Movements among Third World people toward autonomy, self-reliance, and political independence have acknowledged that education is an *enabling* factor in development. In and of itself, education may be a luxury that very few developing societies can afford unless the practical benefits of education can be seen to improve the people's living conditions. In many developing countries (for example, Trinidad and Tobago) there were strong movements towards providing greater accessibility to education at all levels--primary, secondary and tertiary; however, many graduates became unemployed because economic growth did not keep pace with the educational opportunities. This is an example of uneven or unbalanced development: education must work as an essential ingredient for parallel growth with the economy; in other words, national or community planning must include economic and educational development as mutually supporting endeavors in the movement toward decolonization and self-determination.

In the case of northern Canada, the Indian people who live on reserves do not have sufficient resources for either educational or economic development. These reserves are almost totally dependent on Federal funds for their survival. Generally, it is difficult for the people to develop their own local economy because:

1) there is no viable economic base (fishing and trapping can no longer sustain families, and agriculture is impossible because of adverse conditions of climate and soil);

2) viable economies of scale do not apply because of the relatively small population on these reserves (the average being less than 1,000);

3) transportation is extremely difficult by winter roads and expensive by air;

4) proper training is lacking;

5) capital funds are insufficient; and

6) a psychology of dependence undermines initiative.

The political development of Indian people in Canada has been hindered by creating a dependence on the welfare system. Indian leaders are now aware of this but the Federal bureaucracy is too deeply entrenched and unwilling to concede power to Indian leaders. Indeed the treaty rights, especially ownership of lands, have not been honored (Frideres 1983) leading to many current court battles between the Indian peoples and the Federal Government. Provinces similarly underestimate native aspirations and capabilities.

Education plays an important role in the development of leaders with post-secondary educations to understand the complex political and bureaucratic structures of the dominant society. Indian people are striving to develop all levels of education so that leaders may emerge not only through charisma but also through a firm and strong educational background. Teacher training has an important role to play in this effort.

In the movement of a people out of poverty and exploitation, the leaders must come from within the population. They need support from a dedicated, informed, and committed local population. Teachers from the local community play an integral part in shaping the minds and attitudes of the future leaders and followers in these communities; teacher training becomes critical in the move towards the achievement of a better life. In the transmission, shaping, and creation of such values and attitudes among the youth of the community, teachers must feel themselves to be knowledgeable, competent, and confident in order to inculcate modern approaches in these young minds (Grossman and Richert 1988). The training of teachers from these communities serves to prepare personnel with the necessary skills to encourage, direct, inform, and create critical thinking among the youth within an acceptable ideology of Indian development strategies and goals.

For a people in pursuit of self-determination, the cultural values and accumulated wisdom of that society must be transferred to its youth. This is generally facilitated through systems of education--formal, non-formal, and informal. As transformation through education occurs, an unavoidable reflective process is taking place: changes in values and value systems are effected by both the educator (teachers, parents, elders, social workers, or the media) and the educatee (Freire 1973). The greater the diversity (or difference) between the educator and the educatee, the greater the possibility of culture clashes and the imposition of dominant foreign values on the local people. Examples of this can be seen in the effects of colonialism and the consequent proliferation of corresponding European languages in the Third World. Along with these foreign languages comes the hidden or silent seepage of values and attitudes of the dominant colonizer. The accumulated wealth of knowledge, values, attitudes, and beliefs of the indigenous people become subservient to those that are imported. The aboriginal teacher can be of great assistance to the community in directing and assisting the indigenization of the school curriculum. With the training of more Indian teachers, this is beginning to happen, albeit too slowly.

This phenomenon of underdevelopment is generally seen *internationally* with the major actors being nations, multinational corporations, and development banks with their concomitant oppressive instruments of imbalances in trade, aid, ideology, foreign debt, and militarization (Frank 1966). It is also present *intra-nationally*. On a global basis we can see that the plight of the indigenous peoples of the world includes living under third world conditions: the Aborigines of Australia, the Indian of the United States, the Innuit of Greenland, the Sámi of Norway, Sweden and Finland, and the Nenet, Chukchi, Yakut of the USSR, the Massai of Africa, and the Menomic of Brazil. The Indians living on reserves in Northern Canada are no exception to this world-wide devastation of indigenous peoples. (The term *indigenous* refers to those first peoples who are now minorities in their own country).

The cycle that maintains and promotes under-education or miseducation among the Indian peoples of Northern Canada is characterized by poorly educated pupils at the elementary school level who either drop out or struggle through the grades with poor results. Those who survive the system become local teachers, social workers or counsellors or leave the northern communities, become unemployed, or enter forms of employment that have little impact upon youth. The "best and the brightest" generally do not enter teaching or a professional career; hence in Northern Canada, poorly educated students become teachers and the cycle continues. Teachers from Southern Canada compound the problem because many of them are non-Indians who regard their employment in these small and remote communities as temporary. They are seen as transients, as foreigners, with little commitment to education on reserves. Many of these "imported" teachers could not secure employment in an urban area. How can this deplorable situation be changed?

A Teacher-Training Project[2]

In 1971 the province of Manitoba had approximately twenty qualified and certified native teachers. It needed far more. The problem of few native teachers was recognized by native people, the Federal and Provincial governments, and university personnel. In 1975 a program was launched through the cooperation of both governments and Brandon University and called Brandon University Northern Teacher Education Program (BUNTEP). The sole purpose of this project was to train teachers from northern Manitoba who were residents of these communities and had credentials for access to post-secondary education. This project was based on a series of beliefs and assumptions[3] that trained teachers:

　　1) increase learning in students, they link teacher behavior and student achievement;

　　2) inspire students to achieve greater levels of understanding of their culture, their environment, and their traditions;

　　3) are more likely to act in a professional way, that is, they feel more responsible for the intellectual growth and well-being of their students;

　　4) have the same values as the society or community in which they teach, so are more effective, creative, and accepted;

　　5) coming from a particular ethnic group that is educationally disadvantaged serve as role models for the children from that group;

---

[2] The author was one of the first staff members of this project and has maintained close contact with graduates, students, staff, and Indian leaders.

[3] These assumptions are validated to varying degrees through research by such scholars as Brophy and Good (1986), Gagne (1977), Grant (1977), Joyce and Weil (1972), and Rosenshine and Stevens (1986).

6) from a common racial group serve as a source of motivation to children of that race, possibly through a common cultural and linguistic background.

BUNTEP is a part of the Faculty of Education at Brandon University. All regulations that govern the granting of teacher education degrees apply to this special program and the teaching and administrative staff are members of the Faculty of Education. The program is funded jointly by the Federal and Provincial governments. The main project office and senior administrative staff are located on the main campus although the program itself is delivered in various centres for instruction in selected communities in northern Manitoba. Each centre has a resident administrator (who may have teaching responsibilities), some resource materials and other teaching supplies.

In establishing a BUNTEP centre, community support is essential. The community leaders request a centre by making a commitment to provide physical space suitable for a class of up to twenty-five students. There must be accommodation for a resident professor and itinerant travelling personnel. Other prerequisite conditions include sufficient classrooms for practice teaching, co-operation of the school personnel and sufficient funding from the BUNTEP office.

Students in these programs are selected from designated communities and admitted to the university under normal admissions criteria. Then a committee of community members and university personnel reviews applications and selects applicants for interviews. Most of the students are women with children and family responsibilities.

The program offers support to students in three essential areas:

1) *academic assistance* from professors and the centre administrator through additional tutoring, and a course on upgrading and study skills;

2) *counselling* (personal and family) available to students, although on a limited basis;

3) *financial support* covering students' living expenses (travel, day care, clothing, and dependents), and all tuition, fees and books.

The community-based training model has several advantages for aboriginal students: families are not disrupted by a move to an urban centre, students are able to keep in touch with community issues, students who complete the program stay in the community to work, young people may emulate role models provided by their parents (or relatives) who succeed at university education, an already established support system through an extended family and friends assists the student through difficult times, and the students are not alienated by a university bureaucracy and an indifferent urban population.

Some of the disadvantages of this community-based program have been:

1) high turn-over of staff due to rigours of travel and/or living in professional isolation;

2) lack of opportunity for students to learn through the problems of on-campus exposure (large classes, keeping schedules, etc.);

3) no organized avenues for mixing with other university students of different cultures, race, and academic orientation; and absence of major curriculum change in the program.

The program has been successful in: 1) producing aboriginal graduates who are teaching in their communities; 2) demonstrating to native people that, given the appropriate conditions and opportunities, they can succeed; 3) gaining in northern Manitoba an awareness by the native population of educational opportunities and the possibility of moving to autonomy in educational decision-making.

While this program has been evaluated twice by its funders and has been deemed successful, worhwhile, and financially cost-effective, some academics and other skeptics still question its "quality." They continue to imply that its differences make it not as "good" as the program offered on a university campus. And many simply refuse to believe that native peoples can be successful at anything, thus the quality must be lower. Despite such opposition, this and similar programs in Canada have demonstrated that people who live under Third World conditions can improve their lives. Teacher training is a necessary activity for native peoples if they are to throw off the yoke of oppression and move toward self-determination.

Moving Forward

Education as a vehicle for upward social mobility and the achievement of "the good life" is emphasized and promoted by aboriginal peoples. A sound educational basis for elementary schools requires highly trained people from within the culture and community. Approximately one hundred and eighty Indian and northern teachers have graduated since 1975 from the BUNTEP program and the majority of them are currently teaching on reserves. They have changed the conditions of schooling.

The planning process in these small communities is now more comprehensive, with planners aware of local economic development, cultural and social organizations, the political governing body, and education. Professionals plan and organize *together* so that their goals and objectives complement each other: cooperation rather than isolation is the underlying principle.

Indian people on reserves seek to control their own education. This extends beyond fiscal accountability to making suitable curricula, developing and selecting suitable classroom materials, understanding and promoting the cultural/social values of people, and exercising good judgment in the selection of teachers and administrators. Many Indian reserves now have local control of education, and statistics show that their reserve schools have increased the retention rate of pupils (Hull 1987a). In particular, at the elementary school level, where some Indian teachers speak the native language, many youngsters attend classes regularly because they feel comfortable in effective communication with Indian teachers.

To assist responsible administration, Indian people must be trained to fill positions that become available under local control. Although this has been emerging for two decades, in 1989 the Department of Indian and Northern Affairs decided to limit the increases in funding for post-secondary training for Indians (Minister of Indian and Northern Affairs 1989). The government's explanation was "fiscal restraint in a time of scarce funds," but a cynical explanation is that the Federal bureaucracy is unhappy with the success of Indian administration and is attempting to subvert their self-determination. The Federal Department of Indian and Northern Affairs is dependent on the continued colonization of Indian people: if third world conditions are not maintained on reserves, thousands of Euro-Canadians will lose their jobs. The Federal bureaucracy ensures its existence by maintaining and ensuring political impotence of Indian people, including denial of educational opportunity and thus disruption of the movement toward self-determination and self-government.

The continued training of aboriginal teachers in northern Manitoba is improving the levels of educational achievement for the population in these communities, making possible local control over education by chiefs and councils, qualifying more Natives in several professions (medicine, dentistry, law, social work, conselling), and providing successful Indian professionals as role models for the young people.

Several factors still militate against the progressive movement toward decolonization and self-determination: high unemployment, lack of a viable economic base, poor health care and sanitation (reflected in high infant mortality and comparatively lower life expectancy), and the lack of adquate financial resosurces. In other words, while adequate teacher training can assist in the process of development toward self-determination, it is merely an enabling factor within the larger context of education. It must be carefully combined with economic, cultural, social, and political efforts.

During the Oka crisis in the province of Quebec, Archbishop Desmond Tutu of South Africa was invited to visit the Mohawk people on their reserve. He was shown the conditions under which the Mohawks were living; he compared the living conditions with those of black South Africans in the township. In 1987, Chief Louis Stevenson of the Peguis Band of Indians invited the High Commissioner of South Africa to visit his reserve to witness the third world conditions of his people (*Winnipeg Free Press* 1987). Both incidents received national coverage in the media. The Canadian public could no longer feign innocence or ignorance. The national Indian leadership was poised to move ahead in 1990 with reforms in the Canadian constitution, land claims, the legal systems, self-government, and education.

Conclusion

As mentioned in the beginning of this chapter, of the five major areas listed, education received the least attention. Although public school education is accorded some urgency, post-secondary initiatives are minimal. With local control of education and increasing numbers of trained Indian teachers, third world conditions existing among Indian peoples may be eradicated. However, with development and modernization come changes in attitudes, beliefs, technology, and values (Inkeles and Smith 1974). Accomodation to these changes requires new structures, alternate modes of analysis and an acceptable balance between traditional and modern values. While the Canadian power elite must support and enable these changes, the aboriginal peoples of Canada must be recognized as the legitimate architects of their own destiny.

References

Birch, D., and M. Elliott. 1987. Towards a new conception of teacher education. In L. Stewin and J. McCann, ed. *Contemporary Educational Issues: The Canadian Mosaic.* Toronto: Copp Clark Pitman.

Brandt, W. 1980. *North-South: A Program for Survival.* Cambridge, Mass.: The MIT Press.

Brophy, J. E., and T. L. Good. 1986. Teacher behavior and student achievement. In M. C. Wittrock, ed. *Handbook of Research on Teaching.* New York: Macmillan.

Frank, A. G. 1966. The development of underdevelopment. In C. Wilber, ed. *The Political Economy of Development and Underdevelopment.* New York: Random House.

Freire, P. 1971. *Pedagogy of the Oppressed.* New York: Herder and Herder.

_____. 1973. *Education for Critical Consciousness.* New York: Seabury Press.

Frideres, J. S. 1983. *Native People in Canada.* 2nd ed. Toronto: Prentice-Hall.

Gagné, R. M. 1977. *The Conditions of Learning.* Toronto: Holt, Rinehart and Winston.

Goulet, D. 1968. That Third World. *The Centre Magazine* 1(6): 47-55.

_____. 1978. *The Cruel Choice.* New York: Atheneum.

Grant, C. A., ed. 1977. *Multicultural Education: Commitments, Issues and Applications.* Washington D. C.: Associations for Supervision and Curriculum Development.

Grossman, P., and A. Richert. 1988. Unacknowledged knowledge growth: A re-examination of the effects of teacher education. *Teacher and Teacher Education* 4(1): 53-62.

Harrison, D. 1988. *The Sociology of Modernization and Development*. London: Unwin Hyman.

Hull, J. 1987a. *An Overview of Educational Characteristics of Registered Indians in Canada*. Ottawa: Indian and Northern Affairs Canada.

_____. 1987b. *An Overview of Registered Indian Conditions in Manitoba*. Ottawa: Indian and Northern Affairs Canada.

Indian Tribes of Manitoba. 1971. *Wahbung: Our Tomorrows*. Winnipeg: Manitoba Indian Brotherhood.

Inkeles, A., and D. Smith. 1974. *Becoming Modern*. Cambridge, Mass.: Harvard University Press.

Joyce, B. and M. Weil 1972. *Models of Teaching*. Toronto: Prentice-Hall.

Lithwick, N. H., M. Schess, and E. Vernon. 1986. *An Overview of Registered Indian Conditions in Canada*. Ottawa: Indian and Northern Affairs Canada.

Minister of Indian and Northern Affairs Canada. 1989. *Communique: New Policy on the Post-Secondary Student Assistance Program*. 1-8909. Ottawa: Minister's Office.

National Indian Brotherhood. 1972. *Indian Control of Indian Education: A Policy Paper*. Ottawa: National Indian Brotherhood.

National Indian Brotherhood, Assembly of First Nations. 1986. *Tradition and Education: Towards a Vision of Our Future.* Volumes I, II, III. Ottawa: Assembly of First Nations.

Peters, R. S. 1970. *Ethics and Education.* London: Allen and Unwin.

Rosenshine, B., and R. Stevens. 1986. Teaching functions. In M. C. Wittrock, ed. *Handbook of Research on Teaching.* 3rd ed. New York: Macmillan.

Roxborough, I. 1979. *Theories of Underdevelopment.* London: Macmillan.

Winnipeg Free Press. 1987. March 11, p. 1.

MORE THAN 400 YEARS IN CREATION, THE PATH OF AMERICAN INDIAN EDUCATION

Linda Lippitt and Mary Romero

The diverse peoples united under the name of American Indian share with the EuroAmerican society a history that has been evolving since the fifteenth century. This chapter presents the historical contexts of American Indian education, from the religious structures of the pre-colonial era, through policies of assimilation and termination, to the legislative acts of the 1970s and contemporary issues. The chapter also presents a case study of a single school whose first 100 years reflect the national history and whose second 100 years have begun as a statement of success under tribal leadership. Under self-determination, Indian leadership now controls Indian education in the United States. Their solutions to the current educational concerns of their people will shape the path of American Indian education through the twenty-first century.

The People

The people "of the sacred red earth" (Whiteman 1985, 1) had created thousands of indigenous societies before the arrival of Columbus on the eastern shores of North America in 1492. Estimates of the existing Indian population at the time of contact with Europeans vary from a low of 1,148,000 to a high of 18,000,000 (Banks 1987). How and when the first native groups arrived in North America also remains an approximation.

Archaeological evidence indicates that tens of thousands of years ago these first peoples crossed a land bridge between Siberia and Alaska, which is now the water-covered Bering Strait. This migration spread across a continent, creating through the centuries the diverse cultural societies, languages, and belief systems of the historic Indian nations.

Many genesis explanations of tribal groups reject the concept of a wandering race and hold that they were placed directly in their homelands at the time of Creation (Whiteman 1985). The native name of most tribes often translates as "the People" or the "Human Beings;" the Navajo call themselves the *Dineh*--the People, and the Chippewa, *Anishinawbe*--the Original People (American Indian Handbook Committee 1982, 4). Today, there are about 500 recognized American Indian tribes. The Cherokee and the Navajo are the only tribes numbering greater than 100,000 people (Banks 1987).

Contemporary terms for these indigenous tribal groups include American Indian, Native American, and First American. No one term is consistently used. Within the United States, the legal definition of American Indian is stated in the Indian Self Determination and Assistance Act as an American citizen from a federally recognized tribe, band or group of Indians (Public Law 93.638, Section 273.2). All American Indian tribal members and the Eskimos and Aleuts of Alaska are considered Native Americans, but so are Native Hawaiians of Polynesian descent. The term First Americans can be misunderstood, as the term may also apply to the founders and first citizens of the United States. *American Indians, Eskimos and Aleuts* (or Alaska Natives) are the most complete titles used when referring to the native peoples of the United States.

The preliminary 1990 U.S. Census data tallied the most current information available about the American Indian and Alaska Native populations. These groups make up eight-tenths of one percent (0.8%) of the total United States population of 249 million. Approximately 1,960,000 persons identified themselves as members of these groups. They are by far the smallest subgroup of the United States. For comparison, Asian Americans constitute 2.9 percent of the total population; Hispanic Americans, 9.0 percent; and African Americans, 12.1

percent. American Indians and Alaska Natives live in all fifty states, within cities and urban areas, rural areas, reservations, and historic Indian areas of Oklahoma. However, 43 percent live in just four states, Arizona, California, New Mexico, and Oklahoma (U.S. Bureau of the Census 1991).

The History

. . . With minor exceptions the history of Indian education had been primarily the transmission of white American education, little altered, to the Indian child as a one-way process . . . controlled by the non-Indian society . . . its goals primarily aimed at removing the child from his aboriginal culture . . . . (Fuchs and Havighurst 1972, 19)

As summarized above by Fuchs and Havighurst, historically, American institutions charged with the education of Indians had the primary goal of assimilation of Indian children into white society through the removal of these children from their aboriginal culture. No consideration of the indigenous culture of the Indian children was reflected in the curricula of these institutions. Traditional Indian education encompassed far more than the content of a curriculum established by an outside institution. The teacher's historic role was to help ". . . the learner to perceive and to clarify the natural and spiritual worlds and to bring those two worlds into harmonious relationship" (Marashio 1982, 2). For the Pueblo scholar Dr. Rina Swentzell (1982), learning was through doing, figuring out real-life situations and assuming responsibility and participation in a natural course. She wrote that "The word learning, in one Pueblo dialect, is *ha pu weh* which is *to have breath*. Learning, then is to have breath or to be alive!" (p. 29).

This integration of education, spirituality, and community life dissolved as the Europeans advanced their settlements into North America. The Report on Indian Education (U.S. Government 1976) provided a thorough review of the history of government involvement in Indian education. The summation below offers a synopsis of this involvement, as cited by Charles (1981) and expanded by Eder and Reyhner (1988) and Whiteman (1985).

Education Through Church and State

Missionaries arrived with the earliest European contingents, intent on "civilizing" the Indians and assisting with their assimilation into the emerging EuroAmerican society. By 1568, the Jesuits had established a school for Florida Indians on the island of Cuba and the Franciscans had started missions in the Pensacola Bay area of Florida. Protestant churches also involved their ministers and lay people in building churches and schools. Training in religion, vocational arts, and basic academics made up the curriculum of this period for Indian students. Colleges such as Harvard and William and Mary included the education of Indian youth as part of their mission. Religious schooling of the native peoples was the primary source of formalized education by non-Indian peoples during the colonial period. Allegiance to a new religion, cultural values, language, and personal appearance was the price to be paid.

Although religious education also held a central role in non-Indian education during the colonial period, the cost to the native cultures was high. The economic, religious, and political repercussions within the Indian communities varied greatly according to geographical location and historical period, tribal stability, and the social background of the EuroAmericans establishing the system of schooling. In New England, where the establishment of a wide-spread educational system for non-native students was an early priority, the schooling of Indian students was also highly formalized. In areas such as the southern colonies, where literacy rates were low for all populations, the creation of Indian programs was not as highly developed. However, for all of the religious schools, the "fundamental principle necessary for Indian schooling [remained] the need to Christianize and civilize the nations" (Szasz 1988, 5).

The emphasis on Christianity disrupted the very foundation of the tribes. The transmission of cultural values, survival skills, and spiritual understanding, which were the underpinning of their world, was replaced by a patriarchal society based upon a monotheistic world view. This EuroAmerican perspective was intended to replace a multitude of cultural systems evolved over generations to meet particular needs of unique peoples. Traditional policies of child rearing were no longer modeled by tribal members. The role of the community in determining its own educational path was eroded almost to extinction. At the same time, some tribal members did embrace the new system, accepting the very real material benefits provided by boarding schools to children suffering from famine, disease, and other negative results of the social and economic changes. Additionally, competency in the skills and training offered by the educational institutions allowed individuals to prepare themselves as liaisons between their tribes and the developing governments (Szasz 1988).

The first governmental support for American Indian education was a $500 appropriation for Dartmouth College from the Continental Congress in 1775. After the ratification of the U.S. Constitution in 1789, more than 120 governmental treaties with Indian nations contained educational provisions. Despite a constitutional separation of church and state, in 1819, the Civilization Fund was created to allocate funds to religious groups willing to teach Indian students; by 1830, a total of 1,512 students had received aid in 52 institutions. In 1832, a Commissioner of Indian Affairs began operating in the War Department. In just six years, six manual training schools and 87 boarding schools were operated by the federal government to emphasize vocational training. Eleven years later, the Office of Indian Affairs was transferred to the Department of the Interior.

In addition to religious and government schools, there was a significant contribution by tribally run schools. Despite a forced removal from their homelands, the 5 *Civilized Tribes* of Oklahoma (Cherokees, Choctaw, Chickasaws, Creeks, and Seminoles) developed an independent bilingual school system which was funded and administered by the tribes. It successfully served students from primary school to college in the years 1838 to 1860. At the start of the Civil War, the system collapsed, leaving dormant the concept of self-determination in Indian education for another century.

As the westward expansion of white settlers intensified the clash over land and political control, the government policy towards Indian education became more aggressive. In 1873, the Civilization Fund was rescinded, placing greater control of the educational system with the federal government. As the American military campaigns drew to a close and reservations were formed to hold the remaining tribes, schools became a means to accelerate the assimilation of tribal communities. These schools were ". . . designed to devalue the traditional culture and religion of Indian people and to coercively assimilate Indian youth into the dominant society" (Eder and Reyhner 1988, 35). Compulsory school attendance and a standardized curriculum were in place by 1889. The Carlisle Indian Industrial Training School opened in Carlisle, Pennsylvania, as the first off-reservation boarding school in 1879. The boarding school system emphasized vocational training and grew to twenty-five schools by 1900. After the turn of the century, off-reservations schooling gradually gave way to the development of public school systems which included Indian students. In 1912, the public schools enrolled more Indian children than did all of the government schools, effectively transferring most of Indian education from federal to state control.

The Early Reforms

Up until the twentieth century, both church and government schooling attempted to transform Indian youth into active participants in the majority society, neglecting the "multitude of linguistic and cultural differences among Indian peoples, and . . . the varied traditions of child rearing in preparation for adulthood in the tribal communities" (Fuchs and Havighurst 1972, 6). Then, in the early 1900s, scientific and public opinion began to look more favorably at the contributions of the Indian peoples to the broader American society which slowly began to value non-European cultures. During World War I, Indians served in the military, earning respect for their patriotism. Helen Hunt Jackson (1886) educated the public with *A Century of Dishonor*, which documented the failure to honor treaties, land abuses, and the lack of legal rights for the Indian peoples. In 1924, The Snyder Act acknowledged the tribal status of Indian peoples while granting them the rights and responsibilities of citizenship in the United States.

A federal investigation into the education of Indian students resulted in the Merriam (1928) Report which highlighted two areas of concern, the lack of health and educational services and the lack of Indian control. The recommendations of the Merriam Report were implemented in the 1930s under a new Commissioner of Indian Affairs, John Collier. Congress passed the Johnson O'Malley Act in 1934 to provide federal funding to Indian students in state controlled public schools. This funding remains today as an important supplemental source of monies for public schools and is now locally allocated with the guidance of Indian parent committees. Educational reforms included specialized training of teachers of Indian youth, the development and dissemination of bilingual materials, and a growing awareness of cultural concerns within government schools.

From Termination to Self-determination

Following World War II, a shift in public opinion and government policy reversed the pluralistic trends of the 1920s and 1930s. Supportive congressional action of these pre-war years was now viewed as intrusive regimentation. The Indians were to be "freed" by the termination of the unique federal relationship with sovereign tribes. Laws rescinded specialized programs and terminated reservations for the Indian peoples. In 1953, six pieces of federal legislation were passed to further this dissolution of treaty obligations. In 1954, the federal government terminated its relationship with the Klamath tribe in Oregon, the Menominee of Wisconsin, and California tribes. Elimination of tribal standing devastated the tribal members who lost cultural identity, federal benefits, and most importantly, their tribal lands held in common under reservation status.

The building of public schools on reservations was supported by the passage in 1950 of Public Laws 874 and 815 which provided operating funds and building capital respectively. A policy of encouraging the relocation of Indian families off reservation and into more urban areas also increased the number of students in public schools. This further withdrew the federal government from Indian education as public schools are constitutionally the responsibility of state governments.

Indian leadership contested the termination policies, while remaining firmly committed to tribal sovereignty. Increasing awareness of civil rights and attention to equal opportunity for minority groups across the United States bolstered their challenge in the 1960's. The creation of the National Indian Education Association and the Coalition of Indian Controlled School Boards expanded the role of Indian educators as an influential and controlling force in Indian education. Federal education projects such as the preschool program Head Start, Upward Bound, Job Corps, and Vista were authorized under the Economic Opportunity Act of 1964. The Rough Rock Demonstration School, founded in 1966 in the Navajo community of Rough Rock, Arizona, was the first Indian school to truly implement local control under contract with the Bureau of Indian Affairs. Community colleges for the education of Indian students were funded and operated by the Bureau of Indian Affairs in cooperation with Indian leadership.

In 1969 a Special Senate Subcommittee on Indian Education produced the Kennedy (1969) Report, *Indian Education: A National Tragedy, a National Challenge*, which summarized a plight shockingly similar to that found in the Merriam Report of 1928. A second study, the National Study of American Indian Education, as summarized by Fuchs and Havighurst (1972) in *To Live on This Earth*, repeated these findings. This demonstrated lack of an effective educational process for Indian youth inspired passage of the Indian Education Act, Title IV of P. L. 92-318 in 1972 and its amendments in 1975. The law mandated a fundamental shift in policy, reaffirming the cultural validity of the Indian peoples. Community run programs and parental involvement were required. New programs stressed the inclusion of culturally relevant instruction and native language materials.

The era of open support for Indian self-determination began in 1970 when President Nixon officially announced the Indian Self-Determination Policy, a policy which essentially committed the United States federal government to fostering and encouraging self-government among Indian tribes, without the threat of eventual termination. As cited by Banks (1987), the goal of the President's new national policy aimed

> ... to strengthen the Indians' sense of autonomy without threatening the sense of community ... we must assure the Indian that he can assume control of his own life without being separated involuntarily from the tribal group . . . that Indians can become independent of federal control without being cut off from federal concern and federal support. (p. 152)

This national policy set the stage for the passing by Congress of the Indian Self-Determination and Education Assistance Act (P.L. 93-638) in 1975. This act mandated that local tribes be permitted to contract services, including schools, from the Bureau of Indian Affairs. In 1983, after years of public controversy over Indian control and limited success in tribal advancement towards the self-determination policy, President Ronald Reagan publicly endorsed the nation's commitment to tribal sovereignty:

> Tribal governments, like state and local governments, are more aware of the needs and desires of their citizens than is the federal government and should, therefore, have the primary responsibility for meeting those needs. The only effective way for Indian reservations to develop is through tribal governments which are responsive and accountable to their impact. (Department of Interior 1983, 3)

Since the passing of the Indian Self-Determination and Education Assistance Act, there has been a steady increase in the number of tribally operated schools. Currently,

40,000 Native American students nationwide are educated in schools either operated directly by the Bureau of Indian Affairs [103] or funded under self-determination contracts with Indian tribes [67]. Self-determination contracts are authorized under P.L. 93-638; thus, these contracts are often referred to as 638 contracts and schools operated by tribes under 638 contracts are termed contract schools. (Education Department 1988, 133)

Re-Thinking Indian Education

Despite the expanded liberties of self-determination, tribal leaders are constrained by a legacy of social, economic, and educational inequities established by institutional policy over hundreds of years. For Deloria (1974), the "past continues to dominate the present and future" (p. 6). The current educational system to which Indian students have access consists of a choice among government schools, public schools, private schools, and religious schools. Virtually all of these choices are based on an educational model derived from European systems of schooling as adapted for the American society. The curricula, teaching methodologies, and underlying goals reflect an assumed national standard as interpreted regionally by state mandates. Despite compulsory school attendance for Indian youth since 1889, there has been a continually dismal record of achievement among tribal youth as reported in low standardized achievement rates on national elementary, secondary, and college entry exams; continually high dropout and absentee rates in local and national studies; and low success rates in college retention or post-secondary educational endeavors.

Initial reports of the Wells study, *Indian Education From the Tribal Perspective: A Survey of American Indian Tribal Leaders* (New Mexican 1991), parallel the lack of success among tribal youth found in earlier studies. This survey returned by 44.4 percent of the 511 tribal leaders contacted found that 92 percent of all American Indians attend local public schools, primarily in rural areas. Although the majority of the tribal leaders viewed education as a high priority, few felt that they actually had influence in the schools. The advancement of educational reforms must directly involve tribal participation in the public school system. Additional key findings included the following: 52 percent of Indian students entering high school will graduate, but lack of motivation and incentives remain obstacles to achievement; 48 percent of the schools Indian children attend have no Indian teachers; and 70 percent attend schools where their native language is not offered.

Educational studies have repeatedly found that cultural incompatibility between the Indian learner and the instructional method contributes to a lack of student success in education (Klesner 1982, Butterfield 1981, Boloz 1981). A failure to recognize and respond to the special needs of Indian children by teachers and administrators has often led to lowered expectations and accompanying low academic achievement (AIHC 1982). Gilliand and Reyhner (1988) stated in *Teaching the Native American* that conventional approaches to schooling ignore or contradict the native heritage that students bring to school and then called for approaches which recognize the "double advantage of knowing and living in two cultures" (p. 3). Across the nation, emphasis is now being given to the following three educational issues which are seen as initial steps in harmonizing the school setting: cultural relevancy in curriculum development and teacher preparation, first and second language programs, and increasing community control and parental involvement.

The Bureau of Indian Affairs (1980) has acknowledged that ". . . culture includes all aspects of local life and they must all be taken into account in the educational program" (p. 2). These program adjustments reach beyond mere inclusion of traditional and contemporary Indian stories, writings, and histories, to actually teaching from an Indian perspective, melding Western views with traditional ones. Cajete (1986) created an entire science curriculum to demonstrate the feasibility of this method. Martinez (1987) identified peer teaching, games, and programmed instruction as preferred classroom learning strategies of Pueblo, Navajo and Apache seventh graders.

Teachers of the majority culture are now encouraged to learn about the diversity of American Indian communities and the American Indian child before entering the classroom. Expanded and enriched educational strategies are required in a multi-cultural setting. The identification of individual learning styles and relevant strategies for instructional delivery, including computer technology, is underway. High expectations, methods adapted to student needs, and more positive teacher-student interactions are repeatedly stressed as necessary components for educators of Indian children (Klesner 1982, Butterfield 1981, Boloz 1981).

There is now recognition of the strong underpinnings in oral language which the student brings to the classroom (Klesner 1982) and the fact that first language skills transfer to second language usage given "numerous opportunities to test language use" (Boloz 1981, 27). There is also an awareness that content area teachers also function as English language teachers and that instructional delivery must be altered to better serve the language needs of Indian students. Many tribal students are monolingual English students whose vocabulary, diction, and syntax do not mirror standard American English, but whose dialectal use of these linguistic elements is consistent and widespread. Teaching approaches are being developed which show an understanding of the distinct linguistic backgrounds these children bring to their schooling, while still providing opportunities to broaden their experiential background with standard American English.

Developing parental awareness of educational programs within the schools and encouraging parental involvement with decision making is not only philosophically sound, but backed by federal legislative intent. Both P. L. 93-638, the Indian Self-Determination Act, and P. L. 95-561, which provides a specific framework for implementing community control, mandate local support and involvement in education. Tribal leaders, educators, and parents, while embracing the opportunity to develop local control, are still exploring models to assess their specific community needs and to create effective programs for their own youth.

In addition to the questions and controversies which concern the nation as a whole in the development of a quality curriculum to meet the changing needs of youth today, the critical need exists to offer a program which prepares Indian students to successfully make fulfilling life choices in both the Indian world and the broader American society. The Indian schools of the coming decades, whether public, government, or private, will reflect the values, vision, and leadership of the tribal communities in the creation of a new model of education.

Case Study: The Santa Fe Indian School

Searching for the Path: Background and History

Before the 1970 public support for Indian control over decision-making and the promotion of tribal interests, total federal control over all aspects of Indian affairs had existed for nearly two centuries. Federal control over the education of Indians began in the 1800s as a result of treaty responsibilities and other legal agreements between the United States government and Indian tribes. Between 1880 and 1900, the federal government created twenty-five off-reservation Indian boarding schools in fifteen different states. The educational policies and programs of these schools were identical to one another and many of the decisions pertaining to these schools were determined in Washington, D. C. The goal of these schools was assimilation.

It was during this time period that Santa Fe Indian School was founded in 1890, in the north central New Mexico city of Santa Fe. *One House, One Heart, One Voice: Native American Education at Santa Fe Indian School*, a 1987 documentary booklet of the school, summarizes this historic time:

In 1885, Congress appropriated $25,000 for the United States Indian Industrial School in Santa Fe, New Mexico. Prominent merchants, lawyers, and politicians donated a 103 acre site two miles south of town. The school was to serve the New Mexico Pueblos and the Navajo, Apache, Ute, and other tribes, many of whom were reluctant to hand over their children to the government. In 1890, the first students arrived. (Hyer 1987, 3)

Like the other educational institutions of this period, the early Santa Fe Indian School reflected the image of a military institution with uniformed children, some as young as six years old, marching and drilling in battalions and companies. Students came primarily from the Pueblos of New Mexico bringing with them their native languages and a rich Pueblo culture. As implied in the quote above, industrial or vocational training was the central educational program of the school because it was felt that Indians were best suited for manual labor. After the 1930s a national policy supporting and promoting cultural diversity began. The school's military approach switched to one with a greater emphasis on culture and arts. Then World War II erupted and by 1946, Indian education at Santa Fe Indian School began to reemphasize vocational training as a way to prepare students for the job market. Beginning in the 1950s, the federal government began its termination policy in hopes of ceasing its responsibilities towards Indian people. Caught in the midst of this period, Santa Fe Indian School was closed in 1962. Students could transfer to either a public school or to Albuquerque Indian School, a boarding school about sixty miles south of Santa Fe.

Fourteen years later, a deteriorating educational program, dilapidated facilities, and numerous social problems at the Albuquerque site prompted the All Indian Pueblo Council, made up of the Governors of the nineteen New Mexico Pueblos, to contract for the school. In 1977, it became the first contract school in the nation to operate under the 1975 Indian Self-Determination Act. For the first time, tribal leadership determined the direction of the educational process. The Pueblo Governors requested a return to the original Santa Fe campus. In 1981, the move was approved by the Secretary of the Interior. Santa Fe Indian School was reestablished.

Creating the Path: Self-Determination

In the years following, concentrated efforts to improve the quality of the educational program elevated the school to a point of national recognition. In 1987, the Santa Fe Indian School received the U. S. Department of Education *Excellence in Education Award* from the President of the United States. Much of the school's success and its national recognition as a leader in Indian education can be attributed to the following three dominant factors: the direct control and ownership of the school by the Pueblo communities through an all-Indian school board, the consistent strong support of the Pueblo communities, and the high caliber and commitment of its staff. As a result, the Santa Fe Indian School in September of 1988 changed its operation policy from a PL 93-638 contract to a PL 100-297, Title V, Part B grant, which assures greater local community control of the school program.

Today the Santa Fe Indian School continues to attract Indian youth primarily from the nineteen Pueblo communities of New Mexico which represent a total population of about 32,000. Each Pueblo remains politically independent of one another; however, each continues to share a strong commitment to the success of the school. Approximately 560 seventh through twelfth grade students representing sixteen diverse language groups attend and board at Santa Fe Indian School. The school is accredited by the North Central Association of Colleges and Secondary Schools and the New Mexico Department of Education and is a member of the Non-Public Schools Association of New Mexico. In 1989, over $200,000 in competitive scholarships were awarded to Santa Fe Indian School graduates. The school has received numerous national, state, and local awards for outstanding academic and athletic achievement.

To assure continued growth in a direction which best benefits the Indian communities, the school has made a commitment to on-site educational research. Central to each of these initiatives is the solicitation of input from the community and school staff. As summarized in the in-house paper, *New Visions, A Culture Sensitive Approach to Indian Education*

(Merchant, Romero, and Schultz 1991), The Santa Fe Indian School is currently involved in five separate research initiatives:

1) The Competency Testing Project: This project has been identified by the U.S. Department of Education as one of the ten "Showcase Projects" in the nation. Its purpose is to develop a culturally relevant and statistically reliable competency exam which better reflects certain cultural aspects in selected areas of the school curriculum.

2) The Learning Approaches Resource Center (LARC): The Learning Styles Study examined the profiles of learning styles among 489 Pueblo, Navajo, Apache, Hopi, and a small number of Plains Indian students to determine if distinctive patterns of learning, both as a whole and as separate tribal language groups could be identified. The findings of this study have been incorporated into the objectives and methods utilized across the secondary school curriculum.

3) The Cognitive Composition Project: The focus of this project was to improve students' skills in reading, writing, and speaking the English language through development of instructional units, culturally relevant materials, and teacher training in effective instructional strategies. Funding is provided by Apple Computer, Inc., which encourages the study of computer technology in learning to write.

4) The Model Dorm Program: The purpose of this project is to create a more positive living and learning dormitory environment for those students residing in campus dormitories. The major components in this experimental project include training in counseling and parenting skills for both parents and residential advisors, the development of student recreational activities, and the establishment of a communication network to strengthen school and community relations.

5) The Gifted and Talented Research Project: This project is attempting to identify the characteristics of giftedness from a Pueblo perspective. This study was designed as a first step in identifying, nurturing, and developing gifted Pueblo students.

Walking the Path: New Visions

Although Santa Fe Indian School is already recognized nationally for its leadership in Indian education and its successful educational programs, a need to develop and establish an *Indian* school, a school that will reflect the unique values and traditions of the Pueblo people, continues to exist and serve as an impetus for improvement. Far beyond the basic principles of self-determination is the awareness and open recognition that the Santa Fe Indian School has a two-fold purpose: the preservation and proliferation of Pueblo societies, their culture, traditions, and values, and the challenge of providing the best educational opportunities to its 100 percent Native American student body. This duality in the purpose of the Santa Fe Indian School is recognized as being essential for the school's success and survival, as exemplified by its mission statement as well as its school philosophy.

Santa Fe Indian School Mission. The mission of the Santa Fe Indian School is to be responsive to the needs of the Indian community by providing an educational program of continuous awakening and nurturing that reflects the Indian values of respect, harmony and hard work as a basis for making life choices in an Indian and non-Indian world.

Santa Fe Indian School Philosophy: A Special Place. My school is special to me because it is a part of my Indian community. My school is a place where my friends, relatives and other people come together for a short time to learn from one another. It is a place where my people's values are as precious as rain on a dry day, a place where ideas are nurtured as we do the corn in the fields. Here, I learn about the needs and desires of my people and my community. I learn how I can help them through remaining and participating with those I love. We must come together with one voice, one heart, and one mission, to strengthen the Indian way of life...

Santa Fe Indian School has currently undertaken the challenging task of changing the face of Indian education via a culture sensitive approach at Santa Fe Indian School. Considered quite unique and innovative in relation to current local and national practices in Indian education, the school is designing and implementing a comprehensive plan which will create an Indian school for Indian children. It is to be a school that will reflect the unique values and traditions of the Pueblo people, recognizing the everchanging needs and issues of the Indian communities and their impact on the programs of the school. In essence, the Santa Fe Indian School has embodied the principles of self-determination by creating and incorporating an educational program based on the needs and beliefs of the Pueblo people.

Two basic beliefs hold the key to Santa Fe Indian School's future: first, that the future can be influenced through careful decisions based on the sensitive assessment of the needs and values of the Indian communities; and second, that site-based research is essential to discovering effective, alternative approaches in Indian education. These beliefs have evolved as the New Vision, a comprehensive plan for the Santa Fe Indian School.

As part of its comprehensive planning process, the Santa Fe Indian School has established a center for learning and research where 1) the education of Indian people is focused around their needs and dreams and not around federal policy; 2) the research of learning and the consequent development and exploration of effective methods and materials for teaching Indian students are site based; 3) the evaluation of developed programs, methods, and material is immediate and relevant; and 4) the educational resources needed by the Indian communities are identified and utilized.

Six essential components of the comprehensive plan are briefly described below (Merchant, Romero, and Schultz, 1991):

1) *The Center for Planning and Research.* The Santa Fe Indian School Center for Planning and Research plans, conducts, and coordinates all current and future research initiatives and directs the overall research agenda at the school. Primary activities of the Center are solicitation of community input, data

collection and analysis, research coordination, publication and dissemination, funding, and training.

2) *Site-Based Research.* Site-based research serves as the foundation for the comprehensive planning process, exploring and developing effective methods and materials for teaching Indian students which are based on the needs and issues identified by the Indian constituencies. More importantly, research is conducted by Native Americans for Native Americans, thus ensuring that the research process completes a full circle with results reaching and benefitting the Indian people.

3) *Santa Fe Indian School/ University Partnership.* Undertaking a comprehensive planning process and the design of a new model for Indian education is a monumental task. Therefore, the conceptualization and planning requires the expertise and experience of the most reputable universities in a partnership. It also requires that the Santa Fe Indian School draw on all the resources within the school and its communities. An essential concept of this partnership is a collaborative and open communication network between Santa Fe Indian School and a major university concerning the design and implementation of an *Indian* school for Indian children.

4) *Santa Fe Indian School Core Group.* A core group of staff consisting of highly motivated, resourceful teachers, administrators, and others who have demonstrated a commitment to Indian education have assumed an expanded role in identifying and addressing the problems of the future. These individuals are an integral part of the university partnership and simultaneously serve as community/school resource experts and as leaders in the comprehensive planning process.

5) *Advanced Degrees.* The opportunity to earn credit towards advanced degrees through the work contributed to the comprehensive plan will be given to members of the core group through the University Partnership component. Flexibility while maintaining high academic standards and expectations is required of both parties.

6) *Santa Fe Indian School as a Community Resource.* In redesigning the curriculum, the school serves as a resource to the tribal communities and those same communities are a

resource for the school. For example, a group of students under the leadership of qualified staff may wish to undertake an environmental impact study for a tribe. Students could be involved in activities such as monitoring soil, air, and water quality. The resulting data would be useful to the tribe and heighten community awareness at the same time.

The above components of the Santa Fe Indian School comprehensive plan are all guided by a new vision of an Indian school carefully and distinctly designed to reflect the unique values and traditions of the Pueblo people and to meet the needs of its Indian students and communities. Successful establishment of such a school requires the meshing of the best of minds, an exchange of ideas, thoughts and feelings, and a sincere commitment among parties to develop innovative directions in Indian education.

Since the transformation of Santa Fe Indian School from a federally controlled school to a contract school in 1976, a European model of education, similar to other schools across the nation, has been the foundation for its educational program. This European model of education has served its purpose well, as exemplified by the many outstanding student academic accomplishments. However, this model has not been able to provide the foundation needed for reflecting the unique values, traditions, and needs of the Pueblo world.

The President of the Santa Fe Indian School Board and the Executive Director of Indian Affairs for the State of New Mexico, Regis Pecos of Cochiti Pueblo, summarized these feelings with the following statement:

> The philosophy of the school has always been to look within our own communities, to our resources that we have, that for whatever reasons in the past have not been fully utilized. Because no matter what we pursue for the well being of our children, none of that means as much as it does for our people who are developing the needs. Based on those needs, the priorities, and how best we are able to develop programs, the board, as it has done in the past, has valued the input and contributions in our own communities . . . [which] add to the kind of reflections . . . that we as Indian people

ought to have . . . to develop what means most to us and
these should be appropriately reflected in the education
programs for our children. (Gifted and Talented
Research Project 1990, 5)

It is this Pueblo world that has given birth to Santa Fe
Indian School and it is for this Pueblo world that Santa Fe
Indian School must ensure a fertile existence, if it is *itself* to
survive.

Conclusion

The history of American Indian education has evolved for over
400 years, through the religious structures of the pre-colonial
era to the policies of assimilation and termination of the first
part of the twentieth century. National support and
encouragement of the principles of self-determination began in
1970, awakening a nation to the need for Indian control over
decision making and the promotion of tribal interests. Among
tribes within the nation, it awakened the need to initiate new
directions in the realm of education, directions that realize that
Indian youth today are the decision makers of tomorrow. Native
American decision makers must be able to function proficiently
in two diverse worlds, the Indian and non-Indian. As leaders,
they must be aware of and articulate the needs of the Indian
people; they must tactfully and adeptly deliberate natural
resource issues and negotiate land and water rights; they must
understand and advise tribal governments and relate their needs
to national policies; and they must comfortably perform in their
respective capacities in tribal communities. Successful career
and leadership performance with significant contributions to
both worlds will require skills and knowledge in both the Indian
and non-Indian societies.

Providing a rich learning environment to nurture future
leaders of Indian tribes and citizens of a united nation is the
responsibility of today's Indian leaders. The accomplishment of
this task will call for the exploration of diverse educational

methods and strategies to meet the unique learning needs of Indian students. The ultimate challenge is to locate and follow the natural path created by the footsteps of Indian people, so that future generations may continue to walk the same path, adapted for life in the twenty-first century.

References

American Indian Handbook Committee. 1982. *American Indian Education Handbook.* Sacramento: California State Department of Education.

Banks, J. A. 1987. *Teaching Strategies for Ethnic Studies.* 4th ed. Boston: Allyn and Bacon.

Boloz, S. A. 1981. *The glad project: Energizing language.* (ERIC Document Reproduction Service No. ED 214 734).

Bureau of Indian Affairs. 1980. *Teaching guide for reading and language skills and bibliography of Indian materials.* Department of Interior, Aberdeen Area Office. Aberdeen, SD. (ERIC document Reproduction Service No. ED 216 806).

Butterfield, R. 1981. *Thoughts from the shadow of a flame; The Indian reading series: Stories and legends of the Northwest.* Teacher's manual, level V. Portland: Northwest Regional Educational Lab. (ERIC Document Reproduction Service No. ED 258 763).

Cajete, G. A. 1986. Science: A native American perspective, a culturally based science education curriculum. Unpublished doctoral dissertation. Los Angeles: International College.

Charles, R., ed. 1981. *National Education Policies for Aboriginal People.* Ontario Indian Education Council. Ontario, Canada.

Deloria, V. J. 1974. *The Indian Affair.* New York: Friendship Press.

Department of Interior. 1983. *Moving Toward Self Sufficiency for Indian People, Accomplishments 1983-84.* Washington, D.C.: Department of Interior and Department of Health and Human Services.

Eder, J., and J. Reyhner. 1988. The historical background of Indian education. In J. Reyhner, ed. *Teaching the Indian child, a Bilingual/Multicultural Approach.* Billings, MT: Eastern Montana College.

Fuchs, E., and R. J. Havighurst. 1972. *To Live on This Earth: American Indian Education.* New York: Doubleday and Company.

Gifted and Talented Research Project. 1990. Unpublished transcript of the November 5, Advisory Meeting. Santa Fe, NM: Santa Fe Indian School.

Gilliand, H., and J. Reyhner, J. 1988. *Teaching the Native American.* Dubuque, IA: Kendall/Hunt.

Hyer, S. 1987. *One house, one voice, one heart: Native American education at Santa Fe Indian School* (Museum booklet). Santa Fe, NM: National Endowment for the Humanities, the New Mexico Endowment for the Humanities, and the Foundation for Indian Leadership.

Jackson, H. H. 1886. *A Century of Dishonor: A Sketch of the United States Government's Dealings with Some of the Indian Tribes.* Boston: Roberts Brothers.

Kennedy, E., ed. 1969. *Indian Education: A National Tragedy-a National Challenge.* Washington, D.C.: Government Printing Office.

Klesner, M. 1982. *Language arts for native Indian students.* Victoria, Canada: Department of Education, Curriculum Development Branch. (ERIC Document Reproduction Service No. ED 238 630).

Marashio, P. 1982. Enlighten my mind. *Journal of American Indian Education* (February): 2-9.

Martinez, J. A. 1987. Learning styles of seventh grade Native American students. Unpublished doctoral dissertation. Colorado State University.

Merriam L., ed. 1928. *The Problem of Indian Administration.* Baltimore: John Hopkins University Press.

Merchant, B., M. Romero, and H. Schultz. 1991. New visions: A culture sensitive approach to indian education at the Santa Fe Indian School. An unpublished paper, Center for Planning and Research, Santa Fe Indian School.

New Mexican (the). (1991). *Indian Children Attend More Public than Tribal Schools.* Associated Press Report, April 16. Santa Fe.

Szasz, M. C. 1988. *Indian Education in the American Colonies, 1607-1783.* Albuquerque, NM: University of New Mexico Press.

Swentzell, R. N. 1982. A comparison of basic incompatibilities between European/American educational philosophies and traditional Pueblo worldview and value system. Unpublished dissertation. Albuquerque, NM: University of New Mexico.

U.S. Bureau of the Census. 1991. *U.S. Department of Commerce News, cb91-24.* Washington, D.C.: Public Information Office.

U.S. Government. 1976. *Report on Indian Education, Task Force Five: Final Report to the Indian Policy Review Commission.* Washington, D.C.: Government Printing Office.

Whiteman, H. 1985. *American Indian Policy Programs.* U.S. National Report at the 9th Inter-American Indian Congress, October 28 to November 1, Santa Fe, New Mexico.

SECTION III

LONG ESTABLISHED

STIGMAS

LONG ESTABLISHED STIGMAS IN COMPARATIVE EDUCATION: AN INTRODUCTION

Douglas Ray

Discrimination is a way of human life. Schools are responsible for some of the inequality in the world and are one means by which inequality may be transferred from one generation to the next, but in a society where many agencies are responsible for forming attitudes and controlling behaviors, schools may not be successful in breaking through the influences of other institutions like the family to become part of the solution.

The grievances of divided societies often continue through many generations, and may be aggravated by wars in which foreign interests are involved. This situation in evident in several states where civil wars figure in recent experience: India, Ireland, Israel, Spain, the USSR, China, Sudan, and Colombia. Some of these nations have been selected for case studies because their traditional divisions are now being tackled more imaginatively: The Caribbean, Canada, the United States. It is probably better to examine the progressive cases than to lament the failures, so some obvious possibilities were excluded. The "long established grievances" category is here slotted between discussions of "aboriginal status" and treatment of the "foreign born," but this distinction may not be observed in the case studies. Nations may have all three kinds of population divisions.

The Soviet Union. Few nations are so divided linguistically, racially, culturally and religiously as the Soviet Union. It contains several nationalities, ethnic groups, autonomous peoples, provinces, former colonies . . . many of them peoples conquered hundreds of years ago, for the Czar expanded the nation and met rebellions with force.[1] A century ago few of the minority populations had the right to education in their "national" language, for Russian was the imperial tongue. The USSR used education in preference to the sword: schools and even written languages were created for minorities--sometimes for the first time; colleges and universities admitted minority scholars who could then participate in the federal bureaucracy; and progressive constitutions and practices identified the intent to end the old kinds of discrimination. Some minorities became heroes of war and industry. Two major problems remained: there were continuing economic, social, cultural and political advantages for some; and demagogues diverted attention from significant gains. This is a revolution that is not yet finished.

China is often examined over a long period of history--even thousands of years. In this case, the focus is upon the minority peoples that are *not* regarded as part of the Han people. In many cases they live on the fringes of China, perhaps sharing their language, religion, and culture with cousins in other nations: USSR, Korea, Mongolia, Kashmir, India, Burma and Vietnam. Education for the minorities of China links them with the Han people, but their roots in another culture are not severed. Some of the minorities have only recently been introduced to general schooling, and they may still resist sending their children to school long enough for them to become literate. Their interest in another language and sometimes an alphabetic symbolism for writing may make them less proficient in Chinese, and they rarely contribute to the overall community of scholarship in China. In many cases (in Tibet for example) their chief goal is to ensure the survival of their culture, which they want to protect from change as much as possible. The Chinese authorities want to ensure the pervasive impact of Han society, so although minority objectives may be understood and respected, they will not determine policy.

---

[1] The minority peoples stand on the threshold of new political relations since the 1991 failed coup, but minorities remain a concern in most of the new republics.

   The United States' diversity arose from migration from all regions of the world. The focus, however, is upon a single and unshakable problem: that of racism. African American underclass status has its roots in slavery, which officially ended in 1865. The status of descendants of slaves has been studied repeatedly and incisively, always with the conclusion that the hierarchical arrangement remains little changed despite significant advances. Mistreatment continues to be associated with race, with discrimination in many dimensions of society: income, housing, health, and the justice system. Although education can be criticized for contributing to these inequalities, it remains one of the best possible tools for bringing about improvements.

   Segregated schools have officially been forbidden since *Brown vs. Board of Education* in 1954, yet segregation of society, and thereby of neighborhoods, hospitals, employers, jails, and sports clubs remains. Since schools reflect many decisions that can reflect racism (enrollment, employment, curriculum materials, guidance advice, discipline, scholarship recommendations, etc.), it is hard to reverse the determination of the dominant population to retain existing conditions. Some studies show how education might have a ripple effect, ending the century of underclass status that has been the lot of the African American.

   The Eastern Caribbean. Slave societies were to be found in many regions, and among those populations counting a very high proportion of slaves among their ancestors are those of the West Indies. Here the aboriginal population has been almost eliminated, and on most islands entirely so. Indentured laborers from impoverished families brought some Asians and Europeans, especially after the effective end to slave trading in the mid-nineteenth century. Over time, intermarriage blurred racial lines from being typical of its later populations. The eastern Caribbean is now a region where social class structure is important and race is a factor in one's place within the structure, but education is also important. For this reason, the schools acquire a great significance.

   The poverty of the islands means that families sacrifice heavily to send their children to schools, and illiteracy remains a problem. Similarly, teachers may not survive on their pay, and augmenting teaching income by tutoring or selling extra educational materials may sometimes contribute to indifferent records as teachers. Various formulae for providing the necessary services to small populations must be devised, and these educational decisions combine political, economic, and professional judgments in varying parts. The significance of the government's role as umpire is somewhat modified by the prospect of additional funds from various external agencies like the World Bank.

Colombia. The Latin Americans generally ignore race and concentrate upon social class and differences in wealth. Religious differences are more or less confined to agreement with Roman Catholicism or indifference to it, and the only minority languages are those of the aboriginals and some small foreign communities in the larger cities.

Colombia is representative of several of these patterns, and its impressive modernization and urbanization has left some traditional parts of the country well behind, in educational and cultural terms. If this neglect continues, the probable result will be further depopulation of rural areas and problems for the burgeoning cities. The educational systems in this hierarchical and traditionally agricultural society are examined here, using a case study from a relatively progressive rural area. The prognosis is only partly hopeful.

The Sudan. Africa may be more complex than other continents in the interaction of languages, religions, races, cultures, and ideologies. To the extraordinary complications of African migrations are added the recent colonial impact by two Asian and eight European powers. The Sudan is at the center of this matrix, and its size and diversity makes it a continent in miniature. Some of the underclass relationships stem from the legacies of conquest, slavery, or religious conversion. Others are explained more easily by the suspicion of, or hostility to, schooling of traditional societies, in part from poverty, and in part because the efforts of the modernizing sector are bent to eliminate the traditions and provide the best available opportunities to the right people: those who support the government of the day. This convenient rule is complicated by the series of coups and restorations of democracy extending back to independence.

Through all this confusion a central principle emerges: the family determines many of the advantages. In addition, it is useful to be rich, to live in or near the larger cities or towns, to speak Arabic and to practice Islam. Where these rules are in conflict with the standards of equity that Sudan follows in principle, there is concern to do the right thing but not the resources for adequate schooling for all. Of all the nations included in this volume, the Sudanese case study shows most clearly the difficulties of the poor nations of the world.

India. The complexity of Indian society makes it a favorite subject for analysis. Here are to be found three thousand years of foreign invasions, a recent and enduring colonial legacy, the interaction of many religions that were indigenous, sixteen major languages and more than a hundred dialects, and poverty within a state of 750 million people. These challenges have been met in part. India is one of the most dynamic societies in Asia, modernizing and urbanizing rapidly, expanding its educational system in a combination of public and private ventures with the public sector guided by notable attempts at equity. The failures at some tasks are inevitable: personal freedoms cannot easily be reconciled with government programs intended to redress ancient injustices.

The Indian case study focuses upon how modern standards of equity confront the traditions of caste and the ignominy of women and the lower castes, scheduled castes and scheduled tribes. Successive governments have extended quotas to these disadvantaged persons--collectively more than half of the Indian population. Those qualified do not wish to wait forever for their turn for employment. Although India is officially secular, Indians remain among the most religious peoples in the world, so a constitution or a government that defies certain religious traditions--even by introducing affirmative action for the largest groups of oppressed--is in trouble.

Basques, in Spain. The Basques are an ancient people who have lived "forever" on the Spanish-French border and have colonized several parts of the world. In Spain, their heritage was that of an independent people, with ancient recognition of their traditions, status, and creativity. This autonomy climaxed in the last century. During the Spanish Civil War, however, they were brutalized by the first aerial terrorism, stripped of their ancient rights, deprived of their natural leaders, schooled in the language of their conquerors, and deprived of hope. Clandestine education preserved the germ from which their civilization could be restored when the dictatorship of Franco failed to outlive the Generalissimo.

Basques in Spain now have their own schools, teach much of the curriculum in their own language, employ Basque teachers, dominate the economy in their part of Spain, and have significant political independence. The Basques in Spain have had their brush with cultural genocide, and will not soon forget.

Ulster (Northern Ireland) has been a divided society since the implantation of English and Scottish landowners centuries ago. Religious differences, augmented by other cultural and economic barriers and political preferences have kept the ancient divisions in place.

Twenty years of widely publicized insurrection has been met with a series of educational programs intended to ensure that children grew up with more than hate on their minds. The educational gap that once gave some legitimacy to hiring patterns has now been lessened, and there are advocates of merging the schooling systems, ending centuries of official separation.

English education is often equated with that of the whole of Great Britain, or even beyond that of the British Isles. One concern is that the population of England is not exclusively English--in fact it has not been for centuries. The second concern is that the newcomers, whether born in Britain or abroad, are treated as if their expectations of education are of no concern. This is evident in fields like religion and language, in history and literature, and of course in the hiring and promotion practices of most school authorities.

These entrenched discriminations may lessen from actual or proposed changes in the Education Act: funding levels, curricular requirements, location of control, protection against discrimination. There is a potential confrontation between

English (and Scottish) standards and those of the European Community, for although the latter is theoretically excluded from educational debates, the requirements for mobility of labor and citizenship within the Community make some debates and agreements inevitable, and English (and Scottish) educational practices have been challenged in the International Courts.

International Standards. Although international standards are not always respected in these matters, they are used to define an ideal basis for removal of educational barriers. Barriers may take effect at the individual or classroom level, or they may be institutionalized in the bureaucracy of the system. Changes in the systems (like examinations reform) presumably are good to the extent that they reduce such barriers and enhance opportunities. In the nations considered in this section, opportunities have traditionally favored the dominant members of society.

MINORITIES AND EDUCATION
IN THE SOVIET UNION

Douglas Ray

This chapter provides the background against which the present Soviet educational system can be judged. There have been successive changes: an initial expansion of numbers, efforts to bring equal opportunity to girls and women, measures to improve the quality of minority schooling (for both the minority population in any republic and for the education typical within the minority republics), assigning political or social priorities that could augment academic credentials of those entering higher levels of education, and some current attempts to improve education. The emphasis will be on minority status and how progressive reforms were initially welcomed but perceived eventually to fall short of promoting true equality.

Introduction

Few nations have so complex a population structure as the Soviet Union. The vast territory is populated by a range of *peoples* or *minority groups* whose members identify themselves and are recognized to be related by language, religion, ethnicity and sometimes race.[1] These populations are not uniform, for

---

[1] Lerner (1991) examines the legal meanings of group rights and minority groups, showing the difficulties occasioned by treating their rights collectively.

over a long period migrations and intermarriages would undermine group "purity."

Several *peoples* achieved independence in the past and now think of themselves as citizens of a nation state that has been denied its existence (Gerutis 1969). The historical validity of these claims is sometimes reinforced by such cultural characteristics as language (Estonian) and religion (Ukrainian Orthodox). The complexity of the Soviet peoples is probably comparable with that of the rest of Europe or Asia. For example, there are 160 languages (Khanazarov 1989, 13-14).

The boundaries of the Soviet Union are similar to those of the Russian Empire at its greatest extent (between the Congress of Vienna in 1815 and the Bolshevik Revolution in 1917). This huge empire was built in more than three centuries from the tiny Duchy of Moscow (and before that medieval fortress cities such as Novgorod) by a series of aggressive and successful rulers, especially: Ivan III, Ivan IV, Peter I, Catherine II, Alexander I, and Nicholas I (Seton-Watson 1967). Czars imposed Russian rule on territory previously held by neighboring European states such as Sweden and Poland (modern Byelorussia, Ukraine, part of Poland, Lithuania, Latvia, and Estonia), and on Asian lands as vast as Siberia, and the southern steppes of Kazakhstan, and Turkistan. Many subjects of the Empire were cross-boundary *peoples*, divided by a particular border, often victims of the power politics of various periods. Poland, Lithuania, Latvia, Estonia, and Finland were frontier nations that were over-run by Sweden, Prussia, Austria-Hungary, and Tsarist Russia. Some of them reappeared on the maps after the treaties ending the Napoleonic empire, others after World War I. Several had their 1945-1991 status determined by a cynical 1939 treaty between Germany and the USSR, or the equally cynical 1944 Yalta and 1945 Potsdam agreements among the victors of the war against Nazism. The struggles for territories in the east and south east (with China, Afghanistan, Mongolia, Korea, and Japan) were conducted over many centuries (Hoetzsch 1966).

One major difference between the Russian Empire and the Soviet Union is that the latter offered a constitutional right of withdrawing to the fifteen republics that constituted most of its area and population. After delays of some fifty to seventy years and despite vigorous opposition from the Kremlin, the right was exercised in 1990 and 1991. The failed Moscow coup of August 1991 made the separation more possible. However, internal political boundaries can hardly be drawn to reflect ethnic or linguistic territories or historic frontiers. Minority status shifts to new grounds.

Ordinary subjects of the Russian Empire were not citizens who participated in their own government. They were mistreated in a number of respects: most were serfs tied to the land, warriors living on booty, or industrial workers who were essentially slaves--even by the standards of their day (Seton-Watson, 1967). The wealth and beauty of Imperial Russia's major cities was distilled from the sweat of many workers and extortionate taxes. Class differences crossed ethnic and language lines but all poor persons of the Empire period were treated badly, with the minority peoples as an underclass--usually the worst treated of the lot. In the 1860s, for example, "land reform" left most peasants even poorer and tied more closely to their overlords (Hoetzsch 1966).

Under these circumstances, many persecuted individuals left for other lands: the United States or Canada in the nineteenth and early twentieth centuries, now (especially for Soviet citizens of German and Jewish heritage) more likely Germany or Israel. The persecuted were usually identified by some combination of religion, language, and ethnicity.

As in all nations, some of the advantages enjoyed by the favored part of the population arose from discrimination and nepotism. Russian tradition regarded foreign things as either very desirable because they were exotic (as the Italian architects and French painters were respected as the standard setters, particularly in the time of Catherine the Great) or to be treated with suspicion: conservatives sought to arrest the libertarianism apparent from the French Revolution. The Russians were often suspicious of foreign teachers (Johnson 1950). They were even suspicious of descendants of foreigners who had been invited centuries previously to settle and develop empty lands (the Germans immortalized in *The Pied Piper of Hamelin* or the Cossacks invited to defend the Eastern borders).

Often the "others" arrived in flight from religious persecution in another land: long-established minorities of this type include Jews, Hutterites, and Mennonites. There were also the remnants of the French nobility after the revolution. In the early twentieth century, Armenians fleeing Ottoman pogroms similarly sought shelter: many of them have not yet been integrated. At mid-century there were some migrants from Greece, China, Iran, and other states near the Soviet borders. More commonly, there were involuntarily displaced persons from another region of the USSR, who learned to exist in their new surroundings. Some were victims of the Gulags of Stalinism, others were resettled following border changes that accompanied wars or peace treaties. For example, the Yalta treaties gave the USSR a strip of eastern Poland, part of East Prussia with its capital of Konigsburg, Moldavia from Romania, and the Kurile Islands from Japan. The displaced populations of these annexed regions were relocated, and no matter where they went they remained "minorities" such as the Crimean Tartars and the Turks in Fergana. To make their situations worse, minority republics found that they had made room for settlers from other parts of the Soviet Union in their old homes, so that dissenters remained quiet lest they be required to move also.

The discrimination faced by minorities took the form of threats to physical security, denial of "rights" such as land, goods and power, and occasional difficulties arising from actions of citizens who misinterpreted the laws and acted as enforcers. In addition, restrictions arose from bureaucratic delays in approving apartments, assigning workers to jobs of merit, refusing permissions for foreign travel, and similar mean interpretations of policies. The policies were/are often benign.

The ordinary citizens of the USSR experienced a gradual improvement of economic conditions until the last few years. Conversely, their lives were lived under totalitarianism which is now evolving into a more open society. The "Great Power" status of the USSR is historically derived and maintained by military power more effectively than by economic performance, for many smaller nations have a higher GNP. This weakness is reflected in the falling Soviet standard of living and the present popular demand for butter over guns.

Education and Schooling

Several Soviet institutions are well respected among their kind in the world. Among them are the arts, learning in general, and formal education in particular. The USSR has for years placed a surprising priority upon that function (Tomiak 1972). UNESCO reported the percent of GNP spent on public sector education in 1985 to be unusually high--both for typical nations of different regions and for the prosperous G7 industrial nations (Table 1). Only a few exceptional cases reveal a higher financial commitment to education.

This educational consciousness did not spring into existence with the Bolshevik Revolution (Hans 1963). Education in the Russian empire was available to the rich (especially to the boys) and a few of the middle class or poor. By 1917 there was a system of schools in place but resources were short and attendance had not yet become general. Literacy remained well

Table 1. **Total Educational Expenditure** (Percentage of Gross National Product--Low and high spenders by continent, plus G-7 highly industrialized nations and USSR)

Algeria	9.9	Denmark	7.9
Nigeria	1.5	U.S.A.	6.8
Guadeloupe	15.0	Japan	4.9
Dom. Rep.	1.5	Germany	4.4
Paraguay	1.5	France	5.4
Surinam	10.1	U.K.	5.0
Indonesia	1.0	Italy	5.0
Malaysia	6.9	Canada	7.1
Greece	2.9	USSR	7.9

Source: UNESCO 1990, pp. 4-5 to 4-20

below half of the adult population in 1917. And in the eyes of many of the minority groups, the interests of the Tsarist state were entirely *Russian*. Private schools with various purposes and qualities were sporadically created, augmenting the state system. There were excellent universities and technical schools, but enrollments were small.

After the Bolshevik Revolution the interests of the state were quickly redefined to promote the rights of the proletariate. Mass education became important (Tsirul'nikov 1989). This implied opportunity for the poor, the isolated and rural, the minorities inside Russia, and the minority republics. Education for girls and women received attention. Schooling under communism was a great success, and enrolment and literacy expanded very rapidly. Similar improvements in access to secondary and higher education came within the last forty years. Tomiak (1972) offered a generous assessment of this achievement: "In the course of a half-century great progress has been made at all levels and in all aspects of education . . . no other country accomplished as much in a similar period of time" (p. 123). Peschar and Popping (1991) examine recent statistics to determine that equalization of opportunity is greater than that available in three of the five communist nations of their study. More nations need to be included in such comparisons, for this study was confined to Eastern Europe. Dorotich (1969) cautions that the interpretation of history offered in Soviet schools was biased during this period of expansion, with education intended to serve national and party ends. This reorientation of values (including attacks on religions) caused much of the anger of minority parents.

The drive to provide primary education for all included (often for the first time) something of the language and culture of the minorities (Pennar, Bakalo and Bereday 1971). This did not mean that all or even most instruction was in the minority languages: pupils were obliged to learn Russian (Khanazarov 1989). Social education was expected to cement their loyalties to the Soviet Union--not just to their republic (Monoszon 1989, 29). It was felt that education in Russian could be a *lingua franca* for all the peoples of the USSR, giving workers mobility and proficiency, thereby making various state agencies more efficient. Minority parents and their political leaders often saw this as "Russification" (Kolasky 1968) and there were regulations in 1938, 1948, 1954, and 1964 with this intent (Matthews 1982). But the Soviet system provided far more minority language instruction (both for the national minorities outside their republic and for the minority republics themselves) than had been the case under the Tsars, and advocates of schools *exclusively* in minority tongues may have been cranks or the politically ambitious.

Social Education

Four successive spheres of citizenship emerged in the Soviet system. First, the individual was to become a member of the primary group, which was likely to be defined in terms of the classroom, the school, the village, the collective, in preference to language, ethnic group, or religion. At certain periods religious freedom was not available. This aspect of citizenship was based on collectivization ideology (Makarenko 1954). Second, this primary loyalty would then be placed in the context of a broader community, which usually meant nationality and was not necessarily identical with the republic of residence. (For example, Russians were scattered throughout the Soviet Union and their nationality remained constant even after generations of life there--unless they chose another nationality to reinforce their prospects for a job requirement,[2] marriage partner, or some similar consideration. In fact, when presented with such a choice, many minority youth *chose* Russian as their nationality, believing that there were more opportunities for Russians.) The third loyalty was to the Soviet Union (in Czarist times and days of emergency to *Mother Russia*). This primal loyalty strengthened the population to endure the enormous sufferings of famines and bloodshed on their territory (Hoetzsch 1966). The second and third layers of

---

[2] For example, in 1927 the Ukraine required that university appointments be restricted to those who could lecture in Ukrainian (Kolasky 1968).

loyalties were sometimes at odds, but the Kremlin used its authority to Russify the curriculum if regionalism was getting too strong. The fourth loyalty, to the human race, is gradually becoming a widespread force in certain aspects of life. Soviet theory places all particular loyalties into an international idealism, progressing gradually from its appearance as "workers of the world" to a current emphasis on humanism (Monoszon 1989, 29) sometimes identified as international understanding, environmental consciousness, international cooperation, and peace.

Goals of Educational Equality

The initial goals for educational equality of the Soviet Union were connected to class equality. They implied that every person, male or female, was given the right to literacy, an ideal that was addressed by making education free and compulsory for basic education--initially four years. As this goal neared realization, the opportunity for basic education was successively extended to six, seven, eight, ten, and eleven years of free education, accessible to all who had passed the required examinations. Free higher education was also available on the basis of merit, defined mainly by examination results which were capable of being influenced by civic actions and family status (Rultkevich and Filippov 1973). Minimal scholarships were generally available to ensure that family poverty was not an absolute deterrent.

Expansion enabled children of the rural areas and all regions of USSR to participate in schooling on more equal terms (Zajda 1980). Data on these separate but related objectives are harder to find (Tables 2 and 3) and are easily conflated. In truth, the rural areas never achieved equal opportunity for the higher levels of schooling and universities, but selected high achievers were steadily rewarded with opportunities: admission to prestigious institutions and scholarships adequate for all their educational and living expenses. Possibly minority nationalities received less schooling than the Russians living in the minority

Table 2. **Enrollments in General Education Schools in the Union Republics** (millions)

	Total Pop.	Initial Enrollment			
		1914	1940	1970	1984
RSFSR[a]	143.1	5.7	20.6	25.3	17.5
Ukrainian[b]	58.8	2.6	6.8	8.4	6.5
Byelorussian[b]	9.6	0.5	1.7	1.8	1.4
Uzbek[b]	17.9	0.0	1.3	3.3	4.4
Kazakh[b]	15.8	0.1	1.2	3.2	3.0
Georgian[b]	5.2	0.2	0.8	1.0	0.9
Azerbaijan[b]	6.6	0.1	0.7	1.4	1.3
Lithuanian[b]	3.6	0.1	0.4	0.6	0.5
Moldavian[b]	4.1	0.1	0.5	0.8	0.7
Latvian[b]	2.6	0.2	0.3	0.3	0.3
Kirghiz[b]	4.0	0.0	0.3	0.8	0.9
Tadzhik[b]	4.5	0.0	0.3	0.8	1.1
Armenian[b]	3.3	0.0	0.3	0.7	0.6
Turkmen[b]	3.2	0.0	0.3	0.6	0.8
Estonian[b]	1.5	0.1	0.1	0.2	0.2
Total	276.3	9.7	35.6	49.2	40.4

[a]Russian Soviet Federated Socialist Republic [b]Soviet Socialist Republic

Source: Postlethwaite 1988, p. 608

Table 3. **Literacy in Tsarist Russia and the USSR**

		Men	Women	Total
1897	Rural	34.3	9.6	21.7
	Urban	65.5	43.1	55.6
1926	Rural	67.3	35.4	50.6
	Urban	88.0	73.9	80.9
1939	Rural	93.7	79.2	86.3
	Urban	97.6	91.0	94.2
1959	Rural	99.1	97.5	98.2
	Urban	99.5	98.1	98.7

Note: UNESCO 1990 reports no illiteracy in the USSR

Source: Ablin 1963, p. 41

republics, but it is more likely that qualitative differences were the causes of the endemic friction.

Over the first forty years of Communism the drive to provide primary education for all included something of the language and culture of the minorities--often for the first time (Pennar, Bakalo, and Bereday 1971). That did not absolve these pupils of the obligation to learn Russian nor to learn the social education that was expected to cement their loyalties to the Soviet Union. It was felt that Russian would remain the lingua franca for all the peoples of the USSR and this assumption was the basis for requiring that Russian be taught as well as the local nationality language in all republics (Khanazarov 1989). The children in Russian schools (whether in Russia or in the other republics) were more likely to learn international languages like

German, French, and English because they were not *required* to learn Lithuanian or Tadzhik.[3] Their fluency in international languages gave them advantages in economic and political roles that dealt with the world beyond the USSR. This aspect of the minority language question galled minority leaders. The policies and their popular interpretation led to the near extinction of courses in Ukrainian in the Eastern Ukraine and in Byelorussian within that republic. By the early 1980s, several important languages, particularly those of the Slavic family, were facing extinction in their own territories.

The political relationship was more galling than that of linguistic inferiority. For example, the Soviet Constitution of 1936 presented a myth--that the union was voluntary and among equals. In practice, there was always a means of convincing reluctant peoples that their interests were identical with those advocated by the Kremlin. There were enough external fears to galvanize most of the population into cooperation, and until recently memories of the Great Patriotic War (1941-45) were used as a reminder of the importance of strength and vigilance. Fear of the West gradually replaced this ogre. The Soviet army, as used externally in Afghanistan, Hungary, or Czechoslovakia, or domestically in Azerbaijan or Georgia, ensured that the Kremlin's will was understood. The failed coup of 1991 brought this practice to an end, it is to be hoped.

Enrollments from the minority groups within any of the republics and comparisons between republics of the USSR reveal differences that gradually diminished for the early years of schooling but never disappeared in secondary and higher education. In fact, some leaders of minorities would not seek parity of enrollments in subjects or at levels of education that threaten the cultural objectives of *peoples'* autonomy. There were elements of Russification, scientific humanism, and Marxist determinism that intensified in higher levels of studies.

---

[3]   The Russian population continues to expand its proficiency in minority languages, more so for some languages than others (Guboglo 1989).

In many regions the atheist objectives were anathema to religious leaders.

The civic education required in secondary and higher education (and also conducted effectively through youth organizations under the control of the party rather than the schools and regional governments) often reduced the loyalties of the youth toward their linguistic, religious, ethnic, or ideological heritages. The republics or religious groups sought autonomy over the educations of their own children, but they could only make marginal differences in what was prescribed from the Kremlin. Moreover, their potential alternative sources of moral authority were forestalled--for example when religions accepted the offer of the state to provide for the education of priests (Matthews 1982). State scholarships provided during a period when the state was officially atheistic brought the recipients into disrepute.

In some cases, the local state or republic authorities (in the Baltic Republics for example) were allowed to add one year of schooling for children who were not in Russian schools, thereby ensuring they would be competent in both Russian and the minority languages, and of course all the other subjects of the curriculum. Minorities were also frustrated in their attempts to provide the infrastructure for language and cultural survival: projects such as encyclopedia and multi-volume dictionary compilation took decades to publish.

A third means for promoting equal opportunity recognized the validity of the minority aspirations to maintain their own cultures and to express them publicly and symbolically.[4] The USSR created elementary schools where the minority languages could be taught, staffed them with qualified teachers and provided learning materials in the minority languages, then made these minority opportunities available where there were sufficient potential students--either in the

---

[4] The right of minorities to learn in their traditional languages was recognized from the first and defended by Lenin on numerous occasions. Stalin, Khrushchev and Brezhnev periodically returned to Russification, sometimes quite brutally (Kolasky 1968).

great cities or in the republics where the minorities lived in greatest numbers. The development of materials required that linguists and anthropologists work with the traditional populations, finding ways of recording their cultures and codifying their languages. These decisions were made by the authorities rather than by the parents, and the latter sometimes objected to the kind of education that their children were receiving. The minority language programs softened the criticisms that might otherwise have been more widespread.[5]

The result of creating a Soviet education blending Russian and other languages vaulted traditional minorities far past their previous level of schooling, and schooled them far better than their distant cousins (the counterpart minorities across any particular border). This was particularly the case for China, Afghanistan, and Iran. Recent educational data show that Turkey, Romania, and Poland are becoming competitive. In sum, of all nations adjoining the Soviet Union, only the Scandinavians, Korea, and Japan have long established educational performances that apparently outperform the education levels of the minority republics in the USSR (Table 4). Unfortunately, data for the minority populations' enrolments across the whole union--either enrolment or success indicators such as literacy--are incomplete. For parents of minority groups to secure for their children the best education and consequent economic or political opportunities, they would usually have to send them to Russian language schools and universities. For the summit of educational opportunity--such as enrolment in important Moscow or Leningrad universities--the students had to be fluent in Russian.

The wrath of traditionalists from the minorities was more likely to be directed against religious suppression or Russification through language than unhappiness with other

---

[5] Language rescues were most conspicuous for the very small language communities. Larger and potentially rivalling languages like Ukrainian and Uzbek were repressed in order to promote the use of Russian in the schools and media. This transfer occurred even in the capital cities of these minority republics.

Table 4. **Basic Education for Neighbors of the USSR**

	1960/1970		1985	
	M	F	M	F
Finland	100	95	102	101
Sweden	95	96		
Norway	100	100	95	96
Poland	98[a]	97[a]	94[b]	
Romania[a]	96	91		
Turkey	90	58	121	113
Iraq	94	36	105	91
Iran	56	27	122	105
Pakistan	46	13	51	28
China[b]			68	
Korea R.[a]	94	81	98	91
Korea D.R	99	89	104	104
Japan	99[a]	99[a]	102[b]	
Mongolia	79	78	100	103
USSR[a]	98	97	80	

[a]Adult literacy (1970 and 1985) or enrollment ratio for primary education (1960 and 1985) or percent of grade 1, [b]enrollment completing primary education (1985)

Source: UNICEF, 1991, pp. 108-109.

characteristics or the general quality of schooling. Although at some stages Soviet schooling promoted atheism and ideologies such as "the dignity of labor," these objectives brought criticism for diverting attention from proper academic pursuits. As in many other diversified nations, the argument for integration was partly efficiency. Diversity has its advocates, but when financial conditions worsen, the case is harder to sustain.

The opportunity for general changes came as Andropov and then Gorbachev proclaimed the need for change, through reforms known as *Perestroika* (restructuring, rethinking, replanning, renewing) and *Glasnost* (open, openly debated). As the political and economic relationships were freed to find their natural adjustments, the ability of the Kremlin to guide change evaporated. The prospect of change induced various groups to plan a new course. In consequence, diversity rather than integrated planning will try its legs. Education is one of the institutions that was quite completely controlled and, if the Soviet youth would not have paid for it in the numbers actually enroled, subsidized. It may be a victim of downsizing of the bureaucracies and their transfer to the control of the autonomous republics. On the other hand, the transfer may be accomplished smoothly because of the common consent that schools and higher education are vital to future prospects.

Conclusion

Praise for Soviet education is usually focused upon the rapid expansion and democratization of school enrollments, and the success at expanding secondary and higher education for an increasing part of the population--particularly in the 1920s. Approval is sometimes extended for a comprehensive assessment of both quantitative and qualitative achievements. Among the important policies (also in the 1920s) was the acceptance and promotion of language diversity. Ancient differences periodically changed harmony to discord. Events in the relationships between the central and the regional governments have now taken center stage, in events that began as *Perestroika* and *Glasnost*.

Soviet education has been affected along with other aspects of society, government and the economy. Minorities became more confident and strident, particularly after the withdrawal of troops from Afghanistan and Eastern Europe suggested that they would not be used to suppress movements for autonomy. The Baltic republics and Azerbaijan showed that armed forces might still be a factor in achieving change[6] but in August 1991 the Moscow population showed itself capable of facing tanks to promote the new interpretation of democracy. A newly freed press contributes to this debate.

Where does education for minorities fit into these momentous events? The leaders of most republics seem to have assumed control of the education in their regions, resulting in long discussions as the future intrarelationships of the Union are worked out. An important aspect will be the interpretation of minority status of individuals within the "new union" and its various "republics" and that of the status of republics and of their citizens collectively. Although regional languages (for example Lithuanian, Latvian, Estonian, Ukrainian, and Armenian) will supplant Russian as official languages in these autonomous republics or states, Russian will continue to be the lingua franca of the emerging new "union of independent states" and the language of many international contacts and of a substantial artistic importance.[7]

---

[6] Conversely, in Armenia the Red Army's presence was an important factor in limiting the bloodshed.

[7] Germany and Canada are the federal states that concentrate most educational powers with the regional governments (Laender and provinces respectively). See the Mitter and Lessard chapters for the German and Canadian systems for balancing regional and national authority concerning minority education. The United States and Australia maintain a stronger national influence and also leave more autonomy with local decision makers, both professional and private.

The national and ideological content within several subjects will likely evolve for several years, with history, literature and music changing profoundly. Religion will become possible for all and although it may be introduced as a school subject, different authorities will provide various perspectives on how it should be taught. In the worst cases a particular religion may be imposed and religious dissent ignored. Similarly, domestic minorities such as the Jews must seek their *modus vivendi* both within their republic, in other parts of the federation or other regions of the world. Although national associations have been formed by the expatriates in distant lands such as the United States and Canada, their voices will be of limited impact when the decisions are made concerning the emerging republics.

The achievements of international cooperation and solidarity that have been developed through generations of Communist ideology will not likely be abandoned, but will adjust to a new ideology.[8] They stem from traditions of courtesy and hospitality that are widely endorsed by the peoples. Successive governments have merely proclaimed these qualities. Probably they are widely shared within the *peoples* of the region.

---

[8] For example, the commitments to provide technical assistance and military equipment to Marxist leaders in Africa or Cuba have been scaled down to mere symbolism.

References

Ablin, F. 1963. *Education in the USSR. A Collection of Readings from Various Journals.* White Plains, New York: International Arts and Science Press.

Dorotich, D. 1969. History and Soviet education in the 1920s. *International Review of History and Political Science* 6(1): 28-46.

Gerutis, A. 1969. *Lithuania: 700 Years.* New York: Manyland.

Guboglo, M. N. 1989 Factors and tendencies of the development of bilingualism among the Russian population living in the union republics. *Soviet Education* 31(10): 40-73.

Hans, N. 1963. *The Russian Tradition in Education.* London: Routledge and Kegan Paul.

Hoetzsch, O. 1966. *The Evolution of Russia.* London: Harcourt Brace and World.

Johnson, W. H. E. 1950. *Russia's Educational Heritage.* Pittsburgh: Carnegie Institute of Technology.

Khanazarov, K. K. 1989. Bilingualism: A characteristic feature of nations and nationalities under developed socialism. *Soviet Education* 31(10): 11-21.

Kolasky, J. 1968. *Education in Soviet Ukraine.* Toronto: Peter Martin Associates.

Lerner, N. 1991. *Group Rights and Discrimination in International Law.* Dordrecht, The Netherlands: Marinus Nijhoff.

Makarenko, A. S. 1954. *A Book for Parents*. Moscow: Foreign Languages Publishing House.

Matthews, M. 1982. *Education in the Soviet Union*. London: George Allen and Unwin.

Monoszon, E. I. 1989. Development and current status of the theory of Communist upbringing. *Soviet Education* 31(1): 5-49.

Pennar, J., I. Dakalo, and G. Z. F. Bereday. 1971. *Modernization and Diversity in Soviet Education*. New York: Praeger.

Peschar J. L., and R. Popping. 1991. Educational opportunity in five east European countries. *Comparative Education Review* 35(1): 154-169.

Postlethwaite, T. N., ed. 1988. *The Encyclopedia of Comparative Education and National Systems of Education*. New York: Pergamon.

Rutkevich, M. N., and F. R. Filippov. 1973. Principles of the Marxist approach to social structure and social mobility. In M. Yanowitch, and W. A. Fisher (editors and translators), *Social Stratification and Mobility in the USSR*. White Plains, New York: International Arts and Sciences Press.

Seton-Watson, H. 1967. *The Russian Empire 1801-1917*. London: Oxford University Press.

Soviet Education. 1967. Vol IX, No. 12.

Tomiak, J. J. 1972. *The Soviet Union*. Hamden, Conn: Archon.

Tsirul'kikov, A. 1989. What to study? *Soviet Education* 31(8): 3-37.

UNICEF. 1991. *The State of the World's Children*. New York: Oxford University Press.

UNESCO. 1990. *Statistical Yearbook*. Paris: UNESCO.

Zajda, J. I. 1980. *Education in the USSR*. New York: Pergamon.

IMPROVING THE EDUCATION OF CHINA'S
NATIONAL MINORITIES

Jacques Lamontagne

The fifty-five national minorities of China represent a relatively small percentage of the total population, scattered over a large part of the country. The constitution protects their languages and cultures, and a special educational policy is aimed at their catching up with the level of educational development of the Han majority. A closer look reveals disparities between the minorities themselves in terms of educational level and of female/male educational inequality.

The counties of Yunnan Province are among the least educationally advanced and within Yunnan, some minorities in some counties are even more backward. The corrective measures presently taken in those cases focus on more investment in education by the State and on the use of the minority languages and cultures in education.

This chapter looks at the current educational situation of the national minorities in China and notes the progress made over the past forty years, as well as the policies and problems concerning the future educational development of the national minorities.

The National Minorities

Ethnic Identification

Chinese scholars generally refer to Stalin's (1934) definition of nation to refer to the minority ethnic groups in

183

China: "a historically evolved stable community of language, territory, economic life, and psychological make-up manifested in a community or culture" (p. 8). However, Stalin's definition is not entirely applicable to the Chinese national minorities because in a number of cases one or several of the conditions are not present, in particular, a common territory, a common language, and a common culture. Some minorities, such as the Hui, the Man and the Mongols, are scattered over most of the country and therefore are not entirely concentrated in a given territory. There is a lack of a common and unique language among some minorities: the Hui and the Man do not use a language distinct from the Han majority; some Yugu speak a Turkish language, and others speak a Mongolian language; the Jingpo speak a number of languages. In some areas, larger ethnic groups have had a cultural influence on smaller groups, partly assimilating them. Therefore, in identifying the Chinese national minorities, Stalin's definition has been used with some flexibility and to the criteria was added *self-consciousness*, i.e. the idea that a particular ethnic group considers itself distinct from all other ethnic groups.

Before 1949, no thorough ethnographic study had been made of the ethnic minority groups residing on Chinese territory. In the process of identifying the national minorities which began in the fifties, two basic questions were asked: 1) Is the ethnic group distinct from or part of the Han majority? 2) If the group is not part of the Han, is it a nationality by itself, or is it part of a larger nationality? The Chinese government encouraged all ethnic groups in the country to declare their ethnic allegiance. In response, several hundred groups claimed to be specific. These claims were then examined by ethnographers who proceeded to uncover the historical factors that have determined the characteristics of the ethnic groups. Based on the cases analyzed, a number of historical patterns of development were observed:

1) Some Han groups, having settled among non-Han peoples and retained their Chinese culture, claimed to constitute a separate ethnic group.

2) Some non-Han groups, having occupied a given territory alongside Han and having adopted the Chinese

language, nevertheless considered themselves as a national minority.

3) Subgroups of a given ethnic group, having scattered in different regions, but having retained their language and customs, considered themselves to be different from one another.

4) Subgroups of people in a given locality, with different languages and customs, nevertheless considered themselves as only one group.

5) Some nationalities, close in language, customs and history, having acquired individual features, were unable to decide whether they consider themselves as only one group.

In the main, the ethnographic work was accomplished within ten years: in 1956, forty-five national minorities had been officially recognized; the number rose to fifty-three in 1963, and to fifty-five in 1980. There are, however, still some nationalities whose status is not yet clear. They total around 900,000 persons, and include the Tibetans in Pingwu County (Sichuan), the Deng in Zayu County (southeastern Tibet), the Xiaerba in Dinggyê County and Tingri County (southern Tibet), and the Kucong in Honghe Hani-Yi Autonomous Prefecture (Yunnan).

Most of the languages of the national minorities in China belong to two language families: Han-Tibetan (twenty-nine nationalities) and Altai (seventeen nationalities). Other families are South Asian (three), Indo-European (two) and Southern Islands (one). One language has not yet been categorized, and the Hui and the Man use the Han language. In 1949, twenty-one national minorities had their own written language or shared the written language of others. Nine years later, the government had created or systematized written languages for ten other groups, using the Latin alphabet. Five other existing languages were romanized.

Territorial Distribution

The national minorities constitute only 8.0 percent of the total population (Renmin Ribao 1990), but are spread over more than half the country's total area, mostly in outlying or border territories: Heilongjiang, Jilin, Liaoning, Inner Mongolia,

Ningxia, Gansu, Qinghai, Xinjiang, Tibet, Sichuan, Yunnan, Guizhou, Guangxi and Guangdong. These areas are important in terms of defence and for their rich deposits of natural resources. The minorities live mainly in the country's western half. The Han are scattered all over China, but they are mainly concentrated on the eastern plains.

Several minority groups live along China's long borders: Koreans, Hezhe, Ewenke, Oroqen (Northeast); Uygur, Kazak, Kirgiz (Xinjiang); Tibetans, Menba, Luoba (Tibet); Zhuang, Jing (Guangxi). In many instances, the minority groups are on both sides of a border. For example, the Kazak, Kirgiz, Tajik, Tataer, Mongols, Uygur, Dawoer, Ewenke, Oroqen and Hezhe are also found in the USSR; and the Miao, Hani, Dai, Jing, Jingpo, Lahu, Lisu, Wa, Yao, Yi and Zhuang live in Vietnam, Laos, Thailand, and Burma as well. Altogether, China borders on twelve countries.

The fifty-five national minorities totalled 91,200,314 persons at the 1990 census. They vary greatly in numbers, from the Zhuang (seventeen million), to the Hezhe (2,000). In eighteen cases, the population is over one million, and in eight cases, it is less than 10,000. Not being bound by the same birth control measures as the Han, the national minorities are increasing at a much faster rate than the latter: a thirty-five percent increase from 1982 to 1990, vs. eleven percent for the Han.

The National Minority Policy

The People's Republic of China sees itself as a "united country of multiple nationalities"; and a principle of the national minority policy is that all ethnic groups, no matter their size, are to be equal. On the other hand, the nationalities are bound by their obligation to contribute to national unity. Another principle is that each nationality should enjoy the freedom to use and develop its own spoken and written language and to maintain or change its customs. These principles have been set forth since the Common Programme laid down in 1949, which functioned as a provisional constitution, through constitutions adopted by the successive National People's Congresses.

Regional Autonomy

China has a system of regional autonomy comparable to the one in the USSR. However, whereas the republics of the USSR can and do secede, the autonomous areas of China are considered inseparable parts. The principle of regional autonomy is to grant autonomy to areas where there is one or several sizeable minority groups living in a compact community. According to the size and importance of the territory inhabited, the area is called *region*, *prefecture* or *county*, in decreasing order. There are five autonomous regions, twenty-nine autonomous prefectures and seventy-five autonomous counties (including three autonomous *banners* in Inner Mongolia). The autonomous areas cover sixty-four percent of the total area of the country and comprise around ninety percent of all national minority members, as well as around eight percent of the Han.

Autonomous areas enjoy more rights than non-autonomous areas of the corresponding administrative level. These rights extend to administration of the affairs of their nationalities, financial administration, economic development, local security forces, training and employment of local nationality cadres, use and development of the local minority spoken and written languages, development of culture, education and arts, and health and medical services.

Minority Education

The development of the autonomous areas rests a good deal on the development of minority education, in particular on the training of minority cadres. On March 21, 1951, the Ministry of Education issued a decree that provided special arrangements for minority education. To supervise minority education at the provincial and county levels, special offices and personnel would be put in place within the Department of Education at each level. Other measures were special subsidies for minority students; the establishment of schools in remote areas even where there are relatively few pupils; relaxation of the conditions of admission for minority students in secondary schools and institutions of higher education; and the creation of minority normal schools.

The minority education policy was re-appraised at the Beijing Conference on Minority Education, in February 1981. The government policy that ensued laid stress on the following measures to be maintained or taken:

1) to continue teaching in the languages of the minorities in the minority schools;

2) to teach primary and secondary pupils their mother tongues before teaching them Chinese and, eventually, a foreign language;

3) to continue to compile textbooks in minority languages;

4) to set up primary and secondary boarding schools, and to regard these schools as the backbone of all schools for the minorities that live in sparsely populated and remote areas, where the means of transportation are inadequate;

5) to allot additional budgeting at the local level for the school equipment, teachers' salaries and pupils' living conditions in the minority schools; and

6) to maintain the special offices for minority education in the provincial and county Departments of Education, and to strive to recruit as many minority cadres as possible in these offices (Gu 1989).

In 1950 the State elaborated a plan to train minority cadres in large numbers. At that time, nationalities' institutes were set up: 1) to train high and medium-ranking cadres for the minority regions; 2) to conduct research on the problems, languages, history and culture of the national minorities; and 3) to edit and translate books and materials related to the national minorities. There are short and long term programs in the institutes, the former being for on-the-job training of cadres, the latter for cadres who will be expected to be proficient in their mother tongue as well as in the Han language.

Eleven such institutes were set up in various parts of the country. One of them, the Central Institute of Nationalities, is located in Beijing. Its primary function is to train minority cadres above the county level, as well as to train teachers and researchers in nationalities' problems, languages, history and culture, and to assist the other ten nationalities' institutes. The latter, situated in or close to the minority areas of China, primarily handle the training of cadres below the county level. In addition, minority cadre schools, minority normal schools, and minority schools of continuing education for in-service training of teachers have been set up in some provinces. Some institutions of higher education hold special courses to prepare minority applicants for their examinations. The passing scores for minority students in institutions of higher education are lower than for Han students.

The Educational Development of the National Minorities

The 1982 Census revealed that the percentage of illiterates or semi-literates among persons aged twelve or more is higher for the national minorities combined (43) than for the Han majority (31) (Population Census 1985). Moreover, there is a great deal of variation in the level of illiteracy among the fifty-five national minorities (Table 1). The proportion of illiterates and semi-literates is larger than 65 percent for eleven nationalities: Tibetan, Hani, Lisu, Wa, Lahu, Dongxiang, Bulang, Sala, Benglong, Baoan, Luoba. But it is smaller than 30 percent for thirteen other nationalities: Mongol, Korean, Man, Kazak, Gaoshan, Dawoer, Xibo, Uzbek, Russian, Ewenke, Tataer, Oroqen and Hezhe.

The provinces and autonomous regions inhabited by the national minorities with the highest level of illiteracy are mostly Tibet, Qinghai, Gansu and Yunnan. At the other extreme, the provinces and autonomous regions inhabited by the national minorities with the lowest level of illiteracy are mostly Xinjiang, Inner Mongolia, Liaoning, Jilin and Heilongjiang.

Is the level of illiteracy of the national minorities congruent with the *total* level of illiteracy--i.e. the level of the Han *and* of the national minorities combined--in the provinces or autonomous regions where they live? For all inhabitants

Table 1. **Percentage of Illiterates and Semi-Literates among the Fifty-five National Minorities of China, 1982**

Minority	Illiterates and semi-literates	Minority	Literates and semi-literates
Mongol	28	Mulao	33
Hui	41	Qiang	50
Tibetan	74	Bulang	74
Uygur	42	Sala	72
Miao	58	Maonan	29
Yu	62	Gelao	54
Zhuang	31	Xibo	12
Buyi	56	Achang	60
Korean	10	Tajike	46
Man	17	Nu	63
Dong	45	Ubek	17
Yao	47	Russian	18
Bai	41	Ewenke	16
Tujia	33	Benglong	73
Hani	70	Baoan	76
Kazak	22	Yugo	41
Dai	57	Jing	33
Li	41	Tataer	9
Lisu	72	Dulong	61
Wa	69	Orogen	15
She	52	Hezhe	14
Gaoshan	18	Pumi	61
Lahu	82	Menba	44
Shui	62	Luoba	69
Dongxiang	87	Jinuo	51
Naxi	39	Unident.minor[a]	61
Jingpo	61	All nat. minor	43
Kirgiz	39	Han majority	31
Tu	60		
Dawoer	18	Total pop China	32

[a] A Total of 879,201 persons were classified in the category unidentified minorities.

Source: Population Census Office, 1982, p. 24; 1985, pp. 32-33 and 244-247.

combined, the provinces and autonomous regions with the highest percentage (i.e. more than 40 percent) of illiterates and semi-literates are Anhui, Guizhou, Yunnan, Gansu, Qinghai, Ningxia and, especially, Tibet. The level of illiteracy is lowest (i.e. less than 26 percent) in Beijing, Tianjin and Shanghai, plus Shanxi, Liaoning, Jilin, Heilongjiang, Hunan, Guangdong and Guangxi. In general, the level of illiteracy of the national minorities appears to be congruent with the total level of illiteracy of the territory in which they live, notably for the minorities in Tibet, Qinghai, Gansu and Yunnan, where illiteracy is high, and for the minorities in Liaoning, Jilin and Heilongjiang, where illiteracy is low. Exceptions to this tendency are five minorities of Xinjiang--the Kazak, Xibo, Uzbek, Russian and Tataer--whose level of illiteracy is substantially lower than that of all inhabitants of Xinjiang combined.

Thus, in most cases, what might appear to be a difference based on ethnicity may be a difference based on regional socioeconomic development. But this would require a more detailed study, because the congruence is determined by the proportion of national minority people in the various provinces and autonomous regions. The higher that proportion, the closer the minority level of illiteracy will be to the provincial or regional level of illiteracy: this would be the case in Tibet where the proportion of Tibetans to the total population is 96 percent. In the other main areas inhabited by the national minorities, the contribution of each of the minorities to the total result is less influential. The percentages of all national minorities combined to the total population in selected provinces and autonomous regions are: Inner Mongolia 15, Guizhou 26, Yunnan 32, Ningxia 32, Guangxi 38, and Xinjiang 60.

We also note that the national minorities with the lowest level of illiteracy live mostly in highly urbanized provinces and autonomous regions: Xinjiang, Inner Mongolia and, especially, the three northeastern provinces of Liaoning, Jilin, and Heilongjiang. Conversely, the national minorities with the highest level of illiteracy live mostly in less urbanized territories such as Gansu, Tibet, and Yunnan. Exceptionally, Guangxi is not highly urbanized and has a low level of illiteracy. Thus, the degree of urbanization of the territory inhabited could bear some relation with the level of illiteracy of the national minorities (Lamontagne 1986).

Future observations at the county level should take special note of the national minorities whose level of illiteracy is in contrast--being higher or lower--with the level of illiteracy of the rest of the population in the territory they inhabit. Of particular interest will be the study of four advanced minorities--the Kazak, the Gaoshan, the Mongols and the Man--some of whose members live in backward territories. The question to be answered will be: do all clusters of these minorities have a low level of illiteracy, notwithstanding the territory--backward or advanced--they inhabit?

Parts of thirteen intermediate minorities (Hui, Uygur, Miao, Yi, Zhuang, Buyi, Dong, Yao, Tujia, Li, She, Shui and Gelao) live in backward *and* advanced territories. Their geographical dispersion might account for the fact that their level of illiteracy is about average. More detailed observations on these minorities will determine if underneath their overall level of illiteracy lie very different levels reflecting, respectively, the backward and the advanced territories they inhabit.

Backward *and* advanced minorities are found in a total of nine territories: three of them intermediate (Henan, Sichuan and Xinjiang) and six backward (Anhui, Guizhou, Yunnan, Gansu, Qinghai and Ningxia). Intra-provincial comparisons will show to what extent the minorities within a given province share a similar level of illiteracy. This will be an indication of the specific effect of variables *region* and *ethnicity* on illiteracy.

Trends

From 1951 to 1985, the national minorities' percentage of total enrollment increased from 2.2 to 7.1 in the primary schools, from 0.4 to 6.6 in the secondary technical schools, from 2.1 to 8.9 in the teacher training schools, from 2.6 to 4.8 in the general secondary schools, and from 1.4 to 5.5 in the regular institutions of higher education (Department of Planning 1986). Since minority nationalities constitute 8.0 percent of the total population (it was 6.7 percent in 1982), four observations can be derived: 1) in 1951, the national minorities were very much underrepresented in all types of educational institutions; 2) the proportion of national minorities in all types of educational institutions has increased substantially over the past four decades; 3) the national minorities are still significantly underrepresented in the general secondary schools and the regular institutions of higher education; and 4) the national minorities are now slightly overrepresented in the teacher training schools.

Analogous characteristics and trends are found with national minority teachers in the various types of educational institutions, with the exception of technical schools, where national minority teachers are somewhat underrepresented (4.7 percent).

Female/Male Educational Gap

At the national level, the proportion of illiterate and semi-literate females (45 percent) is substantially larger than the proportion of illiterate and semi-literate males (19 percent), and the female/male inequality ratio (i.e. the percentage of illiterate and semi-literate females divided by the percentage of illiterate and semi-literate males) is 2.36. For the national minorities as a whole, the inequality ratio is 1.88. The inequality ratio is relatively small (less than 1.50) among sixteen minorities and relatively large (more than 2.10) among sixteen other minorities. The thirty-two national minorities with a small or a large inequality ratio are shown in Table 2.

With variable *female/male inequality ratio of illiteracy*, we find some incongruences between *region* and *ethnicity* (Table 3). In each of twelve territories, there is at least one national minority whose inequality ratio is small and at least one national minority whose inequality ratio is large. This applies to twenty-seven national minorities--eight backward, thirteen intermediate and six advanced.

More research is needed to explain this variation in the magnitude of gender discrimination concerning education. To ascertain the respective effect of *region* and *ethnicity* on gender discrimination concerning education, a comparative analysis

Table 2. **National Minorities with a Small or a Large Female/Male Inequality Ratio of Illiteracy, 1982**

Minority	Small ratio (−1.50)	%	Minority	Large ratio (+2.10)	%
Dongxiang	1.23	87	Shiu	2.21	62
Lahu	1.12	82	Buyi	2.32	55
Bulang	1.33	74	Qiang	2.15	50
Tibetan	1.42	74	Yao	2.11	47
Benglong	1.35	73	Dong	2.62	45
Lisu	1.48	72	Bai	2.96	41
Luoba	1.27	69	Naxi	2.15	39
Wa	1.33	69	Jing	3.48	33
Nu	1.43	63	Mulao	2.92	33
Jingpo	1.32	61	Tujia	2.42	33
Dulong	1.37	61	Zhuang	2.99	31
Jinuo	1.39	50	Maonan	2.35	29
Uygur	1.17	42	Gaoshan	3.22	18
Dawoer	1.38	18	Russian	3.21	18
Uzbek	1.47	17	Hezhe	2.45	14
Oroqen	1.36	15	Korean	3.43	10

Note: The percentages represent the proportion of illiterates and semi-illiterates among males and females combined.

Source: Population Census Office, 1982, pp. 32-33, 244-247.

would have to be made on the situation of minorities whose inequality ratio is very different although they live in the same territory, and of minorities who live in more than one territory. We might find that the magnitude of gender discrimination for a given minority is the same in all territories it inhabits: this would mean that *ethnicity* has more determining power than *region*. Conversely, a given minority might have a magnitude of female/male inequality that varies between the territories that it inhabits; in this case, variable *region* would outweigh *ethnicity*.

The Current Educational Policy in Yunnan

Yunnan Province is among the poorest areas of China. Its industrial per capita output value (in 1986) is only 368 Yuan compared to the national average of 838 Yuan. In agriculture, the gap is also noteworthy 233 Yuan vs. 438 Yuan. Moreover, within Yunnan, the autonomous areas are in a still less favourable position than the rest of the province. Of the province's 128 counties, nineteen are autonomous and fifty-five are situated within an autonomous prefecture. These seventy-four counties account for 49 percent of the total population of Yunnan. Their share of the gross agricultural output (47 percent) is close to their share of the total population. In the industrial sector, however, their share is much lower (29 percent) (Heberer 1989). There is, then, a double backwardness for the autonomous areas of Yunnan in terms of their economic development. These variations among the autonomous areas and minority groups of Yunnan mean that there are some extremely poor localities and peoples within Yunnan province. According to the 1985 national reform policy, the program of compulsory education should be implemented in stages, taking into account the varying levels of economic and cultural development of the various regions of the country. The more advanced areas could go ahead immediately in the compulsory education program, whereas the backward areas, which in many cases are inhabited by national minority groups, would prolong their compulsory education program.

Table 3. **Disparities in the Female/Male Inequality Ratio of Illiteracy among Various National Minorities Inhabiting a Same Territory, 1982**

Territory	Total level %	Minorities	Total level %	Female/Male[a] Inequality Ratio −1.50	+2.10
Heilongjianj	22	Oroqen	15	−1.36	
		Dawoer	18	−1.38	
		Zhuang	31		+2.99
		Hezhe	14		+2.45
		Korean	10		+3.43
Nei Mongol	31	Tibetan	74	−1.42	
		Oroqen	15	−1.36	
		Dawoer	18	−1.38	
		Zhuang	31		+2.99
		Korean	10		+3.43
Beijing	15	Tibetan	74	−1.42	
Henan	37	Uygur	42	−1.17	
		Zhuang	31		+2.99
		Korean	10		+3.43
Shaanxi	33	Tibetan	74	−1.42	
		Zhuang	31		+2.99
		Korean	10		+3.43
Gansu	48	Dongxiang	87	−1.23	
Qinghai	47	Tibetan	74	−1.42	
		Zhuang	31		+2.99
Xinjiang	31	Dongxiang	87	−1.23	
		Tibetan	74	−1.42	
		Uygur	42	−1.17	
		Uzbek	17	−1.47	
		Dawoer	18	−1.38	
		Zhuang	31		+2.99
		Tujia	33		+2.42
		Russian	18		+3.21

Tibet	73	Luoba	69	-1.27	
		Tibetan	74	-1.42	
		Naxi	39		+2.15
Sichuan	32	Tibetan	74	-1.42	
		Lisu	72	-1.48	
		Buyi	56		+3.32
		Qiang	50		+2.15
		Bai	41		+2.96
		Naxi	39		+2.15
		Tujia	33		+2.42
		Zhuang	31		+2.99
Yunnan	49	Lahu	82	-1.12	
		Bulang	74	-1.33	
		Tibetan	74	-1.42	
		Lisu	72	-1.48	
		Benglong	73	-1.35	
		Wa	69	-1.33	
		Nu	63	-1.43	
		Jingpo	61	-1.37	
		Jinuo	51	-1.39	
		Dulong	61	-1.37	
		Shui	62		+2.21
		Buyi	56		+2.32
		Yao	47		+2.11
		Bai	41		+2.96
		Naxi	39		+2.15
		Tujia	33		+2.42
		Zhuang	31		+2.99
Hunan	24	Uygur	42	-1.17	
		Yao	47		+2.11
		Tujia	33		+2.42
		Zhuang	31		+2.99

[a]The female/male inequality ratio of illiteracy represents the percentage of illiterate and semi-literate females divided by the percentage of illiterate and semi-literate males

Source: Population Census Office, 1985, pp. 32-33, 218-231, and 244-247

Yunnan, taken as a whole, is one of the province-level administrative divisions where illiteracy is the most widespread (49 percent, compared to the national average of 32 percent). Of the total population of Yunnan, 32 percent are members of minority groups (the highest percentage after Tibet, where the Han constitute only 3.8 percent of the population). Moreover, in the total population of China, the national minorities have a substantially higher rate of illiteracy (43 percent) than the Han (31 percent). Consequently, to promote education in Yunnan means to focus on the education of the national minorities of that province, and the educational policy needs to be based on the varying conditions of the national minorities, including their languages, traditions and level of economic development. The autonomous local governments of the minorities are expected to provide their own educational plans for all aspects of the establishment of schools, including school administration, curriculum, language of instruction, and pupil recruitment (Wang 1989).

Vocational and technical education. Parents in the backward areas are not keen on sending their children to school, and there is a high dropout rate among the children who do begin. Since few pupils complete their primary education, and fewer still go on to secondary education, stress must be laid on linking general education with vocational and technical education. The school graduates are expected to return to their villages to develop the local economy and contribute to the progress of their locality.

Boarding schools. In general, the minorities of Yunnan live in backward mountainous regions. School children have to travel long distances every school day, leaving very little time for their homework. Moreover, they do not know the Han language, and would need to spend extra time for their education. To surmount this problem, in the context of limited financial resources, the current policy is to emphasize quality, rather than quantity. In practice, this means the development of boarding and semi-boarding schools for selected children. In those schools, the pupils can concentrate on their studies, since they are no longer burdened with household chores assigned to them at home, and they do not have to travel several hours per day to and from school.

Language of instruction. The policy of attaining proficiency in the Han language through schooling presents different problems for different minorities: 1) For minorities that do not know Han and have their own written language, the minority language is the language of instruction and of textbooks in the lower grades of primary school, and the children learn Han gradually. In the upper grades, the minority language remains the language of instruction while Han textbooks are adopted. 2) For minorities that do not know Han and do not have their own written language, the minority language is the language of instruction and Han textbooks are used. 3) For minorities that know Han, the local population should decide whether the language of instruction is to be Han or the minority language.

Minority teacher training. Minority children are taught both by Han teachers who come from other more developed areas and by a growing contingent of minority teachers who were brought up in the locality and who were given teacher training. There is an obvious advantage to using minority teachers from the point of view of their knowledge of the minority language, history and culture.

Educational Development in Six Counties of Yunnan Province

The following accounts from five somewhat backward counties and one less backward county in Yunnan describe the problems encountered, as well as the corrective measures taken or envisaged for educational development.

Ximeng, Cangyuan, Lancang and Menglian Counties

These four counties in the southwest of Yunnan province border on Burma and are strongly characterized by their ethnic composition (Zhou 1989). Taken as a whole, they comprise twenty-eight national minorities. Of the total population of the four counties (662,772 in 1982), 82 percent belong to a national minority, much more than the provincial average of 32 percent.

The overall percentage of illiteracy of the four counties (72) is much higher than the mean for all the counties of Yunnan combined (52). Among the four counties, the percentage of illiteracy also varies: at 77, Lancang has the highest level, and levels are lower in Cangyuan (59), Ximeng (68), and Menglian (72).

The Wa nationality represents 40 percent of all national minorities in the four counties combined. Also numerous are the Lahu (20 percent) and the Dai, Hani and Yi (5 percent each). The twenty-three other national minorities' share of the population averages one percent each.

The Wa, Lahu and Yi live mainly in the mountains, whereas the Dai and the Han live along the river basin. Although the various nationalities interact in the course of their cultural and economic activities, they tend to live separately in homogeneous mountainous villages, with inconvenient means of transportation. This relative isolation is conducive to the preservation of the minority languages and cultures, although most of them, with the exception of the Dai and the Yi, do not have a written language.

The peasants in the counties still use rudimentary methods of agriculture, such as slash and burn. They do not usually consider it advantageous for their children to go to a faraway school; what is more obvious to them is the fact that school attendance entails additional expenses and deprives them of the help of their children for their work on the farm. Consequently, the rate of school enrollment and the rate of school retention are very low.

Problems. Although most minority children speak only their native language when they begin school, they are spoken to in Han by their teachers and are confronted with Han teaching materials developed for schools nationwide. This turns the children from their desire to learn; indeed, most children do not attend school beyond the first grade. Only about six percent of school-age children complete primary school. The regular school schedule conflicts with the needs of work to be done on the farms. This problem has intensified with the implementation of the agricultural system of responsibility. Altogether, there are fifty-six primary schools in the four counties, half of which are single-teacher schools. Because of a lack of material and human resources, it is impossible to operate all of them properly. Despite an insufficient supply of teachers, the four counties have increased the number of junior and senior secondary schools, as well as of junior secondary school classes affiliated with primary schools. The training of teachers is inadequate: for example, less than three-fifths of Lancang elementary school teachers have a junior middle school teachers' training. The teachers are discontented and insecure because of their low salary and mediocre teaching conditions, so they tend to move away from the minority locality where they were assigned.

Measures. Various measures are being implemented to overcome these problems: 1) part of the education funds are set aside for bonuses and rewards to units or individuals who reach annual goals; 2) in order to raise the retention and passing rates of pupils, boarding and semi-boarding schools are established for the middle and upper grades, and these pupils are given cost-of-living subsidies; 3) teaching materials are compiled, relevant to the economic and cultural life of the minorities but taking into account the main elements of the nationwide curriculum; 4) teachers from outside the area are required to learn the local language and to use it for teaching in the lower grades of the primary schools; 5) the State education budget has been increased for the minority areas more than for the Han areas, and there is increased local funding for education; 6) the number of regular secondary schools is being reduced to concentrate the material and human resources on primary education; and 7) the salaries and living conditions of the teachers are being improved.

The Dai Nationality in Gengma County

In China, as a whole, 57 percent of the Dai people aged twelve years or more are illiterate or semi-literate. This level is not extremely high, but substantially higher than the average level for all national minorities combined (43 percent). The Dai people make up 19 percent of the 182,831 inhabitants of the Gengma Dai-Wa Nationalities Autonomous County (Zhang 1989). They are mostly concentrated in three districts: Mengyong, Mengsa and Mengding, and especially in the latter, which borders on Burma and where their 15,000 is three-fifths of the population.

Problems. Before 1949, there were no schools in the area, but the Dai language was taught to monks in Buddhist monasteries. There are now regular schools, but since the adoption of the Party's policy on religion during the eighties, several monasteries have been restored and many boys go to the Buddhist monasteries to be trained as monks, instead of to the regular schools. Families send their sons to the monasteries to acquire an ecclesiastical name and to improve their status in the community. The abandonment of the regular schools was enhanced with the adoption of the responsibility system in production which had the effect of encouraging families to keep their sons at home and give them work as cowherds. The young girls work at home, are often married by the time they are fifteen and get little schooling.

For the children who enter the regular schools, opinions are divided on which language--Dai or Han--should be taught in the lower grades. Some prefer Han to facilitate and quicken the learning of science and the integration into Chinese society. Others advocate the preservation and development of the Dai culture, arguing that the Dai language already is phoneticized, is easy to learn, and is in accord with the local linguistic environment. Until now, the Dai language has been chosen to overcome illiteracy, the Han language being perceived not only as more difficult, but also as being needless in the work and social life anticipated after schooling, especially since the work recruitment system gives priority to township and city youths waiting for jobs.

There are two types of teachers in the region: outsiders (usually Han or Bai) and Dai. Both types, and especially the Dai, have a poor educational background, often no more than a primary-school level of education.

Because of inadequate finances, the schools are deficient in buildings, facilities and teaching equipment, which is detrimental to the teachers' morale and the quality of their teaching. The outsiders tend to go back where they came from, whereas the local teachers, whose families work on farmlands, have to help on the farm during the busy agricultural period.

Measures. A number of measures have been or are being taken to alleviate these problems: 1) publications and broadcasting are being promoted in the Dai language; 2) the Dai language has become the medium of instruction and of textbooks in the lower grades of primary school, with a gradual transition to Han; 3) opportunites are given to teachers for in-service training; 4) the salaries and benefits of the teachers coming from outside areas have been raised; 5) the State education budget in minority border areas has been raised and the townships and villages are encouraged to finance their own schools; 6) the pupils are enrolled in a township school, instead of a village school, in order to lessen their families' influence; and 7) boys may attend the monasteries during the school vacation, so that they can be initiated as monks and change their names, after which they would return to the regular schools.

Lunan County

Lunan Yi nationality Autonomous County is situated some seventy-five kilometers southeast of Kunming, the capital city of Yunnan Province. The national minorities of Lunan, including the Yi, Miao, Zhuang, Bai and Hui, make up 31 percent of the 197,000 inhabitants of the county (Li 1989).

The percentage of illiterates and semi-literates in Lunan is lower (41) than the average for the counties of Yunnan (52). Enrollment is 2,646 in kindergartens, 29,940 in primary schools and 8,342 in secondary schools. In the schools, the representation of minority children is more or less the same as their percentage in the total population of the county: thirty-eight in the kindergartens, thirty-five in the primary schools and thirty-one in the secondary schools. Despite this proportional representation of the minorities in the schools, various measures have been taken to handle the educational problems specific to the minorities in the county.

Problems and measures. Although the Yi have their own system of writing, only a few know it. That is why the textbooks and the language of instruction have always been in standard Chinese. Pre-school classes have been set up in the schools to facilitate the transfer from the language of the minority to written and spoken standard Chinese.

The bilingual system adopted in the county gives priority to standard Chinese. In practice, this means: 1) to begin instruction in Chinese in the first grade of primary schools in areas where standard Chinese is used daily; and 2) to teach in standard Chinese, with explanations in the minority language, at the lower levels of primary school in areas where standard Chinese is not fully used daily.

In the early 1980s, the county government opened five semi-boarding classes at the senior level in township key schools. In 1984, twenty-four other semi-boarding classes were opened. Children in these classes are given an extra allowance because they originate from very poor families. In 1980, Guishan secondary school, situated in a mountainous area of Lunan County, was designated by Yunnan Province as the secondary boarding school for the province's minorities. In 1987, the school was moved to new school buildings in the county seat. Also in 1987, a vocational secondary school for minority pupils was opened.

In the county there are Yi and Han teachers, some paid by the State, others by the local population. But the number and quality of teachers in the mountainous areas where there are minorities are inadequate. To solve this problem, the following measures have been proposed:

1) when the graduates of teachers schools are assigned, the needs of the minority areas should first be attended to;

2) each Han teacher in the county should teach in a minority area in the county for six years, before being given the status of teacher paid by the State;

3) the quota for the mountainous areas should be twice as high, when distributing the quotas for the change from the status of teacher paid by the local population to the status of teacher paid by the State, in order to reduce the percentage of teachers paid by the local population in the mountainous areas, thus alleviating the expense in those areas;

4) teachers from other provinces should be assigned to the mountainous areas;

5) teachers working among minorities in mountainous areas should get an additional monthly allowance;

6) a basic salary should be assured for the teachers paid by the local population;

7) a basic monthly payment should be assured to retired teachers who have taught for more than ten years.

Summary and Conclusion

The definition of a national minority in China is that of an ethnic group whose members share a culture, language, territory, economic life, and the sense that it is distinct from all other ethnic groups. However, some officially recognized national minorities do not satisfy all of these conditions: in some cases, there is no common language, in others the members are not entirely concentrated in a given territory. The fifty-five national minorities of China, as they are known today, were identified through ethnographic studies carried out mainly in the fifties. They constitute only 8.0 percent of the total population, but are spread over more than half of the country's total area, mostly in outlying or border territories. Totalling more than ninety million persons, the minorities vary greatly in numbers, from 17 million to two thousand.

According to the Constitution, all national minorities are to be equal and are free to maintain or develop their language and culture, but are obligated to contribute to national unity. These principles are translated into a system of regional autonomy and special educational measures for the minorities. Regional autonomy is granted to areas where there is one or several sizeable minority groups living in a compact community.

The objectives of the educational measures for the minorities are to raise their educational level, to increase the number of minority cadres in the minority areas, and to facilitate the use and development of the minority languages.

Illiteracy is more widespread among the national minorities as a whole than among the Han majority, but there is a great deal of variation in the level of illiteracy among the fifty-five minorities, although, in general, this is congruent with the level of illiteracy of the province inhabited. However, backward *and* advanced minorities are found in several territories. Future research on this phenomenon at the county level would reveal more specifically the respective effect of variables *region* and *ethnicity* on the level of illiteracy.

At the national level, the illiteracy level of females is. more than twice as high as males. This female/male discrepancy is smaller among the national minorities as a whole, but it varies a great deal between the minorities. The magnitude of gender discrimination concerning education also varies between minorities inhabiting a same province. Future research on the varying female/male inequality ratio of illiteracy of a given minority that inhabits several territories would reveal the respective effect of variables *region* and *ethnicity* on the ratio.

Over the past four decades, the enrollment of national minorities in all types of educational institutions has increased proportionately more than that of the Han, but the national minorities are still underrepresented in the general secondary schools and in the regular institutions of higher education.

Yunnan Province is among the poorest and least literate areas of China, and half of its population lives in autonomous areas. Its current educational policy focuses on the lower levels of education, on vocational and technical education, and on minority education. The educational facilities and resources being insufficient, the policy now stresses quality education for selected pupils. At the same time, measures are implemented to protect the minority languages at school.

Education is in an especially sorry state in the least developed counties of Yunnan. These are mountainous and remote counties, where minorities represent an overwhelming proportion of the population, where the methods of agriculture are rudimentary, where schools are few and of poor quality, where there are no convenient means of communication, and where the curriculum and language of instruction in schools are hardly adapted to the local educational needs. The measures advocated to break the cycle of poverty and illiteracy in these counties are: 1) more money invested by the State in schools and competent teachers, 2) boarding schools for selected pupils, 3) the use of the minority language as the language of instruction and textbooks in the lower grades, and 4) the return of the school graduates to their locality of origin.

References

Department of Planning, State Education Commission, People's Republic of China. 1986. *Achievement of Education in China. Statistics 1980-1985.* Beijing: People's Education Press.

Gu Mingyuan. 1989. Development and Reform of Education for Minority Nationalities in China. Paper presented at the VIIth World Congress of Comparative Education, 26-30 June at Montreal.

Heberer, Thomas. 1989. *China and Its National Minorities: Autonomy or Assimilation?* Armonk, New York: M.E. Sharpe.

Lamontagne, Jacques. 1986. Educational development in the PRC regional and ethnic disparities. *Issues and Studies: A Journal of China Studies and International Affairs* 22(2): 73-94.

Li Zhi. 1990. *Lunan xian fazhan minzu jiaoyu de zhuyao cuoshi.* (Important Measures for the Development of Minority Education in Lunan County). *Yunnan Jiaoyu* (Education in Yunnan), Nos. 1-2. 3-4.

Population Census Office. 1982. *The 1982 Population Census of China: Major Figures.* The State Council and Department of Population Statistics of the State Statistical Bureau, People's Republic of China. Hong Kong: Economic Information and Agency.

Population Census Office. 1985. *The 1982 Population Census of China: Results of Computer Tabulation.* The State Council and Department of Population Statistics of the State Statistical Bureau, People's Republic of China. Beijing: Statistical Publishing House.

Renmin Ribao (People's Daily). 1990. October 31.

Stalin, Joseph. 1934. *Marxism and the National and Colonial Question.* New York: International Publishers.

Wang Lianfang. 1989. The problem of developing minority education in Yunnan province. *Chinese Education* (Spring): 21-6. Originally published as *Yunnan fazhan minzu jiaoyu de wenti. Hongqi* (Red Flag, 1985, 12: 34-6).

Zhang Yuanqing. 1989. Current Problems of Education and Proposals for Improvement in Dai Nationality Schools in Gengma Dai-Wa Nationalities Autonomous County, Yunnan. *Chinese Education* (Spring): 47-55. Originally published as *Yunnan Sheng Gengma Dai zu zizhixian dangqian Dai zu xuexiao jiaoyu zhong cuizai de wenti he gaijin de jianyi. Minzu lilun yanjiu tongxun* (Bulletin of Studies in Nationality Theory, 1985-June 25, 2: 39-41).

Zhou Gengxin. 1989. Accelerate the pace of educational reform in minority regions primary education in four counties of southwestern Yunnan. *Chinese Education* (Spring): 56-66. Originally published as *Bixu jiakuai shaoshu minxu diqu jiaoyu gaige de bufa Tianxinan si xian chudeng jiaoyu qingkuang diaocha. Minzu Yanjiu* (Nationality Research, 1985, 3: 60-4).

AFRICAN-AMERICAN SOCIETY
AND EDUCATION

Letha A. (Lee) See

The study of social inequality in the United States has properly focussed on the fate of African-Americans. Although other minorities have endured privations based on their language or religion, their identity is in their own hands to some extent: there are no physical barriers to a change of an individual's tongue or faith. This is not so with race. Gender would similarly define identity by nature, but even though women are still treated unequally across almost all racial and ethnic groups, civilized societies increasingly denounce sexual discrimination.[1]

The African-Americans, at twenty-eight million, considerably outnumber the Native Americans (about one million), the Asians, or the mixed race Hispanic community (sixteen million). Their situation still constitutes the "American problem" that has been identified for generations. It should be clear that the problem is only partly theirs to solve, for the society as a whole must change too, and would benefit immensely from its solution.

On the other hand, there is evidence that a minority of African-Americans have succeeded, despite the inferior opportunities available to most of their members. Of course, without their handicap of widespread victimization, these

---

[1] Women who are members of a racial or ethnic underclass are doubly disadvantaged. Black women in the United States have this double disadvantage, evident in several categories of social data.

211

notables would likely have won achievements which were more substantial, earlier, easier, and achievements might have been recognized over a broader range of ventures.

This chapter deals briefly with four aspects of inequality in society to set the context for a discussion of education: income, housing, criminal justice, and health care. Other data on inequality (such as social class) in the United States are drawn upon where appropriate, but this chapter argues that African-Americans exist as a statistically significant sub-group within most of the other categories of disadvantage found in American society--in fact a statistically larger share of disadvantaged categories than would be expected. In short, race does not explain everything, but if you are black and in the United States, it has a pervasive inhibition on opportunities of every kind. Educational programs of schooling and teacher education are then addressed to see where intervention is most promising. Self-help programs are identified, recognizing the difficulties of securing broad public support.

Background to Inequality for African-Americans

African-Americans came to the United States as slaves in most cases. Although they sometimes came via the British colonies of the Caribbean, most came directly from Africa. Although other peoples were sometimes enslaved and the Africans mixed with various other races, slavery remained the dominant experience of their group (more or less exclusively) until the Civil War. From the time that slave trading was abolished during the 1830s (with legislation from several states reinforced by the effective blockade of slaving by the British navy) the numbers of African-Americans have grown by natural causes rather than by continued migration. Only a few thousand have left the U.S. for other nations such as Liberia or Canada.[2] In short, for over 150

---

[2] The 1971 Census of Canada showed 21,000 Blacks, some descended from African slaves in Canada or the West Indies, but most were "freedom seekers" (Hill 1981). About 12,000 former

years the United States has been the only home of African-Americans, and for 125 years they have been citizens. But not equal ones.

Deprived of the vote initially, threatened by lynch mobs until the present generation, denied equal access to many public services in both government and private institutions, the African-American is still not able to enjoy equal status. This inequality remains institutionalized although no longer formalized in law. Most of the social functions of American life create separate categories for white and non-white, and black is both the largest and probably the most disadvantaged group among the latter. At the personal level, racism may not be evident, but almost any set of statistics can be broken into categories that reflect the racial exploitation. Of course, current data do not describe a society that is inevitable or desirable. Since the systems they describe are capable of being changed if there is sufficient social and political will, education has an important role in improving the deplorable conditions revealed in studies of other aspects of society: income, housing, health, and crime.

Income

Economic developments for African-Americans in the United States reflect the continuum of possibilities. Blackwell (1985) asserts that "many segments of the black community experienced major economic progress" between the Civil Rights Act of 1964 and the election of Ronald Reagan in 1980. *U.S. News and World Report* (1986) claimed that the majority of African-Americans are prospering and that they had doubled their proportion in the middle class. But these two articles still portray these gains as insignificant in the context of economic inequality. The Reagan period brought appalling reverses in economic equality for the majority of African-Americans. An Urban League report entitled *The State of Black America* (Swinton 1989) shows per capita income for African-Americans

---

U.S. slaves migrated to Liberia (Webster et al. 1967).

remained steadily at 51 percent of that for whites. The aggregate incomes of both groups continued to grow, but the income gap widened by about $2000. Black family income was only 42 percent that of whites and spelled disaster for large families in the urban setting.

U.S. News and World Report (1986) reported that 1.1 million black males were unemployed in 1985, compared to .5 million in 1970. Half of all black teenagers who had started a job are now unemployed. The explanation offered by the Department of Commerce (1986) is that there are no longer well-paid jobs in manufacturing where unskilled blacks would be employed. In the last fifteen years, of twenty-three million jobs created in the private sector, more than 90 percent were in the service sector.

High unemployment rates among African-Americans are related to the entry of new immigrant groups into the employment force, and to the structural shift from low-skill jobs to jobs requiring technical skills (See 1986). The internationalization of the world's labor force (partly because American businesses are opening factories offshore) points to an increasing need for American youth to have job training and general education. Indirect evidence indicates that investment in public schooling can be partly offset against added costs of long-term unemployment, or can provide a partial solution to the high rate of unemployment among blacks, thereby providing a respectable cost/benefit argument for offering training services.

Black unemployment and poverty are both high, and high relative to the figures for white Americans. The 1986 Census Bureau reports that 33.7 million people (14.4 percent of the U.S. total) are poor. Among African-Americans, the rate is 33.8 percent, for black children 51.1 percent, and for the black elderly 31.7 percent. Blacks are three times as likely as whites to find themselves in poverty. Black families headed by women are twice as likely to be poor. Swinton (1989) contends that not only did African-Americans not share in the recent economic revolution, but the black-white gap is growing. The black poverty rate doubled from 1969 to 1988 (12 percent instead of

6 percent) and unemployment tripled (1.7 million instead of 570,000).

This economic inequality in America reflects upon the marginal participation by African-Americans in the economic community. Not only are there smaller numbers but the nature of the jobs makes workers vulnerable to displacement from automation, technological changes, and shifts to off-shore operations. Unskilled and semi-skilled jobs are disappearing at the rate of 35,000 per week, nearly two million per year. This pressure on the African-American community is curiously functional, for Gans (1974) noted that any social system can ensure that its "dirty work" is done at low wages if there are no alternatives for part of the work force.[3]

African-Americans are losing ground, giving rise to a nation of the truly disadvantaged. Evidently America is growing into two nations, one black, one white; separate and unequal.

Housing

Blackwell (1985) argued that African-American housing should be judged by the standards created and used by the empowered Americans--the whites. By these standards, African-American housing is grossly overcrowded, substandard, and expensive. It contributes to homelessness even as it provides a limited form of housing.

This situation evolved as a succession of Republican administrations shifted the focus from construction of public housing to permitting private landlords to build or convert rental units for eligible families. These changes were followed by a series of rental subsidies (Bell 1970). To reach provisional agreements with landlords, landlords were allowed to subdivide

---

[3] This remark recalls an infamous 1858 address by James H. Hammond in the U.S. Senate during the debate concerning the admission of Kansas to the Union. "In all social systems there must be a class to do the menial duties, to perform the drudgery of life." Hammond concluded that slavery should be legalized in Kansas.

existing apartments into exceedingly small units, resulting in overcrowding becoming commonplace (Forman 1978). The population density in public housing was three times as high for African-Americans as for whites. In 1980, black families were larger than those of whites, but their apartments were smaller. The 1986 Census also indicated that a substantially larger number of ancillary indviduals resided with black families. There are not enough housing units for the African-American population, and the existing units cost too much.

Today's problems arose from the urban renewal programs of the late 1950s and the 1960s, when the goal was to demolish blighted areas and construct new dwellings, office buildings, and highways. African-Americans were forced from their homes and traditional neighborhoods and the reduced number of available housing units became available for the poor in new ghettos (Gilderbloom 1989). The Reagan adminstration added to existing problems by massive cuts in domestic spending, including a large reduction in housing aid. Spending for low income housing fell from $32 billion in 1980 to $7 billion in 1988. This national agenda halted construction of low income housing despite residential density being at its highest levels ever, housing problems at their maximum.

Another consequence of these government housing policies is that some African-Americans have no housing at all. It is estimated that less than 2 percent of new housing guaranteed by Federal Housing Authority (FHA) mortgages is available to African-Americans. For non-government housing, the percentage open to black people is even smaller. One-third of the 23 million African-Americans now live below the poverty line (U.S. Bureau of Census 1988). It is highly probable that they live in desolation and squalor, devoting an increasing portion of their income to rent. Waiting lists for public housing swell dramatically, forcing many cities to close off new applicants.

Inequality is evident in the housing shortage, in racial exclusion, and in homelessness. The exclusion of persons from residential areas because of their race, color, creed, or ethnic attachment, despite their needs and ability to pay denies African-Americans a fundamental right. While complete freedom of selection is never achieved, compulsory or manipulated segregation is inherently wrong, damaging both for the immediate victims and for the general public. Housing segregation leads directly to segregation in other areas of life: schools, churches, hospitals, public accomodation, recreation, welfare and civic activities, and the workplace. Although segregation of schools is a violation of the orders of the Supreme Court, many schools of the north and west are segregated not by law but by racial patterns of residence.

Health

Universal health care is hotly debated in the United States. Conservative ideology suggests that those in need must fail in seeking help from their families and from the marketplace before they can depend on the government for medical assistance (Enthoven 1980, Hornbrook 1983). For poor people, seeking medical care from the marketplace drains them of hope and resources (Trevino and Moss 1983). The numbers are substantial: in 1983 the number of people living in poverty in the United States exceeded the entire population of Argentina, Australia, Canada, Sweden or Taiwan--in fact of all but twenty-three nations in the world. African-Americans represent a large number of those in poverty.

In 1969, 19.9 percent of African-Americans sixty-five years of age or more could not work because of ill health. (Only five percent of whites were in the same situation.) Low incomes for African-Americans explain many of these discrepancies, as they have done throughout the century. At the beginning of this century, white men outlived black men by 15.7 years; white women outlived black women by 16.0 years. These gaps have continued to narrow throughout the century, to become respectively 6.8 and 5.3 years. Significant differences are evident in the proportion of each race that lives beyond the age of 65: 74.8 percent of white and 58.1 percent of African males; 85.7 percent of white and 74.9 percent of African-American females (Statistics of the United States 1986).

Lacking the means to purchase the available health care, the majority of African-Americans die before their white counterparts, often from stress-related diseases such as cancer, strokes, hypertension, cirrhosis of the liver, diabetes, sickle cell anemia, heart disease, and substance abuse (Harwood 1981, Hornbrook 1983). The stress of living in a racist society is manifest not only in forms of disease but in the avenues of enjoyment and escape. African-Americans increasingly drink alcohol and smoke cigarettes despite warnings that these endanger their health. The immediate dangers apply not only to the abusers of these substances but to members of their families, who suffer from financial privation, neglect, family violence, and physical disease.

Poor nutrition is another factor. African-American families, like many impoverished Americans, live on diets that are high in carbohydrates and fats, low in proteins and other essential nutrients. Substance abuses and malnutrition are reflected in many statistics. For example, teenage pregnancy and low infant mortality rates are at levels usually associated with third-and fourth-world nations. One of every fifty black babies is born prematurely or does not survive the first year of life (Black and DeBlassie 1985, Burt and Sonenstein 1985, Gelder and Brandt 1987, Guttmacher 1976, Sai 1978).

The last years of life are fraught with a different deprivation: a substantial proportion of African-American men will never collect social security, despite having paid into the system for all their working lives. The current retirement age is sixty-five but will soon move to sixty-seven in the United States. The average age at death for African-American men is sixty-four, so most will not survive to the dreamed of retirement and leisure years.

Hospitalization and health care are also less available to poor--and thereby to a large sector of African-Americans. Many cannot afford hospitalization, and because U.S. health policies do not adequately address the problem, many African-Americans turn to folk remedies, clinics, and out-reach centers, each of which may be inadequate and too late to help (Hornbrook 1983, See 1989). Currently AIDS has become a killer, for although representing only 12 percent of the American population, blacks have over one quarter of the reported cases.[4] The whole notion of inequality in the United States is interlocked with the health care system and with the health of citizens. Funds for social services have continued to disappear, leaving the minority groups at risk. Direct money for health systems has dwindled, leaving large gaps within the system. Inequalities within the American health care system can be expected to increase and African-Americans will pay a significant toll.

Criminal Justice

African-Americans constitute only 12 percent of the American population, yet in 1981 they made up 48 percent of the total prison population (Bridges and Crutchfield 1986). A study by the *Atlanta Journal Constitution* (Thompson 1989) reported that black men convicted of an offense were at least twice as likely to go to jail as white men convicted for the same crime. The study further reported that between 1985 and 1988, one out of every six black men in Georgia was either in jail, on probation, or on parole. The rate for white men was roughly one in twenty. The study also showed large disparities in sentencing for a particular crime. In one South Georgia circuit the average sentence for burglary was eleven months for white men, and in metropolitan Atlanta the average was nearly seven years for black men. Staples (1984) noted that the numbers of imprisoned African-American, Hispanic and other minority populations have increased five times faster than that of the white population.

How did these curiously different sets of statistics come about? First, there is the view that African-American black males have inherent criminal tendencies. In attempting to resurrect this ancient and questionable bromide, Eysenck (1964) identified what he called the "criminal personality"--a paradigm

---

[4] The Center for Disease Control reports the following cumulative data for AIDS: White 64,618 cases, Black 31,514, Hispanic 17,885, Asians 705, Indians 156, and 280 of unknown cases (U.S. Department of Health Services 1986).

which gained popularity among some sociologists. Moynihan (1965) pointed to a supposed decay inherent within African-American families and culture. Hill (1985) refuted this criminal personality theory, showing it to be empirically unsound. All in all, these theories, once given credence, have been denounced as erroneous, racist, and damaging to African-American families (Myers 1980).

Empirical studies show a positive relationship between African Americans and incarceration rates (Gross and Mauro 1984, Rand Corporation 1983). Surprisingly, these same studies show the relationships to be spurious (J. H. Nagel 1977, W. G. Nagel 1977). Becker and Hills (1980) report that African-American crime is rooted in economic deprivation and racism. They further believe that African-American men have more time to engage in aberrant behavior because teenagers and adults are chronic victims of unemployment. The courts are biased in prosecution and sentencing: African-Americans are more apt to have certain behaviour labeled as deviant, then targeted for criminal prosecution (Radelet and Pierce 1985). African-Americans are more frequently incarcerated than are whites, and there is strong evidence of racial disparity in jail sentences. They constitute only 12 percent of the population but represent 36 percent of the persons jailed in 1988. Bowers (1983) found that the race of both the defendant and the victim affected the likelihood of obtaining an indictment, and Myers and Hagan (1979) report that regardless of the race of the defendant, prosecution may consider white victims to be more credible or their troubles more worthy of full prosecution. This conclusion is supported by research dealing with homicide cases. First, in murders where the victim and defendant did not know each other, individuals accused of killing white people were more likely to be indicted for first degree murder (Foley and Powell 1982). Also, prosecutors were 3.2 times more likely to seek the death penalty for defendants charged with killing whites than they were for defendants charged with killing African-Americans (Radelet and Pierce 1985).

In the sentencing of convicted murderers (Reidel 1986, Baldus, Woodworth and Pulaski 1983, Rand Corporation 1983) African-Americans and Hispanics receive stiffer sentences and serve more time in jail than do whites convicted of similar felonies. In the post-sentencing phase as well, race continues to determine decisions, for black offenders are significantly less likely than whites to have their capital sentences commuted.

When attempting to specify targets to be overhauled, no one phase of the criminal justice system can be held responsible for the existing racial disparities: injustice is pervasive. Researchers emphasize that any corrective action short of overhauling the entire system would grossly oversimplify the huge problem. As a result of this racial myopia, a substantial number of minorities view police departments and the rest of the justice system as enforcers of majority power structure and not as protectors of the non-white community (Staples 1984).

Education

American educational history for African-Americans can be divided into four periods:

1) the slavery period, in which schooling for African-Americans was very unusual and was forbidden in most states;

2) the period between the thirteenth Constitutional Amendment in 1865 extending emancipation everywhere in the U.S.A. and the Brown case in 1954,[5] almost a century of segregated schooling in which the inferior opportunities of African-Americans were reflected directly in low pay and virtual servitude enforced by their lack of market skills;

---

[5] *Brown vs the Board of Education of Topeka Kansas* was a Supreme Court decision that rejected as impossible the earlier official objective of providing segregated but equal school facilities and services for American blacks. In the Brown case, it was ruled that if the African-American schools were different, they would be inherently unequal in status. It was further ordered that the schools should be desegregated "with all deliberate speed" and this process was to be overseen by the federal government. President Eisenhower made it plain that the law would be enforced (Wilkinson III 1979).

3) the early desegregation period, in which there was a struggle to make desegregation work--despite the energetic efforts of many whites to undermine its promise by securing better advantages for their children by fleeing to the suburbs, opting for private education, resisting busing to equalize opportunities, and protesting hiring of African-American teachers in desegregated schools, etc; and

4) the recent period of realism over idealism, in which it was recognized that desegregation is working slowly and poorly. This has given rise to *ad hoc* decisions by many African-American educators and parents to pursue the best available treatment for the children now in the schools rather than (or while continuing) to struggle for the best corporate solution.

Some African-American leaders, parents and teachers are willing to abandon desegregation--in effect opting for a situation like that obtaining before the Brown case. In an effort to boost the self-image of their youth, they seek enrichment programs that are culture specific and offer better role models of high achieving African-American teachers in schools. In effect, they accept segregated schools *if the results are good for their children*, and they doubt that a positive result can come from schools that have been so poorly integrated that separate programs continue to be typical for African-American children. For many years, the vocational programs have been oversubscribed with black children, and the academic programs more or less inaccessible to them, mostly at the behest of the school administrators and guidance persons, but also because of culturally-biased testing programs that are used to provide program advice (Samuda 1975).

School reformers seek changes directed at the whole American population: for the civil rights of all the American minorities to be respected.[6] Of these minorities, it has usually

---

[6] Jesse Jackson referred to this ideal in his "Rainbow Coalition" when he sought the Presidency as the candidate with support from all races. Standifer, as the 1987 guest editor of *Negro Education*, made an eloquent plea on behalf of education,

been claimed that the African-Americans present the greatest challenge because of their numbers and the dismaying need for their school programs to be improved. Simple desegregation, leading to a better understanding and mutual respect, remains a mirage, shimmering and beckoning, but apparently receding as one approaches.

Requirements for Reform

Desegregation has not been abandoned, defeated, nor won. The statistics show that a progressively larger part of the American population attended desegregated schools over most of the period since 1954, with the fastest growth during the sixties and seventies. The 1990 Gallup poll (Elam 1990) shows that a majority (79 percent) of whites and non-whites believe that "black children and other minorities in this community have the same educational opportunities as white children" (p. 47). Although 83 percent of white parents believed this statement, only 56 percent of non-white parents agreed.

Desegregation of pupils was intended to be accompanied by desegregation of the teachers and administrators, and some of the changes in these fields were disastrous to the African-American teaching community, for the most highly qualified and experienced teachers in many communities were whites, and they were the more likely to win jobs as schools were desegregated (Sinowitz 1973).

Curriculum reforms marked a further stage of desegregation, and these changes went through more than two stages in most cases (Gay 1990). The first change was to add minority characters (Black, Chicano, women, non-Christian, etc.) to the curriculum, and these changes gradually overcame the traditional stereotyping of minority occupations as laborers and servants, badly educated and lacking initiative, and making infrequent deferential appearances. There is (or was) a danger that this would be an incomplete change, with the outcome being two separate sets of materials, each positive but each

---

claiming that a better deal for only some victims was no answer.

ignoring the legitimacy of the other, and consequently reinforcing the "two solitudes" that have been identified for American education. The second phase saw all parts of the curriculum become accessible to all minority groups. There was to be an end to stereotypical streaming of African-Americans into vocational courses, athletic programs, and jazz. The third phase (which is not really completed) requires the rethinking of the foundation of school theory to bring genuinely pluralistic content, perspectives, and experiences to the whole population (Banks 1981). No longer would African-American children be the only ones to adjust their cultural objectives. Unfortunately, the schools of America do not respond readily and quickly to these prescriptions for a non-discriminatory society.

The problems of educational streaming are likely to begin in the different opportunities available in homes. When poverty keeps both parents working, often in shift work, and where the culture of poverty is generations old, the preparation of children for schooling may have suffered (for example parents cannot afford to send their children to quality pre-school programs and the prospects of the child seeing parents reading and experiencing stories being read to them are greatly reduced) so the African-American child may be launched poorly in the first years of schooling. Remedial work continues to remove the pupils from participation with the others and the classes are never completely caught up. Some of the answers were sought in technology (mechanical teaching machines, then electronic computers were regarded as significant aids) and in equally mechanical instruction--mastery learning and similar approaches that enabled all students to proceed at their own rate but failed to address the cultural reasons for the problem. Of course, whenever the instruction was individualized, it was equally possible for advantaged children to maximize their lead and arrogate unto themselves a new set of salable skills (McPhail 1985). Slavin (1990) claims that some of the highly touted educational programs are not offering the benefits that many of the consumer school boards assumed would be automatic. In these cases, the clear need for better education for children such as some African-Americans in many communities has given rise to hucksters rather than benefits. Project Head Start is not an example of this failure but its initial hopes were unrealistic.

Although it was dismissed early by some scholars (Jensen 1969) its twenty-five year record marks it as a program that provides reliable enrichment and stimulation for at-risk youngsters who would be likely to fail in the typical school environment. These advantages for Head Start pupils are evident in the first year and diminish in the second and subsequent years, but they still have measurable advantages several years later (Cole and Washington 1986, Gimmett 1989).

Affirmative Action for students is most likely to be justified in those cases where sequential development of knowledge and skills is less essential, or where alternative learning procedures (some of them outside the schools) are readily available for aspects of the program where knowledge is imperfect. In the case of the African-American community, selection and promotion practices fail to take into account their experiences and judge them on what others experience (Samuda 1975). Assumptions about intelligence are based upon this biased information and the minority groups suffer in consequence.

American education is at present perceived to suffer from widespread social or political promotions, with the consequence that many senior students are underachievers, even illiterates. African-Americans are among the adults who have suffered from ineffective school instruction in the past, and those now in school are more likely to be disadvantaged. City core schools usually have the poorest financial support, facilities, and sometimes the poorest teachers--a series of disadvantages more likely to retard the education of black than white youth (Darling-Hammond 1990).

Funding

Raising minimum standards is only effective if there are reasonable prospects for all children to achieve them. Under the Reagan administration national funding of schools was reduced substantially (Verstegen and Clark 1988), and with that cutback the administration gave away its leverage over non-complying states or school boards. Deprived of a significant source of funds in a recession, many poor neighborhoods faced problems. These undermined the chances of African-Americans more than the population as a whole, and the solutions (or lack of solutions) indicated that the poor boards would usually have to find their own solutions. Even large and prosperous cities like New York, Chicago, and Detroit closed schools for several weeks or even months because they had no funds to pay teachers (Cibulka 1987). The more prosperous suburbs of these cities had different boards where schools were attended mainly by white children. No schools were closed there. More general privations hurt the African-American youth most. When the out-of-school services (day-care, birth control clinics, etc.) are also starved for funds, the result is a disproportionate number of drop-outs, lower than potential achievement, and low self-esteem.

Raising minimum standards, rather than simply allowing current minimum standards to be recognized as acceptable, will require pouring millions of dollars into the poorest schools of every city, to improve the facilities, provide more favorable pupil/teacher ratios, boost the numbers of enriching activities, and reduce the interference of crime. All of these changes would be welcomed by the majority of the African-American community. The busing programs of the 1960s and 1970s were not very successful attempts to boost the floor levels of education, for they relied upon the questionable motivation of majority parents to argue for better conditions in the schools to which their children were bused. Instead, white parents admitted that urban core schools were inadequate for their children, and sought a solution by avoiding the effects of busing--at least for their children (Coleman 1975). The trend has continued in various formats (DiBona 1988).

The reality for many African-Americans is that they must now choose, just as the white parents in the busing controversy chose to favor their children over long term policy gains. The most successful, best educated, most prosperous blacks can escape to the suburbs or their brownstones, send their children to desegregated but mainly white schools, and forget about the problems of the poor of America. They know that most of the poor are non-white, and that some of the poorest are African-Americans. They also know that some of the nation's newest non-whites climb quickly from the ranks of poverty to middle or upper class and entrepreneurial success, with superior education playing an important role in this success. The temptation to ensure the future of their own children is very real (Arnez and Jones-Wilson 1988).

Experimental Programs

Is it possible to create a greater determination and demonstrate its success in the largely black communities of some cities? Evidently the answer is at least a qualified yes. Koff and Ward (1990) indicate that incentive payments (offers of free college tuition) created a very large number of high achievers in neighborhoods with traditionally low expectations. Other programs with different kinds of incentives are blossoming in various cities, apparently demonstrating that schools could make a bigger difference if they were given the chance (Richmond 1990). The problem seems to be that for the past several years the amount of funding available to education has been insufficient for all qualified African-American students to attend, let alone receive public scholarships. Richmond hopes that incentive plans would not be confined to academic programs, for important contributions in other fields should also be encouraged. The television program *Fame* suggests one such possibility.

Those with a broader sweep of responsibility need to achieve in the whole system of education the limited gains that receive publicity because they are so unusual--such as transforming all the youth in one slum school into scholarship winners. Partial answers include successful neighborhood schools, elite management of schools under contract, private control of schools (which tolerates rejection of all the difficult cases and can charge well beyond the average per-pupil cost of public schooling, and schools where the parents are closely involved in the operation of many school functions (Henderson 1988). The problem is not so much a lack of solutions as the inability of a badly fractured society to ensure that appropriate solutions are accessible for the schools that are most in need. The huge demand on resources would be hard for the majority to accept.

The growing shortage of qualified teachers is one major concern of American education. It has arisen because a major glut a generation ago left teachers comparatively underpaid; recruiting for the profession declined as teaching conditions deteriorated; enrollments, faculty numbers, and program prestige dropped dramatically in faculties of education (Johnson 1990); and worst of all, many of the current teachers in the U.S. expect to retire in the next few years. There is no way by which all classes can find qualified teachers to replace those retiring within this century. For African-Americans, the spectre of continuing disadvantage in their schools remains, exacerbated by the remaining *de facto* segregation (Eubanks and Parish 1990).

Proposals to reform or upgrade teacher education--such as those advocated by Goodlad[7] or Sizer (1984) have a good prospect of success in the states with money and non-salary assets[8] that will attract a fine teaching force. They are likely to prove politically impossible elsewhere--in fact to be stymied by tax revolts and the various new initiatives concerning tax increases (Pipho 1990). If faculties of education do not have resources sufficient to achieve their avowed objectives of excellence everywhere, it is likely that the disadvantaged of

---

[7] Goodlad (1988) writes of a mission with four aspects: justification is for society's benefit, pedagogical excellence is assumed to be vital, typical schools are to be upgraded to become very fine institutions, and ideals, ethics and legal obligations are to pervade schooling. This public morality stands in contrast to the back to the basics movement, and would achieve far more but likely at a higher cost (Goodlad 1984).

[8] Goodlad (1988) begins his proposals with two expensive postulates: 1) programs for the education of the nation's educators must be viewed by institutions offering them as a major responsibility to society and be adequately supported and promoted and vigorously advanced by the institution's top leadership, and 2) programs for the education of educators must enjoy parity with other campus programs as a legitimate college or university commitment and field of study and service, worthy of rewards for faculty geared to the nature of the field.

society will remain so. Unless programs are specific in their intention to place the last first, African-Americans will view them with continuing caution.

A Question of Will

The World Bank, UNESCO, and other international agencies (Hallak 1990) have suggested certain management reforms and educational priorities that could be applied in the United States. In other nations they are intended to improve the prospects of underutilized human potential by emphasizing basic education and literacy programs for adults who have not attended schools. These reforms were proposed for developing nations, so it is embarrassing for both the U.S. and state governments, and for the most disadvantaged American groups to be faced with arguments for the same kinds of reforms. The solution proposed is that higher education and secondary education should be frozen at their present levels because they are subsidized services for the already advantaged members of society. Parents would be required to pay for advantages if they want them for their children, while public monies are directed toward progressive improvements in access and quality of programs for the least-served parts of the population. In developing nations, this would be the elementary schools. These changes, insist the exponents, have a better cost-benefit ratio and are more democratic. In the United States the secondary schools and colleges are analogous. The effort to make them genuinely accessible and effective is important--not least to African-Americans.

References

Arnez, N. L., and F. C. Jones-Wilson. 1988. A descriptive survey of Black parents in the greater Washington D.C. area who chose to send their children to non-public schools. In D. T. Slaughter and D. J. Johnson, eds. *Visible Now: Blacks in Private Schools.* Westport, CT: Greenwood.

Baldus, D. C., G. Woodworth, and C. Pulaski. 1985. Discrimination in Georgia's capital charging and sentencing system: A preliminary unpublished report submitted by Petitioner, 1983. In *McClesky vs. Kemp,* 753 F. 2nd 877.

Banks, J. A. 1981. *Multiethnic Education: Theory and Practice.* Boston: Allyn and Bacon.

Becker, B. D., and S. M. Hills. 1980. Teenage unemployment: Some evidence of the long run effect on wages. *The Journal of Human Resources* 15: 354-372.

Bell, C. 1970. *The Economics of the Ghetto.* New York: Pegasus.

Black, C., and R. R. DeBlassie. 1985. Adolescent pregnancy: Contributing factors, consequences, treatment, and plausible solutions. *Adolescence* 19(78): 281-289.

Blackwell, J. 1985. *The Black Community: Diversity and Unity,* 2nd ed. New York: Harper and Row.

Bowers, W. J. 1983. The pervasiveness of arbitrariness and discrimination under post-Furman capital statutes. *Journal of Criminal Law and Criminology* 74: 1067.

Bridges G. S., and R. D. Crutchfield. 1986. Racial and ethnic disparities in imprisonment. *Washington Public Policy Notes* 14: 1-5.

Burt, M. R., and F. L. Sonenstein. 1985. Planning programs for pregnant teenagers. *Public Welfare* 43(2): 28-36.

Cibulka, J. G. 1987. Theories of education budgeting: Lessons for the managment of decline. *Educational Administration Quarterly* 23(1): 7-40.

Coleman, J. S. 1975. School desegregation and loss of Whites from large central-city districts. In *U.S. Commission on Civil Rights, School Desegregation: The Courts and Suburban Migration.* Washington D.C.: Government Printing Office.

Darling-Hammond, L. 1990. Achieving our goals: superficial or structural reforms? *Phi Delta Kappan* 72(4): 286-295.

DiBona, J. 1988. The resegregation of schools in small towns and rural areas of North Carolina. *Journal of Negro Education* 57: 43-50.

Elam, S. M. 1990. The 22nd gallup poll of the public's attitudes toward the public schools. *Phi Delta Kappan* 72(1): 41-55.

Enthoven, A. C. 1980. *Health Plan.* Reading, MA: Addison-Wesley.

Eubanks, E. E., and Ralph I. Parish. 1990. Why does the status quo persist? *Phi Delta Kappan* 72(3): 196-197.

Eysenck, H. 1964. *Crime and Personality.* London: Pergamon.

Foley, L. A., and R. S. Powell. 1982. The discretion of prosecutors, judges, juries in capital cases. *Criminal Justice Review* 7: 16.

Forman, R.E. 1978. *Black Ghettos, White Ghetttos, and Slums.* Englewood Cliffs, NJ: Prentice Hall.

Gans, H. 1974. The politics of culture in America. In L. Rainwater, ed. *Social Problems and Public Policy.* Chicago: Aldine.

Gay, G. 1990. Achieving educational equality through school desegregation. *Phi Delta Kappan* 72(1): 56-62.

Gelder, L. V., and P. Brandt. 1987. Teenage pregnancy, beyond sex education: School clinics tackle the teen-pregnancy epidemic. *McCalls* 114(7): 83.

Gilderbloom, H. 1989. America's housing crisis: A sad record for Reagan. *Atlanta Constitution* (editorial, January 29).

Goodlad, J. I. 1984. *A Place Called School: Prospects for the Future.* New York: McGraw-Hill.

_____. 1988. Studying the education of educators: Values-driven inquiry. *Phi Delta Kappan* 70(2): 104-111.

Gross, S. R., and R. Mauro. 1984. Patterns of death: An analysis of racial disparities in criminal sentencing and homicide victimization. *Stanford Law Review* 37: 27.

Guttmacher, (The Allan Guttmacher Institute). 1976. *11 Million Teenagers: What Can be Done About the Epidemic of Adolescent Pregnancies in the U.S.?* New York: Planned Parenthood Federation of America.

Hallak, J. 1990. *Investing in the Future: Setting Educational Priorities in the Developing World.* Paris: International Institute for Educational Planning and Pergamon Press.

Harwood, A. 1981. Introduction: Guidelines for culturally appropriate health care. In A. Harwood, ed. *Ethnicity and Medical Care.* Cambridge, MA: Harvard University Press.

Henderson, A. T. 1988. Parents are a school's best friends. *Phi Delta Kappan* 70(2): 148-153.

Hill, D. 1981. *The Freedom Seekers. Blacks in Early Canada.* Agincourt, Ont.: The Book Society of Canada.

Hill, R. B. 1985. A reassessment of Blacks in crime. *The Western Journal of Black Studies* 9(4): 198-203.

Hornbrook, M. C. 1983. Allocative medicine: Efficiency, disease severity, and the payment mechanisms. *Annals of the American Academy of Political and Social Science* 468: 12-29.

Jensen, A. R. 1969. How much can we boost I.Q. and scholastic achievement? *Harvard Educational Review* 39: 1-123.

Johnson, T. W. 1990. Taking a first step toward reform. *Phi Delta Kappan* 72(3): 202-203.

Koff, R. H., and Deborah Ward. 1990. Philanthropy, the public schools, and the university: A model for at-risk youth. *Phi Delta Kappan* 72(3): 223-226.

McPhail, I. P. 1985. Computer inequities in school uses of microcomputers: Policy implications. *Journal of Negro Education* 54(1): 3-13.

Moynihan, D. P. 1965. *The Negro Family. The Case for National Action.* Washington, D.C.: U.S. Department of Labor, Office of Policy Planning and Research.

Myers, M. A., and J. Hagan. 1979. Private and public trouble: Prosecutors and the allocation of court resources. *Social Problems* 26: 439.

Myers, S., Jr. 1980. Black, White Differentials in Crime Rates. *The Review of Black Political Economy* 10(2): 133-152.

Nagel, J. H. 1977. Crime and incarceration: A reanalysis. *Fels Discussion Paper 122.* School of Public and Urban Policy, Fels Center of Government. Philadelphia: University of Pennsylvania.

Nagel, W. G. 1977. For a moratorium on prison construction. *Crime and Delinquency* 154-172.

Pipho, C. 1990. Taxes and tempers. *Phi Delta Kappan* 72(1): 6-7.

Radelet M. L., and G. L. Pierce. 1985. Race and prosecutorial discretion in homicide cases. *Law and Society Review* 19(4): 587-609.

Rand Corporation. 1983. *Racial Disparities in the Criminal Justice Sytem.* Santa Monica, CA: Rand Corporation.

Richmond, G. 1990. The student incentive plan: Mitigating the legacy of poverty. *Phi Delta Kappan* 72(3): 227-229.

Riedel, M. 1976. Discrimination in the imposition of the death penalty: A comparison of offenders sentenced to die pre-Furman and post-Furman. *Temple Law Quarterly* 49: 261.

Sai, F. A. 1978. Social and pyschosexual problems of African adolescents. In A. S. Parkes, R. V. Short, M. Potts, and M. A. Herberton, eds. *Fertility in Adolescence.* Cambridge, England: Galton Foundation.

Samuda, R. J. 1975. *Psychological Testing of American Minorities.* New York: Harper and Row.

See, L. A. 1986. *Tensions and Tangles Between Afro Americans and Southeast Asian Refugees.* Atlanta, GA: Wright Publishing Company.

_____. 1989. Folk medicine, folk healing and Voodoo in rural health care. Paper presented in August at the University of Maine, Medical College of Augusta.

Sinowitz, B. E. 1973. School integration and the teacher. *Today's Education* 62: 31-33.

Sizer, T. R. 1984. *Horace's Compromise: The Dilemma of the American High School.* Boston: Houghton Mifflin.

Slavin, R. E. 1990. IBM's writing to read: Is it right for reading? *Phi Delta Kappan* 72(3): 214-216.

Standifer, J. A. 1987. The multicultural, nonsexist principle: We can't afford to ignore it. *Journal of Negro Education* 56(4): 471-474.

Staples, R. 1984. American racism and high crime rates: The inextricable connection. *The Western Journal of Black Studies* 8(2): 62-72.

Swinton, D. H. 1989. Economic status of Black Americans. *The State of Black America.* Atlanta: Urban League.

Thompson, T. 1989. Blacks sent to jail more than Whites for same crime. *Atlanta Journal-Constitution* (April 30).

U.S. Bureau of the Census. 1988. *Statistical Abstract of the United States: 1986.* Washington, D.C.: U.S. Government Printing Office.

U.S. Department of Health Services. 1986. *National Health Statistics.* Washington, D.C.: Center for Disease Control.

U.S. News and World Report. 1986. A nation apart (March 17): 18-21.

Verstegen, D. A., and David L. Clark. 1988. The diminution in federal expenditures for education during the Reagan administration. *Phi Delta Kappan* 70(2): 134-138.

Webster, J. B., A. A. Boahen, and H.O. Idowu. 1967. *The Growth of African Civilization: The Revolutionary Years: West Africa since 1980*. London: Longmans Green.

Wilkinson III, J. Harvie. 1979. *From Brown to Bakke: The Supreme Court and School Integration: 1954-1978*. New York: Oxford University Press.

TEACHER TRAINING IN THE
ANGLO-EASTERN CARIBBEAN

K. P. Binda

Introduction

The Anglo-Eastern Caribbean discussed in this chapter consists
of seven relatively small fragmented but densely populated
territories, extending approximately 400 miles longitudinally
from Antigua-Barbuda (just east of Puerto Rico) to Grenada
near Venezuela.

These insular territories range in size from under three
hundred square miles in the case of Dominica to a few hundred
acres in some of the dependencies in the Grenadines. The area
has a cosmopolitan population, the largest ethnic group of
African origin, East Indians mainly in St. Lucia, St. Vincent and
Grenada, as well as Chinese and descendants of the expatriate
white European plantocracy, mulattoes and other mixed races.
The aboriginal inhabitants were exterminated, except for a few
hundreds in a reserve in Dominica.

The Eastern Caribbean had a very turbulent history.
Before the arrival of Columbus the warlike migrating Carib
pushed out the peaceful indigenous Arawaks. Columbus
accidentally stumbled upon the islands and promptly claimed
them for Spain. The lack of precious minerals and hostility of
the Caribs led the Spaniards to abandon the region. England,
Holland, and France, among others, quickly moved in to fill the
void. The territorial fragmentation aided the development of
colonialism and balkanization by the European powers who
fought incessantly for centuries in attempts to claim ownership

of the islands. The nineteenth century brought some stability to the region, but by then colonial exploitation had already left its indelible mark.

The region was now fragmented not only physically but politically and economically. Attempts at forming a West Indies Federation with the British territories collapsed in 1962, and Britain embarked upon a program of decolonization as the islands, which were no longer useful, were becoming a burden upon the British treasury. By the middle of 1980, all but Montserrat were independent nations, politically free, but still shackled under the yoke of economic neocolonialism. All these islands are labelled as Less Developed Countries (LDCs) in the Caribbean, with high levels of poverty, overpopulation, underemployment, and outmigration. Table 1 shows the population, land area and population densities of the seven territories discussed in this chapter.

Table 1. **Population, Land Area, and Population Density**

Territory	Land Area (sq. miles)	1988 Population	Density (persons per sq. mile)
Antiqua/ Barbuda	171	84,000	491.2
St.Kitts-Nevis	104	48,000	461.5
Dominica	290	79,000	272.4
St.Lucia	238	133,000	558.8
St.Vincent	150	108,000	720
Grenada	133	100,000	151.9
Monserrat	39.5	12,000	303.8

The education system in the Anglo-Eastern Caribbean today results from the legacy of rapacious colonialism and historical inertia. It was never the intention of the metropolitan colonial powers to provide quality education for the masses as an illiterate and ignorant populace was easy to control, and was a source of cheap labour for the foreign-owned plantations and other economic enterprises.

The education system was essentially dualistic, elitist, and inherently unequal; children of the poor were denied the same educational opportunities as the children of the wealthy. Desmond Hoyte (1978), President of Guyana, commented that "education in former times was used as an instrument of division and class prejudice in support of the capitalist imperialist system" (p. 10). The poor were made to believe that education would not be of much benefit to them. Brizan (1984), for example, noted that among the first three vehicles identified as contributing to vertical class mobility, in order of priority, education came last with "color and Caucasian features, income and wealth" (p. 280) taking first and second place.

Educational neglect of the masses can still be observed today in the truancy and high illiteracy rates in some schools in the Windward Islands such as in St. Vincent, St. Lucia, Grenada, and Dominica. The illiteracy rate in St. Vincent was reported to be about 38 percent in 1982 and about 40 percent in St. Lucia in 1986 (Binda 1986). The comparatively low educational expenditures today result as much from this legacy as from the precarious and fragile state of the economies of the island states. In 1986-87 St. Lucia spent 24.8 percent or E.C.$39,963,736 of recurrent expenditures for education; Dominica spent 18.62 percent or E.C. $17,058,280 (one $E.C.= Approx. 37 cents U.S.) in the same fiscal year, while St. Vincent averaged around 20 percent, St. Kitts and Nevis averaged around 14 percent, and Antigua around 11 percent in the 1982 fiscal year.

Political independence from Great Britain did not bring economic independence or prosperity as the islands found themselves gripped in a new neo-colonial, core-periphery economic relationship with the metropolitan powers (McCann 1987). The islands are still characterized by the socio-political and economic dualisms. Brizan (1984) noted that right into the 1940s, education in Granada "had made no significant impact upon the social life of the people" (p. 290). Though conditions have improved somewhat, the small elite ruling class still accounts for and consumes the greater share of the national income. Attempts by the island governments to eradicate poverty and lessen the dualisms have not had much success, because in the third world countries "the problems of poverty and income distribution are largely political and institutional in origin" (Todaro 1977, 155). In the Caribbean, these institutions often show stubborn and persistent inertia and rigidity.

Lower income families can least afford the extra costs associated with schooling. The necessity of poor children having to work on the farms or elsewhere to supplement family incomes often proves too much of a burden so they withdraw from school. Lower income children are therefore at a disadvantage even before they start school; they are the first to drop out.

The unequal distribution of incomes and dualistic social structures persist but are now cyclical. Todaro (1977) has stated that the elite ruling class "whether knowingly or not, is in the perpetuation of the international capitalist system of inequality and conformity" (p. 91). The recent invasion of Grenada by American-led forces (well documented by O'Shaughnessy 1984) is perhaps one of the more extreme examples of the perpetuation of the neo-colonial hegemony.

Income redistribution, although one means of lessening the inequalities, causes serious political problems unless accommodated within a growing economy. With limited natural resources and few exportable commodities which are dependent upon variable weather conditions, limited local markets, fluctuating low world prices, and high cost imports as characteristic structural imbalances in their economies, the Caribbean countries face serious setbacks in their attempts to expand and develop their economies. The one bright spot, an expansion of the tourist industry, likewise suffers from the neo-colonial shackles of foreign ownership (Bonisteel 1978, DeBlij and Muller 1988). The World Bank in its economic report on the Caribbean considered these factors "a severe impediment to their economic and political modernization" (Chernick 1978, 4). The World Bank further noted that each of the territories in the Eastern Caribbean "has found economic and political viability an elusive goal" (Chernick 1978, 5). While a variety of policy initiatives have been undertaken to increase living standards and lessen inequalities among the populace, one of the more widely pursued policies has focused upon developments in the education field.

Theories about the relationship between education and economic development have failed to have an impact upon development efforts in the third world. Human resources development (Harbison 1973) has been advanced as the ultimate basis for the wealth of nations.

Developments such as experienced in Japan have not taken place in the Eastern Caribbean territories and quantitative expansion of the educational system has not led to accelerated growth and development. Expansion of the system is constrained by a number of factors; there are inadequate funds for capital expenditures (though foreign aid from agencies such as CIDA do provide some relief), and a shortage of qualified teachers severely affects all the systems of the Eastern Caribbean.

While a quantitative expansion of the education system is still needed in these underdeveloped countries, some like St. Kitts-Nevis, are beginning to look at educational development from a qualitative perspective, and have taken steps to restructure their higher education system, making it more accessible and more equitable, and aligning it with government development policies that would help reduce societal and economic inequalities. Dominica's reorganization of teacher training from college-based to inservice school-based training was designed to improve significantly the quantitative and qualitative aspect of the education system (Dominica Teachers' College 1986).

Education is still considered a tool for socio-economic and political development. This is an explicit policy of the government of St. Kitts and Nevis as noted by the College of Further Education (1988).

The College is expected to provide the educated and skilled personnel required by the developmental policies and strategies of the Government, and for the total development of the Federation of St. Kitts and Nevis. While meeting the needs of the present, the College will also anticipate the needs of the future, and plan and implement educational and training programmes in terms of national planning and developmental goals. The

College shall aim at providing more access to tertiary-
level education and training, than presently available,
and as far as possible at costs within the reach of those
seeking such facilities. The College shall also strive to
meet the needs of the community, including those in
employment and in professions, for further and
continuing education. (p. 2)

The reconceptualization of the education system, however, has
not meant a radical break with existing structures. Even the
revolutionary government in Grenada found this task to be a
very difficult one. The education system still functions as it did
during the colonial past, albeit with some modifications.

Structure of the Education Systems

The education systems in the Anglo-Eastern Caribbean
territories consist of primary, secondary, and tertiary sectors. In
addition, a pre-school or early childhood sector may exist
formally (as in the case of Grenada) or semi-formally (Antigua-
Barbuda). Figure 1 shows the levels of schooling and passage of
students through a typical system--that of St. Kitts-Nevis.

All the territories have a dual system of education:
schools run by both the government and religious organizations.
The governments, however, are responsible for teacher training,
curriculum, supervision and salaries of all the schools--
government and denominational, except the private schools. All
teachers are civil servants.

In the primary schools pupils are assessed and promoted
by teachers until about ages 11, 12, or 13 when they write the
Common Entrance Examination which selects for the limited
places in the secondary schools. In 1986, St. Lucia had a
transition rate of only 29.24 percent (Ministry of Education
1986a) from the final year in the primary school into the
secondary system. In Grenada the rate was 56% in 1983-84. This
means that a significant proportion of students are not receiving
a secondary education.

Figure 1. St. Kitts-Nevis, Education Structure

Institutional Level	Approx Duration	Approx Ages	Exams
Early Childhood	2 years	3-4	
Primary Education	7 years	5-12	Common entrance exam for selection into secondary
Post-Primary Senior Post-primary	4 years	13-16	School Leaving Certificate
Junior secondary	4 years	13-16	"
Secondary	5 years	13-17	GCE CXC (0. Level)
Post-Secondary Teacher education	2 years	18 plus	Basic Certificate
Technological & vocational and management studies	1 year or more	16 plus	or
Health Sciences	1-2 yrs.	18 plus	National Certificate
Arts, Sciences & General Studies (incl. Adult & Continuing Ed.)	2 years	18 plus	and National Diplomas
University of the West Indies	3 years or more	19 and over	University degree

The curricula of both the primary and secondary schools consist of regular academic subjects with some practical courses such as Arts and Crafts, Home Economics, Agriculture, Industrial Arts, Music, and Physical Education. Most pupils who fail to gain entrance into the secondary schools are held over in post-primary classes in the same elementary school where they continue to receive more of the same curriculum with additional inputs of some practical subjects. These students would normally study for an additional three years. At the end of the Post-Primary, a School Leaving Examination is written and a certificate awarded to the successful candidates.

A large proportion of teachers in the schools are untrained and unqualified. Of the 915 teachers in the elementary schools in Grenada in 1986, 476 were untrained and 282 did not possess the minimum academic qualification for entry into the teachers' college. In St. Vincent the teachers' college could find only four qualified people for the 1985 intake--even after lowering the entry requirements. It is not surprising, therefore, that both the quality of instruction and results are dismal. The situation is equally bad in the other territories except St. Kitts-Nevis, where only five untrained teachers were reported in 1987. However, there were seventy-seven substitutes, largely untrained, temporarily teaching in the schools (Ministry of Education 1987a). In Antigua 25 percent of the primary school staff was untrained (Binda 1986). In St. Lucia, St. Vincent and Dominica the situation is even worse. Forty eight percent of all primary staff in St. Lucia (Ministry of Education 1987b) and 70 percent in Dominica (Dominica Teachers' College 1986) and St. Vincent (Ministry of Education 1986b) were untrained. No wonder the failure rates in the schools are very high, a condition, though very bad, that is acceptable as part of the system where full access to secondary education is as yet not possible.

Those who enter the secondary school system face an uphill task with underqualified and untrained teachers who constitute the majority of staff in all the schools in the Anglo-Eastern Caribbean. In 1986, 62 percent of all secondary staff in Grenada were untrained; in Antigua 50 percent were untrained; in St. Lucia about 70 percent were untrained and in St. Vincent the figure was 57 percent (Binda 1986). The failure rate in the

GCE/CXC examinations, the final examinations of the high schools, is also quite high--often reaching over 70 percent.

Many of the problems can be traced to the low educational expenditures, poor, inadequate physical facilities, low teaching salaries and large percentages of unqualified untrained teachers in the schools at both the elementary and secondary levels. But perhaps the root of the problems lay in the process of recruitment and training of teachers, which is constrained and proscribed by economic and political decision making.

Teacher Recruitment and Training

The peripheral, fragile, and marginal economic position of the Anglo-Eastern Caribbean territories in the worldwide economic system and the nature of the socio-economic and political decision making, have not augured well for the education systems in the islands. Underfunding, large numbers of unqualified, untrained personnel, and poor performance (as measured by both internal and external examinations) are endemic features of the education system.

Teaching staffs are recruited either directly by the government concerned or on the recommendations of the denominational boards, and are given their appointments by the Teaching Service Commission in the various islands. The requirements for entry into the teaching service are generally similar throughout the islands, four GCEs at the Ordinary Level with English, or the equivalent CXC. Professional training as a prerequisite for entry into the teaching service in the Anglo-Eastern Caribbean is not a requirement, nor is it mandated though it is desirable; as a result, the majority of teachers initially recruited are untrained.

When new recruits are hired, they are offered a short orientation on teaching for about a week or two before they are sent into the classroom to assume their teaching duties. Sometimes recruitment takes place after the schools reopen because ministry officials may not be certain which teachers will be returning to their classes, because some have found better paid positions or migrated overseas. The new recruits are sent directly into the classrooms as teachers with only the experience they themselves received as pupils, very often from poorly qualified teachers.

The slow increase of trained staff is due to:

1) a high turnover of teachers;

2) school systems not graduating a sufficient number of students with the necessary GCE/CXC passes;

3) teacher training institutions unable to increase significantly the number of trainees because of insufficient staff and inadequate facilities, space, equipment or other resources;

4) limited national resources hindering government's ability to increase significantly spending in this sector; and

5) socio-economic and political decision making (for example, in the presentation of the budget estimates for 1986-87, the Prime Minister of Dominica recognized that education was one of the "most critical" areas but was "not able to increase expenditures" in that sector).

Untrained recruits may be in the classroom for up to ten years before entering the Teachers' College for the two year training program. Earlier entry may depend upon the backlog of untrained teachers in the system. Some teachers in St. Vincent, St. Lucia, and Grenada who lack the minimum entry requirement have been in the classroom without training for even longer than ten years.

Many of these entrants to Teachers' College lack sufficient training in Mathematics, English, or Science, therefore subject content must also be taught. Students are given the opportunity to acquire content in order to meet the University of the West Indies (UWI) requirement before they can graduate. Many of them do not acquire the content passes and consequently do not receive the UWI diploma at the end of the two years of training. Some islands, for example Antigua-Barbuda, offer a local diploma. The status of these people is often unclear even to ministry officials. One ministry official in Antigua said that these teachers are classified as "uncertificated."

Training Programs at the Teachers' College

The Teachers' College training programs across the Caribbean territories are theoretically the same, the structure having been agreed upon by the Biennial Eastern Caribbean Standing Conference on Teacher Education and the University of the West Indies. The Biennial Eastern Caribbean Standing Conference on Teacher Education is the regional educational organization that meets every two years to discuss the syllabus of the UWI program and other educational matters. This body includes personnel from the School of Education, UWI at Cave Hill, Barbados, the Principals of the Teachers' Colleges and senior personnel from the Ministries of Education.

The teacher training program focuses on elementary teacher training and consists of both academic and pedagogic courses run over two years. There are compulsory courses as well as electives and options. These options may vary from island to island, but graduates emerging from any of these programs would have a common background of training. The compulsory courses are jointly assessed by Teachers' College Staffs and the Faculty of Education, University of the West Indies at Barbados. Those who pass the university approved program are presented with a Teachers' Certificate from the University.

A few of the Colleges, for example in St. Kitts-Nevis, St. Lucia, and Antigua-Barbuda, also offer a secondary program for students having the requisite GCE passes. In St. Kitts-Nevis, the Division of Teacher Education, College of Further Education, has also developed a Post-Graduate Diploma in Education for University Graduates. Training for graduate secondary teachers in the Eastern Caribbean, however, is carried out at the University of the West Indies, in Barbados. Figure 2 outlines the program structure at the Division of Teacher Education in St. Kitts-Nevis for 1988-1989.

The entry requirements for the Primary Programme are four passes at GCE "O" (ordinary) Level or CXC General or the equivalent including English. Candidates pursuing the Secondary Program are required to have "O" level passes in both teaching subjects in group B. In 1986-87 there were thirty-one first year students enrolled at the College in St. Kitts, sixteen

Figure 2. **Teacher Training Program, St. Kitts-Nevis**

Primary Program	
Compulsory Subjects	Options (One)
Education Language arts Mathematics Science Social studies Research techniques Health & family life education	Art Music Industrial arts Home economics Introduction to school librarianship

Secondary Program		
Group A (3 subj.)	Group B (2 subj.)	Group C
Use of English Education Contemporary social issues	English Maths Social studies Science	1 option from the primary list

males and fifteen females; and the number of second year students consisted of five males and nineteen females. Females appear to predominate in the teaching service throughout the islands where a large proportion of the teachers practice without the minimum requirements for entry into Teachers' College. For example, in 1987, females constituted 77 percent of primary school teachers in St. Lucia (Ministry of Education 1987b), and 74 percent in St. Kitts-Nevis (Ministry of Education 1987a). Ministry of Education data show that in 1987 73.4 percent of all untrained teachers in St. Lucia were females.

In-Service Training Programs for Untrained Staff

The backlog of large numbers of untrained teachers in the islands led to the development of structured accelerated programs in a number of places. This was necessary since the rate of entry into the Teachers' Colleges was low and the numbers graduating were quite small. When the attrition rate in the teaching service was added, it was quite clear that the backlog would never clear up but rather increase. Various programs were developed. In 1980 Grenada launched the National In-Service Teacher Education Program (NISTEP), for 534 participants at Grenville, St. George's and Carricou. NISTEP's aims were threefold: 1) to upgrade the academic qualifications of the staff, 2) to impart the necessary pedagogic skills required for teaching, and 3) to allow people to specialize in particular areas such as curriculum development or materials development. Participants were released for a day in the week to attend classes and spent a total of six additional weeks during the vacation periods March/April and July/August.

While NISTEP managed to upgrade the skills of some teachers, it did not achieve the anticipated degree of success. Many problems were encountered. Participants were not adequately prepared for this type of training; many only had one or two "O" Level subjects. The lack of adequate resources and teaching staff as well as insufficient instruction and supervision, poor motivation, and delinquent attendance compounded the training problems. Many of these graduates were later found to be deficient in many areas of their training.

A new program called "Inservice Teacher Education Program" (INSTEP) was initiated in 1984. This program runs for two years as a preparation for entry into Teachers' College.Teachers are released for a day from their classroom duties for instruction at Teachers' College. On completion of the preparatory program, graduates spend one full year at Teachers' College. The accelerated one year program was expected to help clear up the backlog of untrained staff but the program encountered the same problems as those faced by NISTEP.

In Dominica the two year in-college teacher training program was completely revamped in 1983 as it became clear that the untrained backlog of teachers would not clear up at the current training rate well into the second decade of the twenty-first century. In place of the two year college program, a three year inservice program was established. The pattern of training involves day release of teachers every two weeks over a three year period as well as utilization of the vacation periods of Easter and August for block training. While the model of training is different from those in the other islands, the UWI program is the one being implemented. College instructors regularly visit trainees in the classroom. At the end of the three year period trainees write their final examinations; and unsuccessful students are allowed to repeat the examinations in the following year.

In St. Vincent, an inservice upgrading program was begun by Teachers' College in 1986 for the untrained and unqualified teachers. Teachers were released for one day to attend college in order to upgrade their content and at the same time receive some professional skills. This pre-college year was expected to produce sufficient numbers of capable people for full time entry into the Teachers' College regular program. This program has faced numerous problems such as poor attendance, motivation of teachers, insufficient numbers of college staff, and inadequate facilities. Moreover, when teachers leave their classrooms to attend the college, chaos prevails in those classrooms without teachers.

St. Vincent Teachers' College with the assistance from the Caribbean Network of Educational Innovation for Development (CARNEID), an affiliate of UNESCO, also launched an innovative program in 1986. Under this program, capable and industrious teachers who showed potential for becoming "master" teachers were selected for training as cooperating teachers and teacher mentors for untrained teachers. This program, while receiving the blessing from the UWI, suffered from serious underfunding.

Among the territories in the Eastern Caribbean St. Lucia has one of the better organized systems of inservice training. This is perhaps understandable given the large numbers of pupils in the schools, about 33,000 primary and 6,000 secondary pupils in 1986 (Ministry of Education 1987c), as well as the large number of teachers. St Lucia has developed a structure for teachers' inservice education which is staffed by a ministry official who is the co-ordinator of all Inservice Training. The island is divided into three school districts which facilitates the offering of inservice programs. The program is designed for untrained teachers who have academic deficiencies, and there are many teachers in this category, some with only one GCE subject or none at all.

The focus on academic upgrading resulted from failure rates of over 50 percent at the Teachers' College. Instructors are university graduates as well as other trained teachers and staff with "A" Levels. Results from the Teachers' College exam in 1986 show that forty out of fifty-one students who wrote the exam passed with eleven being referred (Teachers' College 1986). These results represented a major improvement over previous years.

Notwithstanding the shortcomings, these inservice programs provide a level of training in content and pedagogy needed in these underdeveloped countries. But even these efforts leave the situation critical, as the education systems in the Eastern Caribbean still employ large numbers of untrained and underqualified staff.

To help meet the training needs in the Eastern Caribbean over the last fifteen years, the Organization for Cooperation in Overseas Development (OCOD) has been conducting numerous inservices aimed at improving and upgrading the teaching services both in the areas of content and pedagogy. In many of the territories "the OCOD summer programmes have been the main course of training for these teachers" (OCOD 1989, 2). OCOD has been involved in the upgrading of staff at the Teachers' Colleges as well as in the schools through its Advanced Regional Programmes. It is hoped that this program will produce a cadre of trained personnel who will then conduct training throughout the islands. Due to the existence in the islands of a large number of unqualified teachers without the requisite GCEs, OCOD recently (1989) introduced the Comprehensive Teacher Training Project (CTTP) as a means of upgrading qualifications to GCE level "for entry into Teachers' Training College in these territories thus allowing for a reduction in the backlog of untrained teachers" (OCOD 1989, 2). The program is directed from St. Lucia and consists of the development of distance education modules in the areas of English Language, Mathematics, Social Studies, and Integrated Science. Other international agencies such as the Canadian Teachers' Federation, The United States Agency for

International Development and the British Voluntary Service Overseas are also involved in upgrading teaching staffs in the islands. Such international aid plays a great part in the upgrading of the education systems in the Eastern Caribbean. It is too early to say, however, what impact such aid is having upon the education systems and cultural values in these islands. Poonwassie (1987) has raised the question as to whether agencies such as OCOD tend to breed "dependency instead of promoting development" (p. 148). Governments, nevertheless, appear to welcome such foreign aid as it lessens the burdens on their almost empty treasuries. Moreover, such assistance sometimes constitutes the only structured inservices that are offered in some places.

Conclusion

In the Anglo-Eastern Caribbean the marginal levels of economic activity still largely controlled by a small ruling elite show marked dualisms and inequalities. Underfunding of the educational system, the legacy of both colonial neglect/inertia as well as the nature of local decision making have resulted in an education system with poor physical facilities, lack of equipment and resources, extremely large numbers of untrained and unqualified staff, and underperformance--so much so, that illiteracy is still a major problem in these islands.

The Eastern Caribbean has instituted a common syllabus for teacher training but the large numbers of unqualified people coming out of the secondary schools have necessitated modifications to the teacher training programs by the island governments. Various models of inservice teacher training which include foreign aid are currently in operation in the attempts to reduce the backlog of untrained staff. The cyclic nature of the problems, however, limits these efforts. But unless the islands increase their educational expenditures, as well as make serious attempts to improve socio-economic conditions, the education system may continue to suffer from the problems that currently plague it.

References

Binda, K. 1986. *An Examination of the Education Systems with Particular Reference to Teacher Training and Staffing Requirements in Selected Territories of the Eastern Caribbean and Guyana.* Winnipeg: Organization for Cooperation in Overseas Development.

Bonisteel, R. 1978. *Welcome to Paradise.* Toronto: National Film Board of Canada.

Brizan, G. 1984. *Grenada Island of Conflict.* London: Zed Books.

Chernick, S. 1978. *The Commonwealth Caribbean: The Integrating Experience.* Washington, D.C.: The World Bank.

College of Further Education. 1988-89. *General Information.* St. Kitts and Nevis: College of Further Education.

DeBlij, H., and P. Muller. 1988. *Geography: Regions and Concepts.* New York: John Wiley and Sons.

Dominica Teachers' College. 1986. *Inservice Training.* Dominica: Dominica Teachers' College.

Harbison, F. 1973. *Human Resources as the Wealth of Nations.* New York: Oxford University Press.

Hoyte, D. 1978. *Education for Development.* Georgetown, Guyana: Guyana Teachers' Association.

McCann, L., ed. 1987. *Heartland and Hinterland.* Toronto: Prentice Hall.

Ministry of Education. 1986a. *The Education System and the Catholic Assisted School.* St. Lucia: Ministry of Education.

_____. 1986b. *Statistical Information on Teaching Personnel, St. Vincent and the Grenadines.* St. Vincent: Ministry of Education.

_____. 1987a. *Educational Statistics 1986-87.* St. Kitts-Nevis: Ministry of Education.

_____. 1987b. *Educational Statistics 1986-87.* St. Lucia: Ministry of Education.

_____. 1987c. *Primary and Secondary School Enrollment and Staffing 1963-1986.* St. Lucia: Ministry of Education.

OCOD. 1989. *Report to the Annual General Meeting.* October 14. Winnipeg: Organization for Cooperation in Overseas Development.

O'Shaughnessy, H. 1984. *Grenada: Revolution, Invasion and Aftermath.* London: Sphere Books.

Poonwassie, D. 1987. OCOD in the Caribbean. In D. Clarke, ed. *Report of the Sixth Biennial Caribbean Conference on Teacher Education.* Barbados: University of the West Indies.

Teachers College. 1986. *Summary of Examination Results.* St. Lucia Teachers' College.

Todaro, M. 1977. *Economics for a Developing World: An Introduction to Principles, Problems and Policies for Development.* London: Longman.

United Nations. 1988. *World Population Chart.* New York: United Nations.

TRADITIONAL NEGLECT IN RURAL EDUCATION IN COLOMBIA

Beatriz Franco

The Social and Educative Context

Colombia has a land area of 1.139.000 square kilometers and a population of 29.5 million; it is considered to be a middle income country with an estimated GNP per capita of US$ 1.240 (World Bank 1989). It has a rate of inflation of 23.7 percent a year, regarded as low when compared to 101.5 in Peru, 166.3 in Brazil, or 298.7 in Argentina (World Bank, 1989). Colombia's external debt, 17 million , is also one of the lowest among Latin American countries (108 million in Mexico, 124 in Brazil, 57 in Argentina).

Colombia is a republic with a President elected by the people every four years in a power-sharing agreement provided for rotating the presidency between the Conservative and the Liberal parties. The Colombian Constitution establishes a federal system of government and provides for a parallel educational organization of national, state, municipal, and private school systems (Article 41).

The President appoints a Minister of Education, to whom is delegated the authority to establish educational policy covering all the school systems in the country. Ideally, the national, state, municipal, and private schools will all reflect the ministry's policies and thus unify the educational effort, supporting the development goals of the nation.

Each province has a popularly elected assembly, but its governor is appointed by the president of the republic. The

255

governor appoints a secretary of education to be the province's chief educational officer. The secretary of the province is responsible to the governor and not to the national minister of education, which reduces the minister's control over education in the provinces.

Formal education is structured in a sequence of regular school stages, each with an established curriculum content. There are four levels: pre-school, basic (five years of primary and four of secondary), middle-vocational and intermediate-professional, and higher education. Nonformal education is not structured in regular stages nor does it have a curriculum sequence, nor offer a degree.

Colombia experienced rapid urbanization-industrialization development over the past three decades. In 1987, 67 percent of the population lived in urban areas, in contrast to 1955 when only 31 percent was urban (Ocampo 1987). Industry grew and so did the worker class. Urban poverty rose and marginal zones--associated communities with marginal services--occupied large portions of big cities. The nation's social structure is represented by four social classes: an upper class consisting of 9.2 percent of the population, a middle class of 30.5 percent, a lower class of 60.3 percent and a marginal class representing 6.8 percent (Gutierrez 1988).

The country's development stimulated significant efforts by the government and private institutions to expand and improve educational opportunities. Decentralisation and regionalisation reforms started in the 1970s and have had a certain amount of success (Hanson 1986, 1989). Diversification brought new vocations to secondary schools, with the help of the World Bank (Vespor 1988, Rondinelli et al. 1990). Distance education with innovative methods has been a great contribution to the nation's education (Griffon and Richard 1990, Hallak 1990). The in-service training SENA programs, some of the oldest and largest in Latin America, have been very efficient in training workers for the urban labor force (Jimenez and Kugler 1987, Hallak 1990). The instructional television programs, among the largest in the world (Bishop 1986), have been a significant contribution to elementary schools. Unfortunately most of these programs were directed to strengthen the urban sectors, while ignoring the rural populations.

The underdevelopment of the rural areas has brought thousands of peasant families to the cities. In search for a better life, people abandoned their farms, and with them their peasant values and traditions. In 1951, the primary sector occupied 55 percent of the economic active population with occupations such as agriculture, livestock production, and mining; in 1986 the number was only 34 percent. On the other hand, the secondary sector (manufacturing and construction) climbed from 16 percent to 21 percent, and the tertiary (commerce and services) from 29 percent to 45 percent in the same years (Ocampo 1987).

Disorganized migration to the cities has not only produced serious social, economic, and educational consequences to the whole nation, but it has also exacerbated the contrasts between rich and poor in both urban and rural sectors. Unfortunately, there is not much research to show how education--perhaps more than any other social aspect-- reflects the traditional acute inequality between rural and urban opportunities. A few studies conducted mostly by universities (Parra and Subieta 1983, de Tezanos 1983, Garzón and Caicedo 1985, Cerda 1986) brought the government to realize the magnitude of the problem, and new measures were initiated to improve the educational opportunities in the countryside.

Public and Private Education

The Colombian system of education has been characterized by tensions and conflicts between the State and social groups. While the first intends to establish a national education, the latter groups struggle for autonomy to design their own programs. The public sector provides 86 percent of primary education, 62 percent of secondary, but only 43 percent of pre-school and 40 percent of higher education (Rodriguez 1988). The most prestigious private schools are supported by foreign firms and can afford to import and effectively utilise the most up-to-date teaching materials. They also have the best and the best paid teachers. These schools deliver a very high quality education but the high fees ensure their students come from only a high socio-economic level. Two other important kinds of private schools are run by the Church and sponsored by various national foundations. These also deliver high quality education and reach kids from medium socio-economic levels as they charge lower fees. Compared to private institutions, the condition and maintenance of public schools is deplorable: about 90 percent have no library and almost no teaching materials, 70 percent lack the minimum sanitary requirements and 20 percent of the rooms and desks need to be repaired (Rodriguez 1988).

There is an interesting differentiation that applies throughout Colombia between elite and mass institutions among elementary schools in urban areas. *Colegios* are selective private institutions where parents from upper and middle socioeconomic levels make sure their children get an education suited to their intended life-style. *Escuelas*, on the other hand, are public institutions with low standards, usually attended by marginal children. There are no escuelas in rich areas, and whenever the State builds an escuela in a middle-class neighborhood, people turn it into a colegio. In rural areas, where such differentiation does not exist because the only available institutions are public, the school (through its teachers) reproduces the social differences.

Secondary schools continue this marked differentiation. Traditional *Bachillerato* (high school diploma), offered by most private institutions and obtained by upper and middle classes, leads directly to universities. Vocational Bachillerato, offered in public institutions and taken by low prestige classes, are regarded as a means to get low status occupations with limited incomes, including Normal schools and teaching training. In rural areas secondary education is almost unavailable--the public sector reaches only 5 percent of the population aged 13-18, and the private does not exist (Rodriguez 1988).

The same is the case with universities, concentrated completely in urban centers. The universities are autonomous bodies, governed by their own statutes, under the Ministry's supervision. Whereas tuition is very low in public institutions, it is usually high in the prestigious Catholic universities and higher still in the secular elite ones. Private universities grew in number with the expansion of secondary schools, and as a consequence of financial and political problems in public institutions (Patrinos 1990). Private universities can select comparatively limited goals to prepare their graduates for the best jobs in the public and private sectors, whereas the public sector undertakes to fulfill many more functions including research. Students in private institutions enroll in areas with more social prestige such as administration and economics (30 percent), and engineering and architecture (23 percent), while only 16 percent in education and 13 percent in social sciences (Velez and Caro 1986).

A typical university student belongs to the middle or upper class of a big city, with elementary and secondary education obtained in private institutions. He/she has been brought up within a familial atmosphere where parents, brothers, and close relatives have reached levels of education that are relatively high. It is not surprising that children of construction workers, children from rural areas, and children from marginal urban sectors never reach university and rarely secondary school.

Pre-school education has not been a priority in the Colombian system. Even though in 1960 a section of the Ministry of Education was created for pre-school education, only in 1976 was it incorporated into the national system and seven years later the Ministry established the guidelines (Cerda 1986). The creation of pre-school institutions in urban sectors has followed social and economic phenomena rather than the needs of children. The growing presence of women in productive sectors brought the need for institutions to take care of their children. This is not true in rural areas, where mothers are close to their children even while they are contributing to the local economy--in 1984, of the 1,763,000 children aged 0-6, only 13,000 (less than 1 percent) were reached by pre-school education in rural sectors (DANE 1985). In 1987 with the need to direct more attention to the establishment of pre-school education in rural areas, an agreement was signed by the Ministry of Education and UNICEF (Pulido 1988). Since conditions and characteristics of peasant life are quite different from those in the cities, it was decided to commission a careful study to determine the best programs.

Rural Education and Illiteracy

Apart from elementary school for the children, the only other kind of education available to the peasants in Colombia has been the ACPO (Cultural-Popular Action) radio program. It is a private non-profit organization founded in 1947, utilizing radio in combination with radiophonic schools, textbooks, a weekly newspaper, and locally initiated village study groups. ACPO has become one of the most successful examples of the use of radio (Hallak 1990). Although its major focus was basic literacy, it went beyond to develop in the peasants the understanding and capability necessary to enable them to improve their quality of life. Unfortunately there is no record of the number of peasants that have benefited with this program.

Another successful effort to reach adults in rural and urban areas has been the national literacy campaign *Camina*, started in 1984. The first experiences have brought increased numbers of adult literates and a considerable interest to special education (UNESCO 1986). According to the results of the literacy campaign Camina, from the total enrolled in 1985 there was a drop-out rate of 21 percent in rural areas while 14 percent in urban areas (Rios 1986). The most difficult obstacle to rural school enrollment is motivation. Peasants attach no importance to learning to read and write, preferring more "practical" courses related to domestic economy and production, which knowledge they can apply immediately (Rios 1986).

Despite government efforts to enlarge enrollment in primary education, the number of illiterates among people fifteen and over remain very high (see Table 1). These numbers include "functional illiterates," who have attended primary school for three or less years and have gained very little knowledge. According to Villamil (1982), by the end of the century a fifth of the rural population will still be illiterate (see Table 2).

The relative growth of enrollment in rural areas has dropped dramatically from 50 percent in 1953 to 34 percent in 1983, including the Indian population which represents about one percent of the nation's population (280,500). According to

Table 1. **Colombian Population Aged 15 and Over, Illiterates Same Ages (millions)**

	1938	1951	1964	1973	1983
Population	5.044	6.450	9.329	12.517	15.676
Illiterates	2.223	2.429	2.527	2.578	2.440
Percent	44.07	37.65	27.09	20.56	15.56

Source: DANE 1986

Table 2. **Illiteracy Rates (%) and Population Change with a Projection to the Year 2 000**

	Illiteracy Rates			Illiterate Pop. Decline	
	1970	1980	2000	1970/ 1980	1970/ 2000
Nation	21.0	14.8	5.0	-3.8	-4.8
Urban	15.0	9.7	8.0	-4.7	-9.6
Rural	39.3	31.8	20.5	-2.3	-2.2
Urban employees	32.1	26.7	17.5	-2.0	-2.0
Rural employees	46.6	38.9	27.2	-2.0	-1.8

Source: Villamil 1982

the 1985 Census, 110,000 were illiterate, Spanish was the language of instruction for 93,574, bilingual education was given to 13,988, and only 1,500 received instruction in their native tongue (DANE 1986).

Rural education has been unable to keep students in the schools even in the lower grades. The drop-out percentage in 1983 was 20 for grade one, 16 for grade two and 15 for grade three (DANE 1985). Repetition is also common--statistics show that from 100 students enrolled in grade one in 1983, fifty-six were promoted to grade two, thirty-seven would go to grade three, twenty-one to grade four and 17 would finish grade five (DANE 1985).

The problem for illiterates is not necessarily that they face unemployment because they tend to generate their own work--especially in urban areas. Unemployment percentages in 1978 showed only 4.5 illiterates, 9.4 with completed primary school, 13.3 with secondary school, and 7.8 for people with higher education (DANE 1979). The situation has changed little since then, and the problems continue to be in equality of income and accessibility. For women, the situation has been even worse: while an urban literate woman was making $ Col. 5,728 (about twenty U.S. dollars) a month, an illiterate from a rural area had only $ 1,058 (DANE 1979).

Education in a Typical Rural Province[1]

Boyacá is the Colombian province with the largest proportion of rural population. Like any rural society, the economy in this province is based on the primary sector. 70 percent of the population make their living from agriculture, livestock, and mining. Industry occupies only 10 percent and commerce and

---

[1] The data for this section was taken from statistics gathered in 1978 by The Oficina de Planeación Departamental de Boyacá. The numbers have not changed much since then. The educational opportunities and school conditions described for this province apply for any of the rural areas of Colombia.

services 20 percent. Small holdings are very common in this part of the country. 73 percent of the peasants own less than five hectares, 19 percent between five and nineteen, and only 8 percent own more than twenty hectares. The first group of peasants (73 percent) send children to rural schools: the other two groups can afford to send them to urban schools.

The population of this province is very young. Half of it is under fifteen years of age and the group five to fifteen reaches 30 percent. On the other hand, people sixty years and over are only 6 percent of the total population. 45 percent of rural people aged fifteen to sixty are illiterate (see Table 3). The number goes up to 70 percent when people over sixty are included.

This situation results from the real life isolation of the remote rural areas, where printed materials like books, newspapers, or magazines are hardly found and literacy skills are not considered necessary in order to clear the land, sow or

Table 3. **Population 15-60, Levels of Education**

	Urban	%	Rural	%
Illiterates	25,516	19	186,469	45
Primary: 1	8,965	6	41,483	10
2	14,473	11	76,112	18
3	16,835	12	54,956	13
4	15,114	11	29,217	7
5	23,206	17	18,972	5
Secondary	22,152	16	5,291	1
University	2,159	1	470	-
No data	9,062	7	1,614	-
Total pop.	137,482	100	414,734	100

harvest the crops. These tasks, moral values, and culture are efficiently passed from one generation to the other without the need for schooling. The isolation and lack of interest of the people is so pervasive, that peasants who learned to read and write may have forgotten these skills as they grew older. It is also common to find semi-illiterates, and people who know how to count or add but not to read and write.

In such a milieu, schools seem like foreign institutions trying to teach a strange culture. Teachers are not trained to face the realities of rural life. On one hand, they find illiterate parents who are not equipped to help and encourage their children to deal with school matters, and on the other hand, the children's minds are not prepared to meet the demands of the teacher. Not being able to understand their children's worries, upset parents turn against school believing that learning stops the children's creativity. A very poor peasant woman was extremely worried about the headaches suffered by her children "who have to force their minds in order to fulfill school duties" (Castro 1977, 20).

The impact of schooling becomes more clear when considering the material and human conditions in which teaching is developed. In 1978 rural Boyacá had 1,950 classrooms in 1,500 schools in which 26 percent offered grades one and two, 39 percent grades one to three, 18 percent up to grade four, and only 15 percent the complete primary cycle. There were 1,883 teachers, a ratio of 1.3 teachers per school. The situation in urban Boyacá was quite different: 392 schools with 1,702 classrooms and 1,664 teachers, averaging four teachers per school.

The *Oficina de Planeación de Boyacá* (Boyacá's Planning Office) considers 80 percent of the rural schools to be in bad shape. Only 6 percent have electricity and 5 percent sanitary facilities. A typical school has one classroom with one teacher who teaches simultaneously thirty to thirty-five students from different levels. In more remote areas schools have no walls and perform other functions: to dry and store the tobacco, coffee, etc. "Some children were sitting on the soil using the trunk of a tree as a desk, and others were kneeling trying to trace the vowels on the soil with a small stick" (Castro 1977, 101). The students have only one notebook and one pencil for the whole year as they have to travel long distances to buy them, and sometimes they can not afford them.

The bad shape of the schools does not seem to bother the children, for their houses are not better. Table 4 shows how "modern" facilities hardly exist in these houses. As a general rule, people from Boyacá have only the foundations of a house made of adobe, a straw roof, an earth floor and no windows, one room for people and one for the animals.

From the total enrollment in rural areas in 1978, 38 percent of the children had dropped out and 19 percent were repeating. For grades one and two the situation was more critical, as 57 percent and 26 percent respectively were repeating. The causes for this are not always related with economic demands. Motivation plays a very important part (see Table 5). It would be interesting to see how factors such as "mean" teachers or children's psychological and cultural tensions could also be related to drop-out.

From a pedagogical perspective, it is clear that the contents taught are very limited. Teachers tend to teach the same skills over and over for the new students, forgetting about the more advanced. The whole process appears to be an extension of grade one. A student who has taken grades one to three in a rural school has learned the same as a grade one child of an urban school. The system can not expect any more from teachers: given the conditions they do what they can.

Table 4. **Facilities in the Houses**

	# Houses	%
Running water	13,621	9
Electricity	4,411	3
Washroom	3,483	2
Toilet	3,299	2
Latrine	6,809	4

Table 5. **Causes of Drop-Out**

	Number	%
No parents' interest	2,760	24
Need to work	2,557	22
Have moved	2,529	21
Long distances	1,590	13
Illness	1,547	13
Others	768	7

The teaching force in Boyacá is fairly young. 53 percent are less than thirty years of age and 80 percent are under 40. In this province, teaching is primarily a feminine task as the number of female teachers doubles the number of males. 64 percent of rural teachers are Normal school graduates, 6 percent finished high school, 27 percent have some secondary school education and 3 percent completed only primary school. In urban areas, 80 percent have the Normal school degree. Compared to other rural provinces where half of the teachers have only finished elementary school, Boyaca's teaching staff can be considered very good.

The rural school continues to be a cultural shock for teachers, most of whom have been trained in urban centers to serve urban populations. The social and intellectual isolation in which they live and work does not motivate them to read, communicate, or to study and preserve their own culture. Teachers think of peasants as abominable. "They smell like manure, they are dirty and coarse. They send their children to school in rags without shoes or sandals to cover their lousy feet" reports a teacher after five years in a rural school. On the weekends, she goes on, "When I go to town, I am afraid of meeting with my urban colleagues, they look at me in such a way that I could feel the shame of my inferiority" (Castro 1977, 53). Cultural tensions are also suffered by parents who are afraid of teachers. Peasants think of teachers as their enemies, as strangers who are driving their children away from them.

Teachers' salaries are paid by categories which depend on the place of work, degrees obtained and courses taken. Amounts for elementary school teachers are high in relation to the minimum salary, but not when compared to secondary school and university teachers. Since most of rural elementary school teachers have the lowest category (or do not fit in any, see Table 6) they have very reduced incomes. In fact, their monthly salary is only triple the salary of a peon.

Table 6 also shows that the teachers with the best category are in urban areas. Not only the training opportunities but the social contact give urban teachers many more possibilities for promotion. For rural teachers the chances of a promotion or a transfer to an urban center are very poor since they lack training and influence.

Rural teachers feel intellectually close to the middle class, but relegated to inferior levels because of their income. When asked about their social class, 61 percent of the teachers claimed to belong to the middle and 29 percent to the middle-upper, only 5 percent admitted they belong to the low class. This ambivalence of status causes unhappiness and mediocrity for teachers in the place of work and in their lives.

Table 6. **Categories for Elementary School Teachers**

	Urban		Rural		Total
	No.	%	No.	%	No.
Category 1	749	74	266	26	1015
Category 2	714	43	931	57	1645
Category 3	81	18	358	82	439
Category 4	25	20	100	80	125
No category	95	29	228	71	323
Total	1664	47	1883	53	3547

Conclusion

Teaching in rural Colombia has been a very hard task. The isolation and poverty of rural schools, when compared with urban schools, is a shame for a nation that is undergoing a relatively fast development. What makes this extreme inequality is not the lack of institutions or the lack of a curriculum, but the conditions of the schools and the social and cultural differences of teachers, parents and children.

The situation appears to be changing with new programs introduced by the Ministry of Education a few years ago, focussed primarily on promoting rural education. The National Plan for Development in 1986, calls for a "change with equity." Its main objective is to define and strengthen the national identity through the promotion of regional values and an effective cultural participation of marginal areas (Pulido 1988). One of the Plan's successes, *Escuela Nueva* (New School), has been given excellent evaluations (Berry 1988). It relates the process teaching-learning to the concepts of rurality and actual life of the peasants and their children. It also involves the community in educational activities. Teacher training is also directing attention to rural areas and to the role of the teacher as an agent of cultural transformation (Gantiva 1988), and a new reform is being introduced to Normal schools.

The prospect for a better future in education in the rural areas is comforting, although there is yet a long way to go, and the results are still to be seen.

References

Berry, A. 1988. *Education, employment and development in Colombia: Phase I Report.* Doc. 3: Colombian educational priorities and capacity. Ottawa: CIDA.

Bishop, G. 1986. *Innovations in Education.* London: Macmillan.

Castro, G. 1977. *Colombia Amarga.* Bogotá: Carlos Valencia Editores.

Cerda, H. 1986. *La Institución Preescolar.* Bogotá: CED, Universidad Santo Tomás.

DANE. 1979. *Encuesta Hogar 1978.* Bogotá: Departamento Administrativo Nacional de Estadísticas.

_____. 1985. *50 Años de Estadísticas Educativas.* Bogotá: Departamento Administrativo Nacional de Estadísticas.

_____. 1986. *XV Censo Nacional de Población y Vivienda.* Bogotá: Departamento Administrativo Nacional de Estadísticas.

Gantiva, J. 1988. El movimiento pedagógico en Colombia. *Educación y Cultura* 16: 52-59.

Garzón, M., and R. Caicedo. 1985. *Algunas Características de la Educación Rural en Colombia en el Quinquenio 1978-1982.* Cali, Colombia: Universidad del Valle.

Griffon, N., and M. Richard. 1990. Éducation à distance et développement de la communauté en Colombie. *Revue Canadienne d'Études du Développement* 11(1): 61-80.

Gutiérrez, H. 1988. 50 años en la economía colombiana. *Revista Javeriana* 531: 21-45.

Hallak, J. 1990. *Investing in the Future: Setting Educational Priorities in the Developing World.* Paris: UNESCO, International Institute for Educational Planning.

Hanson, E. M. 1986. *Educational Reform and Administrative Development: The Cases of Colombia and Venezuela.* Stanford University, CA: Hoover Institution Press.

_____. 1989. Decentralisation and regionalisation in educational administration: Comparisons of Venezuela, Colombia and Spain. *Comparative Education* 25(1): 41-55.

Jiménez, E., and B. Kugler. 1987. The earning impacts of training duration in a developing country. An ordered probit selection model of Colombia's SENA. *The Journal of Human Resources* 22(2): 228-247.

Ocampo, J. A. 1987. La consolidación del capitalismo moderno. In J. A. Ocampo, ed. *Historia Económica de Colombia.* Bogotá: Siglo XXI.

Oficina de Planeación Departamental de Boyacá. 1979. *Estadísticas de la Oficina de Planeación.* Tunja, Boyacá.

Parra, R., and L. Zubieta. 1983. *La Imagen del Maestro en la Escuela Campesina.* Bogotá: Centro de Investigaciones, Universidad Pedagógica Nacional.

Patrinos, H. A. 1990. The privatization of higher education in Colombia: Effects on quality and equity. *Higher Education* 20: 161-173.

Pulido, O. 1988. Las políticas culturales de Colombia. *Educación y Cultura* 16: 38-47.

Rios, L. S. 1986. *El Plan Nacional de Alfabetización "Camina."* Seminario-taller Latinoamericano sobre evaluación de programas de alfabetización y educación de adultos. Bogotá: Ministerio de Educación Nacional.

Rodríguez, A. 1988. La educación colombiana: Datos y cifras. *Educación y Cultura* 16: 5-14.

Rondinelli, D. A., J. Middleton, and A. M. Vespoor. 1990. *Planning Education Reforms in Developing Countries.* London: Duke University Press.

Tezanos (de), A. 1983. *Escuela y Comunidad: Un Problema de Sentido.* Bogotá: Centro de Investigaciones, Universidad Pedagógica Nacional.

UNESCO. 1986. *International Yearbook of Education. Primary Education on the Threshold of the Twenty-First Century.* Paris: International Bureau of Education.

Velez, E., and B. Caro. 1986. *Postgrado en América Latina: Investigaciones Sobre el Caso de Colombia.* Caracas: CRESALC-UNESCO.

Vespoor, A. M. 1988. *Pathways to Change: Improving the Quality of Education in Developing Countries.* Washington, D.C.: Education and Training Department, World Bank.

World Bank. 1989. *World Development Report.* New York: Oxford University Press.

THE SUDAN AND MINORITY EDUCATION

Azza A. M. Ibrahim

The Sudan is the largest nation in Africa (2,505,000 square kilometers) and the fourth most populous (20,950,000) (UNESCO 1986). Its population is a typical African mixture of different races and peoples. There are the three main religious loyalties of the continent (Islamic, Christian and pagan), and important linguistic differences are found as within many African nations. Said (1965) described Sudan as "Africa in miniature." In this chapter, the majority/minority concerns are claimed to be similar to those faced by many other African nations. The Sudan's present situation makes the questions of minority status unusually important, for there is hardship in the land and people with the least standing will fare worst in the competition for wealth, food, medical care, or schooling and other comparative luxuries. How long this situation will continue is not known, but some form of competition for power and resources is centuries old.

The Dominant Traditions

The Arabic and Islamic influence grew slowly but meaningfully, largely through intermarriage, with the Arabian conquerors of Sudan steadily penetrating the psyche of the people. This led to Arab predominance in the fifteenth and sixteenth centuries. This demonstrated the power of Islam to absorb other cultures and the power of Africa to absorb Arab society. During the process, the pre-Islamic culture and civilization were integrated

273

into classical Arabic and Islam, resulting in a unique product. The word "Arab" in the Sudan has always referred a culture rather than a race or ethnic group. And the whole of the country is so interspersed with people of. Hamitic, Nilotic, Nubian, Negroid and mixed races that there is no clear racial or ethnic boundary.

Nevertheless, since there is a convention in the literature to divide the Sudan into the African South and the Arab North, and to identify some language, religious, and cultural traditions with these regions, that convention will be followed. It is supported by political reality.

In pre-Islamic times there were two main aboriginal groups. The brown or Mediterranean race consisted mainly of Nubians and Beja, and their subdivisions. The Negro or Negroids are divided into the Ingessana of Central Sudan, the Nuba in Nuba Mountains, in Kordofan and some tribes of Darfur Province in Western Sudan. The Southern ethnic composition was the Nilotics, Nilo-Hamitic and Sudanic, who are also divided into a number of tribes that speak different languages and belong to different sub-cultures, believe in different religions and practice different ways of life (Ali 1989). The 597 tribes are classified into fifty-six groups (Said 1965).

Principal Sources of Differences in Status and Rights

One of the concerns for Sudan is that it borders upon nine states: Egypt, Libya, Chad, Central African Republic, Zaire, Uganda, Kenya, Ethiopia and (across the Red Sea) Saudi Arabia. This situation makes it highly vulnerable to instability beyond its borders. The most serious external dangers appear to come from the warfare of Libya and Chad, and that between Ethiopia and Eritrea. These wars have resulted in more than one million refugees seeking safety in Sudan, with consequent difficulties in providing services.

A second consideration arose from the very large size and diversity of Sudan. Its geography varies from desert in the

Figure 1. Map of Sudan

North, tropical forests in the South, a swampy area in the south east, a vast and fertile plain in the center, and a series of rivercultures. This diversity gave rise to different livelihoods, associated cultures and levels of prosperity. Quarrels for the best opportunities among a mobile population have been endemic throughout history, and the period since independence has not been different. There has been civil war in the South since independence, with the exception of an interval of peace from 1972 to 1983. Even for those sections of the population not directly affected by this bloodshed, there have been displacements and arrested aspirations. Until the population can be more effectively united, these kinds of quarrels can be expected to prevent the most rapid possible progress. Too many of the youth are involved in defence during the time when their idealism and energy could be used effectively for nation building.

During the last decade, some parts of the Sudan experienced several consecutive years of drought. As a result, not only was the economic base for agriculture or herding destroyed, but some groups were reduced to the status of landless migrants, wandering in search of food, or taking jobs that would enable them to survive. Lacking good educations in most cases, they had nothing but their bodies to offer on the labour market, and in the cities they became labourers, maids, and (if necessary) thieves.

Economic development is another aspect of the differentiation of opportunity throughout Sudan. Although traditionally four Sudanese out of five are farmers of some kind, the nature of agriculture is dictated by rainfall and fertility. Cattle herders can survive where cash crops would fail, and some cultures are geared more to survival than to achieving prosperity. Almost 95 percent of the exports are produced by the agricultural group, and some 40 percent of the GNP. The World Bank (1990) indicates that no real economic growth took place between 1965 and 1988.

Industrial innovations and urbanization have been limited. There are the usual movements of some rural populations to central locations where they do not necessarily participate in modern occupations. These movements disrupt traditional expectations in rural areas by removing the youth upon whom the families depend for security in old age. They disrupt the city dwellers and the government by their attempts to establish homes in locations that they can afford, to learn the skills associated with modernity, and to manage their money effectively. The frustration of the peasants and cattle herders when they fail to reach their high expectations often leads to crime and a demand for more social services including education, medical care, housing, and community facilities.

Industry is still not well developed, contributing less than 10 percent of GNP, but the small number of employees is expanding exponentially, reaching 42,000 in 1971 (Lees and Brooks 1977). Industry is for local consumption: mainly food processing, textiles, footwear, sugar, and other light industries. Oil has been discovered but not developed. Industrialists are concerned that the capital for expansion may be denied to them because of the large foreign debt that Sudan contracted progressively in dealing with modernization of agriculture, transportation and the military. Although Sudan's external debt reached eight billion dollars by 1988 (much lower than the debt of Nigeria or other "least developed nations" with larger populations) it will be hard to repay because this debt is 72 percent of the GNP--but this fraction is also lower than some other nations (World Bank 1990). Expansion of new industries is difficult and risky: many would face stiff competition from previously established sources of similar goods and perhaps sources with fewer transportation problems. The differences in the economic development of various parts of the population are reflected in the educational opportunities of all regions.

The language situation is very complex. Not even linguists nor the official statisticians are aware of the precise situation. Uncertainty about the exact number arises partly because new languages are occasionally still to be found and partly because so little is known about some of the generally listed languages that it cannot be ascertained whether they are distinct languages or only dialects (Hair quoted by Ali 1989). Some of these languages are shared by other nations. Of all languages, Arabic is the most widely spoken (51 percent in 1956 Census) and the rest spoke a mixture of 112 languages (114 according to other sources mentioned by Ali 1989).

The Mobility of the Sudanese People

The International Labour Office (1976) reports that the population of the Sudan is mobile to an extraordinary degree:

> We estimate that upwards of 1 million men and women are on the move every year in search of income-earning opportunities. In addition, the Sudan has a large number of nomads who move with their cattle in rhythm with the seasons. Thus, every year, one in four persons in the adult population migrates in search of work or in the course of work from one rural area to another and from rural areas to urban centres. (p. xxii)

These forms of migration are categorized as nomadism (the most traditional form of mobility); rural/urban mobility, and seasonal labour movement either in agricultural or industrial projects; and international mobility, which is particularly significant among the highly qualified Sudanese. Either the Arab nations or the Western world are their principal destinations. The nomadic populations are mainly concentrated in Kassala, Darfur, Kordofan, Bahr El Gazal and Upper Nile. The reasons for this mobility (apart from refugee movements) are largely economic but for the international mobility they are partly political. Some regions have very much better economic opportunities than others, and for highly skilled persons the choice of employers may be very restricted. The International Labour Office (1976/68, 19) reported a range of household incomes of over 100 percent in 1967 and it is likely that this gap has remained.

In the nineteenth century, European colonialism and missionary activities of British and German origin were significant, with the colonial activities most pronounced in the North and the Christian missions in the South. In various ways, these two activities continue to influence cultures, including education. Where mission schools traditionally emphasized scriptures, they have now become similar to the national schools. Practical knowledge is included but there is an emphasis on the preparation of youth for secondary and higher education. The colonial activities promoted education by making a range of civil service jobs available to Sudanese with the required qualifications. The Colonial Office was responsible for tipping policy toward support of the North and against the South by its policy of divide and rule. (The Northerners were no longer allowed to trade in the South, and visas were required for all journeys. Only Missionaries were allowed to enter the South, a decision based on their claim that they would be able to suppress the slave trade through salvation.) This policy was pursued even farther when Arabic was banned from the South where English was to become the lingua franca (Said 1965).

The colonial regime contributed to one of the major political concerns for the Sudan. In the North, there was the gradual establishment of the infrastructure and development that would be necessary for colonialism to function. To the roads and buildings of military significance were added schools which would produce the clerks and managers that kept things working properly. In short, the differences in education contributed to the persisting distrust between North and South, or at least to some of the unequal opportunities between the populations of each region. This tradition of hostility and suspicion between the two regions increased when the Southerners were excluded from both pre- and post-independence political activities.

Sudan has been unstable politically, both in its colonial and independent eras. Before the conquest of the present Sudan by Mohammed Alli Pasha in 1822, to establish a Turko-Egyptian rule, the country was divided into different kingdoms, sultanates, and tribes. The Turko-Egyptian rule continued until 1881, when it was overthrown by Mohammed Ahmad, Al Mahdi, whose rule continued until the Sudan was reconquered in 1899 by the Anglo-Egyptians under the leadership of Lord Kitchener of Khartoum. The Sudan became self-governing in 1954 and independent in 1956. Since then there has been a series of parliamentary democracies and military dictatorships (see Figure 2).

Figure 2. The Sudanese Governments, 1956-1990

Parliamentary Democracy	Jan. 1, 1955-Nov.17, 1958
Military Rule	Nov. 17, 1958-Oct.21, 1964
Parliamentary Democracy	Oct. 21, 1964-May 25, 1969
Military Rule	May 25, 1969-April 6, 1985
Parliamentary Democracy	April 6, 1985-June 30, 1989
Military Rule	June 30, 1989-

These various governments represented a wide variety of ideologies, ranging from socialism to fundamentalist "Muslim Brothers." There has been more continuity in the support for education than in some of the other aspects of government policy.

Values that Guide Sudanese Education

There are different sources of values in the Sudan, some of them official for the state but not universally enforced, some popularly rooted and perhaps widely followed, and some stemming from different religions and consequently not powerful for those who do not share the particular faith. In these respects, Sudan is more or less typical of Africa and of some nations in other continents.

Equality

Islam has an intense passion for equality: it demands that equality should be universal and complete, not limited to one race or one nation, to one house or one city. It also demands that equality embrace a wider sphere than merely economic interests, to which Islam charges that the teachings of the materialistic West are confined.

Mankind is essentially one body, with members mutually responsible and interdependent--a body in which there are no isolated and outcast societies. It proclaimed that there is no virtue except in good deeds and no nobility except in piety.

A few examples from theology make the point effectively:

> Allah--*I shall not waste the work of any one of you who works, male or female, you belong to one another.* (Suva 3-193)
>
> *We have ennobled the sons of Adam . . . ., we have given them preference over much of that which we have created.* (Swa 17:72)

They were ennobled by their nature, not by their persons or their races or their tribes. And that nobility attached to all men, producing absolute equality. . . .

The Prophet (peace be upon him) said

> *you all belong to Adam, and Adam was created from clay. Human beings are equal like comb teeth.*

Islam has also proclaimed a complete equality between men and women except in some incidental matters connected with physical differences or some responsibilities.

The prophet (peace be upon him) also contended

> *Education is a must for everybody, man or woman. You need to get education, even if it has to be in China.*

Equality in all things to all humans is the objective, mutual responsibilities are paramount and important in all fields, unity of body and soul is sought in the individual and public institutions. Fourteen centuries ago these ideas concerning equality and educational opportunity were revolutionary, they were then ambitions to which humanity had never aspired.

Male Orientation

Many of the populations of the Sudan are paternal and male oriented, macho in their valuing of humans. Equality may be sought and proclaimed, but it will not lead to precisely identical treatment. Nothing in the school curriculum will eliminate sex-bias and stereotyping, for that is introduced from the family and reinforced by many community forces. Men are always favoured, highly ranked in both the family and society. Neither maximum educational credentials nor a top career gives a woman complete social independence, for she must have the shadow of a man--her father, husband or brother--to protect her from society's suspicions. Only one function gives her maximum security in the family: giving birth to a son, for the male heir is important and highly prestigious, not only for Islamic inheritance rules but also as the future guide and guardian. These deeply rooted attitudes cannot be changed without intervention through education. Appropriate considerations are required both in the schools and in adult education, for otherwise proposing equality of educational chances will not work.

Although there are differences within the Sudanese population concerning the desired education for each gender, these differences cannot be described with great precision for the required data on access to different programs are not complete.

National Laws Augment Islam

The Sudan is an Islamic nation both officially and according to the practice of the majority of its citizens. Equality of status is fundamental to the religion. This implies equality of race, ethnicity, and gender as well as education as a human right.

Sudan has more recently subscribed to the general principles of the *Universal Declaration of Human Rights* (1948) and subsequent UN proclamations and declarations, even though these endorsements may describe long term objectives rather than current practice. Among them are universal, free, and compulsory primary education, which Sudan embraced as a signator at the Addis Ababa Unesco conference in 1961, where the goal of Universal Primary Education was proclaimed for Africa. Free and varied secondary education, accessible to the qualified, higher education accessible on merit, and continuing educational opportunities for those unable to secure schooling as children are practised, but opportunities are still constrained. Progress toward fully realizing these goals has been steady since independence in 1956, but sometimes expansion has been bought at the price of disparity. Discrimination may result inadvertently from the failure of minorities to promote their welfare.

Education in the Sudan

Schooling begins at seven in the Sudan, and is free but not sufficiently available for every child to find a place. The system includes six years of elementary schooling, then an examination determines if and which type of secondary schooling may be taken (see Figure 3). The academic secondary school consists of a lower and an upper section, each three years long, and each terminating with an external examination that determines the educational prospects for the following stage.

The upper secondary includes another choice for those denied academic schooling: they can take a four year technical or a four year teacher training course. For those shifted from the schools at a still earlier stage, there are two year vocational training courses of a relatively informal nature conducted in youth vocational centers (Sudan Ministry of Education 1985).

The major problem with Sudanese education is that there are not enough resources to accomplish what is desired by the government and by a large majority of the older students. Without these resources, the teachers do their best to prepare their best students for the small number of available academic places instead of seeking to make education fit the modest vocational prospects.

A large number of students drop out and repeat courses, but at every level teachers try hard to ensure that their most

Figure 3. The Sudanese Official Educational System

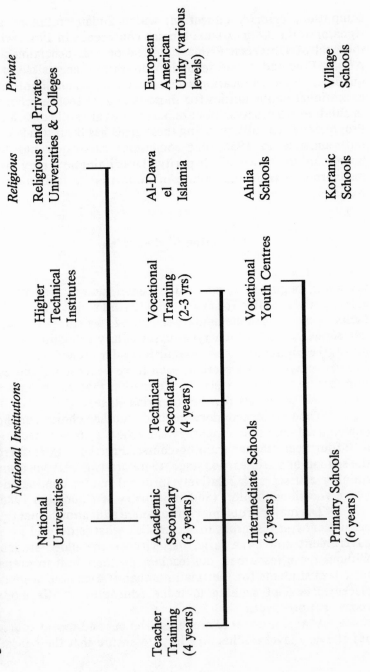

	National Institutions		Religious	Private
National Universities	Higher Technical Institutes		Religious and Private Universities & Colleges	
Teacher Training (4 years)	Academic Secondary (3 years)	Technical Secondary (4 years)	Vocational Training (2-3 yrs)	Al-Dawa el Islamia	European American Unity (various levels)
	Intermediate Schools (3 years)	Vocational Youth Centres	Ahlia Schools	
	Primary Schools (6 years)		Koranic Schools	Village Schools

promising pupils have a good chance of passing the dreaded examinations. Well-to-do and enlightened parents try to maximize the prospects of their children's success by buying extra classes and by taking their children to the best private schools. Children of poor or rural families have little chance against these kinds of competition. Of course, the competition intensifies as the student progresses through each set of examinations. Sanyal, Yaici and Mallasi (1987) indicate that one fifth of rural children attend primary school, two thirds of urban do so. While only 2.6 percent of rural children go to secondary school, 41 percent of urban do so.

Unfortunately, the hidden costs of "free education" (books, uniforms, transportation, and the lost income from the jobs that children can do) make it hard to afford for middle class families and impossible for the poorest. In fact, the free educational system has become one in which various incidental costs make the difference between success and failure. The objective of universal primary education, once identified for 1990, seems unlikely to be realized this century, and the expansion of other phases of education is similarly being rescheduled.

In all these cut-backs, Sudan is like many other nations of the third world (Shaeffer 1990). The best education is selective and of international standard. The system for the poor is expanding but not meeting expectations for quality of instruction. The present situation is unlikely to improve unless there is an increase in Sudan's economic productivity, the external payments position, and political relations with donor states. Without such improvements, there is a low prospect of education addressing its major concerns.

Regrettably, the wages of teachers are so low that they are often tempted to take offers of work elsewhere, and the better qualified they are, the more persuasive are these wage gaps. Sudan has a major brain drain, through the loss of teachers and other intellectuals.

The schooling traditions of North and South were markedly different. In the South, there were no Islamic and Arabic schools and no other religion or culture sponsored formal education before the arrival of Christian missions in the late nineteenth century. This was a highly diversified collection rather than a system (Hamilton 1935). These continued unopposed until 1957. Although for a time after independence, it was intended that the Christian schools would also form part of the state system, only a few of them survive.

The traditional Islamic schools were based largely upon the Koran (*Khalwa*), but there was substantial attention to arithmetic and reading. In the higher level colleges, there was the Institute of Islamic Studies in Omuderman, which is now upgraded to The Islamic University. These Khalwas have now been incorporated into the Sudanese system. Their disappearance has been a pity, for they traditionally provided a very cheap form of basic education for a large part of the population. However, a new Moslem school has arisen in response to the gaps of the state educational system. Al-Dawa el Islamia are a form of elitist, selective private schools for Moslems (for the most part) with high tuition fees and rigorous academic standards. They follow the national curriculum with a further emphasis upon Arabic and Islamic studies.

Another form of private education is the traditional system of Ahlia schools, which was intended to be a cooling valve for those who failed to pass their entry examinations to junior or upper secondary schools. They follow the national curriculum, but they charge fees and normally have the weaker students from well-to-do families. These schools can only be found in the capital and some of the big towns. This type of school is permitted (or even welcomed) by the government, for it relieves the pressure upon the Ministry of Education to increase places for marginal students.

Similarly, these kinds of institutions are being welcomed at the level of higher education, because they enable more students to be accommodated without government expense. These expensive academies are only located in the capital area. Although some of them are able to maintain high standards, there is no policy from the National Council for Higher Education to perform rigorous academic evaluations or to impose selection standards for their students before permitting such academies to be opened. One concern is that this policy might open the door to undesirable colleges being opened, or services being duplicated and quality being neglected. However, unless such academies exist, parents may be in a position to send their children to similar institutions in other nations, causing a heavy drain of foreign currency. That would have an even greater negative impact upon the Sudanese government and society. The effect of education abroad for the students is another point that would require systematic evaluation. Altbach (1971) indicates that foreign education for the social elite ensures cultural dependency.

Higher education has an international curriculum and procedures. Khartoum Memorial College was started as a preparation college for degrees set externally by The University of London. Recently, the objectives of providing academic leadership to the nation have included research and publication programs, but the preparation of a well educated but relatively small body of students remains the priority. After 1975, there was rapid expansion of higher education, with the opening of new universities in Gezira and Juba, both of which are community oriented, with a special focus on the problems of rural life. Khartoum High Technical Institute, with a large variety of technical qualifications and specializations, was upgraded in 1990 to a fourth university. Four additional regional universities are now being established.

At the private level, Ahfad Girls' College and Ahlia (both in Omdurman) provide services at the higher level. Cairo University--Khartoum branch also exists under the sponsorship and supervision of Egyptians.

In short, there are quantitative and qualitative differences in education that contribute to unequal opportunities in Sudanese life, and those with a religious basis are likely to continue.

The Curriculum

Three important characteristics of the Sudanese school curriculum address minority rights. Firstly, there are attempts to promote the national curriculum in all regions, for all groups, and as free education. This is intended to reduce the numbers of children denied education and the benefits accruing from it. Secondly, equivalent forms of instruction are recognized and perhaps encouraged. These are offered in some schools that are not government sponsored nor controlled, organized on the basis of language or religion. Some of them use different forms of pedagogy initiated by others and conducted by agreement. Thirdly, Sudanese education supposedly endorses the UNESCO Declaration of 1974 on international education, by which education is expected to promote international understanding, cooperation and peace, and human rights and fundamental freedoms. Although work on this massive task continues, priority has been given to expanding the numbers of school places. However, it might be noted that this objective seems to be supported by Islamic traditions and scriptures and there is an influential Islamic interpretation of the Universal Declaration of Human Rights.

Cultural Policy in the Sudan

The objectives of Sudanese Cultural Policy with respect to equality and education were updated in 1979, reflecting most of the internationally proclaimed targets for that period:

1. Education was to be given a democratic direction, so as to afford equal opportunities for all Sudanese.
2. Adult education was to be effective within six years for those who missed the opportunity for basic education.
3. Elementary education was to become compulsory.
4. A scientific, planning-conscious, industrial mentality was to be introduced, to permit the comprehensive development of society.
5. The countryside was to be developed, making the whole population sedentary rather than nomadic.
6. The capacity to innovate was to be developed in everybody.
7. Intelligent receptiveness of international experience was to be introduced.
8. Literature and the arts were to be promoted and made more accessible.

9. Sports training, hobbies and leisure activities were to promote self-education. (Abdel Hai 1982, 22)

Equality of Opportunity in Education

The extent of equality in the schools and higher education system of Sudan can be associated with several variables: region, wealth, socio-economic status, gender, language, and religion.

It should be noted initially that the Sudan has a sharply diminishing proportion of the age group enrolled in schools or higher education, and that enrollment in even the first grade is less than the number of youth of appropriate age. These data are summarized in Table 1.

The first kind of inequality is evident from these data: a significant number of Sudanese youth are being denied an opportunity to attend schools, essentially because the nation is too poor to provide for all. If one estimates this discrimination from the enrolment/age cohort, the figures for the Sudan are approximately the same as many other African nations: about fifty five percent do not attend primary education, seventy percent have no secondary education, and about ninety-seven percent have no higher education (Sudan, 1984). However, these figures are gradually improving.

An approximation for the success in macro-educational objectives for the past is provided by the literacy rate for adults. Nationally, the figure is about 20 percent. A related figure is the drop-out or wastage rate, which has been traditionally high throughout Sudan. Out of a total student population of 141,900 in grade six in 1973, 63,700 arrived at grade nine in 1976, a loss of 78,200. The maximum loss occurred between grade six and seven (55 percent) when the national examination took place. Average drop out between grades six and seven during the period 1972-80 was 56.5 percent. More than half of the grade six fail to "pass" the examination. The average flow from grade nine to ten has been 53.9 percent, a slightly higher success ratio than that between primary and lower secondary. Within the higher secondary school there is a very high level of repetition

Table 1. Enrollment in Sudanese Schools and Higher Education, and Proportion of Age Cohort Enrolled (Percent of age cohort for 1981)

	Total	Percent
Primary	1,476,300	38.8
Junior Secondary	276,767	22.9
Senior Secondary	136,651	13.0
Technical Secondary	15,545	1.5
Teacher Training	4,723	0.5
University	33,432	3.5
Advanced Technical	2,488	2.1

Source: UNESCO 1989

of studies in an effort to prepare for the examinations that determine access to higher education (Sanyal, Taici, and Mallasi 1987).

Public expenditure for all three levels of education were 15.6 percent of the national budget, and 5.6 percent of GDP (Sanyal, Taici and Mallasi 1987). The share devoted to higher education alone has been falling, from 4.6 to 3.5 percent between 1977/78 and 1980/81. Formerly, higher education received a larger budget than either primary or secondary schooling. Considering the rapid decline in enrollments at each level, the cost per student rises dramatically with the advances through the levels of education.

The second measure of equality is the significance of gender on educational opportunity. It is clear that nationally the enrollment of girls is substantially less than boys, and this is true for all levels of education but not necessarily for all programs. Interesting conclusions might come from combining data for gender with those for ethnicity or language, but these data are not available. Gender selection is summarized in Table 2.

According to UNESCO (1989) women were less than 20 percent of the students in higher education, with most of them in teacher and nursing training programs.

Table 2. **Gender and Educational Opportunity**

		Enrolment Ratio % Male	Female
Primary	1980/81	44.5	32.6
	1983/84	51.4	39.1
Secondary Intermediate	1983/84	28.4	23.3
Senior			
Academic		28.4	23.3
Teacher training		22.0	16.0

Source: Sudan Ministry of Education 1984, UNESCO 1989

The third measure in equality of opportunity is that of region in the nation (Table 3). It is evident that those with the best prospects are in Nile Province (75.4 percent) and the least in Lakes (11.6 percent). More precise data are not available but would likely show that the smallest towns and rural areas are least well served by educational services.

Social class cannot be measured directly from the available figures. It is reflected in part by private schooling, for the richer families are more likely to send their children to the good private schools. It is clear that not all private schools offer programs of equal quality. The best schools are of two types, those with an international curriculum and those with a classical Moslem program. Both are inaccessible to poor families. A further measure is the enrollments in alternative forms of secondary and higher education, which emphasize vocational training and immediate access to the labour market. These are the institutions of second choice: those who have the opportunity for academic secondary or universities will not be

Table 3. **Enrolment Ratios by Province (%), 1980/81**

Province	Primary	Secondary Intermediate	Higher
Lakes	12.2	7.7	1.1
Jonglei	21.3	12.9	6.0
E. & W. Equatoria	53.8	30.0	8.3
S. Kordofan	34.9	11.5	4.6
N. Kordofan	30.0	18.3	10.1
S. Darfur	18.9	7.3	3.9
N. Darfur	27.8	12.8	6.1
Blue Nile	42.0	21.6	7.2
Red Sea	20.6	14.5	15.5
West Nile	31.7	19.4	9.7
Kassala	31.1	19.4	9.5
Northern	73.6	53.7	32.8
Nile	75.4	46.3	25.0
Gizera	64.6	33.5	22.8
Khartoum	67.4	30.8	31.0
Overall	38.8	22.9	13.0

Source: Sanyal, Yaici, and Mallasi 1987

found here. They are attended by scholars who passed the requisite examinations but failed to find a place in the academic schools, and their vocational destiny is to be technicians and members of the near professions.

Recently, the government has expanded opportunities in these schools and reduced the rate of expansion of the academic institutions. For example, the number of teachers in technical schools increased between 1977/78 and 1980/81 from 435 to 684. The number of primary teachers has increased from 34,988 in 1977/78 to 42,611 in 1980-81. The number of teacher training institutes grew between 1977/78 and 1980/81 from fifteen to eighteen, with the number of teachers growing from 488 to 695.

The teacher/pupil ratio in primary schools was 1:35 in 1980/81, but varied from 1:25 in Northern Province to 1:62 in East Equatoria. At the intermediate level, enrollment increased from 10,612 in 1970/78 to 12,323 in 1980/81--an average annual rate of 5.1 percent. Academic secondary teacher/pupil ratios range from 1:17 in Jonglei and 1:40 in South Kordofan, with 1:31 nationally. The Jonglei figure is low, not because there are many teachers but because pupils are so few.

Conclusion

Inequality in educational opportunity is an obvious outcome of the selection of students that is required by the education system of the Sudan. The question of inequity is not so clear. Each individual or group may feel that his/her/its share of the available spaces was less than fair, or that the share was systematically of lower quality. Different aspects of the inequity can be summarized:

1. *Overall selection.* 60 percent of the youth do not complete primary education. 85% do not complete secondary education 97 percent do not complete higher education.

2. *Gender selection.* In general, the female students are disadvantaged, progressively more so in the senior levels of studies and the most prestigious programs. Although they are

slightly more numerous than males for the whole population, they make up only about 40 percent of the students.

3. *Language selection.* The members of the Arabic language community have the best prospects of finding educational opportunities. All other language groups must learn Arabic before the full range of education is open to them.

4. *Ethnic group selection.* Arab ethnicity is the most favoured group for all levels of schooling. However, the question of equity on the basis of language seems to answer most of the questions that could be related to ethnicity, and Arabic is primarily a cultural designation, with language as one of its most obvious characteristics. A factor related to ethnicity is the government policy of attracting all Sudanese to sedentary locations (thereby ending nomadism) and encouraging many minority groups to adopt the major cultural patterns, including the Arabic language (Abdel Hai 1982). The emphasis upon regionalization contained in the 1982 Presidential Decree of Regionalization of Higher Education does not imply that ethnicity will be promoted.

5. *Religious Selection.* Religion is likely to be a strong factor in determining educational opportunity, for the only religion taught in the national school curriculum is Islam. Mission schools and Coptic Christian schools exist, in parallel to the state system.

6. *Wealth and Socio-economic class.* The poor are most obviously disadvantaged and the rich are clearly likely to find education for their children. The middle class probably spend a very large part of their income in the private sector, paying additional tuition and the hidden costs of "free education." The lower income earners of the middle class probably find it necessary to borrow money to secure the education of their children. Nevertheless, the middle class is an important political pressure for the improvement of the state system.

7. *Rural/Urban Selection.* The rural students are particularly likely to be disadvantaged educationally, for their parents may oppose the development of schools because of the impact of education upon their lifestyle (for example in the case of nomads). The small size of schools and possibly the lower quality of teaching may make it more difficult for rural pupils

to pass the competitive examinations that determine their prospects at successive levels of education.

8. *Regional differences*. Recognizing the inequity of having the best educational opportunities (both private and public) in the capital area and a few large towns, an attempt has been made to promote regional equity. This has included the foundation of some regional colleges and universities. New institutions require a very large initial investment and the policy is consequently being pursued with caution. The differences will remain an important characteristic of Sudanese education for a long time.

In summary, it has been necessary for the Sudan to promote expansion of education and to ensure that its best educated citizens contribute to the welfare of their compatriates. This has required more money and more sacrifice than many poor nations could (or would) afford. By trying both to expand all forms of education and to maintain or improve the quality of instruction, minorities have sometimes been left unprotected. This is neither unique to Sudan among African nations, nor unusual in the poorer nations of the world. The difference between good intentions and acceptable results is partly explained by lack of resources, but perhaps by ineffective use of those resources that are available. The Sudan will likely be a test case of the new strategies and renewed will that was implied in the Jomtien conference of 1990 (UNESCO et al. 1990).

References

Abdel Hai, M. 1982. *Cultural Policy in the Sudan.* Paris: UNESCO.

Ali, Bakri M. 1989. Education, language and national integration in the Sudan. Ph.D Thesis, University of London, Institute of Education.

Altbach, P. G. 1971. Education and Neocolonialism: A note. *Comparative Education Review* 15(June): 237-239.

Hair, P. E. H. 1966. Layman's guide to the languages of the Sudan Republic. *Sudan, Notes and Records.* Vol. 15, Khartoum.

Hamilton, F. A. de C. 1935. *The Anglo-Egyptian Sudan from Within.* London: Faber and Faber.

International Labour Office. 1968. *Household Budget Survey for Sudan, 1967/68.* Khartoum, ILO: Geneva.

_____. 1976. *Growth, Employment and Equity: A Comprehensive Strategy for the Sudan.* ILO: Geneva.

Lees, F. A., and H. C. Brooks. 1977. *The Economic and Political Development of the Sudan.* London: Macmillan.

Said, B. M. 1965. *The Sudan, Crossroads of Africa.* London: Bodley Head.

Sanyal, B. C., L. Taici, and I. Mallasi. 1987. *From College to Work: The Case of the Sudan.* Paris: International Institute for Educational Planning.

Shaeffer, S. 1990. *Educational Change in Indonesia: A Case Study of Three Innovations.* Ottawa: International Development Research Corporation.

Sudan Ministry of Education. 1984. *Educational Statistics, 1983/84*. Khartoum.

_____. 1985. *Educational Statistics, 1984/85*. Khartoum.

UNESCO. 1986. *UNESCO Statistical Digest 1986*. Paris: UNESCO.

_____. 1989. *UNESCO Statistical Yearbook 1989*. Paris: UNESCO.

UNESCO, UNDP, UNICEF, and World Bank. 1990. *Education for All, Final Report*. Paris: UNESCO.

World Bank. 1990. *World Development Report*. Washington: World Bank.

MULTICULTURAL EDUCATION FOR
THE DIVERSE GROUPS IN BAHRAIN

Aman Attieh

This chapter explores the extent to which the government of Bahrain has provided adequate schooling to its minority communities, including a large immigrant population, in order to integrate them into the social mainstream. To this end, it examines 1) the socio-economic status of these multi-national, ethnic and religious groups; 2) the extent of educational access; and 3) the extent to which the existing curricula depict and incorporate multi-national, ethnic and religious content.

Population Profile

Equal access focuses upon the divergent socio-economic, religious and ethnic profiles of the population, the social status of the various population groups and the perceptions and relationships established toward one another. In the absence of a set of school access statistics that breaks down student distribution along national, religious, sectarian and sex lines, it becomes necessary to draw on other relevant data.

Population census that are readily accessible on Bahrain's national or religious populations are not consistent in chronology or uniform in their data. Most sources report for certain base years the numbers of Bahraini and non-Bahrainis. In 1988, an estimated medium projection of the total population was 421,040, of which non-Bahrainis constituted at least one-third, a ratio which has held constant since the early 1980s (Franklin

1985). Yet, the work force reverses this distribution, showing 78 percent foreign nationals and 22 percent Bahraini (Arab Communicators 1988-89). Some unofficial sources report even more foreign workers.

All told, Bahrain has a heterogeneous population composition spread along ethnic, religious or sectarian, tribal, and national lines on the one dimension, with rural and urban, rich and poor being other measures. Ethnically, the Arab Bahrainis, and other Arab nationals (especially Egyptians, Lebanese, Palestinians, Syrians, Omanis, Yemenis, and Saudis) have been the dominant community.[1] The Asians (Indians, Pakistanis, Filipinos, Koreans, Sri Lankans, and Thais) rank second, followed by a substantial Iranian community, most of whom are naturalized citizens, and finally by Baluchis (Kurian 1990).[2] There is also a small but very influential coterie of Western professionals and technocrats: Americans, British and other Europeans, with Americans the majority and the most celebrated among them.

Moslems form the largest religious group, both domestic and foreign, constituting 85 percent of the population. They are, however, divided into two major sects, Sunni and Shi'i, the estimated ratios being consistently given as 40 percent to 60 percent respectively for the total population, but one-third to two-thirds if only the native population is taken into account (Kurian 1990). The Sunni population is advantaged

---

[1] The 1991 Gulf war may soon effect changes among Arab nationals. The loyalties of Palestinians, some Christian Lebanese, Sudanese, and Yemenis have become suspect by all Arab Gulf States (Bahrain, Kuwait, Qatar, Saudi-Arabia and the United Arab Emirates) due to the support of many of their nationals to Iraq in this war, and their work contracts are not being renewed by Saudi-Arabia and Kuwait. Other Arab Gulf States (including Bahrain) may follow suit.

[2] Many Indians and Pakistanis are permanent residents, some descended from settlers of previous centuries. Filipinos, Koreans, Sri Lankans and Thais are migrants from about the 1970s and are guest workers of limited tenure.

economically, socially, and politically, and is represented by two pivotal constituencies: the ruling family of Al-Khalifah and its select circle, and the *Huwalah*. The former comprise kinsfolk, tribal allies, and most of the wealthiest families, the majority of whose ancestors migrated to Bahrain after 1783 in successive waves from Northeast and Central Arabia. The Huwalah, of strong mercantile tradition, are of Arab descent and originally from the Gulf area, but a few centuries ago settled the principal southern coastal towns of Iran in pursuit of prosperity, then repatriated to Bahrain after its oil boom improved the economic conditions. This community[3] is greatly affected by Persian stock and culture, and its members are bilingual in Arabic and Persian.

The Shi'is, referred to as *Baharnah*, who are also Arab, constitute the indigenous population of Bahrain. They do not boast of Bedouin lineage but have always been sedentary, inhabiting mainly a large number of villages and hamlets, though they now form a large presence in Manama, the capital city. Despite their numerical superiority, the Shi'is view themselves as a "deprived minority"; this stems from their experiences of political oppression, which date from occupation by the ruling family's tribe in 1783 (Al-Tajir 1983), and their subsequent restricted access to the decision and policy-making process and limited control of the country's wealth and expanding resources (Franklin 1985). In addition, there is another small group of non-Arab Shi'is, whose mother tongue is Farsi and who hail from Iran, though they have not always formed a coherent group with other Arab Shi'is.

The Sunnis and Shi'is in Bahrain have traditionally chosen to remain geographically and socially segregated from each other, despite the minuscule size of the country. Their social integration and political rapprochement began in the 1950s and culminated after independence in 1971. Clamors for political pluralism, expansion of schooling, and reinforcement of other modernizing, social, and employment agencies united

---

[3] Most Arab authors state this source, but some claim the migration was from Persia.

them in a common challenge to the legitimacy of the monolithic Al-Khalifah rule. They also generated a degree of socioeconomic and neighbourhood homogeneity among the growing urban Sunni and Shi'i working and educated middle classes. Their political rapprochement collapsed under the strain of political turbulences and sectarian passions following the Iranian Revolution.[4] Since then Sunnis and Shi'is have looked askance at each other's political loyalties, recreating the rift between them.

There are also non-Moslem religious minorities, numbering in descending order Hindus and other non-monotheistic adherents, Christians of eighteen distinctive sects, Jews, Baha'is and Parsee communities (Horner 1978). Most members of these monotheistic minorities are resident aliens; a few are citizens.

Despite daily interactions among members of these diverse groups living and working in a compact area, national, ethnic and religious fault lines still result in doubts about "the other" with respect to authority, incomes and permissions, parity of treatment and human rights.

Broadly speaking, Shi'is regard Sunnis--symbolized by the government--as political and economic predators: the Sunnis, gravitating around their ruling patrons, are considered the major beneficiaries of the country's wealth, exploiters of "communal land-ownership" (an orchestrated scheme of purchasing soaring real estate; see Lawson 1989, 5-9), discriminating against Shi'is in employment and unduly favoring Sunnis and foreign subjects, even the unqualified. In addition, they consider Sunnis as deceptive in their political promises, forestalling the reinstatement of the country's suspended constitution and a democratic parliament that reflects popular sentiments, fair representation, and labour concerns. Finally, Shi'is charge that the brutal suppression, harassment, intimidation, torturing, and imprisonment that were inflicted on members of their community and arbitrarily at times, during the

---

[4] Until Bahrain's independence, Iran claimed the region, based on history extending from the Persian empire and intermittent political control until the eighteenth century.

decade following the Khomeini revolution as a response to some coreligionist dissenters, have continued to muzzle them to the present day.

The Sunni image of the Shiʿis is no more positive. Shiʿis are perceived as perpetuating the ghost of a victimized minority that continually contends for power on the basis of old grievances which have little or no relation to present time practices and policies. In Sunni eyes, Shiʿis have occupied the lower echelons of the occupational structure because they have not taken advantage of the education and training available to Bahraini citizens to qualify for better job opportunities. Additionally, they have been unreliable in their civil duties, the main political agitators, national dissenters and terrorists, suspects for disloyalty to the ruling family and national interests, traitors who supported the Khomeini revolution, to reprise against Sunnis, opportunists and isolates from the social order who are galvanized around the encumbering and misguiding authority of their ʿUlama (religious scholars) (Khuri 1980).

The attitude of the Bahrainis toward expatriates has been dubious, depending on one's economic posture and interest. Since the discovery of oil in the 1930s, Bahrain has recruited expatriate labour at all occupational levels because the indigenous work force was unable quantitatively and qualitatively to meet the challenges of the petroleum and related industries and the need for services in an expanding modern economic sector.

While most Bahraini workers disapprove of expatriates, Bahraini entrepreneurs openly import their work force--even for skills that are domestically available. This policy has so far been to their advantage: a lack of wage regulation encourages bargaining with cheap foreign labour which will be reliable, hard working and un-political--prompted, by fear of losing their jobs and facing deportation and privation in their home country (Haliday 1977, Lawson 1989).

On the other hand, national labour wants to restrict and reduce dependency on foreigners in the private sector (Lawson 1989) as the government has done in the public sector, a process referred to as "Bahrainization." As the non-national labour force has become increasingly evident, Bahraini toleration has been waning and in some cases has turned xenophobic (Lawson 1989). In the last fifteen years, foreign labour has dominated most occupations in the private sector: technical, skilled, management, professional, services, and unskilled labour (Franklin 1985). Consequently many Bahrainis perceive foreigners--especially holders of white color jobs--as competing with them, even displacing them from their right to employment and livelihood in their own homeland.

According to an informant, there is also foreign competition in the cultural arena. Many Bahraini families decry the more permissive sexual liaisons that are becoming clandestinely widespread between their sons and men and foreign female nationals, especially the Filipins. These liaisons not only pose a threat to the indigenous sexual mores but have also delayed marriage, elevating this phenomena to a social issue affecting their daughters and women of marriageable age.

Since the establishment of a new economic order generated by the discovery of oil, Bahraini citizens have faced deliberate or situational discrimination from foreign owners and technocrats of that industry. From the 1930s many unskilled Bahrainis became low wage laborers in the oil industry as their traditional subsistence economy and the pearl-fishing declined. Subsequently, unemployed Bahrainis had either to accept unskilled jobs or acquire new training (Franklin 1985). Moreover, nationals in the oil industry became highly politicized and displayed their activism through sit-ins and strikes between 1941 and 1968, when their discontent and economic grievances with the managements of the foreign petroleum companies and the British authorities concerning low wages, poor working conditions, and discriminatory practices when compared to the non-nationals: British, Americans, and Indians (Khalaf 1985).

Nonetheless, Bahrainis who strove to assert their human and labour rights would sometimes deny these same rights to others. There is a dramatic gap in wages and benefits between the non-nationals in the private sector, particularly those who occupy the unskilled, semi-skilled, and blue-collar jobs, and middle-class occupations. While preferential treatment is accorded Europeans and Americans (high salaries, housing and benefits designed to lure them to live in what is considered a hardship area), migrant Asian workers receive extremely low wages, are abused and dehumanized by their Bahraini contractors (Aruri 1987). They are disdained, cursed, considered the dregs of Bahraini society, and relegated to inferior economic and social conditions and physical and social segregation. They lead a deprived existence, their lives are wretched, their overcrowded communal housing in labour camps is deplorable, and their meagre monthly salaries range between $75-100 from which they send remittances to their dependents at home (Bahraini Citizen 1985). It is expected that these 1985 salaries would have doubled by now.

In early 1984, members of an Indian and Pakistani labour camp, where ten men shared a room, struck to protest their working conditions. The precipitating factor was lack of drinking water in a desert location with no shade. To that incident the owner of the construction company responded that it was merely an oversight (Bahraini Citizen 1985). Guest workers usually react to similar incidents in silence in order to avoid deportation, and with resignation because any dispute with their superiors leads to more discrimination, humiliation, and denial of basic human rights (Aruri 1987, Haliday 1977). This gloomy picture is reminiscent of the conditions of American migrant laborers of the 1930s and 40s in Steinbeck's *Grapes of Wrath*. Housing conditions for foreign females (mostly domestics or retail clerks) tend to be somewhat better since most of them live within the employer's residence complex. Yet both male and female guest workers in these occupations are categorically denied the company of their immediate family, spouses, and dependents (Aruri 1987).

The status of citizenship is fundamental to multi-ethnic and religious communities seeking access to full rights, benefits, services, resources, social mobility, political and social networks in the country. Prior to independence, while Bahrain was undergoing its formative stage towards nationhood, many residents belonging to all the categories listed above, both indigenous and foreign, were given the opportunity to apply for and receive Bahraini citizenship, but a large percentage did not. This lack of enthusiasm to change passports then was partly due to the uncertainty of the economic future of both their original and current countries (in the case of Indians and Pakistanis of Bahrain), and partly due to foreigners' ambivalence concerning their own social status and cultural identity in Bahrain (as in the case of the Indians, Pakistanis and the Huwalah). After independence, however, citizenship became a very significant and sensitive issue. For example, some Huwalah families are now denied citizenship despite proof that their family traced its origins to Bahrain, simply because they had vacated their claims.

Access to Schooling

Against this background, the extent to which students of national, ethnic and religious groups have access to education might be better assessed. The 1973 Constitution of Bahrain includes two articles addressing this point (Blaustein and Franz 1990). Article 4 proclaims "liberty, equality, security, tranquillity, education, social solidarity and equal opportunities for all citizens (to be) the pillars of society guaranteed by the State." Section (a) of Article 7 ensures "educational services and cultural services for citizens" and upholds that "primary education shall be compulsory and free in accordance with the law."

Bahrain has exceeded the obligation to provide free schooling by extending it beyond the primary cycle of six years as stipulated by the constitution, to include intermediate and secondary levels for all citizens. Moreover, despite the lack of an official pronouncement or commitment to education beyond the primary cycle, access to free education up to the secondary level is open to nationals and non-nationals who legally reside in the country. Even illegal residents take advantage of it without danger of being deported on that account.

Bahrain has lagged in enforcing compulsory attendance for primary schooling, despite the availability of financial resources and the wide expansion of educational facilities throughout the country during the last twenty years. Figures of a decade ago show that only 43 percent of boys and 42 percent of girls of the eligible age group were enrolled in the first grade (Al-Misnad 1985). Even though current school statistics demonstrate a considerable increase of intake (between 10 percent and 15 percent) absenteeism remains high. Such a low intake rate, slightly depressed by wastage of 1.5 percent drop-out rate in primary education (Al-Misnad 1985) continues the threat posed by the country's current 26 percent illiteracy rate and limits the pool of students that filter to the higher intermediate and secondary stages.

While failure to enforce attendance legislation has adversely affected the national population at large, effects have been greater on certain segments of the population. One classification divides Bahraini nationals into seven population groups in terms of access to formal education, ranging down from 1) the Al-Khalifah family, 2) urban Sunnis, 3) urban Arab Shi'is, 4) urban Persian Shi'is, 5) rural Arab Shi'is, 6) Sunnis of tribal origin, and 7) the rural Arab Shi'is living in suburban settlements (Khuri 1980). This sequence is analogous to their income scale. The government, in the decades following independence, has attempted to replace the unwieldy minority group affiliations with concepts of "nationhood" and "citizenship" by expanding the supply of education among all communities, with the goal of redressing long-standing inequities in educational access and quality of life between social classes, rural/urban and Shi'i/Sunni communities. It has increased schooling capacity at all levels, established teacher centers, operated literacy and adult education programs, utilized the media (closed and open circuit television and radio programming) to provide practical vocational skills, offered distance instruction in reading, writing, and the English language, furnished mobile and permanent libraries, and raised awareness for maternal, health and child care. The gap among the lower and higher social groups remains wide (Lawson 1989) and will not soon narrow.

Several factors inhibited the participation of the lowest two social groups in the educational enterprise. The marginality of Sunnis of tribal origin in the education system was largely self-imposed in order to resist cultural assimilation. It stemmed from the group's perspective on the distinctiveness of its bedouin culture and strong pride in its lofty traditions and *modus vivendi* vis-à-vis the emerging new social order (Khuri

1980). Hence this group deliberately wanted to differentiate itself from the others by discouraging its youth from attending schools beyond basic elementary education.

The same pattern of resistance against becoming members of a modern educated citizenry can be discerned among the suburban rural Shiʿis. According to an anonymous 1989 informant, the new secularly-oriented state schools have gradually but steadily eroded and displaced a long entrenched educational heritage of Shiʿi teaching and value systems activated by private initiative and supervised by community control through the traditional learning institutions of the *Kuttābs* and *Mādaris*. Historically, these institutions preserved the social identity and religious knowledge of this minority amidst the vast Sunni majority. Present public schools are suspected by conservative Shiʿis of weakening the community's heritage and cultural identity. Thus, parents, particularly the uneducated, chose not to enroll their children for fear of this cultural corrosion, deeming these schools to have unnecessary harmful effects. In support of this position Khuri (1980) states that this group has "turned inward, enclosing themselves within their traditional communities" (p. 146) instead of attempting to adapt themselves like their village Shiʿi counterparts to the changing lifestyle that was brought about by the accelerated modernization process of Bahrain.

The attitude of some Shiʿis towards the government (discussed earlier) makes them dubious of state-controlled public schools. From the standpoint of religion, these schools do not symbolize nor express the way of life of "true Islam" but rather represent, socially and politically, an elite that some Shiʿis consider to have usurped their rightful possession and control of the land and its resources and now control the schools, thus affecting Shiʿi attendance and absenteeism.

School attendance is also impeded in a family-owned operation where children are considered a valuable asset in the labour force among Shiʿis village community, so the government's laxity in enforcing school attendance and child labour laws encourages absenteeism. Rural, village Shiʿis who are interested in and/or eligible to pursue higher education face the formidable obstacle of leaving home for the urban and suburban areas (where most of these institutions are concentrated), thus contributing to a shortage of manpower needed to sustain the family's income and economy.

Another hindrance to primary school attendance and the attainment of further education are the problems of gender discrimination and seclusion of women which are endemic to traditional societies. It is reported that the lowest enrollment ratio of females is that of the Sunni of tribal origin, followed by the rural suburban Shiʿis. Grim statistics indicate that the gender gap in the former group starts with the ratio of one female for two males at the early stages of education and widens progressively to the striking ratio of 1:20 (Khuri 1980). It is expected that this gap would by now have narrowed.

Regarding the village Shiʿis, low female enrollment becomes serious at the post-secondary level. In addition to paying tuition fees, daughters seeking college education must travel some distance away from home because it is only available in urban centers. This puts them at a disadvantage, for parents traditionally supervise their daughters closely to ensure their safety and proper conduct. Even the other option (village-based females may reside in the city in government owned, free of charge, segregated-sex facilities, operated according to the moral and ethical codes of Islam) works against them. Cultural norms hold that it is not socially accepted for unmarried females to live away from home, so their guardians will not forgo these values for the sake of higher education. This seclusion, combined with the widespread practice of early female marriage, has serious implications for education and employment opportunities for girls in the lowest three social categories. Many families see no value to female formal education since their short participation before marriage hardly contributes to economic returns.

Another disadvantaged group has an educational profile and access to schooling that is hardly discussed in the accessible literature. Members of this group are very limited in number and are descendants of the old-time labor force (some from the slave trade era) of early pre-independent Bahrain. They are of Omani, Sudanese, Pakistani, Indian, and Baluchi origin. They are not citizens but are entitled to live in Bahrain. To what extent they gain access to the gamut of educational services remains vague. Regardless, poverty obliges many to drop out of school for employment in order to augment their families' meagre incomes.

Finally, a factor that retards attainment of further education and cuts across social class, sectarian, and ethnic groups, is ambivalence about the real utility of higher education. Despite traditional respect for knowledge and learning in Bahrain, education and higher degrees do not necessarily translate to acquiring wealth and/or high ranking jobs. On the less positive note, the government of Bahrain discriminates positively by hiring Sunnis of tribal descent for high ranking positions in the area of security, defense, and law despite their low educational attainments (Khuri 1980). Consequently, many impatient young men, guided by the successes of non-college businessmen of the previous generation, drop-out from school to seek their fortunes. They venture into private enterprise by setting up companies, which, if successful, are normally much more materially rewarding than the delayed gratification of graduating from an institution of higher education and obtaining employment in a government agency with limited income. If the companies are not successful, these drop-outs form a pool of unemployed who become dependent in their kinfolks.

Those who continue in the public schools share the problem of lower quality instruction when compared to private schools, as well as stiff competition in the marketplace with the more privileged and the rich.

As for the expatriate student body, statistics of a decade ago report a figure of only 2 percent of the primary school population (Al-Misnad 1985).[5] It is expected that they will have doubled or tripled by 1990. This extremely low ratio, despite the increasing numbers of expatriate workers during the last fifteen years, results from prohibition of entry for dependents of blue-collar workers and labourers. Thus the non-national student population mostly represents children of white-collar

---

[5] The names, levels, affiliation, control and tuition of these private institutions is provided in Arab Communicators (1988-89, pp. 40, 190).

employees, including teachers and university professors, who flock to the best schooling offered in the country: private education.

Private education, which is regulated by and run under the purview of the government (Article 7 of the Constitution), is more prestigious than its State counterpart and symbolizes pluralism not reflected in the latter, albeit flavoured with preferential class status. The establishment of private schools is consistent with the spirit of the Constitution which recognizes that "People are equal in human dignity" (Article 18 of the Constitution), and their primary function is to cater to the educational, cultural, language, and spiritual needs of the dependents for the diverse national and religious groups not adequately provided for in the public schools. Private schools are national and foreign, secular and religious. Those that have a religious orientation, however, practice freedom of religion. Thus religious instruction is not compulsory for students who are affiliated with another religion or denomination, though they are, in some cases, provided with the chance to study their particular religion. For example, the British school, St. Christopher, teaches Arabic to Arab nationals and Islamic studies to its Moslem students.

Modeled after Western educational programs, these private schools are sponsored under various auspices: Bahraini, Arab and Moslem, American, British and Anglican, Indian, Pakistani, Catholic, French non-college-bound and Japanese.[6] It is interesting to note that the Shi'is do not presently sponsor a private school despite their majority status and religious partisanship. The majority of students enrolled in each school reflect the cultural orientation and national affiliation of the institution, and individual schools implement the standard curriculum leading to either the national secondary school exit examination of their respective country or its equivalent as in the case of the United States, thus insuring smooth transition and promotion for their students when they return home. The

---

[6]   A list of the names, levels, affiliations, controls and tuitions of these private institutions can be found in *Arab Communicators* (1988-89, pp. 40, 190).

fierce sense of competition prevailing among these schools is responsible for their lofty academic standards, high-quality students, rich extracurricular activities, and good support services including considerable proficiency in foreign languages and English; the latter has become the *lingua franca* in the private sector. Non-Arab foreign student education is curtailed beyond secondary education, mainly because of the language barrier they face at the college level, thus far education institutions at the tertiary level operated by foreign groups are non-existent.

Despite the private schools' prestigious status, they are at the same time a double-edged sword. On the one hand, their advantages in terms of providing students with wider access to quality programs cannot be over-emphasized; however, due to their high tuition they have become class-centred, catering to the elite of highly paid expatriates and rich nationals. Consequently, the latter have a better chance to afford the tuition charges of higher education at home or obtain scholarships for education abroad, and upon graduation, to land well-paying jobs. In contrast, graduates of government schools have fewer prospects for further education and training and hence less marketability, especially for those of the lower income group. Thus the dual school system has contributed to a bifurcation in Bahrain's education system and in the quality training of its student population.

Curriculum

In examining the extent and tone of multi-ethnic, religious, and cultural content in textbooks, one may adopt or adapt one of the established procedures for quantitative and/or qualitative analysis. This study adopts James A. Banks' typologies for qualitative evaluation because they have encapsulated the literature on multicultural education into various models which adequately serve to assess the case of Bahrain.

In his 1988 article, "Approaches to Multicultural Curriculum Reform," Banks classifies the inclusion of ethnic content of a given curriculum into four typologies of spiralling and progressive nature, each building upon the other. The leanest of all four typologies is "The Contributions Approach," which is generally concomitant with ethnic movement revival and is characterized by incorporating into the curriculum ethnic heroes, holidays, and discrete cultural events of non-mainstream groups as peripheral appendages to the core program of studies, whose basic character remains constant. The second is referred to as "The Ethnic Additive Approach," where ethnic content is expanded to include concepts, themes and perspectives, still without altering the established curriculum. The third is the "The Transformation Approach," where the structure of the curriculum is altered and new strategies and materials are incorporated to assist students in recognizing how various groups perceive the concepts, issues, events and perspectives under study. Finally the "The Social Action Approach" moves beyond the recognition stage to application. It encourages students to think, empowering them to take a course of action to reduce prejudice and to prepare for future political efficacy. Decisions and actions taken by students are based on gathering pertinent data, analyzing their own values and beliefs, and synthesizing their knowledge. However, Banks notes that there may be variations of these typologies.

   To demonstrate how these typologies might be applied in studying the Bahraini curriculum, two elementary education textbooks that were accessible and are in current use in government schools were studied. One is for religious education, the other a history textbook. Elementary schools are important in this study because secondary education is relatively exceptional. These books examine how they deal with diversity, whether ethnic, religious or national, in Bahraini society and its Arab-Islamic past.

Textbook (1) "al-Tarbiyah al-Islāmiyyah"[7]

Contents. This textbook contains, in this sequence, the title page, the picture of the head of State, Emir al-Shaykh Essa bin Salman Al-Khalifah, the preface by the authors, the main body of the textbook, and finally the table of contents. The main body consists of six main sections under the following headings: the Glorious Qur'an, The Prophet's Traditions or Sayings (*al-'Ahādīth al-Nabawiyyah al-Sharīfah*), Beliefs (*al-ʿAqīdah*), Observances (*al-ʿIbādāt*), The Moral Character of a Moslem (*Khulq al-Muslim*), and the Biographies of Religious Figures (*al-Sīrah*). Common features in all sections is the inner textual organization of the topic under study and questions for discussion. Other features that appear in some sections are introductory statements, the moral or educational implication of the topic, a religious anthem and a play.

Observations and Comments. With the exception of the section on the biographies, all the other five sections deal with topics that are largely non-controversial within the two contentious Islamic body politics in Bahrain. They assiduously cultivate the corpus of authoritative teachings and the righteous order, both spiritually and practically, with which all Sunni and Shiʿi adherents of the faith agree and which they actually practice.

Section one, entitled the Qur'an, entails three whole Suras or chapters, most of a fourth Sura, and their explanations. Despite the fact that some Moslem sects rely heavily on sources besides the Qur'an for spiritual guidance, regulation of human relations and social behaviour, for example, *Kitāb al-Jafr* among the Shiʿi Twelvers, and *Kitāb al-Hikmah* among the Druze, and the numerous *Tarīqahs* among the different Sufi Orders, all Moslems consider the Qur'an to be the most holy, perfect and exalted of all revealed sources in this regard since it is the embodiment of the word of Allah.

---

[7] *Islamic Education* for the fifth grade elementary (ʿĀmir et al. 1988).

The section on *Hadīth*, the traditions and sayings of the Prophet, centers on four of them and enjoins students to use them as their exemplars in everyday life. While there are some variations between Sunni and Shiᶜi Hadith, the Hadiths selected here are common to both. They are extremely appropriate in terms of theme and relevance to the students' age group--dealing with topics such as the importance of literacy (reading and writing) and of learning and communicating the Qur'an, the prominent role of mothers in life, the importance of reciprocity and cohesiveness among the brotherhood of believers, the effect of friends and paying heed to their selection, and finally the prohibition of taking oaths except by God. As can be seen, all address moral, ethical, and righteous behaviour, yet one wonders about the absence of Traditions from different dogmas between splinter Moslem groups such as a particular Tradition related to the question of the Prophet's succession. In the context of the Sunni-Shiᶜi schism, it is not only "what" Tradition texts each sect had canonized, but more importantly, "how" they are expounded. The Sunnis adhere as closely as possible to the literal interpretation of Qur'anic and Tradition texts while the Shiᶜis resort more to the process of *Ta'wīl*, an esoteric textual interpretation promulgated by a belief in the existence of a hidden or deeper meaning locked in the Qur'an and Hadith.

Of closer interest to the subject of this article is the Tradition that urges brotherhood among Moslems saying, "The believers in their friendliness, mercy and compassion are likened unto a body which, if one of its organs is in pain, the rest of them respond in vigilance." It eloquently represents the epitome of mutual, communal responsibility and solidarity among its adherents, where the support network is based on a strong organic relationship in a family unit, transcending geographical, racial, ethnic, and sexual boundaries. Students can learn much from this Tradition, and the book is to be commended for treating brotherhood in the widest sense among the Islamic *Ummah* (community) which is consistent with its religious prescription. Soon, however, the reader realizes that the authors' choice in illustrating the applicability of this altruistic concept is disappointing. The only example of brotherhood they offer is the Gulf Cooperation Council, a political and economic body for mutual cooperation that has been established among the Arab Gulf states, overlooking reference to some more needy Moslems (e.g. Nigerians, Yemenis, Bangladeshis, Pakistanis, Sudanese, and the destitute Palestinians). It is futile to speculate as to whether this omission was unconscious, but it has serious implications. Since Bahrain itself is a formal member of the Gulf Cooperation Council, this example, from both religious and intellectual stances, reduces the broader dimension that this Tradition calls for. The "Brethren" in this example form an exclusive group from the standpoint of a common history, geography, culture, language, ethnicity and even more significant, wealth. Moreover, the "other" is actually an extension of the "we." One only hopes that teachers draw other relevant examples of different racial, ethnic, sex, and even religious backgrounds to the attention of students while teaching this topic.

The second section, on Beliefs, concentrates on only three: belief in Angels, in the heavenly books or scriptures, and in the day of judgment. Of these the belief in the revealed books, as the title suggests, injects a form of multi-religious content. It concentrates on The Old Testament (*al-Tawrāh*) and The New Testament (*al-'Injīl*), which are considered in Islam as the eternal Truth, and equal in status, nature, substance, and function with the Holy Qur'an, and ends by urging every Moslem to believe in all three scriptures. Despite equal esteem being bestowed on all three scriptures, an Islamic-centric viewpoint is discerned immediately, for this notion of egalitarian status rests firmly on the notion of exact identities among these three holy books (they originate from the same source, Allah, contain identical messages, and are delivered by one Angel, Gabriel, albeit to three of God's messengers, Moses, Jesus and Mohammad, at different times). Moslems are not required or expected to read the Old and New Testaments. Thus, if fifth graders become curious to read those scriptures, in which it is incumbent upon them to believe, the Moslem teacher would need to simplify a rather complex perspective maintained in Islam. This perspective holds that these two scriptures, unlike the Qur'an, do not constitute a physical reality that can be recognized by the senses, even though they share abstract characteristics that present an ideal, incorporeal form that exists eternally with Allah in the metaphysical realm. However, the existing forms of Old and New Testament texts are at variance with Islam in some doctrinal issues (for example, the question regarding the divine nature of Christ and the Trinity, the status of the Prophet Muhammad as the seal of all Prophets). Islam therefore considers these scriptures as corrupted embodiments of the True revelation and thus insulates Moslem students from learning them.

The third section on Observances focuses on almsgiving and the manner in which missed prayers are to be fulfilled. Of these two, the former constitutes a better focus for analysis since it has implications for multi-cultural content. This section very adequately synthesizes in simple discourse aspects that regulate and govern almsgiving in terms of concept, types, timing, and amount. Once again Bahraini students are exposed at a relatively young age to yet another humanitarian ethos of sharing one's material possessions with needy and poor Muslims. The observance of almsgiving constitutes one of the five basic pillars, *'Arkān* of Islam, the aim of which is to be mindful of the deprived, narrow economic inequalities, and foster social welfare in order to bring about a more egalitarian order.

Theorists and practitioners who are concerned with injustice and inequity in the distribution of resources to individuals and groups will appreciate the attention to detail of this Islamic decree of more than 1400 years ago. The precise determination of the amount of alms and payment of food provisions, livestock, gold, silver, and bill notes is impressive. The maximum amount to be paid is set as one-fourth of each tenth of net property or profit at year's end, which is valued, in this textbook for present-day Bahrain, at eighty-five grams of gold or 595 grams of silver, and it is stipulated that the value of money or bank notes is to be equated to either of these indicators. As generous or viable as this practice may be in wealth distribution, its message to fifth graders may be mixed. On the one hand the book deals with very general terms: its universal overtone applies to a range of beneficiaries of multi-colour, racial, ethnic, and sex groups in the Muslim world. Yet minority group ideologists may argue that broad statements do not refer to specific groups, so they mask concern for minority groups. Moreover, one must question the extent to which present circumstances comply with the tradition of almsgiving, in view of the fact that Bahrain has a strong and active economy but many foreign labourers (including Moslems) live in decrepit conditions, poverty, and deprivation. Thus, is almsgiving on the wane because it is now the responsibility of individuals, replacing the medieval state-run institution referred to as *Bait al-Māl* (The Treasury), where the amassing, incoming, and dispensation of alms were regulated?

The section on the moral character of a Moslem covers these topics: the honouring of guests, moderation in eating and drinking, Islam as the religion of works, the etiquette of visitations, and ascertaining the veracity of news. Islam, the religion of works, conjures up a dimension of multiculturalism. This passage asserts that Islam urges work and diligence and combats laziness and indolence and draws on the occupation of two archetypal figures, the Prophet Mohammed and the Prophet David, the former as a shepherd boy and a merchant, and the latter as an armour maker. Within the context of present day Bahrain, the occupations discussed and portrayed are those of a ship pilot, a carpenter, and a car mechanic. A picture of a plot of farmland with two persons at work is included with no intimation as to the farming occupation. Several observations can be made here: most of the passage concentrates on the semi-skilled trades; trades such as carpentry are on an equal footing with piloting a ship, in terms of worth and dignity, and all these occupations are linked with the essential process of nation building, a very praiseworthy message in reinforcing the need for such skills among native Bahrainis. Still, however, the passage is confined to the Arabs of Bahrain, enhanced by the use of Arab names and drawings of natives. It evades mention of the size and contributions of the non-native labour groups which play key roles in Bahrain's economy, and typically fill all types and levels of occupations, including these very ones. Was this grave omission motivated by a benign but deliberate attempt to present Arab role models in these poorly paid occupations to fifth graders who may not continue their education beyond the elementary level, or was it a deliberate case of Arab-centric perspective. From a multi-cultural perspective, this topic was not seized upon to enrich the textbook with content regarding various groups and their contributions.

The last section on the biographies is devoted to four religious figures: The Prophet Muhammad, ʿAʾishah (one of the Prophet's wives), the second Caliph ʿUmar, and Moses. The largest number of pages focus on Moses, the least on ʿAʾishah. These accounts highlight their deeds, contributions and sacrifices made to the community, thereby serving as role models to fifth graders. This section includes a role model of a female and a male from another ethnic group, the Jews, and another religion, Judaism. Nevertheless, this section is not sensitive to Shiʿi students. The veneration of ʿAʾishah by the Sunni is absent among Shiʿis, for whom ʿAʾishah is considered an anti-hero who actively polarized the Moslem community into two camps after which the schism in Islam was irreparable, those against ʿAlī, and those with ʿAlī or his partisans, referred to in Arabic as *Shiʿat ʿAlī* or partisan. Moreover, she joined battle against ʿAlī in order to weaken his position as a Caliph. With the passage of time, Shiʿis gathered copious accounts (many of them unfounded) about ʿAʾishah to tarnish her name and degrade her status and role in Islam. Less aggravating, yet nonetheless not appreciated by Shiʿis, is the Caliph ʿUmar. Like the Caliph who preceded him and the one that succeeded him, ʿUmar is regarded by Shiʿis to have robbed ʿAlī of his rightful succession to the Caliphate, which explains why the latter became the fourth Caliph in line instead of the first. There is a skirting reference to ʿAlī in the account of ʿUmar. However, it is cast in a context of ʿUmar's qualities of selflessness and humility.

Textbook (2) "al-Tārīkh"[8]

Contents. This text includes the title page, the picture of the ruler, the preface by authors, the body of the text and finally the table of contents. Arab-Islamic medieval history occupies

---

[8] *History* for sixth grade elementary (Halil et al. 1984).

the entire body of the book. It consists of three main units covering sixty-three pages; the first unit with six parts, is devoted to the Umayyad State, 660-750 AD (twenty-six pages), the second unit with five parts focuses on the ʿAbbasid Period, 750-1258 AD (twenty pages), and the third with two major subdivisions on the Umayyad State in Spain, 711-1492 AD (six pages) and the Fatimid State in Egypt, 909-1171 AD (ten pages) discusses them as movements independent from the Abbasid State. Bahrain occupies a part in the first two units. Each part in each unit concludes with a set of student activities and questions, then each main unit concludes with broader questions and activities.

Observations and Comments. These units provide an overview of Islamic history in terms of religious motivation, events, causes, consequences, accomplishments of institutions and dynasties as well as achievements of individuals. The textbook rarely injects any critical perspective of history. It is traditional where reports narrate the accomplishments of the dominant groups and their supporters. Their conquests, administrations, and rules are justified as reinstating hegemony over contentious, troublesome groups. Regrettably, the considerations and the plight of the subordinate groups, suppressed minorities or oppressed people (e.g. the Persians, the Berbers, the Arab Christians in the fertile Crescent, the Copts in Egypt, the Jews, various splinter Shiʿis groups, the Black slaves, the Spaniards, women and others) are either marginal or completely relegated to oblivion.

The two largest indigenous "minorities" in modern day Bahrain, the Shiʿi and women here deserve special attention in this historical context. It seems curious and unsound pedagogy-- particularly for the elementary level--to dismiss past accounts of the familiar and the immediate, i.e. the Shiʿis variety which forms the majority of Bahrain's population, while it dedicates one of its part to a less familiar and distant group of Shiʿis, i.e. the Fatimids of Egypt. Altogether, the scattered references of the former variety of Shiʿi are five, and the longer ones amount to two lines, at best. Three references allude to the disgruntled leaders of these opposition groups or subversive movements, and their attempts at undermining the political status quo or established norms. The other two are extremely sympathetic to the plight of the house of ᶜAlī. The death and the martyrdom of Husein and the House of ᶜAlī are curiously ignored despite its significance to the genesis of the Shiᶜi dogma, its ethos, and particularly the concept of the doctrine of *Imamate*. In commemoration of this event Bahraini Shiᶜis relive annually the plight of the House of ᶜAlī and the death of Husein during the Islamic month of *Muharram*, through expressive mourning and the enactment of passion plays. Undoubtedly, this oversight intensifies a sense of alienation among Bahraini Shiᶜis because their extension back in the history of Islam is being denied, probably contributing to their low participation rate in education.

Likewise, the history of women is hardly revealed in this textbook. History here is taught in terms of men's actions and development. However, we know that there were women who were actors in shaping Moslem history. For example, this textbook chronicles the great achievement and significance of the most illustrious Moslem Caliph, the Abbasid Haroun al-Rasheed, but fails to mention the humanitarian accomplishments of Zubaidah, his wife, who established a chain of inns and water fountains throughout parts of Moslem State en route to the pilgrimage at Mecca from funds that came under her personal control, in order to reduce the hardships of travel usually encountered by Moslems while performing this religious duty. Even if the history of Islam is not imbued with women's "grand" deeds and performances as defined by men, one questions why there is so little mention of their daily lives and existence: their routine, deprivations, sorrows, thoughts, struggles, and exhilarations. Fortunately, two such statements inform us that "preferred entertainment among women during the zenith of the Abbasid state were archery and dancing" and that "women participated with men in pursuing knowledge and establishing schools, libraries and laboratories in every city in Spain." Women, Moslem or minority women, provided the continuity in their communities and shared in many tasks, sublime or banal, against which men in the spotlight of this textbook performed their noble or ignoble acts. The relative absence of women in this textbook not only deprives school girls of female role models but it also robs all students, male and female alike, from learning about the whole sense and texture of authentic life in medieval Islam.

The questions for discussion in the Islamic Education textbook are directly content-based, elicit recall of information presented, or even require rote memorization. There were no questions or activities that encourage students to express their personal opinion or biases. The history textbook fared a little better. The discussion questions included other activities such as information gathering in the library and group interaction which may expand students' horizons and help them surmise and formulate some new thoughts.

In sum, these two textbooks provide very limited overt multi-cultural content when compared with the ideal proposed by James Banks. The Islamic Education textbook borders on the "Contributions Approach"--the most skimpy of Banks' four models. The history textbook appears not to be found in Banks' configuration. It may be appropriate to suggest another model: "The Benign Neglect Approach," where negative judgment assertions about groups do not exist, partly because the groups hardly exist.

Secondary education represents a broader, more internationalized picture, assumed to be vital to the leaders of society. An examination of several course outlines and their textbooks shows a substantial quantitative and qualitative difference from those of basic education. Unfortunately since attendance declines so dramatically at this level, the majority of youth (whether nationals or expatriate) are unlikely to be well informed about the knowledge, skills and attitudes conducive to multiculturalism in Bahrain.

Conclusion

Based on the investigations presented, most readers will agree that improvements regarding the quality of life should be provided for Bahrain's poorer foreign and indigenous population, acess to schooling should be and has been extended to the disadvantaged and subordinate citizen groups, and that multi-ethnic content should be but has not been boosted--particularly at the elementary level.

There remain the dilemmas of implementing such reforms. To what extent is the host country responsible for providing free education for anyone other than its citizens, and particularly to its poor guest workers and their dependents? Does enhancing the chances of all groups and individuals, minority (foreign born or domestic) and majority, to share in and contribute to the socio-economic and political order of the mainstream culture, enfringe on freedom of choice and self-empowerment of these various pluralistic groups and their life styles--as may be the case with the tribal Sunnis? To what extent should diversity and multicultural content in the curriculum be allowed: at what point does ethnic hegemony or cultural separatism conflict with national consciousness and the collective ethos?

Assuming that multicultural education modelled after Banks' "Transformation Approach" or "Social Action Approach" were adopted in Bahrain tomorrow, would this guarantee an egalitarian society? Recent history gives us the example of Lebanon whose constitution formally subscribed to the cultural mosaic theory and delegated to its pluralistic groups the "cultural empowerment" described by Freire and Macedo as "emancipatory literacy": a "Vehicle by which the oppressed are equipped with the necessary tools to reappropriate their history, culture and language practices." The negative consequences of the Lebanese experiment are well known. Similarly, the "benign neglect" approach, reflected until recently in the public school curriculum of the USA, was not very successful at reducing group antagonisms or assimilating them. Only the future, dictated by the events of the 1990-91 Gulf War and other regional developments, will determine which way Bahrain will develop.

Bahrain is a modern Islamic Arab state, and its modernity is reflected in the diversity of its economic activities. Continued prosperity depends upon expatriate workers, some of them highly educated and earning incomes expected by international experts. International incomes for the service industries are not high, and Bahrain has thousands of guest workers in these occupations. Without them, its economy would collapse. There is a potential disagreement between the foreign experts and the unskilled, with the Bahrainis dependent upon both and unable to control them without dismissals and perhaps deportations.

The contribution of education to the amelioration of these differences depends upon several qualities that Bahrain is able to provide. First, free and sophisticated education at the secondary level is available to those who wish to enroll. The value systems of other cultures, including their religions, receive official respect and are more likely to be ignored than attacked. Official respect accounts for instruction in the precepts of other religions in schools attended by non-Islamic expatriates. Other languages are taught and sometimes used as the media of instruction. Many of the teachers are expatriates.

But educational proposals do not quickly affect all the population and the feelings of the street may be decisive in the short run. Recent history includes many unresolved grievances of part of the population: religious sects, traditionally oriented minorities, women, etc. Popular misunderstandings of the official position can affect the outcome, and some Bahraini minorities have traditional grievances.

Guest workers are always aware that they live and work in an Arab and Islamic society where the Bahraini argue about how education, the economy and society should be organized. These arguments take place in the sheltered environment of an autocratic court and in the public domain, with no necessary connection between the two. Despite the problems of human rights and discrimination, Bahrain appears to be an economically satisfying workspot for unskilled workers from South Asia, poor Arab nations in Africa and Asia, and also for technically sophisticated workers from any part of the world.

References

ᶜĀmir, M. M., M. S. ᶜAbd Al-Latīf, and S. K. Muhammad. 1988. *Al-Tarbiyah al-Islāmiyyah.* The State of Bahrain: Ministry of Education and Instruction.

Al-Misnad, S. 1985. *The Development of Modern Education in the Gulf.* London, Ithaca: Cornell University Press.

Al-Tajir, M. A. 1983. *Language and Linguistic Origins in Bahrain.* Norfolk, England: Kegan Paul International.

Arab Communicators. 1988-89. *Bahrain: Business Directory.* 9th ed. Bahrain Arab Printing and Publishing House.

Aruri, N. H. 1987. Disaster Human Rights in the Arab World. Middle East Report. *MERIP Reports* (November-December), 17.

Bahraini Citizen. 1985. The rulers are afraid of their own people. *MERIP Reports* (May), 15.

Banks, J. 1988. Approaches to multicultural curriculum; reform. *Multicultural Leadership* 1(2): 1-4. Edmons, Washington: Educational Materials and Services Center.

Blaustein, A., and G. Flanz, eds. 1990. *Constitutions of the Countries of the New World.* New York: Oceana Publications.

Franklin, R. 1985. Migrant labor and the politics of development in Bahrain. Middle East Research and Information Project. *MERIP Reports* (May), 132.

Haliday, F. 1977. Labor migration in the Middle East. *MERIP Reports* (August), 59.

Ḥalil, A., A. A. Mawzah, M. H. Riḍā, and A. R. Nabawiyy Al-Fardān, 1984. *Al-Tārīkh*. The State of Bahrain, Ministry of Education and Instruction.

Horner, N. 1978. *Present day Christianity in the Gulf States and the Arabian Peninsula*. Occasional Bulletin of Missionary Research, 2.

Khalaf, A. H. 1985. Labor Movements in Bahrain, *MERIP Reports*, 24-25.

Khuri, F. 1980. *Tribe and State in Bahrain*. Chicago: Chicago University Press.

Kurian, G., ed. 1990. *Encyclopedia of the Third World*. London: Europa Publications Limited, Vol. 1, 126.

Lawson, F. 1989. *The Modernization of Autocracy*. Boulder, Colorado: Westview Press.

INEQUALITY AND EDUCATION IN INDIA: THE CASE OF THE SCHEDULED CASTES

Ratna Ghosh and Abdulaziz Talbani

Discourse on the concept of inequality can be traced back to Aristotle, with a strong influence from nineteenth century liberalism and twentieth century socialism. The notion of inequality in modern India has been influenced by both these conceptions and is reflected in the principles of equality of status and equality of opportunity.

Inequalities in society arise from a fundamental root-- the inequality of power (Hicks 1960). Inequalities exist in most societies because power relations are characterized by domination. The sources of inequality and power are many, with the most obvious ones in contemporary society being gender, race, and class. India adds the distinctive category of caste. Inequalities in power relations, which are particularly characteristic of the caste system, result in sharp economic, educational, and consequently, status differences. Religious sanctions have helped maintain the status quo so that power was concentrated in small upper caste elite groups while the lower castes internalized their subordinate situation and were unable to strive for change. The lowest castes were "Untouchables" and were referred to as *Scheduled Castes*.[1] Along with Scheduled

---

[1] *Scheduled Castes* were identified by the British as "Untouchable" Hindu castes attached to the Government of India Act, 1935, for their statutory safeguards and benefits. The term was used by the Indian Government at Independence. Scheduled Castes and Tribes are often referred to together.

327

Tribes, they form 23.5 percent of the total population (Census of India 1981) and have been the most underprivileged groups in India.

All modern societies value equality and strive to remove inequalities through various means. Education attempts to remove existing barriers to equality in society. Can education change society? Many contemporary studies demonstrate that education perpetuates inequalities (for example, Bowles and Gintis 1976). Yet education continues to offer hope as an equalizing force. In India, education was looked upon by national leaders at Independence as the vehicle for transmitting the values which underlie the new social order.

The potential of education to change society must be seen within its social framework. Because there are several aspects of inequality in India, this chapter will discuss the evolution of caste stratification (and inferiorization of women insofar as they suffer from the double burden of gender and caste) in Indian society. It will examine the concept of equality in modern India and its strong emphasis in the Indian Constitution. Finally, it will examine the role of education in the sponsored mobility of Scheduled Castes.

Caste and Inequality

Perhaps the most extreme manifestation of any system of inequalities is the caste system as found in India. While social and economic inequality is not unique to India, there is no comparison to caste as the basis for discrimination.[2] Beteille (1983) points out both the existential and normative aspects in this form of inequality: great discrepancies existed in social

---

[2] Berreman (1960) has applied the term caste to Blacks in the United States. Beteille (1983) argues that in traditional Hindu society, the normative and existential orders were consistent, whereas in the United States, discrimination against Blacks goes against the egalitarian ideology. Myrdal (1944) made a similar argument.

distance among castes, in educational opportunities, wealth, incomes, and earnings. In traditional Indian society, hierarchy permeated every sphere of life but especially the Hindu legal order: the "Dharmashastras are unparalleled among texts of their kind for the consistency with which they make the case for inequality" (Beteille 1983, 18). Because this normative order was considered desirable, these inequalities were maintained.

Interpretations of the origin and development of the caste system differ. According to Sivaramayya (1983), the earliest reference to castes is found in the *Rigveda* in the second millennium B.C., at which time they were "fluid . . . without organization and internal hierarchy" (p. 28 quoting Renou 1959). Between 200 B.C. and A.D. 200 castes became classified into a rigid socio-legal order characterized by a descending scale of social and legal status and fixed from birth. The texts were compiled by the *Brahmins* who ranked themselves on the top of the scale, followed by the *Kshatriyas* (warriors), *Vaishyas* (traders and farmers), and *Shudras* (servitors). Certain groups considered untouchables were outside the four-tier caste hierarchy.

Chakravarti (1983) points out that as a sociological category *caste* refers to an endogamous group practising a traditional occupation. Another explanation is that the caste system organizes Hindu religious rituals involving the top three castes. Those groups which were involved in other tasks (which were called polluted) were excluded. As Dumont (1970) points out, the concept of purity is a fundamental principle of caste which led to segregation based on division of labour. According to Bose (1975), the caste system was supported by the economic order in which the occupation was connected to a specific caste. Weber (1967) maintained that inequality of birth was rationalized through the religious concepts of rebirth and *karma*.

Inequality in the status of women and men is a universal phenomenon. In India, the dependence on a son for attaining spiritual salvation for the Hindu male underscores the importance of the male child and undermines the status of the daughter. In addition, the denial of inheritance of property rights to females (except in the few matrilineal groups), and their exclusion from reading (the scriptures) further explains their status position. Sivaramayya (1983) points out the paradox of the high caste Hindu woman: the higher they were in the caste hierarchy the greater was their disability. For example, while divorce and widow remarriage was permitted and practised among the lower castes, these were not allowed among the higher castes.[3]

In the nineteenth century, contact with Western learning and liberal ideology prompted a criticism of inequality in traditional Indian society. But the commitment to equality in the nationalist period produced a tension between the Indian attack on the institutional foundations of inequality and the use of social inequalities by the colonialist power to defend imperialism (Beteille 1983). This ambivalence prevented a more pervasive critique of inequality during the colonial period.

Concept of Equality in Modern India

At Independence, India inherited a society with extreme inequalities, stemming from its own traditional rigid stratification, sanctioned by a socio-religious order, and from its colonial status. The hierarchical and inegalitarian social order and social handicaps prevented lower castes and women from being educated and from owning land. Colonialism introduced new government and military hierarchies and a market economy. The new economic forces created new hierarchies through land distribution in rural areas and extreme differences in earnings in urban areas. The combination of tradition and lack of political and economic power has made upward mobility for lower classes/castes virtually impossible. Independence was achieved, but the inherited social order remained for a time rooted in the days of the raj.

---

[3] In fact, *suttee* (a widow burning herself to death on her husband's funeral pyre) was widely encouraged until banned by progressive leaders. It still takes place occasionally.

The basic values which underlie the current social order--liberty, equality, justice, and fraternity--are not indigenous to Indian society (Ghosh and Talbani 1989). In independent India the attempts to create equality were constitutional and legislative, but also economic and educational. The problems in India are immense: the need for economic growth must be balanced by the need for redistribution to promote equality. The balance is difficult to achieve because the modern requirement of equality (i.e. opportunity for all) may conflict with special traditional opportunities for some. The constraints for an egalitarian ideology at independence were both ideological and material: the inegalitarian values and beliefs of the traditional hierarchical order did not fit well with the democratic concept of distributive justice.

India became Independent in 1947 and its 1950 Constitution was the first major legal proclamation to discard traditionally sanctioned caste segregation, discrimination, and inequality. India adopted a modern international ideology of equality and justice which was totally opposed to its traditions. The preamble to the Constitution emphasizes economic and political justice and equality of opportunity and status. The strategy was not merely to abolish the historic disabilities but also to create abilities for those who had been denied opportunities through institutional discrimination. The normative response to this in the Constitution was, first, to guarantee the right to equality for all through the provision of Fundamental Rights; and second, to eliminate existing inequalities through Directive Principles of State Policy.

The concept of equality radically opposes the traditional order because it implies *equality of opportunity*, not just access to certain political rights. The move for India was between two polar extremes: from an ascriptive order to an achieved status. The question with equality of opportunity is whether, as Rawls (1971) suggests, the advantages of inborn ability which can lead to a meritocracy is any less arbitrary than social or caste advantages of birth. Rawls' idea of "fair equality of opportunity" suggests that those with natural ability should not be deprived because of their social circumstances while those with less ability should not be deprived of a range of opportunities.

Equality is hardly served by treating all people in an equal manner when they do not have equal abilities and conditions. "The idea is to redress the bias of contingencies in the direction of equality" (Rawls 1971, 100-1). It was with a similar principle in mind that national leaders at Independence sought for equality of opportunity on the one hand, and special new and enriched opportunities (educational and economic) for those groups which historically were far behind. This dilemma of balancing opportunities based on merit with compensatory, protective discrimination policies, built in problems which still shake the Indian system severely.

The Constitution

The concept of equality in the Constitution incorporates three major principles of equality (Sivaramayya 1983, 33): the numerical or egalitarian, the meritorian, and the proportional. The first principle (reflected in equal voting rights) is based on the equality of human worth irrespective of need or merit; for example all children have a right to an education. But this principle cannot be applied to the extent that everyone receives the same education and reaches equal levels because they do not possess the same capabilities (merit). Where sorting is necessary for different types of jobs, and resources and opportunities are not available for everyone, the principle of merit is applied on the assumption that the best person is selected for the good of society. However, in societies where extreme inequalities exist, the merit principle tends to perpetuate, rather than eradicate, inequalities because historical discrimination has set some groups so far behind that they cannot compete on an equal basis. The education of Scheduled Castes in India poses this problem because they have been denied equal access to education and other social services, severely limiting their life chances and leaving them socio-economically disadvantaged when compared to the upper castes. In order to repair this situation, the Constitution introduced protective discrimination based on the principle of proportional equality. In this, a relevant criterion (such as caste) is used so that benefits are proportionate to the disability suffered by a group.

Fundamental Rights in the Constitution begin with the right to equality and several articles deal with it. Discrimination is illegal on grounds of religion, race, caste, sex, or place of birth (Article 15), and equality of opportunity is guaranteed (Article 16). Equality before the law and equal protection of the laws (Article 14) condemn discrimination in both substantive and procedural ways. The equality rights exist in favour of the individual whereas protective discrimination is for groups.

"Untouchability" is abolished and its practice is forbidden in any form (Article 17). Article 46 of the Directive Principles of State Policy says:

> The State shall promote with special care the educational and economic interests of the weaker sections of the people, and in particular, of the Scheduled Castes and Scheduled Tribes, and shall protect them from social injustice and all forms of exploitation. (Sivaramayya 1983, 40)

Positive discrimination represents a major policy for equalizing political, economic, and educational opportunities to underprivileged classes in India (Patil 1989). This policy encompasses all public service areas and is applied in practice through the reservation of a given block of places for particular groups: the *Policy of Reservations*. Article 335 reiterates the upholding of claims of Scheduled Castes and Tribes in making appointments to services consistent with the maintenance of efficiency. For the overall development of Scheduled Castes and Tribes, federal and state governments envisaged three major areas to be encompassed by the policy. Firstly, seats were reserved in the legislations to boost the political participation of the underprivileged. According to the Constitution seats are reserved in the Lok Sabah (Lower House) and state assemblies for ten years at a time. Secondly, reservations were made (with no Constitutional time limits) in government jobs aimed at uplifting economic conditions. Thirdly, preferential treatment made educational opportunities accessible to Scheduled Castes and Tribes.

In 1951, the First Amendment to the Constitution added to Article 15 special provisions for the admission of Scheduled Castes and Tribes to any educational institution run by the State. Accordingly, in 1954, the States were asked to reserve 20 per cent of seats for Scheduled Castes and Tribes for admission in educational institutions--provided they fulfilled the minimum criteria.[4] In 1962, the reservation quota had been raised slightly, to 15 percent for Scheduled Castes and 7.5 percent for Scheduled Tribes in All-India open competitions. Recruitment is direct in class III and IV posts (clerks and manual workers) and is fixed according to the proportion of Scheduled Castes and Tribes in that particular area.

State governments also have their own policies to equalize opportunities for Scheduled Castes and Scheduled Tribes, with departments established to oversee welfare programs. In 1951, the Bihar government, for the first time in Indian history, identified 109 castes considered to be economically backward. These castes were added to those who had already been recognized as Scheduled Castes and Scheduled Tribes. Except for Scheduled Castes and Tribes, an income of less than 500 rupees monthly was prescribed to qualify for reservations (Bharti 1990).

The attempt to remove disabilities through the abolishment of Untouchability (Article 17) was strengthened by the *Untouchability (Offences) Act* (1955) which made the enforcement of religious disabilities an offence. Twenty years later Scheduled Castes continued to suffer from their social disabilities and the 1955 Act was strengthened to the *Protection of Civil Rights Act* (1976) in order to more effectively enforce their civil rights.

---

[4] To facilitate their adequate representation, concessions such as (i) relaxation of age limit, (ii) relaxation in the standard of suitability, (iii) selection, provided they are not found unfit for the post, (iv) relaxation of the qualification regarding experience in the case of direct recruitment only, whenever necessary and (v) inclusion of scientific and technical posts up to the lowest grade of group (India 1987, 208).

The legal attempts to eradicate historical disabilities were coupled with measures to reduce socio-economic inequalities and the adoption of a broad policy of distribution of resources and benefits (b and c of Article 39). Article 41 specifies that the state should provide, within its economic capacity, provisions for the right to an education, etc.

The Indian Constitution is exemplary in its attempt to provide for equality and in its attempt to balance the requirement of equal opportunity for all with special opportunities for those historically exploited. The problem is the gulf between *de jure* and *de facto*: equality laws confronted with the reality of extreme inequalities. Although the formal provisions for protective discrimination in India are among the most far reaching in the modern world, their objectives remain controversial.

In four decades of Independence, India has industrialized much of its economy. In this economic transition from an agrarian to an industrialized society, the castes increasingly coincide with economic classes. The social system changes more slowly than the economic modernization, so it has continued to maintain old inequalities based on caste and created new ones on the basis of class. Protective discrimination or affirmative action in education and jobs arouses bitter controversy in India. It has provoked heated debates in parliament and violence in educational institutions and in streets. It contributed to the defeat of the Singh government in 1990. The reservation of seats for underprivileged groups in jobs and higher education is resented by teachers, peers, and the general public.

National Commissions

In 1971 the Mungeri Lal Commission listed 128 castes as Other Backward Classes and 93 as Middle Backward Classes, taking into account social status, educational backwardness, adequacy of representation in government services and their share in trade, commerce, industry, etc. The Commission recommended 26 percent reservations for jobs and 24 percent for educational institutions (Bharti 1990). Another commission, chaired by B. P. Mandal, was established in 1978 with a broad mandate to investigate matters of discrimination and protection of civil rights (India 1987).

Mandal submitted the Commission's report in 1981 to the Indira Gandhi government. It listed 3,743 communities as Other Backward Classes and placed their proportion at 52 percent of the country's population. While allowing the Scheduled Castes and Tribes to continue their traditional reservations fixed at equal to their proportion in the population (22.5 percent), the Mandal Commission was constrained by a 1963 Supreme Court ruling that more than 50 percent reservation was unconstitutional (Bharti 1990). So only 27 percent was recommended as the reservation for 3,743 lower castes that are officially designated in the constitution as Other Backward Classes (even though they constitute 52 percent of the population). But this 27 percent of all Federal and State government jobs, and in openings in educational institutions, when added to 22.5 percent of openings that had already been reserved for Scheduled Castes and Tribes, would mean that 49.5 percent of all government jobs would be subject to quotas. Fearing a backlash, the Mandal recommendations were not implemented by the Indira Gandhi government.

Educational Opportunity and Sponsored Mobility

As seen above, several Constitutional and legislative measures improved equality of participation in various areas of national life. In education, however, the elitist system of colonial education continued after Independence, with a small minority enjoying access to the best available services. The failure of the system to implement the values of a new egalitarian ideology brought public pressure to appoint the first national Education Commission 17 years after Independence (Ghosh and Talbani 1989). Its *National Policy on Education* (1968) envisaged a radical transformation of the education system to expand educational opportunities and cultivate social values, among other aims. Eighteen years after its adoption, India was still experiencing extreme inequalities and casteism, among other tremendous social strains. The second *National Policy on Education* was announced in 1986 and its major thrust was to achieve equality in the distribution of education, especially for disadvantaged groups such as Scheduled Castes and Tribes and women.

Children from Scheduled Castes did not attend schools at all at the beginning of the nineteenth century. Concern about their status and disabilities began to grow during the renaissance of Hindu society, due to contact with the west in the nineteenth and twentieth century. The first breakthrough came in 1858 when, despite bitter and active opposition by many caste Hindu groups, the Court of Directors threw open government schools to the members of Scheduled Castes. After Independence, Constitutional protection and government legislation paved the way for equalizing educational opportunities for Scheduled Castes and Scheduled Tribes (India 1987). Positive discrimination entitled these groups to special scholarships and maintenance grants. In an attempt to improve the participation of Scheduled Castes and Scheduled Tribes in services, the Union and state governments provide pre-examination training for various competitive examinations, such as the Indian Administrative Service (IAS), the Indian Foreign Service (IFS), and other service exams.

Post-matriculation scholarships were started in 1944-45 to provide financial assistance to backward classes. Now the assistance is provided to the family with monthly earnings of less than 750 rupees. Similarly, girls' hostels are built and book banks make textbooks available to the students. Since 1977-78, the government provided pre-matriculation scholarships for children working in very menial jobs.

To ensure that Scheduled Castes and Scheduled Tribes have better educational opportunities, the *National Education Policy* of 1986 proposed specific measures such as incentives to parents of children up to the age of fourteen to compensate for the foregone income of school children, which is often an important source of income for lower class families. It devised scholarship schemes, improved facilities like hostels, strengthened training for Scheduled Caste teachers, and proposed adult and non-formal education centres. To update information about these classes, a very ambitious program of micro-planning (India Government 1986) charted the educational shortcomings of schools. The micro-planning aims to improve the quality of instruction in schools by providing the basic needs of schools and thereby to arrest the rate of dropouts. For underachieving children a program of remedial coaching has been proposed.

Impact of Education

The government has attempted to make educational opportunities available to underprivileged classes. What has been the impact of these measures? Most of the backward classes have the misfortune of being doubly handicapped, with their underprivileged status sanctioned by traditions, thus economic deprivation is accepted without question by them and without ascribing guilt by the larger society. On the other hand, they are ghettoised in poverty zones in rural areas and shanty towns where the depressing environment and the "culture of poverty" numbs aspirations and motivation to change their conditions.

Literacy. India has the largest population of illiterates (440 million) in the world (Patil 1989). Literacy is also caste-biased. The 1981 census data show literacy for the whole country to be 36 percent, but only 21 percent for Scheduled Castes and 16 percent for Scheduled Tribes. The highest rate of literacy is found among urban males and lowest among rural females. Women suffer most and Scheduled Caste and Scheduled Tribe females have only 11 percent and 8 percent literacy rates respectively (Census of India 1981). As a group, Scheduled Caste women in rural areas are the most disadvantaged in the country.

Education Levels. The statistics concerning the expansion of the educational system (Table 1) show that expansion of middle schools was almost three times that of elementary schools, and at the higher secondary level more than double that of elementary schools. The quantitative discrepancy directly affects the access of Scheduled Caste students to education.

Table 1. **Expansion of Education (millions)**

	1950–51	1982–83	Increase 82-83/50-51
Primary	230.0	690.0	280%
Middle	13.4	123.3	720%
Secondary/High	7.3	53.3	630%

Source: Government of India 1986

For Scheduled Caste students, the enrollment ratios between 1979 and 1986 indicate a substantial improvement (see Table 2), although it is the male rather than the female students who have made the progress. The ratio increased from ninety-eight to 115 for boys (as a proportion of the number of youth in the appropriate age cohort) and from fifty-one to sixty-six for girls. The gap for Scheduled Tribes is even wider.

Although the gap in retention rate between Scheduled Caste students and the general population is improving, drop-out is a serious problem for students of this group. Scheduled

Table 2. **Enrollment of Scheduled Class Students (thousands)**

Class	1979 Total	Girls	1986 Total	Girls	SC/Total
I - V	10,114	3,533	15,040	5,874	17.35%
VI-VIII	1,846	496	4,064	1,270	14.94%
IX-X	764	171	1,539	414	13.41%
XI-XII			394	93	11.45%

Source: India 1980, 1989

Caste students continue to be more illiterate, largely rural, and poor. Poverty is a major factor in their poor school performance, repeated failure and drop-out rates. They tend to cluster in inferior educational institutions, where they secure inadequate basic qualifications to utilize the reserved admission in higher education and employment that would otherwise be theirs.

Similarly there is disparity within government sectors regarding the distribution of educational services affecting the quality of education (Ghosh and Talbani 1989). There are three tiers of government schools: public, Sainik, and Central schools. The Sainik schools are reserved for the children of military personnel and Central schools are for the children of government officials. These two categories of schools provide high quality education, comparable to elite private schools. The government provides all the necessary facilities for them. Public schools are usually underfunded, staffed with underpaid and underqualified teachers and lacking even essential facilities (India Government 1985). This disparity within the government schools organizes the mobility patterns of students who go through the system. Scheduled Castes/Scheduled Tribes typically have some access to public schools where quality of education is consistently very poor.

Hence, despite the fact that education is "free and compulsory," many children belonging to Scheduled Castes have never been to school, and a majority of those who have attended will drop out before completing elementary school (India Government 1985, Ghosh and Talbani 1989, Bose 1970).

Employment. Has the spread of education, the special facilities and reservations brought fundamental change in the pattern of inequality for Scheduled Castes? Equality of opportunity should translate into the ability of the educational system to recruit and retain pupils from the disadvantaged sections of society. If that is successful, then equality of opportunity would lead to results which should be evident in the job market.

Table 3 shows underemployment of Scheduled Castes/Scheduled Tribes in almost all the classes of government jobs, even in class IV category jobs. A comparison of years 1956,

Table 3. Scheduled Castes/Scheduled Tribes Employed by the Central Government (thousands)

Class	Year	Total	Employees Sched.Castes	%	Employees Sched.Tribes	%
I	1956	6233	44	0.71	6	0.10
	1963	14177	250	1.61	29	0.20
	1983	53165	3574	6.72	761	1.43
II	1956	14455	290	2.00	56	0.39
	1963	23756	707	2.98	53	0.22
	1983	62600	6368	10.17	922	1.47
III	1956	642651	45181	7.03	3990	0.62
	1963	916452	84714	9.24	8906	1.08
	1983	2128746	311070	14.61	88149	4.14
IV	1956	759570	167239	22.02	18497	2.43
	1963	881556	151176	17.15	30890	3.50
	1983	1303005	255053	19.57	71812	5.51

Legend: Class I: Highest Executives. Class II: Supervisors with some clerical responsibilities. Class III: Clerks. Class IV: Manual Workers, Messengers, etc.

Source: India 1963, 1987

1963, and 1983 shows a marginal change in the employment status of Scheduled Castes/Scheduled Tribes, particularly in the higher classifications. For example, Scheduled Castes/ Scheduled Tribes representation in class I employment in 1983 is only 6.72 and 1.43 respectively, much less than the quota reserved for these two groups (15 and 7.5 percent). This indicates that the government's efforts to improve participation of Scheduled Castes/Scheduled Tribes in the economic sector have achieved marginal success. However, it seems to be worse for Scheduled Tribes, who are inhabiting regions which are geographically remote from urban centres. Apparently, geographical remoteness has hindered their participation in the economic process of the country.

Table 4 figures for the prestigious Indian Administrative Service (IAS) and the Indian Police Service (IPS) indicate representation of Scheduled Castes and Tribes to be far smaller than their proportion in the national population. A similar discrepancy exists in all occupational mobility trends. Within castes, the social status of castes plays an important role in the individual's mobility and capability to derive benefit from available opportunities. Persons in upper castes have more chances of economic mobility than those in the lower ones. The upper castes occupy the positions of landlords and rich peasants.

Table 4. **Scheduled Castes/Scheduled Tribes Representation in Prestigious Jobs of Central Government**

Class	Total Employees	Scheduled Castes Employees	%	Scheduled Tribes Employees	%
IAS	4,236	404	9.54	181	4.27
IPS	2,198	330	10.40	77	3.50

Source: India 1987

Conclusion

Given the limited effectiveness of quotas for *Scheduled Castes and Tribes*, why would the government follow a similar policy for *Other Backward Classes*? There is evidently a contradiction in the government's simultaneous goals of industrialization and equalizing opportunities for large numbers of disadvantaged groups at the same time. India is still an agrarian country. The per person income is meager and available resources go to the development of the industrial sector. The agricultural sector has developed slowly, so there is no significant improvement in the conditions of underdeveloped rural classes. Efforts to modernize agriculture have been minimal and cannot bring about structural changes in this sector: for example, land reforms and changes in the relationship between landowners and labourers. The agricultural labourers still work in primitive conditions with no social and economic protection. The government's development policies have not directly benefitted the masses of people, specially the Scheduled Castes and Tribes, who are concentrated in rural areas. The principal beneficiaries of development are upper and middle classes.

Prime Minister V. P. Singh promised to implement the Mandal Commission's recommendations soon after he came to office in 1988. The announcement provoked violent reaction in the country, partly from the seventeen million educated unemployed (Johnson and Pratap 1990). Students and the educated unemployed were frustrated with what was for them severe institutional discrimination in already constricted educational and employment spheres. For many this was a politically motivated decision rather than an attempt to equalize opportunities for Other Backward Classes (Shastri 1990). Others questioned why, as in the case of Scheduled Castes/Scheduled Tribes (where the proportion of reservation reflected their percentage in the population) the same principle was not followed for the Other Backward Classes--for which only 27 percent of the places were being reserved for 52 percent of the national population.

Many explanations are behind student reaction against reservations. Within the context of economic development, the slow pace of growth offers a limited number of job openings. The government is still a major employer and there is too much stress on its capability to hire people. The private sector is not affected by the policy of quotas. Yet, in tough economic times, the high unemployment rate, coupled with the government's policy to implement some recommendations of the Mandal Report, has instigated rebellion severe enough to contribute to the toppling of the V. P. Singh government in November 1990.

The upper class backlash against reservation has renewed national debate: what should be the basis of quota? and how long should it be continued? Quotas in jobs and education seem to be a different issue from quotas in legislatures. The latter did not create much stir. But since quotas in jobs affect seventeen million people among the educated unemployed, it is difficult to keep the anger from spilling into bloodshed.

It may be argued that even with the policy of quotas, Scheduled Castes/Scheduled Tribes have made slow progress, so without reservations lower castes have a meagre chance of higher levels of education and entry into jobs to which they have traditionally been denied access. At the time of Independence the policy of reservations was meant to redress the history of inequality. However, after forty three years, it seems that the system is not promoting substantial equality, nor is it making a significant change in their mobility.

There is considerable evidence (Jencks 1972, Bowles and Gintis 1976, Coleman et al. 1966) that access to education and, therefore, employment opportunities, are largely determined by social class (and gender), and in India, also by caste (see for example Beteille 1983, Kumar 1987). Empirical studies also show that efforts to equalize opportunities, and compensatory schemes (as in the United States of America) within the educational system have not had significant effects. In India, the government has attempted to approach the problem of Scheduled Castes and Tribes in a multifaceted way, thereby giving equality of opportunity a dynamic character. Beginning with legislation and rights to support them, educational and employment privileges through structural changes have been attempted. These measures were unable to bring a fundamental change to inequality in India because of the new inequalities that have emerged while the traditional ones are being tackled. Constitutional changes have altered the dynamics between caste, class, and power. This has led to class differences which correlate closely with caste differences. In the narrow spectrum of education, the unevenness of educational development, and the advances in sectors like higher education which do not benefit the masses have contributed to the problem. The dilemma is tremendous: how much equality is possible within a structure of socio-economic disparities? Is it necessarily a negative concept that is prejudiced against the deprived (Karlekar 1983, 247)? Equality of opportunity must have substance to be more than a formal ideal. "The principle of proportionality is a principle of social possibility" (Mohanty 1983, 285). Equality is essentially proscribed by a country's historical experience, socio-economic structure and stage of development.

References

Beteille, A. 1983. Introduction. In A. Beteille, ed. *Equality and Inequality: Theory and Practice.* Delhi: Oxford University Press.

Berreman, G. D. 1960. Caste in India and the United States. *The American Journal of Sociology* 66(2): 120-127.

Bharti, I. 1990. Politics of anti-reservation stir. *Economic and Political Weekly* (February 10): 309-310.

Bose, A. 1970. Education among Scheduled Castes. *Man in India* 50(1): 209-239.

Bose, N. K. 1975. *The Structure of Hindu Society.* Translated by Andre Beteille. Orient: Longman.

Bowles, S., and H. Gintis. 1976. *Schooling in Capitalist America.* New York: Basic Books.

Census of India. 1981. Government of India.

Chakravarti, A. 1983. Some aspects of inequality in rural India: A sociological perspective. In A. Beteille, ed. *Equality and Inequality: Theory and Practice.* Delhi: Oxford University Press.

Coleman, J. S., E. Q. Campbell, C. J. Hobson, J. McPartland, A. M. Mood, F. D. Weinfeld, and R. L. York. 1966. *Equality of Educational Opportunities.* Washington, D.C.: U.S. Government Printing Office.

Dumont, L. 1970. *Homo Hierarchicus.* Chicago: University of Chicago Press.

Ghosh, R., and A. Talbani. 1989. *Educational Policy in India: Its Evolution and Content.* Montreal: McGill University.

Hicks, J. R. 1960. *The Social Framework. An Introduction to Economics.* Oxford: Clarendon Press.

India. 1963. *A Reference Annual.* Delhi: Government of India.

_____. 1980. *4th All-India Educational Survey, 1978-79.* Delhi (July): NCERT.

_____. 1987. *A Reference Annual.* Delhi: Government of India.

_____. 1989. *5th All-India Educational Survey, 1986.* Delhi: NCERT.

India Government. 1985. *Challenge of Education: A Policy Perspective.* New Delhi: Ministry of Education.

_____. 1986. *National Policy of Education.* New Delhi: Ministry of Education.

Jencks, C. 1972. *Inequality. A Reassessment of the Effect of Family and Schooling in America.* New York: Basic Books.

Johnson, M., and A. Pratap. 1990. *Times,* October 8, p. 48.

Karlekar, M. 1983. Education and inequality. In A. Beteille, ed. *Equality and Inequality.* Delhi: Oxford University Press.

Kumar, K. 1987. Reproduction or change? Education and elites in India. In R. Ghosh and M. Zachariah, eds. *Education and the Process of Change.* New Delhi: Sage Publications.

Mohanty, M. 1983. Towards a political theory of inequality. In A. Beteille, ed. *Equality and Inequality: Theory and Practice*. Delhi: Oxford University Press.

Myrdal, G. 1944. *The American Dilemma, the Negro Problem and Modern Democracy*. New York: Harper.

Patil, S. 1989. Mobilising Scheduled Castes and Scheduled Tribes. *Economic and Political Weekly* (September 2-9): 2002-2006.

Rawls, J. 1971. *A Theory of Justice*. Cambridge, Mass.: Belknap Press of Harvard University Press.

Renou, L. 1959. *The Civilization of Ancient India*. 2nd ed. Calcutta: Sushil Gupta.

Shastri, P. D. 1990. All reservations are evil. *The Tribune* (August 24): 5.

Sivaramayya, B. 1983. Equality and inequality: The legal framework. In A. Beteille, ed. *Equality and Inequality: Theory and Practice*. Delhi: Oxford University Press.

Weber, M. 1967. *The Religion of India*. Translated and edited by H. H. Gerth and D. Martindale. Glencoe, Ill.: Free Press.

THE BASQUES IN SPAIN

Norma Tarrow

The Basques as an Indigenous
and Persecuted Minority

The present Basque autonomous community (BAC) of Spain is only a part of the historic Basque homeland (*Euskal Herria*) spread over four provinces in north east Spain (Navarra has opted to remain outside the BAC) and three more in south west France. This chapter is limited to the three provinces in Spain (Alava, Vizcaya, Guipúcoa). A brief historic and linguistic summary is followed by a review of the history of the Basques as an indigenous minority and (from 1936-1975) as a long standing persecuted minority. The current situation, viewed as the initial system of privilege and underclass is discussed both from the perspectives of the Basques and the "new" minorities in the region past and present. *Assimilation* and *accommodation* models are analysed and prospects for the future suggested.

Language

The Basques identify themselves as a people through their language, *Euskara*. Euskara "evolved *in situ* and is a living remnant of the languages spoken in Western Europe during the Mesolithic and Neolithic times, millenniums before the relatively modern evolution of Indo-European language groups" (Frank, Eguzkitza, and Bloom, n.d., 1). These scholars also point out the "ancient character of the language," identified as "an archaic anomaly in Europe and as a linguistic monument in

349

Spain and France." Euskara has an extremely complex syntax, and bears no resemblance to any other modern language. Historically, its speakers came from the rural and less educated segment of the population. Although maintained through the Middle Ages and the early years of Spanish unification, the language did not expand. Considered archaic, with little written literature, and handicapped by its diglossic situation in relation to Castilian, it had begun to disappear by the nineteenth century, when it was regenerated through a brief literary spurt.

History

The origin of the "oldest race surviving in Europe" (Gallop 1970, 9) has puzzled ethnologists for two centuries and is still an enigma. Considered fully autochthonous, since neither people nor language can be traced to any other region, there is evidence of the presence of the Basque population and language for many centuries before the Roman era (Tarrow 1985). They were a pastoral people who, after contact with the Romans, began to devote themselves to agriculture. A series of invasions in the fifth century left the Visigoths in control of the area and another side of Basque character began to be recognized. "In this, their prehistorical period little is known of them beyond the fact that they had established a reputation for violence and ferocity remarkable even in the Dark Ages" (Gallop 1970, 10). While Arab domination of most of Spain affected the province of Alava, the majority of the region, with its natural protection of almost impassable mountains and a rural economy that did not appear worth the necessary battles, was not conquered by the Muslims. By 1016, the Kingdom of *Pamplona* (later Navarra), embracing all of the Basque region, was created, marking the one brief moment of political unification in Basque history. From the eleventh century, Basque society (structured around exploitation of the land) underwent a revolutionary process of urbanization (abetted by the influx of pilgrims along the Way of Saint James), industrialization, and a series of wars between the clans. From this time there are well-authenticated references to the Basques (Arzak 1984, Larrea and Mieza 1985, Collins 1986).

Since the Middle Ages, the legal and administrative structure of the Basque region was based on an elaborate system of *fueros* (rights and privileges) specific to each province, which reinforced both the ethno-cultural and linguistic distinctiveness of the Basques and their internal inter-territorial differences. They had freedom of trade--extending to concluding foreign treaties in certain areas. They were exempt from military service and the king was neither owner of the land nor able to impose taxes on his Basque subjects. For any of his orders to be valid they had to have the consent of the Basque Assembly. The fueros were jealously guarded and every attempt to interfere with them was met with firm resistance. In this sense they were privileged not only by the standards of Spain but also in comparison to most of Europe at the time. As renowned contrabandists, they controlled the roads in and out of France, exacting tribute from the hordes of pilgrims and others who crossed their territory.

The fifteenth century marriage of Ferdinand and Isabella set the stage for the unification of Spain and its linguistic Castilianization. The Basque fueros came into conflict with the increasing centralization of the State. The loss of these fueros after the Second Carlist War led to a nationalist movement, complicated by internal dissention deriving from socio-economic, political, and linguistic differences among the individual provinces. The granting of autonomy by the Second Spanish Republic in 1936 applied only to *Guipúzcoa* and *Vizcaya*, as the Basques had already been split by the military uprising (with Alava and Navarra siding with Franco). Violent fighting during the Civil War took place in the Basque region, with the name of *Guernica* becoming a symbol for Basque martyrdom. The Basques finally surrendered and their government went into exile. The repression following the 1935 revolutionary insurrections did not crush nationalist spirit, but rather pushed it farther to the left, to an extreme separatist and anti-Spanish philosophy. After the Civil War, the nationalist movement appeared to be politically crushed, but sentiment inspired the minds and hearts of Basque youth, an effect lasting to the present.

> For the Basques, the Spanish Civil War was one of those rare psychological moments in history when an entire culture passes through an experience of the deepest significance, and is never quite the same again. Time after time, the leaders of the culture find themselves returning to that experience as they search for ways to make Basques more aware of their ethnic heritage and of their existence as human beings. (Clark 1979, 76)

From then until the last years of the Franco regime, repression was the order of the day. First to feel Franco's wrath were the Basque priests who led the nationalist movement and taught in Basque schools. Many were summarily moved to other regions, imprisoned, and even put to death. With repression extending to imprisonment, torture and/or death, political leaders went into exile. The vitality of the Basque community was dealt a severe blow, as the diaspora of 80,000 included almost all of the intellectual leaders. Twenty thousand Basque children were evacuated in 1937 to Europe, Mexico, and the USSR. Those who returned fell under Franco's Decree of Responsibility, with marked identity papers and police surveillance and harassment for years. It was in this climate that ETA (*Euzkadi Ta Azkatasuna*) was born.[1] This strongly nationalist group, whose acts of terrorism still garner international publicity, demands a Basque nation as a separate political state (Clark 1981, Frank, Eguzkitza, and Bloom, n.d., Legaretta 1985, Medhurst 1987).

Responses of Society

For the forty years of the Franco regime, the Basques were clearly denied full status, and they endured persistent inequality in both social and political realms. Since the State was the abuser, such persecution was technically legal--no matter how unjust. Since the responses of society--in terms of policies

---

[1] For a better understanding of Basque nationalism, see also Douglass (1985), Clark (1981, 1985), Payne (1975), Heiberg (1975), and Heiberg (1982).

and programs--were solely dictated by the central government, clearly these too reinforced the situation of inequality, as an unremitting policy of assimilation was enforced.

Basque nationalism leaned heavily on linguistic identification, so destroying the Basque language as a functioning communication medium was of highest priority. Embarking on a policy of linguistic genocide, the use of Euskara was prohibited in all public places under the threat of jail sentences. Although prior Spanish regimes had subtly fostered Castilianization, prior to Franco, Euskara had never been subject to political repression. The educational system was a particular target of official policy. Schools were not permitted to teach Euskara; priests were prohibited from sermonizing in it; Basque-speaking teachers were dismissed or transferred to other regions and non-Basque speaking replacements sent in; and children were punished for speaking the language. Basque names were erased from public registries, graves, and public buildings. Nationalist parties and cultural clubs were outlawed.

> On the other hand the process of fighting back prompted quite successful efforts to give the Basque tongue a new lease on life. From the 1950s onwards, nationalist political groups and (especially in rural areas) the Roman Catholic Church encouraged the development of special part-time schools--or ikastolas-- dedicated to the propagation of the local language and culture. Despite police surveillance or harassment,their number grew and contributed substantially to the dissemination of Basque. (Medhurst 1987, 5)

In fact, by the early 1970s, officials began to look the other way as long as the *ikastolas* did not "encourage" political activism. By 1977, over 40,000 students were involved. "The ikastola system represented a true popular movement (parent financed, with strong church support, and parent involvement in matters of curriculum and administration) and by 1975, the Franco government, recognizing the inevitable, officially acknowledged it" (Tarrow 1985).

In sum, during the period 1936-1976, the Basques certainly "qualified" as a long standing minority in the nation of Spain, subjected to political and social inequality and a policy of *assimilation* dedicated to annihilating their language and culture. This situation is very different today.

The Basques and the Initial Stage of a Permanent System of Privilege and Underclass

History (The Transition to Autonomy)

Industrialization in Spain concentrated in Catalonia and in the Basque provinces of Viscaya and Guipúzcoa. The process of economic and social modernization and the large scale non-Basque immigration accompanying it challenged basic Basque values.

> The huge influx of immigrants in the 1950s and 1960s wrought a change in the balance of Basques to non-Basques and of Euskara speakers to non-Euskara speakers, resulting in the increased growth of what is now a large industrial working class or *terciarizada*. The newcomers were primarily from provinces with a strong Castilian culture which tended to discourage rather than encourage assimilation. This, of course, led to a further decline in the distinctively Basque identity of the region. It also had the effect of intensifying the efforts of nationalists to "rebasquize" the area, thereby encouraging a polarization between the indigenes and the immigrants. This tendency is reinforced by the social geography, in that the immigrants are, for the most part, isolated in separate new housing tracts. (Tarrow 1985, 257)

The rural Basque provinces of Alava and Navarra, which were not threatened by modernization and immigration (also with fewer Euskara speakers) had less reason to be defensive about safeguarding Basque language and culture. They had been less supportive of the autonomy efforts of the 1930s and 1940s and sided with Francoist forces during the Civil War, sharpening the dichotomy between two rural provinces and the two industrial ones which had sided with the Republic.

Under the *Constitution* of 1978, the Basque region was granted autonomy--accepted by public referendum in three provinces (but not Navarra) to form the Basque Automomous Community (BAC). The Constitution set the tone for the balance of cultural pluralism and social cohesion under the new democracy. In their 1979 *Statute of Autonomy*, the Basque government conferred *co-official* status on Euskara.[2] Between 1979 and 1983, the seventeen autonomous communities which make up the Spanish State were constituted, with only six of them (including the BAC) gaining almost full authority over educational matters. The democratized Spanish state now accommodates three indigenous cultures and languages (*Catalan* in Catalonia, *Gallego* in Galicia, and *Euskara* in the Basque region) and delegates regulatory authority to the autonomous governments.

In 1980, *Royal Decree 2808* transferred to the BAC all aspects of education not reserved to the state. The state retains authority for structuring the educational system, expediting degrees, establishing basic educational requirements, grants and scholarships, economic planning, agreements on private education, teacher certification, and high inspection. All other educational functions are delegated to the autonomous government.

Responses of Society

When autonomy was finally achieved, the Basque government recognized that half the residents of the BAC were

---

[2] The Constitution specifically avoids the use of the term "co-official," indicating only that regional languages shall "also be regarded as official in their region." This is a subtle but very important difference between the Constitution and the Statute of Autonomy.

Castilian speaking immigrants (See next section). Outside Guipúzcoa, only a minority of native Basques could speak the language; relatively little had been published in the language; it was of low prestige, archaic, and needed updating and standardization of the various dialects. The recuperation of language and culture have been a major focus of the autonomous government. Just as Franco viewed the educational system as the means to *assimilate* the Basques into the national culture, the Basques view it as the major focus of their efforts to *accommodate* to their unique indigenous language and culture. We next examine these efforts in terms of curriculum, access, teacher preparation and selection, and then summarize accomplishments and look at the resistance by some of the "new" minorities.

Curriculum

Under the language normalization law, three models of instruction for developing fluency in the language were established: *Model A* (instruction in Spanish with Euskara as a second language). *Model B* (bilingual), and *Model D* (instruction in Euskara with Spanish as a second language). If students want a model not available in their school, the government pays the cost of transport to the nearest school. Enrollment in Model A schools is diminishing, while Models B and D are growing, seen by Basque authorities as an indication of increased interest in learning Euskara.

Although general curriculum guides place heavy emphasis on language instruction, the low level of language competency of BAC teachers requires all curriculum guides to be bilingual. Classroom materials and textbooks in Euskara are increasingly being introduced at all levels and in all subjects. Perhaps in reaction to years of neglect, social studies in lower grades and geography and history in upper grades emphasize Basque history and geography--at the expense of other topics. Other aspects of Basque culture, including sports such as *pelote* (Basque handball) and competitions in stone lifting, woodchopping, etc, as well as traditional dances, poetry competitions, and *txistu* (Basque flute) playing are available through schools and/or community organizations.

Access

Although they had been receiving public funds (challenged by the central government[3]) the ikastolas are presently in a transition period--about to officially join the public school network. Their expansion has been phenomenal (McNair 1980). These schools now serve 70,000 students--and no longer all Euskara speaking. Vila (1986) reports that for 46 percent of children in ikastolas 1982-83, Castilian was the mother tongue. Thus there is a need to develop and adopt different teaching methods for native Spanish or Euskara

---

[3] In the BAC, the passage of the central (Socialist) government's 1983 LODE (Organic Law on the Right to Education) was feared as a death blow to the ikastolas, which, although operating independently (similarly to private schools) were considered public schools by the Basque government and therefore eligible for public funds. Under LODE, to be eligible for public funds, ikastolas would have to conform to certain regulations required of all public schools or "centros concertados" such as employing only teachers who had passed the national *oposiciones*. LODE was challenged in the courts by the Basque government (who lost the case) and the Basque government's 1983 EIKE (Euskal Ikastolen Erakundea), which established public school status for the ikastolas, was challenged by the central government (which lost its case). This six year battle appears to be finally approaching resolution. In December, 1988, an agreement was signed with 127 *ikastolas* prepared to be incorporated in the public school network as of 1989-90, leading to the creation of the new "Basque Public School." A "transition" period was established, during which the majority of the ikastolas are surrendering their "patrimony" (turning over to the government all their buildings and equipment) while the details are worked out for officially integrating the ikastolas into the public school network.

speakers. According to the Director of one of the major ikastolas, some of the ikastolas are using Model B (bilingual) although the majority prefer Model D (Euskara as the language of instruction, with Spanish as a second language) gradually introducing Euskara for Spanish speakers in the preschool stage, with all instruction in Euskara from age six. By the third year of EGB (elementary school) Spanish as second language is introduced (Torrealdai 1989, personal interview).

Teacher Preparation and Selection

In 1977, as the government was about to embark on a program of recuperating the Basque language (to a large degree through the educational system), more than 95 percent of the teachers could not speak Euskara! In order to Basquize children, it was necessary to 'Basquize' the teaching force (e.g., to train some who could speak Euskara to teach, and those who were teaching to speak Euskara). Thus, the *Magisterios* (teacher training institutions) began requiring the study of Euskara and now expect competency in Euskara of all future teachers. However, the drop in the European birth rate has recently had an impact on the Basque region, reducing the number of teaching positions available, which (combined with the lifelong teaching positions of the majority immigrants from other regions of Spain) impedes the process of infusing new Basque-speaking teachers into the system. The focus is therefore on *IRALE* (in-service program of literacy training and Basquization of the teaching staff in after-school courses subsidized by the Basque government). About three thousand teachers take courses during the school year and about two thousand in summer session. There is also a special year-long but limited enrollment intensive language program. The language can also be studied in *Euskaltegis* (language schools offered by other organizations). The goal is for teachers to reach the level of competence signified by earning the Certificate of Proficiency (*EGA*). The Confederation of Ikastolas (1989) remains very critical of the level of language proficiency in Basque of many of the teachers (even those with the EGA Certificate of Proficiency).

While secondary school teachers are trained at the university, pre-service training of elementary school teachers is the responsibility of the Magisterios. They offer a three year course that permits five specializations: Human Sciences, Science, Spanish Language, Preschool and Basque Language. Policy states that, except for the two language programs, all courses are to be taught in both languages. At the beginning of the first year there is a required intensive, hundred-hour course in Euskara. Further courses are required each of the three years. The Confederation of Ikastolas (1989) is also critical of pre-service teacher training, pointing out that even the linguistic capability of teachers at preschool and elementary levels is better than at *Enseñanzas Media* (intermediate level-ages eleven to fourteen), which, under the present structure, falls under the responsibility of the university.

Accomplishments and Goals

Vila (1986) notes that the situation of Euskara varies by area. Although its incorporation in the administration, mass media etc. provides motivation to learn this increasingly prestigious language, it is still threatened and vulnerable. Knowledge of the language has spread but its spoken use has not. Fishman (1989) points out that the Basque government needs to clarify its goals. If they are striving for language spread, they have accomplished a great deal. If they intend to accomplish language shift (e.g. use of Euskara as a mother tongue) they need to aim for those institutions closest to the socialization of the young child, rather than the more glamorous media.

Protests

There is not, however, unanimity in the Basque region on the goal of Basquization. Approximately half the people are "immigrants" in the region although citizens of Spain. While some have chosen to assimilate into their adopted "land," to learn or see that their children learn the language, there are others who, for various reasons, choose not to do so. Some find the language too difficult, too limited in its utility, while others stand on a matter of principle--as Spanish citizens in a region of Spain. An interview with a professor at the Church-run university provided the following information:

> Attendance in Model A schools is decreasing--not because there aren't children but parents worry about integration (and job possibilities for their children) and send them to Models B or D for practical reasons. H.B. (Herri Batasuna ultra-nationalist political party) representatives sit at school registration and coax parents into Models B and D. Remember the poorer people are in public schools--and easily convinced. The richer people choose private schools or Model A. For teachers, there are fewer Model A classes and some of them are losing their teaching posts and being assigned other work.

The "New" Minorities and the Initial Stage of a Permanent System of Privilege and Underclass

Euskara is no longer on the "endangered species list" of minority languages. As their language and culture have been strengthened, the Basques have developed a more secure sense of the "self"--prerequisite to a positive concept of the "other." A minority in Spain, the Basques are not and do not function as minorities within their region--but rather as the "privileged" class in "the initial stage of a permanent system of privilege and underclass."

The "New" Minorities

The new underclass is made up of three different groups who are and do function as minorities in the BAC: immigrants from other parts of Spain, gypsies, and the recent foreign immigrants from third world countries of Latin America, Asia, Africa and the Middle East.

Spanish "immigrants." According to García-Gonzáles (1986) two hundred thousand persons migrated to the Basque region from 1950-75. Seventy percent are working class, with low level education and minimal qualifications, living in industrial belts, subemployed or unemployed, ethnically bifurcated, socially rejected and subject to ethnocentric prejudice (as *maketos*), linguistic and cultural difficulties, and social conflict. They lack the necessary special support or attention essential to successful policies of ethno-cultural pluralism. Their children represent 27.5 percent of the population. García-González recommends an in-depth study and creation of special services for both first and second generation immigrants, as well as programs to foster comprehension and respect for different cultures and values.

Gypsies (Gitanos). One of the first minority groups to receive compensatory education programming is not a new immigrant group, for Gypsies migrated to Spain five centuries ago. Yet this group is the most marginalized, persecuted, and educationally disadvantaged of all the different cultural groups in the country (and in Europe). A significant percentage of gypsy children are not in school during the years of "compulsory" schooling. Those who are schooled still are identified by high levels of illiteracy, absenteeism, and drop-out. Few go on to secondary schooling. For example, in 1989 there was only one gypsy student in secondary education (vocational) in all of the BAC (Alfaro 1989, personal interview). In the BAC, there has been little official interest in the demographics of the gypsy population. On the basis of interviews with a sample of the gypsy population, Grupo Pass (1987a, 1987b) estimates that seven thousand gypsies live in the BAC. Currently three funded studies (in Alava, Guipúzcoa, and Vizcaya) are seeking to find out how many reside in the BAC, where they are and what are their needs.[4] A

---

[4] One of the motivations for undertaking these surveys appears to be that the Portuguese government in response to Council of Europe recommendations and a directive, has indicated a willingness to fund and supply teachers of

Escuela Puente Gitana of Guipúzcoa can account for over three hundred children in forty-eight different schools. It estimates that there are at least another one hundred school-age children not attending school (Seminario Escolarización 1989, Iribar et al. 1989).

Foreign immigrants. Territorially based minorities in Europe (such as the Basques and the Welsh) have long been oppressed by the nation states in which they are located. This response to oppression has often been one of nationalistic antagonism, which may easily become a chauvinistic parochialism. However, the fact of the territorial base makes their position significantly different from those minorities without one. Few doubt that they belong; their feeling of oppression is based on other factors, principally linguistic, cultural, religious and economic. For the other minorities, who share these oppressions, a further one is added. This is the widely held view that these minorities not only do not belong but should not be in Europe. (Jones and Kimberly 1986, 22)

The Basques have been through a difficult period (1936-1976) but even in their blackest moments, no one doubted that they "belonged." This kind of oppression is, however, the lot of a relatively new group in the region. Until relatively recently, Spain was a country of emigration (first to Latin America and the Pacific, and later to western Europe). The *Instituto Español de Emigración* traditionally concerned itself almost exclusively with maintaining Spanish language and culture in the host countries receiving these Spanish citizens. In the mid 1970s, however, Spain began receiving immigration--primarily from Latin America, Africa, the Middle East, and Portugal. This was induced by several factors including the restrictions on

---

Portuguese language, once Portuguese children have been identified. In the BAC many of the Portuguese children are gypsies.

immigration by other western European nations, Canada, and the U.S. political and economic events; the cessation of internal rural-urban migration (opening low-level jobs for immigrants); and very loose border controls until 1985.

In July, 1985 the *Law on the Rights and Liberties of Foreigners* was implemented throughout Spain. While reinforcing the rights of legal immigrants with permission to work, it marginalized and undermined the security of the undocumented immigrants. Available data is questionable, with no breakdown of the data for the immigrant population by provinces or regions. Thus, it is difficult to estimate how many of these have found their way to the BAC. In the BAC there appear to be at least five thousand Portuguese, an indeterminate number of gypsies (many also Portuguese), an Arab population (primarily in Bilbao), and a sizeable Filipino community.

Responses of Society

The first stage of responding to the needs of minorities requires recognition of the existence of these communities, their linguistic, cultural and religious differences, and their problems in their adopted land. The second stage involves *compensatory programs*, designed to assimilate the child into the majority culture--often by focusing on needed language skills, and often at the expense of his or her own language and culture. Compensatory programs may be seen as a *transition* between the ideology of *assimilation* and the next level of *accommodation*, when *minority language and culture programs* legitimize, and possibly safeguard the linguistic and cultural heritage of subordinate groups. It remains for a possible third stage of *multicultural* (or *intercultural*) education programs to sensitize all children to the languages and cultures of subordinate groups, to view *cultural pluralism* positively and to actively encourage interaction and interchange between cultures to the mutual enhancement of each. This is termed "celebration of cultural difference."

Access

Theoretically, all minority students have the same access to education as Basques. Spanish immigrants are enrolling in ikastolas, which previously had been available only to Euskara speakers (in essence, children of Basque parents) and selective in their acceptance policy (with priority to children whose siblings were students or alumni). The majority are in public or Church-supported schools. Their drop-out rate before secondary graduation is much higher than that of the Basque population. One special program reaching some of these drop-outs is described under "Curriculum" below.

Foreign immigrant children who are learning Spanish rarely opt for the ikastolas, where instruction is usually in Euskara. They are, however, required to study Euskara as a second language (or bilingually) in the public schools. Many foreign children are in private schools, often supported by their home country--particularly those from Germany, Japan, England, and France. Children from third world countries, in general, are in public or Church-supported schools. At the present time, there is only one small program dealing with home language instruction, which is also described under "Curriculum" below.

Again, theoretically, gypsy children have access to the public school system, and some are entering "integrated" schools--particularly in the Bilbao area.[5] *Chabolistas* (clans living in more primitive conditions) tend to send their children to one of the two *Escuelas Puentes* in the Basque region (in Vitoria and San Sebastián). According to the Director of the latter school, there are one hundred seven children matriculated. One group contains regular attendees (sixty to seventy). A

---

[5] Escuelas Puentes, started on a national level in the 1970s, were intended as transitional schools for gypsy children to prepare them to enter the regular system. In practice, very few of them made the transition and these schools have been phasing out in most of Spain. These tend to be *apayados* (from more settled gypsy families).

second group tends to come on alternate days so that there about twenty at a time of this group in school. Most of these children leave school by age eleven. As already mentioned, in 1989 there was only one gypsy in secondary school in the entire BAC--and he was in the vocational track.

Curriculum

In the Escuela Puente Gitana the students range from age two to fourteen. The youngest children are brought by their older sisters (or the sisters would not be able to come to school) and are in the nursery. The academic level is very low and there is no attempt to follow formal curriculum. They teach arithmetic, reading and writing but the school is not considered an environment of work--rather play, painting, eating, building social relationships and "passing time." The school day has four hours in the morning, lunch, and one hour in the afternoon. There is little possibility to work with parents as they are not in the area. Four teachers who volunteered to develop this school used a small grant from the government to complete a survey of the gypsy community in the province. Recognizing the need to sensitize teachers and students in the schools accepting these gypsy children, these teachers also wrote a small grant proposal to provide workshops for teachers in those schools. At the time of interview and observation there had been no response to this proposal (Alfaro 1989, personal interview).

PETRA is a program that contains a significant percentage of children of immigrants from other parts of Spain. It was started in 1985 in cooperation with the Council of Europe as part of a European network of transition programs helping young people enter the working world at a standardized level of auxiliary technician. The program covers four areas--basic training, job training, social integration, and culture and leisure. Participants meet in groups of sixteen to twenty for six hours daily over a one year period. The emphasis is on practical training, with theory taught as needed (Department of Education, Universities, and Research 1988a). Evaluation of this program was begun in 1989.

Evaluation led to plans for expansion of Vitoria's program for fourteen to sixteen year-old "dropouts" to four other cities. The evaluation noted that immigrant status of the parents is not a determinant but is a significant factor in the academic failure of these young people (Department of Education 1986, 1988, 1988b).

As of 1989-90, there were no special programs in operation for foreign immigrant children. There are plans for a program called *Minorías Etnicas*. The *intended* populations for this *proposed* program include gypsies, Portuguese (many of whom are gypsies) and Magrebes (Arabs from Morocco, Algiers, and the Middle East). The only concrete proposal was for the Department of Education officially to employ (part-time) an Egyptian teacher currently teaching Arabic in a program initiated by the Arab *collectivo* in Vitoria. Several compensatory programs proposed for September 1989 included school lunch programs, parent education, early school entry and experimental programs (proposed by the teachers of schools in marginal areas and designed to meet their specific needs) (Cuacagoytea 1989, personal interview).

Teacher Preparation and Selection

Interviews conducted and questionnaires administered in teacher training institutions indicate that nothing in the pre-service training of teachers prepares them for the reality of a multicultural classroom--either in terms of the language or culture of the specific minority groups they will encounter or of the research, methodology, and materials available in this field.

As for teacher selection, the Basque region is just beginning to recover from the "artificial insemination" of non-Basque teachers in their schools, as the holdovers from the Franco era reach the age or retirement. Intent on replacing them with Basques or Basque-speakers, there is not now, nor is there likely to be, an effort to attract non-Basques into the teaching force.

Discussion and Conclusion

Following a lengthy period of linguistic and cultural repression based on an *assimilation* ideology, the Basque government moved to an *accommodation* ideology and assertive policies to recoup their language and cultural heritage. Legislation, educational programs, teacher preparation and curriculum materials have been utilized in implementing these policies-- within the parameters imposed by national legislation and directives. Evaluation studies have been utilized to justify intensification of efforts in these areas. There is not unanimous approval of the language normalization program in the region, although protests have not escalated.

The formerly oppressed subordinate group has effectively become the dominant group within the region. Having only recently experienced the effects of an assimilation ideology, one might expect that the Basques might reject this approach in dealing with their "new" minorities. There is still great fear, however, that these cultures and languages will dilute the attempts to reclaim the Basque heritage. Authorities in the Basque region appear to have been so focused on the problems of their own vulnerable language and culture that they have only begun to address the needs of the "new" minorities. For children of Spanish and foreign immigrants, the educational responses are usually directed at integration of these children into a Basque society--and competency in the Basque language is viewed as the major means of accomplishing this integration through compensatory programs. For Gypsy children, they seem to have adopted exactly the opposite approach--discounting possible integration and providing separate facilities to assist in their socialization.

Basque education officials have just dipped a toe into the waters of compensatory programming with several beginning in September 1989. In some of these cases the government appears to play a reactive role--recognizing the problem and providing some support after the initiative has been taken by non-official agencies or groups. Compensatory programs tend to afford a feeling of self-righteousness, of "doing something" for "them," but the ultimate goal is usually assimilation into the dominant culture. Legitimization of other cultures and languages is practically non-existent on an official level. Based on interviews, questionnaires, examination of curriculum guides, texts, etc. there appears to be no attempt to teach non-minority children (or educate teachers) about minority cultures. Intercultural Education (in the sense proposed by the Council of Europe to all its member states) dealing with such concepts as discrimination, stereotyping and prejudice, requiring that all members of the community examine their own attitudes, beliefs, and behaviour in relation to other cultures, that welcomes interaction and interchange between cultures (Rey 1986)--remains for some future time. It appears, at this initial stage of a system of privilege and underclass, that the next step (to a celebration or a valuing of cultural differences) may be a long time in coming.

References

Arzak, J. I. 1984. *Historia del País Vasco*. San Sebastián: Luis Haranburu.

Clark, R. P. 1979. *The Basques: The Franco Years and Beyond*. Reno: University of Nevada Press.

_____ 1981. Language and politics in Spain's Basque provinces. *West European Politics* 4(1): 85-103.

_____. 1985. Dimensions of Basque political culture in post-Franco Spain. In W. Douglass, ed. *Basque Politics: A Case Study in Ethnic Nationalism*. Reno: University of Nevada Press.

Collins, R. 1986. *The Basques*. Oxford: Basil Blackwell.

Department of Education (Universities and Research). 1986. *Proyecto del Centro de Educación Compensatoria para Jóvenes Desescolarizados de 14 a 16 Años del Municipio de Vitoria-Gasteiz*. Vitoria: Central Publications Service of the Basque Government.

_____. 1988. *Diseño Curricular del Centro de Educación Compensatoria de Vitoria-Gasteiz. Tres Años de Experiencia*. Vitoria (December): Central Publications Service of the Basque Government.

_____. 1988a. *Job Initiation Programme (PETRA)*. Vitoria: Central Publications Services of the Basque Government.

_____. 1988b. *Jóvenes Hacia el Futuro*. Vitoria: Central Publications Service of the Basque Government.

Confederación de Ikastolas. 1989. *Diseño de la Escuela Vasca: Los Apuntes para Debate Interno*. Donostia: Confederación de Ikastolas de Euskal Herria.

Douglass, W. 1985. Introduction. In W. Douglass, ed. *Basque Politics: A Case Study in Ethnic Nationalism*. Reno: University of Nevada Press.

El País. 1989. Las ikastolas a punto de integrarse en la red pública. March 8, p. 1.

Fishman. J. 1989. Why the school is ineffective in reversing language shift (RLS). Paper presented at the First Congress of the Basque Public Schools, Bilbao.

Frank, R., A. Eguzkitza, and L. Bloom. n.d. *The Basque Language: Past, Present and Future*. University of Iowa Press.

Gallop, R. [1930]. 1970. *A Book of the Basques*. Reno: University of Nevada Press.

García-González, J. A. 1986. Inmigración e integración. In Department of Labor, Health, and Social Security, *Psicosociología del Adolescente Vasco*. Vitoria: Central Publications Service of the Basque Government.

Grupo Pass. 1987a. *La Comunidad Gitana de Donostialdea*. Bilbao: Orinoco Artes Gráficas.

_____. 1987b. *La Comunidad Gitana del Gran Bilbao*. Bilbao: Orinoco Artes Gráficas.

Heiberg, M. 1975. Insiders/outsiders: Basque nationalism. *Archives Européenes de Sociologie* 15(1): 169-193.

Heiberg, M. 1982. Urban politics and rural culture: Basque nationalism. In S. Rokkan and D. Urwin, eds. *The Politics of Territorial Identity*. Beverly Hills, CA: Sage.

Iribar, J, E. Eskurdia, F. Barrenetxea, and A. Alfaro 1989. Seminario sobre la escolarización de la minoría étnica gitana (June), San Sebastián.

Jones, C., and K. Kimberly. 1986. *Intercultural Education: Concept, Context, Curriculum Practice.* Strasbourg: Council of Europe.

Larrea, M. A., and R. Mieza. 1985. *Introduction to the History of the Basque Country.* Spain: Ediciones Beramar.

Legaretta, D. 1985. *The Guernica Generation.* Reno: University of Nevada Press.

McNair, J. 1980. The contribution of the schools to the restoration of regional autonomy in Spain. *Comparative Education* 16(1): 33-44.

Medhurst, K. (1987) *The Basques and the Catalans.* Minority Rights Group Report 9. London: Minority Rights Group.

Rey, M. 1986. *Training Teachers in Intercultural Education.* Strasbourg: Council of Europe.

Seminario Escolarización. 1989. Situación y problemática de la escolarización de niños/as de la minoría étnica gitana de Guipuzcoa (September), San Sebastián.

Tarrow, N. B. 1985. The autonomous Basque community of Spain: Language, culture, and education. In C. Brock and W. Tulasiewicz, eds. *Cultural Identity and Educational Policy.* London: Croom Helm.

Vila, I. 1986. Bilingual education in the Basque country. *Journal of Multilingual and Multicultural Development* 7(2&3): 123-145.

EDUCATION IN A DIVIDED SOCIETY: THE CASE OF NORTHERN IRELAND

Andrew S. Hughes

The most commanding aspect of life in Northern Ireland is the presence of two communities labelled variously Catholic and Protestant, republican and loyalist, Irish and British, with none of the tags being sufficient to capture the essence of what it is that unites either group or distinguishes it from the other. Still, the rigid division of the population into just two communities stands in stark contrast to societies where multiculturalism is at least tacitly accepted if not whole-heartedly embraced and is vividly illustrated by the story of the outsider who strays into one of Belfast's less savory neighbourhoods only to be accosted by a gang of young people in paramilitary attire. "What religion are you?" the outsider is asked. "I'm an atheist," she says. "Yes, yes!" comes the impatient response, "but are you a Protestant atheist or a Catholic atheist?"

For most of the world, the prevailing image of Northern Ireland is that of the bombs, bullets, riots, and assassinations of the evening television news. For those who live there, "the Troubles" serve as a backdrop against which they play their various parts. For most people, it is only rarely that the apparently routine violence thrusts itself upon centre stage in any sustained way. Yet it is pervasive and pernicious, and never far from the consciousness of everyday being. To outsiders, Northern Ireland is a dangerous place inhabited by a violent people but this is an image which offends both communities to say nothing of causing untold economic hardship through its negative impact upon outside investment. Even at the height of violence in the early seventies, the death rate attributable to civil strife was lower than the typical murder rate in most of the world's larger cities. The crime rate today is lower than that of the United Kingdom as a whole and the number of deaths related to civil disturbances in 1989 was scarcely half that of the city of Montreal. However, for a society in which there was but a single murder in 1965 the escalation in violence has been a traumatic experience although one it is learning to live with, even to the point where both government and terrorists speak of "acceptable levels of violence." In October of 1988 many commentators expressed moral outrage not at the fact that the IRA had detonated a 300lb semtex bomb in the centre of Belfast, but rather, that it had been done without providing sufficient advanced warning. Clearly, terrorists and authorities are developing a code of ethics for the conduct of institutionalized violence. But for the vast majority of Northern Ireland's citizens, there is no acceptable level of violence and to indulge in such rhetoric is, in the local parlance, "to commit murder with your tongue."

Nevertheless, while the society is largely united in its opposition to violence it is bitterly divided in its aspirations for the future. The seventeenth-century plantation of Ulster may have begun before that of Virginia but in the ensuing centuries there has been no common ideal to meld together the planter and the indigenous populations and what was Catholic and Irish and what was Protestant and British at the beginning of the seventeenth century remains essentially so today. The people of Northern Ireland constitute what Hugh MacLennan so eloquently described (in Canada) as two solitudes. In spite of their joint occupation of the same small territory, or perhaps because of it, their ethno-religious identity has served to separate them. All major social institutions are now affected by segregation--especially marriage, education, work and housing, with inevitable structural alienation and disaffection (Spencer 1987).

Segregation in Schooling

With but a few exceptions, children in Northern Ireland attend schools which may be reasonably characterized as either Catholic or Protestant. Attempts were made early in the history of Northern Ireland to establish an essentially non-denominational system of public education but the proposals found favour with neither the Catholic nor the Protestant churches and both groups retained the responsibility for the education of their own communities. Over the years, however, fiscal pressures have pushed both groups into a relationship with the state. Thereby, there has emerged a system of segregated schooling, both strands of which are supported largely from the public purse. *Controlled* schools are paid for fully by the government and are attended almost exclusively by Protestants. *Maintained* schools are attended almost exclusively by Catholics and are government funded to the extent of 100 percent of operating expenses and 85 percent of capital expenditures. The price in both cases has been government representation on the management boards of schools in both systems, more so in the case of controlled schools and less so in the case of maintained schools. For clarity, and also because it is true in all practical terms, I shall refer here to Catholic schools and Protestant schools. Quite simply, Protestant children (99.5 percent) attend "protestant" schools and Catholic children (98 percent) attend "catholic" schools. Crossover between the systems is minimal and in a substantial majority of schools there are no members of the other religion whatsoever (Greer 1980).

In the context of "the Troubles," the dual school system is often targeted as a source of division and divisiveness. It is sometimes seen as dysfunctional in the sense that it contributes to the on-going tribalism that divides the society and it has been depicted as a significant source of what is referred to as cultural and social apartheid.

The cultural apartheid thesis suggests "the possibility that significantly different activities, emphasis and values are encouraged within the two sets of schools" (Darby and Dunn 1987, 86). Such evidence as there is, and it is scant, lends only minimal support to the hypothesis. Indeed, the preponderance of evidence points to two remarkably similar systems:

> Curricular practices such as streaming, the presence or absence of an integrated curriculum, the use of project materials and school broadcasts were similar on both sets of schools; there was little to distinguish them across a wide range of diverse characteristics including the educational qualifications of staff and the work profiles of Principals; although some sports were exclusively played in one system--notably Gaelic games in Catholic schools and rugby and cricket in Protestant schools-- sports like soccer, basketball and netball were popular in all schools; Protestant and Catholic children were equally likely to experience corporal punishment, and their parents were equally likely to be discouraged from close involvement in school affairs. Both, in effect, had a common and rather conservative approach to the organisation and administration of education. (Darby and Dunn 1987, 87)

Still, the Irish language is taught in most Catholic schools and in no Protestant ones and middle-aged Protestants are sometimes inclined to wonder why they learned of the Treaty of Waitangi and the Durham Report as they journeyed across all of the pink-coloured parts of the world map (the British empire, and now the Commonwealth, were pink in many school atlases) yet learned virtually nothing of Ulster and Ireland.

Beyond this there is the fact of separateness itself. The social apartheid thesis suggests that "the very separation of Catholics and Protestants into different schools itself encourages suspicion and hostility" (Darby and Dunn 1987, 87). Young people cannot help but assume that since they are assigned to different systems, there must be something different about the populations that inhabit those systems. Intuitively it would seem quite clear that the friendship patterns that develop, the loyalties that are shaped, the peer and teacher influence that is exerted, are those of their co-religionists. There is a strong belief that this truncated range of social interaction establishes a foundation upon which the society later builds a superstructure of political, demographic, recreational and social segregation, to say nothing of serving as a breeding ground for sectarianism. Yet, there is little evidence to confirm that such consequences emanate from a segregated system. Indeed, evidence from other jurisdictions where religiously segregated education is experienced does not point to such dire consequences. But even if segregated schooling does not contribute to intergroup hostility in Northern Ireland, it certainly does nothing to lessen the mistrust and misapprehension that characterizes the relationship between the two communities.

Integrated Schooling

In the fall of 1988, the Northern Ireland government announced proposals to extend what it called "religiously integrated" education. For the most part the proposals consist of financial arrangements that will facilitate the creation of new integrated schools and the expansion of those that already exist. By late 1988 there were ten such schools in the Province.

In spite of the widespread sympathy for integrated education among the general populace, church leaders in both communities have reacted in a hostile fashion to what they see as preferential treatment for a wholly new educational sector. The principal of a leading Catholic school has described the proposals as "tantamount to an all-out declaration of war on the Catholic system" while a Protestant leader has spoken of the same proposals "as a means of destroying Ulster resistance to the Anglo-Irish Agreement and a united Ireland" (Clarke 1988, H2). It would seem that little has changed from 1921 when proposals for a non-denominational school system in the newly created Northern Irish state evoked the response that the "only satisfactory system of education for Catholics is one wherein Catholic children are taught in Catholic schools by Catholic teachers under Catholic auspices." Protestant protagonists of the same era warned that the same proposals would allow for "a bolshevist or an atheist or a Roman Catholic to become a teacher in a Protestant school" (Bowman 1988, B3). In 1980, the Chilver

Report on teacher education proposed that two Catholic colleges be amalgamated with the major non-denominational (*de facto* Protestant) college with a number of religious and structural guarantees. The result was an outcry from the Catholic Church (Dunn 1986). In such an atmosphere, the proponents of integrated schooling have not found the terrain particularly fertile, at least not until the recent round of troubles and the emergence of the belief that segregated schooling might in some way be contributing to broader community violence and that, even if this is not the case, it is certainly not serving as a forum in which a resolution may be sought.

As planned integrated education has developed in Northern Ireland it has cultivated an attachment to certain principles. First, these are not secular schools. Each would seek to be recognized as "a Christian institution designed for the children of Christian parents" (Spencer 1987, 109). The desire is to make this clear to non-Christian believers such as Jews, Muslims, and Hindus as well as to discourage those who are hostile to or disaffected with organized religion from seeing integrated schooling as a refuge from theocracy. Generally speaking, the leaders of the integrated schooling movement see it as contributing to the development in young people with a grounding in their own Christian religion while fostering an understanding of "the other" Christian community.

> The integrated school certainly aims to transmit the vast secular and religious culture which is held in common by the two major communities, and to stress that they *do* hold it in common. But it has two further aims. It seeks to nurture within each pupil what is specific to the tradition of his own community. And it aims to show each pupil something of the specific tradition of the other community, so that cognitively he/she at least knows and understands, and at best respects and appreciates it. (Spencer 1987, 108)

In addition to its overtly Christian character, integrated education is also clearly committed to tenets of equality of status, parental participation, and voluntary involvement.

Equality of status is pursued culturally through the school curriculum by emphasizing the equal treatment of the secular and religious values and traditions of the two communities, and structurally by attending to the demographic composition of the school. The goal is to establish a 50:50 ratio in the student body between the two Christian groups with a 60:40 rule limit for recruitment in any one year with the same sorts of principles governing staffing. "Deep parental involvement" is sought, partly to avoid a situation where parents expose their children to the experience of integration without having the experience themselves. Deep involvement not only ensures the sort of success evident when communities are profoundly committed to their schools but it also ensures that parents must be prepared to do what they want their children to do (Spencer 1987). The result might well be that the experience of integration becomes a focal point in the life experience not only of children between the ages of four and eighteen but also for the same fourteen years in life experience of their parents who may range in age from their twenties to their fifties.

Over the years there have been calls for compulsory integrated education, all of them resisted by the leaders of the movement for integrated education. They have insisted that the success of integrated schooling relies upon parental self-selection. In creating the option of voluntary integration, restricted though it is as yet, the leaders believe that they have broken the stranglehold of what had been *de facto* compulsory segregated education since the inception of the Northern Irish state. On the other hand, the voluntary nature of integration exposes it to the criticism that it fosters the liberal dispositions of already liberally-minded members of the middle-classes while doing nothing to free the lower classes of the hostility spawned and nurtured in their respective ghettos.

Social Interaction and the Resolution
of Societal Conflict

So far, attempts to promote mutual understanding through integrated education have been limited to the ten schools established between 1974 and 1989. Still, the separation initiated in the school system is viewed as the basis of the separation of the communities in other social institutions such as marriage and work, simply because of the absence of significant social interaction between the two groups. Efforts to overcome this lack of significant social interaction have been made in the form of inter-school links of various sorts and through a variety of out-of-school contact schemes.

One of the curious features of life in Northern Ireland is that while the two communities may be overtly hostile to each other, such hostility seldom manifests itself in relations between individuals which are often cordial and friendly, and nearly always more than civil. Such cordiality makes it a relatively simple matter for individuals such as school teachers to orchestrate interaction among themselves and their pupils. Orchestrate is the right term because such interactions are rarely spontaneous. Nevertheless, there are many examples of inter-school links, all of which would be familiar to neighbouring schools in many parts of the world. There is the sharing of sports facilities, libraries, and computer laboratories. Sometimes pupils wishing to take a subject not offered by their own school, particularly at an advanced level, may do so in one of "the other" schools. Occasionally, there is the sharing of teachers and there are instances of joint adventure sports weekends. More often, teachers work collaboratively in curriculum development and other professional activities. However, in the total scheme of things, "it would be true to say that inter-school contact is very limited indeed" (Dunn, Darby, and Mullan 1984, 41). But one wonders if this limited interaction is any less in this segregated system than in most systems where, apart from the usual rounds of sports activities, science fairs, and music festivals, inter-school contact is, indeed, a rare commodity. Of course, the stress of the Northern Ireland situation may well be creating the expectation that schools ought to be playing a greater role in helping resolve society's problems.

Many schools, led by principals and parents' groups, have strongly resisted the view that the schools should be used as instruments of social reconstruction, or, indeed, that they ought to be held responsible in any way for the social and political ills of the society. Many principals and teachers see their schools as havens of sanity in a sea of madness and, therefore, seek to shut out "the Troubles," thereby creating an atmosphere that at least approaches normality. They wish their pupils to have something approaching a normal school experience and hence, perhaps, the seemingly inordinate emphasis that many schools place upon success in public examinations. And, of course, there is a need to take account of the life worlds of young people. At a meeting I attended in September 1988 concerned with exploring the possibility of creating another integrated school, one parent reminded the others there, to say nothing of the professional educators, that young people, whether Catholic or Protestant, are much more consumed by the work of Michael Jackson or Iron Maiden than by the latest twist in "the Troubles."

Still, educational leaders, particularly academics, have identified a role for schools in both the creation and the solution of the Northern Irish problem. In the early days of the recent troubles, Malcolm Skilbeck (1973), who was then at the New University of Ulster, concluded from his observations that teachers in Northern Ireland were "the naive bearers of a sectarian culture" and he espoused the view that schools must deliberately and systematically respond to rapidly changing social and cultural circumstances, seeking to anticipate, assess, and influence them. He contrasts this view with that of schools simply reflecting basic societal trends, or preserving elements of culture, or, indeed, ignoring the issues of the broader society.

Adhering to Skilbeck's orientation, there has been a few major curriculum projects which have sought to encourage personal awareness and mutual understanding in social relationships among young people in Northern Ireland. Illustrative of these is The Schools Cultural Studies Project (1980) which was initiated by Skilbeck at the New University of

Ulster with financial support from the Rowntree Trust and the Department of Education for Northern Ireland.
 In its conception, the architects of the project thought that

> in the pervasive crudities of the violence . . . the schools were either contributing to the violence by simply doing nothing about it, or failing to contribute to the peace by not taking a more positive institutional stance. (O'Connor 1980, 263)

Based on the analysis of social and political issues using a values clarification approach, the SCSP has suffered the fate of most of its counterparts. It failed to become an examination subject, a fatal flaw for any aspiring program in those islands. It never penetrated the boundaries of the grammar schools where the leaders of the two communities are educated and ended up as what is pejoratively termed "a soft option." It succeeded best in the secondary intermediate schools in a second class and second best environment where it was often considered legitimate to allow pupils to "go with their enthusiasms," and was often used only for remedial purposes (O'Connor 1980).
 Outside of school, there has also been a variety of schemes designed to bring about direct contact between Catholic and Protestant children. The most widespread of these are the "community relations holidays" where approximately equal numbers of Catholic and Protestant children are brought together outside of their own environment for a period of between five days and six weeks (Trew 1989). In 1987 and 1988 these schemes involved approximately 6000 children in holidays in Europe and North America. Such schemes are funded by well meaning individuals from many parts of the world as well as by Northern Ireland government agencies. All have an unswerving faith that simple exposure to members of "the other group" will have a positive impact on community relations. The evidence points to a pleasant interlude in the lives of many deprived children, but not one that extends back into the lives that they lead in their segregated communities. Finnegan (1985) tells of one nine year old Protestant boy about to embark upon a trip to the United States who was flabbergasted to know that he might

have to stay with Catholics. His mother assuaged his fears by explaining that these were American Catholics and would not hurt him.

These various schemes, whether school-based or out-of-school, are rooted in an attachment to the "contact hypothesis" which holds that prejudice may be reduced when there is equal status contact between groups in pursuit of a common goal. However, as developed in the United States, the contact hypothesis has tended to assume that "the fundamental problem of intergroup conflict is individual prejudice" and, furthermore, "the effective remedy is education which will change attitudes and alter behaviour" (Trew 1989, 153). This may well be so in "the development of friendship between neighbours," but it may have "very little relevance to the development of strategies that allow for the peaceful coexistence of members of groups divided on genuine and apparently irreconcilable differences in political goals and aspirations" (Trew 1989, 156) and hence it may have very little to do with the circumstances of Northern Ireland.

The Selective Nature of Schooling

While segregation along religious lines may distinguish educational experience of the young people, it is their subjection to a system of selective secondary education which, more than anything else, serves to make their educational experiences similar.

Before the Second World War only a small number of children pursued formal education beyond the elementary school which dealt with children up to the age of fourteen. Following the War, the secondary education sector expanded considerably but not uniformly. The grammar schools which had been the major providers of secondary education were expanded and continued with their emphasis of providing an academic education aimed at university entrance or, at least, entry into the white collar work force. In addition, there was created a system of secondary intermediate schools which served youngsters destined to enter the workforce at the earliest possible opportunity. For the most part, the type of school that a child ended up in was dependent upon performance in what was and is commonly referred to as the "qualifying examination." Quite simply, one had to "qualify" for a place in a grammar school through the *11 plus*[1] examination. Failure to "qualify" over the past forty years has meant being consigned to the secondary intermediate system which is clearly second class and second rate--unless one's family had the means to purchase one of the fee-paying places retained by the grammar schools which are deemed "first-rate." Today the system is referred to as the "transfer system" though the children and their parents know all too well that where one transfers to is dependent on whether one "passes" the qualifying examination.

This was the system very much in evidence in England and Wales following the 1944 Education Reform Act until swept away in the Comprehensive Reform Movement of the 1960s which attempted to provide equality of educational opportunity by eliminating selection at 11 plus--with the intention of replacing it with election at 14 plus or 16 plus. The recent resurgence of interest in grammar school education in England and Wales has been grist for the mills of Northern Ireland's conservative educators on both sides of the religious divide as they point to their Province's unwillingness to abandon selection as a wise past decision (Sockett 1987).

Certainly, there have been serious reservations expressed about the selection examination and

> the case for a fairer comprehensive system of education has long been conceded in the rest of the UK, but with a Conservative Minister defending the status quo in the Province, an early change of policy seems unlikely. But the 11 plus remains an iniquitous system which is both educationally unsound and emotionally disturbing. (*Belfast Telegraph* 1987, editorial)

---

[1] *The examination traditionally given to children after their eleventh birthday to determine admission to particular forms of secondary education.*

For the proponents of comprehensive education the preponderance of evidence concerning selection seems overwhelmingly to favour its abolition. Among their major concerns is that children who do not gain access to grammar schools are labelled as failures before their twelfth birthday; the process of selection is itself flawed lacking any significant measure of validity and reliability; and its very existence leads to cramming and coaching in the elementary school whose "curriculum dog is wagged by the selection tail" (Sockett 1987, 76). All of this is to say nothing of the stress placed upon children and families in a society of limited economic opportunity where paramount importance is often placed upon educational credentials. Even the chief inspector of schools has said that he is not persuaded that "were we to move for sound educational reasons to a non-selective system, we would not lose anything of real worth" (Wallace quoted in Daly 1987).

With access to types of schooling restricted by the selection process, there inevitably arise questions concerning the extent to which the discriminations made between those who will attend grammar schools and those who will attend secondary intermediate schools are equitable, and this is especially so with respect to social class, gender and religion.

Access and Attainment

Certainly there can be little doubt but that the transfer process at age eleven serves to further divide an already divided society, with religious divisions being further deepened and then compounded by those of class and gender. In particular, it is abundantly evident that the tests of verbal reasoning such as those used in the "qualifying" examinations favor the children from higher socioeconomic groups and disadvantage those from the lower groups. Ultimately, more than half the children from families where the parents are non-manual workers end up in grammar schools. Of the children of manual workers, barely one-sixth makes it (Wilson 1987). The successful group is then sponsored through the grammar school system until a further culling at age eighteen discards those deemed not suitable for the universities.

It is also quite clear that, in the transfer process, boys and girls have been treated quite differently. As a group, girls have traditionally outperformed boys in the qualifying tests. However, for many years there was a practice of treating boys and girls as separate populations and according them equal numbers of grammar school places. This particular practice was outlawed by the High Court in 1988 and places are now meant to be awarded to grammar schools exclusively on the basis of merit. The long term result may well be the significant underrepresentation of boys in the grammar school populations and perhaps even in the universities. This particular interpretation of the concept of equity will be of considerable interest to equity advocates in other jurisdictions, especially in North America.

In addition to the social class and gender concerns, the matter of religion also raises its head with respect to access to grammar school education. Proportionally, fewer Catholics (26 percent) spend some part of their secondary education in grammar schools than do Protestants (35 percent) (Livingstone 1987). This can basically be accounted for in three ways. First, among those children who earn a place in grammar school and subsequently choose not to attend there is a higher proportion of Catholics. Often this is simply because of the absence of a Catholic grammar school within easy commuting distance. Second, a larger proportion of Catholics opt not to seek a grammar school place. Third, of those children who are not successful in the qualifying examination but end up attending grammar schools as fee-payers, a much greater proportion are Protestants. The end result of this underrepresentation of Catholics in the grammar schools is that, in a system dominated by publicly sponsored examinations, access to which is in many ways controlled by the grammar schools, Catholics tend to leave school less well qualified than Protestants.

For the young people of Northern Ireland, as for many of their European counterparts, educational attainment is usually addressed in terms of school leavers' qualifications. Simply put, *attainment* is measured in terms of the number of passes achieved in nationally sponsored examinations. Until the very recent introduction of the General Certificate of Secondary Education these were the General Certificate of Education (GCE) at the "ordinary" and "advanced" levels, and the Certificate of Secondary Education (CSE). Although not mutually exclusive, the GCE examinations have been the preferred route for the grammar schools as they provide the basis for university entrance. For grammar school pupils, CSE has been treated very much as a sort of consolation prize.

Sometimes very flattering but crude comparisons have been made between educational performance in Northern Ireland and the other regions of the United Kingdom. Generally, they are used to show that a greater proportion of pupils in Northern Ireland achieve success in the GCE advanced level examinations than is the case in Britain as a whole. For example, in 1983-84 some 22.5 percent of school leavers in Northern Ireland earned one or more A-levels while the comparable figures in England and Wales were 17.2 and 16.1 respectively. What is only seldom pointed out is that the profile of performance is one of two extremes with not only a higher proportion of Northern Ireland students gaining one or more A-levels but also a much higher proportion achieving no GCE or CSE qualification of any kind. In the same year, 22.4 percent of Northern Ireland students left schools with no qualifications while in England and Wales the figures were 9.5 percent and 17.7 percent.

In terms of sorting and selecting their charges for their differing stations in life, the two types of examinations and the two types of school in which they are pursued seem to do their jobs remarkably well. In the grammar schools, less than 1.5 percent of pupils fail to achieve some sort of examination qualification. Of those consigned to secondary intermediate schools less than 5 percent ever achieve the elusive one A-level (Wilson 1987). "In educational terms, Northern Ireland has very poorly served the vast majority of its school leavers" (Cormack, Miller, and Osborne 1987, 10-11).

Conclusion

The social, political and economic circumstances of the 1970s and the 1980s have caused most societies to examine seriously the relationship of their schools to policies of national development. In Northern Ireland, the adult population reflects upon its segregated school experience and inevitably wonders if therein lies the source of its community divisions; if "the Troubles" that began this time around in 1969 might have been avoided if the Province's children had been educated together; if a community reconciliation could be effected had they but shared a common educational experience. Perhaps! But reconciliation requires elements that are fundamentally reconcilable. To be Catholic, republican and Irish may not be reconcilable with being Protestant, loyalist and British. In 1990 there is no ideal that can cast these traits in a subordinate role (as did the foreign wars in 1914 and in 1939) though some look to the evolution of the European Community as providing one possible means whereby the divisions in Ulster will simply be superseded. To look to schooling in Northern Ireland, itself a manifestation of deep-seated divisions, as a means of resolving the same deep-seated divisions, may be as facile as it is naive. Nevertheless, the expectations of schools are high in many quarters. In the context of historical inertia and contemporary interest the best estimate of success may have been provided by those teachers who sense that they are of but little influence in the totality of determining factors.

References

Belfast Telegraph. 1987. Editorial. February, 23.

Bowman, J. 1988. Chance to overcome classroom apartheid. *The Sunday Times* (Northern Ireland Edition) October 9, B3.

Clarke, L. 1988. Ulster takes a new lesson in integration. *The Sunday Times* (Northern Ireland Edition), October 9, H2.

Cormack, R. J., R. L. Miller, and R. D. Osborne. 1987. Introduction. In R. D. Osborne, R. J. Cormack and R. L. Miller, eds. *Education and Policy in Northern Ireland.* Belfast: Policy Research Institute.

Daly, P. 1987. School effectiveness and pupils' performance in Northern Ireland. In Osborne, Cormack and Miller, eds. *Education and Policy in Northern Ireland.* Belfast: Policy Research Institute.

Darby J., and S. Dunn. 1987. Segregated schools: the research evidence. In Osborne, Cormack and Miller, eds. *Education and Policy in Northern Ireland.* Belfast: Policy Research Institute.

Dunn, S. 1986. *Education and the Conflict in Northern Ireland: A Guide to the Literature.* Coleraine: Centre for the Study of Conflict, University of Ulster.

Dunn, S., J. Darby, and K. Mullan. 1984. *Schools Together?* Coleraine: Centre for the Study of Conflict, University of Ulster.

Finnegan, A. 1985. Evaluation of a holiday scheme for Northern Irish children: Selected case studies. Unpublished B.A. dissertation, the Queen's University of Belfast.

Greer, J. E., and E. P. McElhinney. 1980. *Teaching Religion in Ireland: An Introduction for Teachers.* Coleraine: Education Centre, the New University of Ulster.

Livingstone, J. 1987. Equality of opportunity of education in Northern Ireland. In Osborne, Cormack and Miller, eds. *Education and Policy in Northern Ireland.* Belfast: Policy Research Institute.

O'Connor, S. 1980. Chocolate cream soldiers: Evaluating an experiment in non-sectarian education in Northern Ireland. *Journal of Curriculum Studies* 12(3): 263-266.

Schools Cultural Studies Project. (1980). *Cultural and Social Studies for Secondary Schools: Teachers' Handbook.* Belfast: Association of Teachers of Cultural and Social Studies.

Skilbeck, M. (1973). The school and cultural development. *The Northern Teacher* 11(1): 13-18.

Sockett, H. (1987). Comprehensive education in Northern Ireland: the continuing debate. In Osborne, Cormack and Miller, eds. *Education and Policy in Northern Ireland.* Belfast: Policy Research Institute.

Spencer, A. E. C. W. 1987. Arguments for an integrated schools system. In Osborne, Cormack and Miller, eds. *Education and Policy in Northern Ireland.* Belfast: Policy Research Institute.

Trew, K. (1989). Evaluating the impact of contact schemes for Catholic and Protestant children. In J. Harbison, ed. *Growing Up in Northern Ireland.* Belfast: Stranmillis College.

Wilson, J. A. (1987). Selection for Secondary School. In Osborne, Cormack and Miller, eds. *Education and Policy in Northern Ireland.* Belfast: Policy Research Institute.

NATION STATES, DIVERSITY AND INTERCULTURALISM: ISSUES FOR BRITISH EDUCATION

Jagdish Gundara and Crispin Jones

This chapter develops some of the major issues in intercultural education as they are manifested within the British context.[1] Although reference will be made to current English[2] educational policy and practice in relation to national diversity, the principal purpose is to examine some of the issues that underpin such policy and practice but which are seldom analyzed. The consequences of this, in England at least, are profound. Much of the work in relation to education in and for multicultural society in Britain contains internal contradictions, and, more importantly, neither reduces the discriminatory and prejudiced behaviour of many white pupils, teachers, and

---

[1] An earlier version of this chapter appeared in Alladin and Bacchus (1990). Development of this work is currently being undertaken by the Centre for Multicultural Education, University of London. We are grateful to Keith Kimberley and Paul Whelan for their helpful comments.

[2] *Britain, England* and *the United Kingdom* refer to different national entities. As discussed later in the chapter, the problem is that the English conflate the terms, ignoring the existence of not just the Welsh, Scottish, and Irish nationalities within the United Kingdom, but also other non-territorial British groups such as Afro-Caribbeans.

students nor improves the educational attainments of many groups of minority students.

The debate about definitional terms in relation to concepts of the nation state and pluralism is examined first, in order to clarify the context within which the educational debate takes place. Then follows an analysis of the ways in which the concept of multiculturalism may be best examined. The model chosen is based on an investigation of social group discrimination within nation state contexts, initially using a model derived from the comparative education work of Nicholas Hans (1949). In turn this leads to a taxonomic arrangement by which state responses to diversity might be analyzed. The analytical and conceptual structures derived from these analyses are then used to examine current educational policy and practice in Britain, including a critique of the "new right" radicalism and its influence on such educational policies.

Theoretical Model

Confusion often arises over the use of the terms Briton, Britain and British, especially when they are used by the English. To many English people, English/British, England/Britain are synonyms. Clarification of this, a task that the Scots, the Welsh and the other British minorities find non-problematic, leads to a re-examination of concepts of the nation, nationality(ies), nationalism and the nation state. It is a more helpful starting point than the more usual multicultural, multiracial, and multiethnic in relation to education, although those terms do need scrutiny. Through the concept of the nation these terms achieve their full resonance.

Thus we would argue that most nation states are stratified polyethnic states using a variety of mechanisms to maintain their social and economic stratification, usually presented with an accompanying rhetoric emphasising societal cohesion. Such stratification has operationalising criteria extending beyond class/status and gender, *because* of the way in which the modern nation state is structurally and ideologically constructed. It is not surprising that the modern nation state is based on a fallacious ideal-typical model of a small scale society because the modern unitary nation state disguises its predatory[3] origins by attempting to demonstrate a hegemonic unity in terms of its citizens' allegiances and affiliations.

Such a unity codifies the social and economic arrangements of the dominant group(s) and legitimates an unequal set of socio-economic arrangements. Within this model, members of a nation state should share one or more of the following characteristics: 1) the same language and economic arrangements; 2) a common history; 3) if religion is present, it should be one accepted, if not believed in, by all; 4) a common set of cultural practices, which include aesthetic preferences; and so on (Hans 1949). Groups that fail to meet these and similar criteria are seen as "the other" or as "alien" to the nation and potentially divisive. Consequently, there is a tendency to locate such groups at the periphery of the nation, to refuse to accept them but to tolerate them to a degree that is dependent on the economic and socio-political needs of the dominant groups or groups within that nation. Such dominant groups often see themselves as the legitimately constituted nation, and use the "others" to maintain such an ideological fiction. The dominant may take extreme positions that would be repudiated by civilized society or it may simply reflect popular fears and discrimination. Such a perspective helps to position many minority ethnic and racial groups at the periphery of the nation, in cultural, political, and economic, as well as spatial terms.

This is currently well illustrated in France, where recent electoral successes by an extreme right wing party were built upon such excluding and exclusive concepts of the nation (Marnham 1989). Sadly, such success has led the Socialist

---

[3] By the term "predatory," we imply the manner in which the modern nation state has developed through time by the incorporation of other territorial groups. Examples of this would be the French nation state and the Bretons, or the English nation state and the Welsh. These modern examples resemble earlier, often forgotten annexations, e.g. the Friesians in the Netherlands.

government to weigh tightening immigration controls and expelling more illegal immigrants. It is worth noting that illegal immigration, although seemingly unexceptional, is very likely to be seen and experienced by many in the French Muslim community. It "justifies" their greater harassment by various national agencies, particularly the police.[4]

This process has a long history in the British context. The denial of a capacity to belong to the nation leads to marginalization of groups, some because they can be "racially" defined (as is the case with Black people in the British context), and others as "different" (the case of the Irish) (Hechter 1975). This has clear implications for both British cities, within which live the great majority of Britain's black and different populations, and for the education that is provided in them. This is because of the spatial consequences that can arise from the increase in intra-collective communication and associated greater status solidarity that results from rejection by, and/or hostility from dominant and/or majority groups within British society. In other words, ghetto formation, in both its physical and spiritual manifestations, remains an active element in British urban society.

Immigrant groups (using the term in its correct sense) in Britain are often marginalized by the dominant groups within the nation state.[5] Their socio-spatial marginalisation is reinforced by legislation concerning their status in British society. Thus, successive British governments have introduced ever more complex immigration and nationality laws, supposedly to preserve the nation from being "swamped" by alien cultures. This legislative framework has become one which few other nation states would wish. Indeed, if the subordinated groups are defined out of the concept of the nation, and can

---

[4] This problem is not confined to France. There has been a fierce debate within Italy about the need to strengthen immigration controls and to police them more effectively.

[5] The plural used is deliberate, as the marginalisation is not solely the province of one dominant elite.

only belong through a process of self-denial and rejection of their own identity, it is difficult to see how such exclusive states can do otherwise. What is surprising and a cause of serious concern is the marginalisation of certain groups within the British nation state who are *not* immigrant: many black British citizens remain as marginalized as their immigrant ancestors, unlike white British citizens with similar origins.

Thus racist stratification in Britain sustains and creates national divisions that result in advantaged and disadvantaged groups having unequal access to power and resources. The reproduction of this structure through the education system helps to ensure its inter-generational continuation.[6] An example of this process can be seen in the history and contemporary position of the long established black community in Liverpool. Still often regarded as in some way not British, primarily because they are black, they are economically and socially marginalised within a city that is disadvantaged vis-a-vis the South East dominated British nation state. The educational attainment of Liverpool blacks continues to remain at a very low level, despite their community's efforts to make the education system more responsive to their educational needs (Department of Education and Science (DES) 1985).

This increasing ethnic and racial socio-spatial differentiation in the cities of Britain has serious implications for inner city school populations. For example, in Tower Hamlets, an inner city borough in London, 46 percent of the primary pupils speak a language other than English as their first language. There are twenty-nine schools (out of a total of ninety-five) where the majority of pupils have a home language other than English and at least two where none of the children have English as their home language (Tower Hamlets 1988). This is a trend which the open admissions policies introduced by the 1988 Education Act is likely to intensify because white parents may avoid sending their children to schools with a high

---

[6] This is not to argue for this form of stratification as being the sole factor in inequalities within society. Class/status and gender are clearly equally important areas for analysis.

percentage of black pupils.[7] "Segregated" schools for black and white children are, in the vast majority of cases, as inherently unequal in England as they were (are) in the United States.[8]

Such examples demonstrate that within metropolitan democratic societies like Britain, peripheral groups seldom have sufficient access to significant institutions to bring about a reallocation of power and resources. Such groups consequently remain unrepresented, under-represented or tokenistically represented in the dominant social institutions. A survey by the Inner London Education Authority (ILEA 1985) of its school governors well demonstrates this point. It found that although Afro-Caribbean pupils constituted 15.6 percent of the school population, only 2.7 percent of school governors were from that group. A similar picture (11.7 percent: 1.7 percent) was apparent in relation to the Asian community. This lack of adequate representation usually implies a lack of power, although there are exceptions (Castells 1983).

The nature of the epistemological stance taken in relation to an individual's or a group's perception of objective interests is important.[9] What is implied by group silence in the face of denial of access and resources?

Only detailed empirical case-by-case studies have given any useful pointers. One useful British example is Peter Saunders' (1980) examination of urban politics in Croydon, a Conservative-party-dominated local authority in outer London, which indicated that all such responses were possible. As he states:

---

[7] Parents who move their children from multiracial to monoracial (white) schools are not breaking Britain's Race Relations Act, according to the Department of Education and Science. This claim may be tested in the courts.

[8] If the minority community itself sets up a separate school, as is beginning to happen in Britain, a different set of outcomes may occur.

[9] This matter is discussed, *inter alia*, in Lukes (1974).

Put another way, it seems that grievances are often subjectively recognised, but that they fail to surface in the political system because of fatalism (it would not do any good to protest), fear (what would happen to us if we did protest?) and exclusion (how can we protest?). (p. 295)

Such a seemingly unhelpful finding emphasises the complexity of the issues involved, particularly when groups and/or individuals seek to speak for "their" community.

The issue for minority groups attempting to make their voices heard in education seems to be one of constructing an anti-hegemonic ideology that offers the possibility of successful intervention and/or protest. Unfortunately, much of what passes for multiculturalism does not attempt this. Walzer's (1982) note in relation to the United States has equal validity in the British context: "But ethnic pluralism, as it developed in the United States, cannot plausibly be characterised as an antistate ideology. Its advocates did not challenge the authority of the federal government" (p. 11).

The consequences of our analysis are clear. The multicultural, plural nature of the modern state becomes a major problem for those states whose cohesion is defined in terms of the core values of an exclusivist dominant group. Within Britain, the Welsh and the Scots look with envy at Separatist movements in the USSR and Spain.

These examples raise a more fundamental set of questions: can the modern polyethnic and culturally plural nation state survive in its current guise? how should a national education system deal with this issue? In order to address these questions more systematically, the concept of diversity has to be clarified, a task to which we now turn.

The nature of the modern nation state is more problematic than is often maintained in educational discourse. So are the elements that traditionally have been seen as its constituents. Their problematic position is seen as such from both the left and the right. For Professor Roger Scruton (1982), a well-known British right wing radical critic of progressive views of multiculturalism, the criteria for multiculturalism are also the criteria for the unitary nation state: "language, religion, custom, associations and traditions of political order--in short, all those forces that generate nations" (p. 14). The use of the singular rather than the plural for language, religion, and custom is significant. If pluralised, the terms that Scruton uses may develop a new reality, beyond the mythology of the modern nation state. Using such terms in an attempt to understand the pressures affecting national education systems are not new. Over forty years ago, Nicholas Hans (1949) identified religious, linguistic, geographical, racial, and political "factors" as significant for a range of educational issues.

Such a framework has often been the basis for analyses of multiculturalism by British writers. However, we would include a wider range of significant categories to permit a more sophisticated analysis of societal diversity and to critique the simple polarities that are frequently used to define and divide the population.

Our framework would define national diversity in terms of *axes* of social and national division rather than simple polarities, which are often based on a simple "them" and "us" division. The axes intersect amongst themselves, bringing about a greater range of potential diversities within a given society. Thus, social categories such as class, status, gender, sexual orientation, race, language, religion, disability and spatial location or territoriality can be used in very different ways, reflecting the individual or institutional attitude towards the unitary nation state.

Educational Implications

Such a model helps in our analysis of the genesis of stereotypes in the wider society and the educational stereotypes that they foster and engender. Of particular significance are concepts of intelligence and educability, which have been differentially ascribed to groups within the nation on the basis of stereotypes. For example, in many British schools, Afro-Caribbean boys are seen as "non-academic" students although supposedly good at certain types of games. Even the games are supported by stereotypes: it took many years before British Afro-Caribbean professional football players could be seen as anything but fast offensive players, devoid of the temperament and skills that make a good defensive player.

Green's work on classroom interactions, reported in the Swann Report (DES 1985) clearly revealed how the teachers' stereotypes of minority students were a significant factor in their interactions with such students, usually but not always to the student's detriment. This can lead to a seeming confirmation of the stereotype, a self- fulfilling prophecy. Such practice contributes to the poor educational attainments of many minority group children in British schools.

The educational attainment of minority group children is based on notions of success and excellence that are defined in majority cultural terms. This is clearly a complex area. However, given the massive increase in assessment in British schools that is being brought about through the implementation of the 1988 Education Act, it is likely to be a significant issue for the next few years.

National diversity is ignored and/or parodied through such educational arrangements and stereotypes, but such factors are not the sole contributors to poor educational attainment. School organisation, the curriculum, teaching styles--indeed the whole pedagogy of the school seldom challenges the dominant assertions about the diversity within British society. If the dominant assertions go unchallenged, working class children may be regarded as stupid: and their parents as uncaring about their childrens' education; stereotypical gender roles for both boys and girls may be reinforced; religions other than Christianity may be still regarded as peripheral. Such a list could go on and on. These few examples reveal the potential value of a taxonomic framework for the effective analysis of the racism, xenophobia, prejudice, and discrimination. It also demonstrates that struggles over gender and class/status oppression within (and between) nation states are interlinked with those over, say, race, religion, and language. It enables a more effective analysis of practical issues, creating potential for more successful intervention and reform.

Multiculturalism in Britain has often been presented as over-simplified and atheoretical.[10] Social and educational policy and practice in relation to societal diversity, whatever the political stance that has been taken, has been consequently oversimplified and often ineffective.

Taxonomic frameworks for analysis such as that of Street-Porter (1976), although invaluable in their time, need reworking in terms of current knowledge. Her framework was used mechanistically (for example, by the ILEA),[11] reminiscent of how Piaget's developmental theories were misrepresented in initial teacher training in Britain in the 1960s and 1970s.

Reworking the taxonomies is also needed for two reasons: 1) they often ignore the fact that Britain, like other European nation states, has always been a multicultural society and has not just recently become one, 2) they fail to bind education about educational disadvantage and poor attainment as issues of multiculturalism in education to a broader set of educational issues such as equality of educational opportunity and outcomes, educational entitlements and issues relating to more general democratic and human rights.[12]

However, the taxonomies contain valuable elements, most noticeably the recognition of the power of the minority communities to alter educational policy and practice affecting their members.

Such a re-evaluation also points not so much to a framework of societal and educational response to diversity on a continuum from assimilation, through integration, cultural

---

[10] Of course it could be argued that some of the writing in the area has been excessively and unhelpfully theoretical.

[11] See for example the taxonomic analysis in ILEA (1983), parts 2 through 5.

[12] Much of the debate about anti-racist education within the British context during the 1980s ignored, or was unaware of the significance of the black minorities' interventions in policy debates throughout the 1970s and early 1980s.

pluralism, and anti-racism, but to an *oscillating polarity*, between separation/segregation and assimilation, or put another way, between pluralism and "unitarianism." Such a model is one on which British practice can be better located, as it allows for the backward and forward nature of British educational policy and practice in this area.

Such a taxonomy can be used to explore briefly the way in which the various interested parties in British education changed and renegotiated their roles in the light of changing educational policies and practices. Although the motive force for such changes may have laid outside the educational debate, an attempt will be made to interweave the two themes.

Policies of the 1970s and Early 1980s

Up until the 1980s, most educational policy in relation to societal diversity followed the Street-Porter model. Social and educational policy gradually accepted cultural pluralism and acknowledged the racism and xenophobia in the wider society. The apogee of this movement in education was the publication in 1985 of the official governmental enquiry into the educational performance of minority groups within the British educational system. This report, entitled *Education for All*, or more usually, the *Swann Report*, is a valuable source, summarising much of what had and had not been achieved over the previous two decades.

However, many of its main recommendations were disregarded by the government, which was guided by the ideological shifts in political thinking at that time. For the move to the right was in fact a more complex set of realignments and repositionings of the Conservative Government, and the Conservative Party and its supporters.

There are at least three elements in this ideological restructuring. The first was market libertarianism. Often associated with the monetarist economic writings of Hayek (1954), it placed an unusual reliance on the power of the market to minimize inefficiency, create wealth, and benefit all in differing degrees. In other words, certain forms of inequality, particularly economic inequality, were seen as a necessary part of the market's regulatory power. As Sir Keith Joseph (one time Minister of Education in the Conservative administration) said,

> The blind, unplanned, uncoordinated wisdom of the market . . . is overwhelmingly superior to the well researched, rational, systematic, well meaning, co-operative, science based, forward looking, statistically respectable plans of governments . . . (Quoted in Lawton 1989, 35)

This opposed most aspects of the social consensus that had prevailed in Britain since 1944. From the Conservative perspective, if there were problems with educational attainment, untrammelled market forces (such as a voucher policy where parents could pick and choose an education to their liking) would quickly restore efficiency into the system.

The second element demonstrated that Conservative supporters *did* want to interfere with the market when they thought it was essential in order to maintain the greater values of social order and national sovereignty. In respect of diversity, where the workings of a free market might encourage temporary in-migration in order to keep wages down, this strand of conservatism wished for ever stronger immigration controls to keep "visible" minorities from entering the country. Many even encouraged the "repatriation" of those already here and they made little or no distinction between British black or immigrant. If these Conservatives had an educational policy, it defended white English culture, promoted its ascendency, and reinforced assimilation into this culture.

For much of the 1960s and 1970s, the educational views of these Conservatives were seldom considered seriously. However, they gained wider support within the Conservative administration and the mass media as the right wing counter to what was increasingly being seen as the "loony left."

In education, they first opposed antiracist education, particularly as espoused by Labour controlled local education authorities such as the ILEA and the London Boroughs of Brent and Haringey. These Authorities' policies on gender were also seen as threatening to all those values which "every Englishman [*sic*] held dear." Policies relating to gays and lesbians were seen as intended to turn all children into gays and lesbians. As the Hillgate Group (1986) asserted, in a document that clearly influenced the 1988 Education Act, there was a real worry that "traditional" values were being destroyed with schools "preaching on behalf of homosexuality, sexual license and social indiscipline" (p. 4).

Thirdly, the Conservatives were more tolerant on religious matters, recognising similar reactionary tendencies within the range of faiths of British inner city schools. However, religious tolerance went against the spirit of assimilation, so their tolerance was seldom more than provisional, as the 1988 Education Act showed.

The fourth strand conflicts with this traditional conservativism and is shared by some parties. This strand is meritocratic, and is based on the assumption that if the race is fair, the losers deserve to lose and the winners deserve all the prizes. To this group, tradition is worthless unless it supports efficiency, modernisation and the development of a meritocracy. Such a meritocracy is not egalitarian but within it, people, and by implication, school children, get their just deserts.

Clearly, there is much in common with the market-led strand of thinking, with debate on the degree to which government should intervene. In education, it questions anything that cannot demonstrate its contribution to the economic growth of the society. Given the innate conservatism of most education systems, this perspective led in the early 1980s to removal of huge areas of educational activity away from the Department of Education and Science and also from schools and to the huge expansion of vocational education and training, partly induced by political worries about the high levels of youth unemployment.

Opposition to this system splitting was belated and often equally disastrous. There was a demand to stick with the educational consensual policies of the 1960s and 1970s, with their stress on relevance, mixed ability teaching, and the non-selective comprehensive secondary school. As this system had not worked for many minority school students, few supported the "consensus," while nostalgia for grammar schools disguised the fact that they had never really been a significant instrument for working class social mobility and would offer very little to minority communities, either in terms of access and outcome. And when the electorate returned a Conservative government with an even bigger majority in 1987, the "consensus" was quickly attacked. There was little specific minority protest. Subsequently opposition moved away from consensus toward a more social democratic educational model in the hope of capturing the middle ground of educational politics. This policy will be tested at the next General Election, likely to be held in 1992. In the meantime the schooling system grapples with the details of the new Education Act and has little time to assess alternative strategies.

The Education Reform (1987) and the Education Act (1988)

The return to social policies based on assimilation has largely gone unchallenged, given the electoral unpopularity of pluralism within England. When the government introduced the Educational Reform Bill in 1987, incorporating much of the educational thinking that had emerged within the Conservative party over nearly a decade in office, the opposition to it was often ill-organised and inefficient.

The consequence is an Education Act which is likely to do little to enhance the educational aspirations of minority parents and pupils. The introduction of inherently unfair market forces into education will very likely parallel and ultimately strengthen those forces which maintain many minority group adults in unemployment or poorly paid work. The return to "traditional" (i.e. English white male middle class) values within the curriculum will further alienate many children from their schooling. Worse, it will alienate them from their own communities as they attempt to assimilate into a society which does not want them and into an epistemological system in which they have no place or voice. And if the education system is seen as more meritocratic, failure within it will bring about even greater stigmatisation than there is at present. These changes implicitly espouse assimilation, which is likely to continue and deepen current educational inequalities.

An evolving literature (e.g. Jones 1990) details the consequences for education of this shift in political and educational thinking that has taken place over the last decade. As elsewhere, the initiatives that have resulted from it may mark the end of a process of change rather than its beginning. If the concept of an oscillating polarity has value, which factors might return pluralism to the British educational agenda? One possibility is Britain's developing relations with its European partners.

1989 will go down in the history books in a very similar way to 1848,[13] because of the extraordinary power of nationalism within the European context, the powerful emotions that such nationalism can engender, and the dramatic speed with which its message travels.

---

[13] In January 1848, in Palermo, Italy, the people came onto the streets to protest against the incompetence of their ruler, Ferdinand II of Naples. In the months that followed, the demonstrations spread across Italy and by the end of the year, few parts of Europe had not been shaken by rebellion, revolution, or protest. In France, the Second Republic had been established, in Austria-Hungary, Metternich was forced out of office, while in Britain, the activities of the Chartists made fear of revolution a major concern of government. (1848 also saw the publication of the Communist Manifesto). A primary focus of this continental revolution was national aspirations faced with inflexible and conservative authoritarianism. Yet by 1849, counter-revolutions had regained for the authoritarians much of the power lost in 1848. The very speed of the changes had been too great for permanence.

Europe's Challenge

Thus as England moves towards a narrow exclusivist definition of the British nation, events within the Soviet Union, Eastern Europe, and the European Community are moving in an opposite direction, pulling Britain and other European Community states towards greater unity, posing further questions to those raised in the previous sections and countering to those aspects of current British educational policy that encourage assimilationism. Nationality and nationalism, which pose very real questions for all shades of political and educational opinion within the Community, are seen as best resolved by greater plurality within as well as between the nation states that make it up.

This is not new. Britain has always hoped that certain *between* nation state issues could be resolved through the mechanisms of the Community, for example those relating to Spain and Gibraltar and Northern Ireland and the Republic of Ireland. What Britain (or at least its current government) is loath to accept, is a plurality *within* the nation state: the aspirations of the Scots in Scotland or the British Afro-Caribbean in England.

However, dramatic recent events in the USSR and Yugoslavia do little to change the assimilationist tendencies enshrined in the 1988 Education Act, although they have long-term consequences. Current arguments within the European Community over education still centre on the legality of Community involvement in educational work in the first place, as it is a power reserved to the nation states by the original Treaty of Rome. However, European concern with the educational fate of migrants and other minorities has frequently kept the educational debate within the Community flourishing, even if conducted without too much overt reference to formal schooling.

As an example of the value of such debate, concern about language within the Community led to a series of legally binding European Community Directives about language and the language rights (including educational entitlements) of minorities that counter the recent direction of the British government. "Market forces" and the "neutrality of the meritocracy" are not enough to match the linguistic and associated educational rights of migrants and other national minorities.

Current minority educational inadequacies are blamed upon inadequate national governmental responses, which have been inadequate for years (e.g. the national case studies in Gundara, Jones and Kimberley 1982). This counterbalancing debate strengthens the opposition within the British nation state. Most recently, a vast European Community initiative for language teaching, the *Lingua Project*, was bitterly opposed by Britain on the grounds that it dealt with education.[14] Although the British view was technically correct, the project had the enthusiastic backing of other states and has been adopted. Its implementation will support   linguistic plurality and the educational needs of bilingual learners in mainstream British education.

Perhaps most important of all is the nature of the new European society that is emerging as the Community moves towards 1992 and greater economic and political union. The assimilationist ideology of the British nation state and the 1988 Education Act is widely decried by E.C. partners as being outmoded and unrealistic. The world view of the British electorate is increasingly shaped within a Community context.

Some consequences of this change are already apparent. The "Eurospeak" phrase for pluralistic initiatives in relation to education, "intercultural education,"[15] has enabled educationists across the Community and within the wider European context that is supported by the Council of Europe, to exchange

---

[14] This ambitious and expensive (200 million ECU) program was approved by the EC Education Council in May 1988 only after prolonged and acrimonious debate about the right of the EC to be involved in schools. For details of the actual Lingua Project, see *Eurydice Info* (1989).

[15] For accounts of this concept, see Batelaan (1983), and Jones and Kimberley (1986, 1990).

contexts and practice within common frame of reference. This potential for development and change extends beyond educationists. Minorities, for example the Romany, have made new groupings that transcend national boundaries, giving them the potential to intervene both at the national and the European levels. It also has the potential to enable minorities to gain a platform in their own right, avoiding, if they wish, the device of using the nation state of origin as their sponsor.

Thus, a new world begins to counter the old. As educational policy in Britain moves in the direction of assimilation, Europe helps those forces within British education who desire a more pluralistic perspective. To predict the outcome of this debate is beyond the scope of this chapter. Its prospect provides an opportunity to end on a modestly optimistic note.

References

Alladin M., and K. Bacchus, eds. 1990. *Education, Politics and State in Multicultural Societies.* Needham Heights: Ginn Press.

Batelaan, P. 1983. *The Practice of Intercultural Education.* London: Commission for Racial Equality.

Castells, M. 1983. *The City and the Grassroots.* London: Arnold.

DES. 1985. Education for All (The Swann Report). London: HMSO, Department of Education and Science.

Eurydice Info. 1989. December, no. 8.

Gundara, J., C. Jones, and K. Kimberley. 1982. *The Marginalisation and Pauperisation of the Second Generation of Migrants in France, the Federal Republic of Germany and Great Britain, Relating to the Education of the Children of Migrants.* Final Report and Three National Case Studies. Brussels: Commission of the European Communities.

Hans, N. 1949. *Comparative Education.* London: Routledge.

Hayek, F. A., ed. 1954. *Capitalism and the Historians.* Chicago: University of Chicago Press.

Hechter, M. 1975. *Internal Colonialism: The Celtic Fringe in British National Development.* Berkeley: University of California Press.

Hillgate Group. 1986. *Whose School? A Radical Manifesto.* London: The Hillgate Group.

ILEA. 1983. *Race, Sex and Class.* London: Inner London Education Authority.

_____. 1985. *Survey of Governing Bodies*. RS 998/85, July. London: ILEA Research and Statistics Branch Report.

Jones, C., and K. Kimberley, eds. 1986. *Intercultural Education: Concept, Context, Curriculum*. Strasbourg: Council of Europe.

_____. 1990. *Intercultural Perspectives on the National Curriculum for England and Wales*. London: Centre for Multicultural Education, Institute of Education.

Jones, K. 1989. *Right Turn: The Conservative Revolution in Education*. London: Hutchinson.

Lawton, D., ed. 1989. *The Education Reform Act: Choice and Control*. London: Hodder & Stoughton.

Lukes, S. 1974. *Power: A Radical View*. London: Macmillan.

Marnham, P. 1989. French extremists gain from hostility towards Muslims. *The Independent*, December 5.

Saunders, P. 1980. *Urban Politics*. Harmondsworth: Penguin.

Scruton, R. 1982. Thinkers of the left: E. P. Thompson. *Salisbury Review* Autumn(1): 14.

Street-Porter, R. 1976. *Race, Children and Cities*. Milton Keynes: Open University Press.

Tower Hamlets. 1988. *Tower Hamlets Education: Getting It Right. Draft Development Plan*. London: London Borough of Tower Hamlets.

Walzer, M. 1982. Pluralism in political perspective. In M. Walzer et al., *The Politics of Ethnicity*. Cambridge, Mass.: Belknap Press/Harvard University Press.

SECTION IV

INTEGRATION OF RECENT

IMMIGRANTS

INTEGRATION OF RECENT IMMIGRANTS THROUGH SCHOOLING: AN INTRODUCTION

Douglas Ray

Recent immigrants are identified by the authors of this section as those who are foreign born and their dependent children. There are substantial numbers of such migrants in some large nations (the U.S.A., Germany, France, and Canada) and a very large proportion of the population in certain small nations (Israel, Bahrain). Several other nations with the same characteristics have been discussed in Sections II and/or III (Australia, India, Sudan, Britain) where the focus was directed to different aspects of their divided populations.

France is a society with very different traditions. Because metropolitan France has long recognized that regional differences were important to the quality of education that might be available, the national system undertook to equalize opportunities to the extent possible with a uniform curriculum, teachers with similar qualifications, identical examinations, and a system of subsidies. But that system acquired an increased significance when it was applied to overseas colonies and possessions. When colonies won their independence, some of their populations chose to remain French, and many of them have since come to France--particularly from the Mahgreb but also from central Africa and from Vietnam, Cambodia, and Laos. These populations do not fit easily into   metropolitan France. Despite their proficiency in French and in the subjects that they studied in schools, they are not fully accepted by the French, partly because they want to retain some of their.identity (as did the Jews, Gypsies, Huguenots, Alsatians, and Corsicans) for a life that may extend over many generations in France.

413

How can such new minorities be protected and to what extent must they be integrated into metropolitan cultures and institutions? For perhaps a greater degree than ever before, the French educational community has been decentralized, liberated to try those things that common sense and experience suggest might be useful, and subsequently endorsed by the establishment. This is particularly important in the education of teachers from the minority communities.

France is discussed only from the perspective of foreign born minorities. The large immigrant population is technically French, for De Gaulle disposed of the French Empire by making all colonies into *departements* of France--the equivalent of Corsica. Citizens were thereby entitled to migrate to metropolitan France, and the educational systems of their youth in the colonies theoretically provided the same standards as were available in Paris or Burgundy. This equal status was not accepted by traditionalists among the French populace and racial tensions existed in those locations where a large migrant population settled. The tensions were particularly high when the migrants were not descended directly from French *colons* (colonizing settlers) of an earlier generation but were the colonials--perhaps of another race.

The questions of how to deal with these divisions within French society are complex and concern education at several levels. One of the most important goals is to ensure that the schools now attended by the migrants are as well taught as possible, and the decision was made to ensure that the teachers would be, or would include, members of the minority communities. The teacher education programs of France were unable to meet the requirements for this kind of professional and new programs were set up and allowed to experiment. This is an unprecedented departure from the tradition of control of teacher education by the French government.

Jeannine Bardonnet-Ditte has directed the Paris version of the experiment, with significant independence to adapt and invent the needed courses. The requirements for a basic level of French language and civic education, mathematics and science are to be met, but the migrants also expect that their teachers will know and teach something of the traditions from the former *departements*. It may be significant that there are many objectives which appear to resemble the programs for *Sámi* in Scandinavia, Cree in Manitoba, Basques in Spain, and *Gastarbeiter* in Germany.

Germany has the most complicated and extensive set of divisions in Europe, divisions that have grown in magnitude as a result of four recent changes in Europe.

1) The German economic miracle demanded more workers, and the population was no longer growing, so millions of foreign workers were invited to provide the extra muscle. These guest workers (Gastarbeiter) were mainly from Turkey, Yugoslavia, Greece, and Italy. They were not given German citizenship but were expected to return with their savings to retire in their villages. When they stayed for twenty years and more, and had children born and educated in Germany, their repatriation was doubtful.

2) The European Community decided that all its citizens would enjoy mobility of employment opportunity, so the ambitious from many nations moved to more prosperous Germany.

3) The reunification of Germany in 1990 meant a new group of Germans had the right to seek work anywhere in the nation.

4) An ancient tradition that Germans abroad are welcome to return meant that thousands, perhaps millions, of ethnic Germans from Eastern Europe and the Soviet Union might seek repatriation in the land of their ancestors. This movement has already begun.

The educational consequence of this economic and political *mélange* is not yet clearly defined. Mitter notes that it is ludicrous to deny German status to Gastarbeiter and their children while extending such rights to families that lived for generations or even centuries in a foreign nation. The rest of Europe has different expectations that Germany may be obliged to accept.

The educational responses of different *Laender* (provinces or states) to the four challenges are varied and sometimes predictable from the socio-political views of the ruling party. The policies on languages may also reflect the nation of birth more than the existence of sufficient teachers to provide instruction in the language of the Gastarbeiter. The question of civic education is even more complicated, given the expectation that some of the foreign born are to remain citizens of a country that they may never have seen.

The United States is the most famous "nation of immigrants" and it theoretically never closes the doors to those in need of refuge. In fact, the ambitious flock to the United States, for even if the jobs available are physically demanding and poorly paid, or demand professional qualifications competitive with the best in the world, there are migrants to be found who can and will succeed in them. Of course such migrants compete with those already in line for the available jobs, causing some resentment. The substantial gap between well and poorly qualified migrants means that they need very different educational responses for themselves and their children in the United States. Bilingual educational programs are intended to help the children learn in their mother tongue until they become proficient in English, but in some cases the transitional courses are being used to maintain a language and culture until it acquires a semi-legal status for regional use. The other part of the educational process is to ensure that newcomers are not victimized, so civic and social educational programs are intended to develop positive models. Naturally these programs have implications for both native-born and foreign-born pupils.

Canada is another nation of immigrants, and recently the migration has been more from Asia and the Caribbean than from traditional European sources. Languages and religions have become increasingly diversified. The response has been to avoid discrimination by Constitutional and legal protection, and to promote opportunities for the newcomers by education in the Official Languages of Canada (English and French) and often in the heritage languages of the youth. More than fifty languages are taught in a few school boards and there are often ten or more. Civic and cultural education has similarly been diversified to ensure that all children identify with the school's objectives and have a chance to excel in some aspects of the program. Teacher education has been extended to ensure cultural competence and pedagogical resources for some of the profession.

Bahrain. Very small nations like the Arab oil producing states may have relatively large foreign born populations introduced on a temporary basis. In the case of Bahrain (which has a strongly divided domestic population), guest workers are sometimes allowed to bring their families and send their children to school, but they have no prospect of becoming citizens. Certain guest workers have high salaries and respect but others toil in menial jobs. The education in state schools is intended for Islamic Arabs, and early drop-outs are still high. Private schools offer educationally conscious families an international standard of technical competence. Visitors who accept national, religious and linguistic objectives may attend schools free of charge, but their right to other forms of education (even at their own expense) is subject to control by the state.

Israel. The nation with the highest ratio of foreign born/total population in the world is Israel. That has been the character of its Jewish population from 1948 when the nation was founded by action of the United Nations. Since then the migrants have come in cohorts, founders from Europe and the United States, then Arab nations including North Africa, other Asian nations, the USSR, and Ethiopia. The early years were marked by attempts to socialize migrants according to the idealism that was widely shared by the founders, but over time this has been replaced by a more tolerant attitude. Education still promotes the Hebrew language, religion, and civic education thought necessary for citizenship, and undertakes excellence by international standards in technical education, science, and similar studies.

Section IV emphasizes the experimental character of much education for migrants. Not only do these nations differ in detail among themselves, but often internally also. Many practices have evolved in only a generation or two. Many of these nations offer educational programs for "traditional grievances" that are not offered by nations listed in Section III. These differences cannot easily be dismissed. Although some of the nations differ in the objectives of their migration policies

(Canada from Bahrain or Germany for example) the common aspects of their programs are also important.

Comparisons of the results of various policies and interaction among the legal debates (concerning refugees for example) and the educational policies concerning assimilation or integration of migrants would be desirable. There is only skimpy research as the basis for educational policies concerning millions of people in more than a dozen nations. This gives little comfort to the professionals who are still seeking to do their best.

INTEGRATION OF IMMIGRANTS INTO THE FRENCH SCHOOL SYSTEM: THE LAST TWENTY YEARS

Jeannine Bardonnet-Ditte

Migration had a dramatic impact on the French education system, especially in the early 1970s. The traditionally centralized French system had to face the sudden mass intrusion of non-francophone children in the elementary schools. The response was to create an educational sub-system, which after twenty years of pragmatic (rather than centrally controlled) response, conforms to the needs of the immigrants' children. This progressive adaptation is analyzed through the evolution of the *Centres de Formation et d'Information Scolaire pour les Enfants Immigrants*--CEFISEM (Centers of Training and Information for the Schooling of Immigrant Children).

Given the centralization that characterized France longer than most other countries of Europe, the effects of the "Decentralization Law" of 1982 break with tradition. However, CEFISEM generally conform with nationally defined objectives, programs and methods, for their students will always teach in schools where national objectives, programs, and methods obtain.

The CEFISEM have developed objectives and methods which reflect official policies and also the concerns of recent immigrants. It would be worth knowing if this empiricism--relatively rare in France--has served the national desire for maximum schooling for all children. In other words, do the policies of the past twenty years serve better the needs of foreign children than when migrants were simply assimilated

419

into the French school population, and submitted to the same learning demands?

The CEFISEM were created where immigration was most intense. Soon, teachers realized they could not assimilate the non-francophone students without compromising the success of either the immigrant or the French students. In 1970, The Ministry created "initiation classes" for elementary schools by simply ratifying local initiatives. In these, the non-francophones were taught the French language before being sent to regular classes with their French age peers. The Minister authorized a large number of initiatives, recognizing the creative ideas of local authorities and teachers. Now these initiatives were to be rationalized, just as similar action in 1973 officially established the structure for initiating non-francophones into the secondary school.

Since then, a board of teachers, guided by the equality principles from *The Declaration of Human Rights (1789)*, has confronted the technical difficulties in the insertion of non-francophones into the school system. The structures of initiation could become closed, as has been defended by some because of their "effectiveness" and by the "feeling of security" that they give to the students; but attacked by others as "ghettoes" where teachers have to solve problems that the Ministry cannot. Alternatively, they could be open, with students free to attend progressively more of the activities of their French peers, and to receive French lessons. The creation of specific structures for initiation was dictated by the shortage of qualified teachers and has never been accompanied by strict ministerial instructions. These criteria have produced flexible measures, which progressively accomodate to the needs of the students and to the professional capacities of teachers to teach the program.

It soon seemed that professional success depended upon teachers receiving adapted training, so the Ministry of Education started the progressive creation of the CEFISEM where required. In 1976, the centres of Douai, Grenoble, Paris and Aix-Marseille were established close to the Normal Schools of these areas. The Ministry created twenty-four CEFISEM in ten years--practically one for each academy.

Official guidelines do not define the precise missions of these centres. Based on general mandates, they proposed contents that they considered to be appropriate to the needs of the school teachers and professors of the colleges. In fact, the CEFISEM have always maintained the common references of official instructions issued for the whole French system. In 1970, they recommended that the initiation classes in elementary schools should adapt the methods of teaching French as a second language to non-francophones. In 1973, they called of priority to the oral language and for "the learning of a current French, indispensable for a day-to-day life."

But (probably fortunately) these recommendations were too schematic to influence the coherent national training policies, as defined in the Normal Schools for the training of teachers for a general educational system. Moreover, through diplomatic relations between France and the immigrant countries, the teaching of mother tongues and cultures of the migrants was imposed on the schools, either by integrating or by deferring classes, but again without clear objectives or consultation of teachers and professors.

By March 1986 the activities of the CEFISEM had been outlined in *the policies of integration in the schools.* In a political speech by the National Minister of Education the proposed changes were:

1) inserting immediately all children into the educational system,

2) teaching of French and other basic subjects and skills,

3) appointing professors with training of French as a second language,

4) communicating with the families,

5) differentiating linguistic difficulties to match them more closely with specific pedagogy,

6) distinguishing linguistic differences from more general difficulties which are treated within a common frame, and

7) promoting interest for cultures other than French--as "needed in a world with increasing common international affairs."

These official mandates derived from the local political desire for a firm integration. They also reflected the abundant and disorganized richness of the work of CEFISEM during their first decade. In fact, during the period 1976-1986, the CEFISEM tried to clarify the needs in teacher training by following closely the evolution of the immigrant chidren, establishing relations with universities, and visiting the association in charge of immigrants to France. Each CEFISEM has built its unique responses on the bases of its own resources and local problems--to the point that in 1982 the Ministry advised the professors of the centres to create a "tour de France" among the CEFISEM institutions, with students being given the opportunity to work for a few days with partners from different places. This was never before seen in France except in higher levels of university research.

In any case, it is now possible to claim that through the varied creativity of the CEFISEM, the initial mistakes have been corrected. These institutions have progressively developed diversified methods, to meet the general needs of instruction while reflecting the specific cultural differences of the peoples they address.

The central task of the CEFISEM in 1976 was to train teachers and professors of five academies to initiate specific arrival classes for the non-francophone immigrants. These courses focussed on sensitive methods for accelerating the teaching of French. At that time, the CEFISEM naively believed that the methodology for teaching French as a second language could be applied to the particular case of the immigrant children--a scientific simplicity reflected also in Ministerial mandates.

In reality, the foreign children found themselves living in a familiar environment where both cultures were more or less valued. Immigrants of the same nationality might have different aspirations, even when they attended the same initiation classes. For them (as for the French children) socio-economic differences among families are reflected in the development of linguistic ability.

These remarks have quickly driven the CEFISEM to enlarge and diversify the contents of the stages. Certainly, it was agreed to seek scientific information which would better project the characteristics of the French linguistic system and distinguish it from the system of the immigrants' countries of origin. Indeed, technical instruction was needed if French were to become an effective tool of communication in everyday life, and a factor in autonomy in communication. This technical component needed progressively more theoretical references, so that universities increasingly contributed to the functionality of the language. It was necessary to enrich the work of pedagogic formation, particularly by showing that French is learned in all situations, not only in those devoted to learning.

Stimulated by the experiences of student-teachers, drawing upon research in sociology of education and educational socio-linguistics, and thanks to exchanges among CEFISEM, it was soon realized that an apparently specific and even marginal difficulty was in fact a main problem in the educational system, and it concerned all teachers.

How to teach French to the migrant children could not be effectively answered from reflections about the differences between the French used by family and school and the mutual interference. This problem goes beyond the study of language as a technical tool of communication, and introduced the CEFISEM into the more complex field of language as a vehicle for proclaiming, upholding, and communicating culture, reinforcing expression by such means as costumes, plastic arts, and music.

Doubters would accuse the CEFISEM of encouraging multi-cultural practices in the schools, which were targeted as intercultural pedagogy. The Paris CEFISEM took part in a movement directed to the teachers about valuing the cultural identity of both *ourselves* and *others*; focusing on family values, establishing the links between these and the schools, then looking for the success of the children in the school. At the same time, the CEFISEM realized the risk of exoticism, and introduced cultural anthropology into the university research.

Children of some socio-economic groups are almost equally "foreigners" to the language and to the expectations of French culture. The newcomers would require years to become capable of handling the language as a tool of communication; even if they entered normal classes in schools of colleges, they would still face difficulties. The CEFISEM realized the need of providing some pedagogical and social assistance to all teachers and professors who had significant numbers of migrant children in their classrooms, promoting in the schools and colleges studies of their local condition, and working directly with the several associations in charge of the migrant families, literacy classes, kindergartens, etc.

Working with the Normal Schools and the Permanent Group for Fighting Illiteracy, the CEFISEM now provide instruction for all who want to learn, recognizing that children do not succeed in school without the involvement of their families. The task is complicated by the inter-institutional gaps within French society, and by evolution of programs after centralization was replaced by an educational partnership.

The CEFISEM identified several difficulties arising from the teaching of the language and culture of origin:

1) intervention in the schools to decide with the teachers about the organization and curriculum that would minimize the marginalization of children, or their opportunity to learn French in an integrated classroom;

2) courses of language and culture. Teachers that arrive in France need to become familiar with the objectives and methods of the French system so that their students will not be disturbed by huge differences between the two types of teaching;

3) open courses are required, both for general teachers and for teachers of the language and culture of origin; and

4) courses of French language and culture should be accessible to foreign teachers.

The CEFISEM should draw upon general research so that French teachers introduce cultures without stereotyped folklore or exoticism. They would be aware that present cultures introduce distortions and that these are accompanied by a growing list of legends concerning the descendants of earlier migrations.

A new perspective on the problem of education for immigrant children has been outlined. From a foundation in the theoretical field of *language as a communicative tool* and also from language as a *vehicle of a culture*, the CEFISEM addresses language as a *generator of culture.* Although these three dimensions of the topic have always been reflected in the work of the CEFISEM, the urgency of schooling problems, the increasing number and diversity of foreign people, the evolution of international political agreements, and continuing foreign tourism of France, are all factors which explain why there is pressure for action and/or research.

The objective is to define the best schooling for foreign and French born children, so that all may benefit from the mixture of cultures introduced by historical events. In the process, the *origin of a culture* became less significant than its *potential contribution.*

How can society--not only the schools--move toward a French culture that is enriched by the cultures of the immigrants? This question shows the intention to integrate the immigrants without assimilating them. It is essentially the question of any European culture enriched by the culture of another continent.

Such an important question has humanitarian, political and educational dimensions. The school has the mission of opening the minds of youth to future ways of thinking. The CEFISEM deplores the disinterest by primary school teachers who have been trained by secondary school teachers to ignore the influence of qualified professors in economics, international politics, and cultural anthropology. This lack of scholarly reinforcement requires CEFISEM to solve day-to-day difficulties, thereby endangering their training task, although the Ministry is now emphasizing that role.

Foreign born children have increased in numbers sufficient to force the French educational system to deal with their problems. They have made the system acknowledge its important but ill-defined imperfections in the acculturation and learning programs.

When the French Parliament enacted the *Decentralization Law* of 1982, directing schools to open their doors to all social levels (among other things), it enabled several foreigners to establish links with the schools, the local authorities, and the associated world. At the present time, all children (including French) with school difficulties are gaining a place within the multiple organizations linked with the schools and participating in programs that support learning.

The young immigrants now entering their second generation have revealed culture to be a living reality of plural contributions. France has gained from extending its interests beyond its hexagonal borders to reflect a more European way of thinking.

But have immigrants succeeded in the school system they helped to integrate? Has their social and professional integration been promoted in the work of the schools? France cannot answer these questions alone. But the French tradition made universities the guardians of *culture* without attention to the *vocational future of French students*, schools provided general knowledge followed by a brief introduction to a professional formation, and teachers dedicated themselves to the children's service rather than the interests of business. It would be difficult to reject these traditions and evaluate schooling on the basis of the vocational success of graduates.

Why is there a recent need for "jobs for everybody?" In 1981 the "Orientation for higher education" law recommended that universities engage fully in the professional orientation of the students. In 1985 the National Ministry of Education asked schools to emphasize job training, recognizing the social uneasiness about the rising unemployment of youth. Meanwhile, professional colleges, which boast real links with the world of work, have not gained prestige equivalent to the detached but traditional general colleges.

Within this typically French context, one can understand the discreet studies that have been completed. For example, local statistical studies suggest that in comparable socio-economic levels, foreign children have success comparable to that of the French. Their success by the age of twelve is more substantial when they have started kindergarten in France than when they started in their own country.

There is a belief also that foreign children are more likely to be oriented to technical areas than are typical French families, who usually favor longer general studies despite the uncertain outcomes of them. But let us be cautious: how can the tasks of the schools be isolated from the other influences of society? We do not know what impact these contexts have upon the integration of the children.

The conclusion goes with an advance hypotheses: if French public opinion comes to believe that the presence of foreign children will enrich the schools (as we have argued here), if it comes to understand that the immigrants contribute positively to the evolution of the country, then the future aspirations of the two populations will coincide and their hopes will be enlarged and strengthened.

The CEFISEM have confirmed this message in the schools. It is the schools' turn to consolidate public opinion. If they use their technical authorities for justifying the insertion of foreign students, they should also make use of their public influence for helping these same children feel part of a country which commemorates the Bicentenary of the Declaration of Human Rights. This recognition, we believe, is the fundamental condition that foreign children wish for, for it enables them to participate in an integrated French society.

EDUCATIONAL ISSUES IN THE MULTICULTURAL SOCIETY OF GERMANY

Wolfgang Mitter

Basic Considerations:
The Scopes of Multiculturalism

Present-day Germany must be defined as a "multicultural society," although this is contested by "conservative" politicians and ideologists. Their denials extend from feelings of latent indifference and reservation to manifest intolerance and hostility against "strangers" or "foreigners." Although irrational and demagogic, such attitudes are rooted in a narrow perception of what constitutes "German society." This is because:

1) German history is perceived in terms of apparent homogeneity and "monoculturalism" to be traced back to the strength of particularism and to the historically oscillating relations of many Germans to their own national identity. Therefore they fail to take into account, for instance, the remarkable contributions of Huguenots in Prussia and the other former German principalities and Polish miners in the Ruhr-District to the formation of modern "German culture." They ignore the German-Jewish relations and their tragic termination by the Nazi totalitarianism (Spaich 1981, Smolicz 1990).

2) The debate on cultural identity is narrowed to the legal and political status of "German citizens"--the official line of West German (and since 1990 all-German) legislation and policy up to now. Accordingly, the "multinational" component of multiculturalism in present-day Germany (there are 4.6

million "migrants") is reduced to the "foreigners' issue," whereby the illusion of "temporariness" is maintained, as if the bulk of foreigners might leave Germany in the foreseeable future (Cropley 1982).

3) The mental configuration of "Germanity" (*Deutschtum*) which is embedded in the heritage of Romanticism (and has influenced East Central and Eastern Europe), has survived and is today an essential constituent of national identity. It is based on the irrational and vague criteria of descent and ancestry and not on the rational criterion of place of birth used by the French. This explains why "ethnic Germans" (*Volksdeutsche*) immigrating from the Soviet Union and Eastern Europe are accorded German citizenship without any restrictions, while children of migrants who were born in Germany are denied this claim.

All these three views which exist in German society affect educational processes: identifying the legal status of students and teachers; regulating access to the education system, in particular to institutions at the higher education level; developing and implementing curricula and textbooks, particularly in the subjects of German, history, and social studies; controlling parents in school committees, etc. Language teaching has to face the paradox that many children of "Russia-Germans" (*Russlanddeutsche*) must be taught their German "mother tongue" after arriving in Germany, while an increasing number of migrants' children who were born in Germany have a near perfect command of the German language. School instruction must be prepared to cope with both cases.

Beyond these historically based political and educational practices, there is the basic question of cultural identity as one of a people's essential basic rights. Therefore multiculturalism, in its most frequent appearance of "bi-culturalism," must be derived from the evidence that all aspects of "cultures" point to the superordinate notion of "culture" which comprises people's relation to nature, society, to themselves as individuals and to the divine or metaphysical sphere. Culture can be structured in various ways, according to the seeker's curiosity, self-awareness, and action. Social analysts usually classify by social class, age-group, educational standard, political status, religious commitment, ethnic descent, and national loyalty (Mitter 1984).

"Multiculturalism" in this chapter means the narrower sense of "multiethnicity" and "multinationality" with their impacts on education. Multinationality is related to the concept of "nation" or "national group" (nationality), as used by political science and focussed on the feature of national commitment and solidarity. Multiethnicity is identified as a concept rooted in cultural anthropology and cultural sociology. Its features are defined as language, life-styles, and customs. All three terms assume the coexistence of different value systems. In many cases the commitment of a people's values to ethnic or national coherence is linked with religious confession.

While mentioning the criteria of multiethnicity and multinationality, we must not forget their close and complex action among the criteria mentioned above. For instance, the neglect of the interdependence between social class and ethnicity can lead to serious errors. "Foreigners'" or "immigrants'" education usually is associated with schools and educational issues affecting lower classes. The majority of "migrants" in Germany are of peasant descent, having come from their rural homes to metropolitan cities. The bulk of "first generation" Turks have come to Germany from Anatolian villages, not from Istanbul. There is a two-fold problem resulting from the social concern for schooling. On the one hand, such children confront a cultural environment which differs fundamentally from that of their origins and the behaviour patterns of their families. On the other hand, unless special care is taken in their school, the culture shock leads to weak scholastic achievement and consequently to repetition, school failure, or transfer to a remedial school. Such a situation can be aggravated by the practice of foreign students being combined with "native" students with quite different educational problems. Such is the case in some *Hauptschulen* (secondary modern schools) in Germany. In these secondary schools there are classes consisting of migrant workers' children and children from disturbed homes, very often associated with unemployed parents.

This unhappy circumstance can be contrasted with cities with large multinational communities of business executives, engineers, doctors, university teachers, and other professionals. Unless their children can attend their own local schools, they go to special international schools. These children often have to cope with individual adjustment difficulties, but these are comparatively easy to overcome through private remedial instruction or special educational measures typical of international schools (individual or small-group language courses, etc.). The success of these schools is rooted in above average teaching/learning conditions, extraordinary financial contributions by parents, and the motivation of students and parents.

Multiethnicity as a Topical Issue

German multiethnicity consists of four major relationships: Indigenous minorities, Ethnic Germans (Volksdeutsche) having resettled from the Soviet Union and Eastern Europe, people seeking asylum, and migrants.

Multiethnicity includes relations between the non-German groups, but in its constitutional and legal meaning in Germany, the term "minority" is only applied to the first community. On the other hand, migrants constitute the largest non-German category and claim the most attention from politicians, administrators, educators and the public. Due to the particular position that migrants have attained in the German society, they will be given the most extensive attention.

Indigenous Minorities

Until the reunification of Germany (October 3, 1990) the Danish community was the only indigenous non-German ethnic group to enjoy a special status, including the right to maintain Danish-medium schools. These institutions are run privately (Mahler/Steindl 1983) by the "Danish School Association" (*Dänischer Schulverein*). At the same time they are highly subsidised by the Land of Schleswig-Holstein. German-medium schools to the North of the German-Danish border receive reciprocal treatment (Reich 1986) for reasons rooted in the long history of this border region. Schools were an important factor in the conflicts between the two "mother nations" which even escalated into wars, particularly in the nineteenth century. Since 1945, the relations have gradually improved and reached the satisfactory state which they enjoy today. They give a positive example of how bi-ethnic issues can be settled.

While the Danish minority is typical of the solution in a border region, the Sorbian minority in Eastern Germany (in the East of Saxony and the Southeast of Brandenburg) represents the remainder of a formerly widespread ethnic group, occupying part of the territory between the rivers Elbe and Oder (Urban 1980). In contrast to the other tribal and political units in that region, the Sorbs have survived, though gradually being assimilated into the German majority. The German Democratic Republic (GDR) favoured their survival by safeguarding bilingualism in administration and education. For instance, the Education Act of February 1965 confirmed preceding provisions for Sorbian-medium primary and secondary state schools. However, minority policy was promoted at the cost of the autonomous cultural agencies that the Sorbian community had built up in the nineteenth and beginning twentieth centuries. Although the Laender (provinces or states) of Saxony and Brandenburg have made explicit provisions for maintaining the Sorbs' right to run their own schools, the future of this ethnic group depends upon its strength to resist assimilation.

The Ethnic German "Resettlers"

The ethnic Germans (Volksdeutsche) are those who, since the beginning of the seventies (and particularly as a concomitant of *Perestroika*) have been allowed by their governments to resettle in Germany where their ancestors had come from centuries ago. In certain cases, German communities in the Soviet Union, Poland, and Romania went back to the thirteenth century.

The resettlers are automatically given German citizenship when crossing the border, including all rights and duties involved. However, school children often have a poor command of German due to their use in school and home of another language (often reinforced by social pressures before resettlement against speaking German even at home).

The need to integrate these children into the German (until 1990 West German) society and educational system has led to the establishment of one-year and two-year special courses, sometimes with boarding provisions. Recently a few private religious schools have been established by Mennonite ethnically German communities from Russia and other parts of the Soviet Union. These ethnic German resettlers are "temporary" minorities, whose special problems are the non-fulfilled expectations of people who "return" to the country of their ancestors.

People Seeking Asylum

Certain problems have emerged with people who have come to Germany as political refugees, in particular during the past twenty years. The children of those refugees who have been given political asylum are required (like the migrants' children) to attend school. Educational provisions for them usually take place within the framework of regular German-medium school classes.

In recent years the problems with refugee seekers have increased because of the continual stream of newcomers and the relatively liberal interpretation of admission for "non-acknowledged" refugees.

The Migrants

In contrast to the hitherto-mentioned minority groups, the migrants form part of the "foreign population" (Mitter 1984, 1986). While the Federal Statistical Office allocates all persons of non-German citizenship to this category, in educational and social policy the term "foreign" is usually applied only to the "migrants." They are numerically dominant and in socioeconomic and political terms the most significant group of the "foreign population." That means that the official termin- ology of educational policy neglects two subgroups of "minor" importance. First, there are numerous and growing communities of foreign diplomats, business executives, engineers, doctors, university teachers, particularly in the large cities. Schooling of their children has been already tackled above. Secondly, there are foreign workers who either belong to very small ethnic groups or whose children merge into German schools because they speak German or a similar language (Dutch children). Education authorities take no special measures for these groups.

Two categories of "foreign" children have assured rights in Germany. There are children of workers from the "European Community" and those where Germany has bilateral agreements: Greece, Italy, Portugal, Spain, Turkey, and Yugoslavia.

Reunification has confronted Germany with an additional group of foreign workers who are actually migrants although they do not officially enjoy this status. GDR authorities have invited and employed some foreign workers, mostly from Vietnam and Mozambique. Since reunification the majority of these migrants have left Germany, while those who have stayed are being included in the "migrants' policy" of the Federal Government. Their situation differs from that of the "West German migrants" insofar as they have come to (East) Germany without their families, so "multicultural education" is limited to their further vocational training. The following considerations concentrate on the "West German" variation.

The Socioeconomic and Political Framework

The socioeconomic and political background conditions of migrant workers must be investigated in the mirror of their forty years of history. They first arrived in the Federal Republic in the early 1950s, to provide an additional work force. After a period of economic expansion, the 1970s experienced the "oil crisis," leading to the Federal government asking the Federal Authority of Labour to stop recruiting foreign workers. One of the unwanted side-effects of this measure was that it motivated the vast majority of workers who had already arrived in the Federal Republic to stay. Migrant workers' numbers stabilized. Moreover, the Italians, Greeks, Spaniards, and Portuguese are not affected by the restriction on foreign workers: full freedom of movement is available to inhabitants of the "European Community."

The economic recessions and the rationalisation of industry in the late 1970s brought increasing unemployment to migrant workers. The government again encouraged migrants to return to their home countries in 1983 and 1984, by offering immediate cash for their rights to unemployment and other insurances (McRae 1980). However, this incentive did not work: the migrants usually stayed. Since 1984 there has been an increase reflecting improved employment prospects for migrants. In spite of the brief recruitment stop, the number of migrants has nearly doubled.

This increase stems mostly from the arrival of migrant workers' families, first wives with small children, then older children (Mahler/Steindl 1983). The Foreigners Act (*Auslaendergesetz*) of 1965 granted residence permits to foreigners' wives and all family members up to their sixteenth year. This right has been subsequently extended to migrants'older children. This relatively liberal interpretation of the Foreigners' Act, as handled by the regional and local authorities, was widely supported by the public and by the courts. Article 6 of the Basic Law (Constitution of the Federal Republic of Germany) promulgated that marriage and family are particularly protected by the State, so attempts by the Federal Minister of the Interior to lower the age of migrants' arriving children to six years had only partial success.

The ethnic composition of the migrant population has shifted from Italians (prevailing among the migrants in the 1950s and early 1960s) to Turks and Yugoslavs. Turks have become almost one third of the migrant population (1.5 million). This demographic trend discloses the complexity of the issue. The legal provisions refer to the overall category of "foreigners," as exemplified by the Foreigners' Act of 1965. Even in its narrower interpretation (confined to the migrants of the aforementioned six European countries) the summary classification provides no real understanding of what the West

German society has to cope with. The use of "foreigner" or "migrant" insinuates that there is a homogeneous group which does not exist.

Migrants differ from nation to nation in fairly specific ways. The societal systems of the home countries, e.g. in Turkey, Greece, and Yugoslavia, differ from one another and internally. They are culturally and religiously diversified. Three countries (Italy, Spain, Portugal) are Roman Catholic; Greeks are Orthodox Christians; the largest group of migrants (the Turks) are mostly Muslims; and the Yugoslavs combine all three. Languages are similarly complicated: linguistic diversities exist from country to country, but also inside the individual nations (e.g. the Kurds among the Turkish group, and the "Yugoslavs" Serbocroat, Slovenian, Macedonian and Albanian). Any dissolution of the Yugoslav state would complicate this issue even more. In this context, membership in the EC affects the general legal provisions as well as specific regulations.

Migrant Children and Youngsters

Policy issues in Germany are decided according to their place in a federal constitution. There is a network of laws and guidelines comprising legal and social provisions such as residence permits, unemployment insurance, and social welfare. Within this framework, educational matters are the full responsibility of the Laender. The duration of compulsory school attendance (nine or ten years) falls into the "cultural responsibility" (*Kulturhoheit*) of the Laender, so they determine the stages of primary education, lower secondary education, and the school-bound forms of upper secondary education. It is only higher education, job-bound vocational education, and further vocational education which are jurisdictions shared by the Federal and Laender governments. Pre-school education is a traditional domain of non-governmental agencies (churches etc.) and local communities.

The legal provisions for the education of migrants are totally embedded in this overall structure, enabling political strategies and administrative measures practised in the individual Laender to differ. Such diversities include organisational as well as curricular matters that may be traced back to controversial approaches to how to harmonise the core values of "integration" and "cultural identity" (Cropley 1982, 52). There is a wide consensus about the validity of both values. However, when education policies of the Laender are transferred from general guidelines and directives into everyday operations of the schools, they have to set priorities. This process is widely influenced by the political philosophies governing the individual Laender. There is a "Christian Democrat" and a "Social Democrat" model. Party-bound philosophies with regional and local attitudes and interests give a spectrum of nuances to West German policies in the education of migrants. The (re-)establishment of the Laender in East Germany will extend this diversity.

The challenge of educating migrants' children has been taken seriously by the (old) Federal Republic of Germany, promoting continuous efforts of the Laender to achieve sufficient uniformity in handling the necessary tasks and measures (Mahler/Steindl 1983). Such coordination has come from the Standing Conference of Laender Ministers of Education and Culture, formed in 1948 (before the Federal Republic of Germany). The need for unanimity in conference resolutions entails great pressure for compromise, but slows decision-making or even prevents reasonable solutions. There is a further critical point: the Standing Conference can only recommend; there is no binding effect on the decision of the Laender. Considering the problem area of educating a diversified population, one has to acknowledge that the Standing Conference has been rather successful, particularly for its Resolution of April 4th, 1976; amended October 26th, 1979 (Mahler/Steindl 1981, 203-207). All the West German Laender have accepted and incorporated this resolution in their respective laws and decrees:

> It is essential to enable the foreign students to acquire the German language and to reach German school-leaving certificates as well as to maintain and to improve the knowledge in the mother-tongue. At the same time the educational measures are to pay a contribution to the social integration of the foreign

students as long as they stay in the Federal Republic; moreover, they serve the purpose of maintaining their linguistic and cultural identity. (Preamble)

Summing up, there are four issues of general concern for the education of migrants' children and youngsters in Germany. The first deals with the international dimension of the education of migrants. Considering that all member countries of the European Community are more or less involved in this matter, the Federal and Laender authorities pay great attention to the activities of this supranational organisation. Its resolutions and recommendations are regarded as important incentives to the solution of concrete problems in Germany. Among them the "Guideline of the Council concerning the Schooling of Migrant Workers' Children" of July 25th, 1977 (full version documented in Mahler/Steindl 1983, 210) paved the way for regular consultation among the member states. Within a broader geographical context, the eighteen national Ministers of Education of the Council of Europe had adopted a similar resolution on November 8th, 1974 (full version documented in Mahler/Steindl 1983, 207–210).

Second, endeavors to reach and extend bilateral co-operation with the authorities of the migrants' home countries have been greatly encouraged by the Standing Conference of Laender Ministers of Education and Culture. Within the framework of existing "cultural agreements," bilateral commissions have been established; in the meantime they have developed into permanent forums of discussion about all matters concerning education and schooling of foreign students. Between 1974 and 1980 such joint commissions have been constituted with Yugoslavia, Greece, Turkey, Italy, Spain and Portugal.

One should not be surprised to learn that the individual counterparts emphasise specific interests. Divergent attitudes result from different expectations with regard to the youngsters' return to their home countries. These range from Italy which seems to favour the integration of their migrants in Germany, to Greece whose governments, irrespective of their ideological orientations, have emphatically stressed the continuing adherence of their compatriots to the Greek nation. These divergent views explain differences in the instruction of the vernacular. Specific cultural and civic knowledge in the learning areas of history and geography is discussed for these children.

For Turkish children, religious instruction raises a special problem. German Laender have refrained from including religious instruction for Muslim students in the curricula because of the incompatibility of certain component parts of the Islamic religion (e.g. the individual and social position of women) and the value order laid down in the Basic Law of the Federal Republic and the Constitutions of the Laender. On the other hand, the attendance of Koranic Schools by Turkish children and youngsters is suspected to produce effects in civic and moral education contrary to the goals and objectives of German schooling.

Third, there is a distinct impact of the expectations of the migrants' home countries upon private schools. Conflicts emerge when the foreign initiators' philosophy collides with Article 7 of the Basic Law which requires that private schools, particularly at the primary level, must observe the educational goals and objectives which are valid for the public school system. Recognition of private primary schools, moreover, is dependent on "a special pedagogic interest" to be confirmed by the educational authority. In this constitutional and legal context, the Danish schools in Schleswig Holstein and the Sorbian schools in Brandenburg and Saxony have been acknowledged; the second group consists of schools whose students are very likely to stay in Germany only temporarily i.e. American, French, British, and Japanese institutions. For migrants, Greeks have been exceptionally active in opening private schools and there is one German-Italian private school run by the Catholic Church. The ongoing encouragement by the Greek government has provoked caution by some educational authorities. In this context we touch again the problem of how to harmonise integration and cultural identity as educational core values (Rist 1978). While, on the one hand, the adherents of private schools refer to better opportunities for preparing the youngsters for their return, the opponents argue that in fact many or most of such students are likely to stay in Germany. Their needs are best served by adjusting to the German labour market and career system in general.

Fourthly, there are important activities of the Federal Laender Commission for Educational Planning and the Promotion of Research. It was established in 1970 by an agreement between the Federal and the Laender governments. During the past twenty years it has launched a great number of pilot projects at various levels for the education of migrants' children. Moreover, the Laender themselves have been active in this field.

Specific Problem Areas

According to the Resolutions taken by the Standing Conference of Laender Ministers of Education and Culture, the EC Guideline of 1977 and the constitutional and legal provisions made by the individual Laender, the formal education of migrants' children and youngsters is bound to the main goals of integration and maintenance of cultural identity. These two goals have been pursued by various strategies which are rooted in Laender's different priority settings. The differences are recently being reduced, as recognised by the handling of the language of instruction. In general, Laender emphasise all migrants' children acquiring both the German language and their mother tongue, subject to certain restrictions.[1]

Migrants' children are assisted in coping with German schooling conditions by organisational arrangements (Cropley 1982):

1) There are one-year and two-year preparatory classes in which instruction in the vernacular language is provided not

---

[1]   The Federal Republic respects the official Turkish doctrine that Turkey is a monolingual country which means that Kurdish and other non-Turkish speaking children have to learn Turkish in German schools because of their national citizenship, so they cannot study their mother tongues. For practical reasons (size of classes, availability of teachers, etc.) mother tongue tuition is usually limited to the dominant languages of the children's home countries. This restricts the language program for those Yugoslav children who do not belong to the Serbocroat-speaking community.

only in the specific "language" subject (Italian, Greek, etc.), but also in some other subjects, such as Social Studies and, in some cases, Mathematics. Such preparatory classes exist in all Laender except Hesse where migrants' children are immediately admitted to regular German classes.

2) In large cities and other districts with concentrated migrant   populations, "national classes" have been established. They offer migrants' children a bilingual instruction in separate units, then the "regular" instructional language gradually glides from the vernacular to German. Such "national" (bilingual) classes last from four to six years.

3) In Bavaria there are special "national" classes which comprise the whole compulsory school attendance of nine years.

The Laender of Bavaria and Hesse represent the two extreme wings of the spectrum (Mahler/Steindl 1983). Hesse (with its long Social Democrat tradition from 1945 to 1987 and since 1991 again) strongly favours early integration. Bavaria (with its continuous majority of the conservative Christian Social Union) has always emphasised the option for "national classes." All the Laender have provided options for migrants' children to enter regular German classes when their knowledge of the language is sufficient. This is most important at the transition from primary school to selective secondary education (Grammar Schools/*Gymnasien*, Intermediate Schools/*Realschulen*). Such transition has been facilitated by youngsters choosing their vernacular language as a regular school subject instead of learning a second "foreign" language; that means, for example, that a Turkish student who has taken English as the first foreign language, chooses Turkish instead of French as a second one. Children living in areas with a concentration of migrants, particularly in the large cities, benefit most from these provisions (McLauglin/Graf 1985).

The language issue is complicated when youngsters do not enter school at the beginning of the primary level, but at a later stage. The later a student arrives in Germany, the more difficult is the adjustment to the prerequisites of the German school. Fluency in German usually turns out to be only one of the disturbing factors. The most complicated cases involve youngsters who move "to and from," which often leads to virtual illiteracy in both languages. Special problems are also posed by youngsters who have completed compulsory school attendance in their home countries. In large cities special classes have been established for this group, where teachers introduce their students to their new environment and to some basic knowledge of German. These fluctuations arise from economic needs, in that fathers and mothers are both employed so they leave their children in the care of the grand-parents. It is also rooted in the permanent uncertainty of migrants: will they stay or return? (Most of them actually stay in Germany).

Teachers and Teacher Training

Teachers who are capable and willing to educate migrant workers' children may be German or native language teachers who are usually appointed temporary contracts (Cropley 1982).

A number of universities and colleges of education have introduced special courses for German teachers, dealing with the specific issues of educating migrants' children. Courses in the educational foundations link with optional language courses at elementary and advanced levels (McLauglin/Graf 1985). These efforts are far from satisfactory because the activities are primarily the initiatives of individual professors or lecturers. In-service training has become the main qualification for teachers of migrants' children. In-service institutes or centres now exist in all the Laender, but they are often restricted to special tasks, e.g. instruction in preparatory or "national" classes. Such initiatives solve only part of the problems, for the education of migrants' children affects the whole of schools and all teachers. Neglect of this dimension in teacher training and teaching practice leads to highly trained and committed teachers finding themselves frustrated among an indifferent environment.

Since the beginning of the 1970s the Laender have appointed "native language" teachers with two functions: to teach the vernacular language to "their" children, and to awaken and maintain their cultural identity. There are two categories of native language teachers: persons directly appointed by German authorities (often married women of foreign descent with permanent residence in Germany), and teachers delegated by their own Ministries of Education for a period of three to five years. Such appointments result from a bilateral agreement between Germany and counterparts. Native language teachers initially lacked effective preparation for their task at German schools, so in-service training institutes have offered courses to this group too. These activities are often linked with the production of teaching and learning aids (textbooks, handbooks for teachers, etc.).

Considerations Concerning the State of the Art

Although this chapter has been focussed on the state school system (which in Germany comprises the vast majority of schools) non-governmental institutions also face the problems. Particular attention has been given by the churches to pre-school education. Unions and other professional associations assist with vocational and further education.

Two incompatible perspectives disrupt the orderly development of education policy. First, the Federal Republic of Germany still defines itself as a "non-immigration country" (McRae 1980, 119) while the everyday practices in classrooms and other educational places are oriented towards patterns of "multicultural education." This educational contradiction is caused by the commitment of many educational policy makers and classroom practitioners to this task, and by the unlikely prospect that most migrants will return to their home countries.

The "non-immigration" doctrine also justifies the official emphasis on "integration" and "re-integration" (which is shared by the governments of the most home countries, with the most emphatic representative of the re-integration philosophy being Greece). Politicians often expect and advocate integration and re-integration in particular in rhetorical speeches. However, educationists must be sceptical about such expectations. Neither goal can be realized in the normal German school day, which is overloaded for all concerned--children, parents and teachers.

Conclusion

The reunification of Germany has induced a new dimension of multiculturalism. It would be too extreme to infer the emergence of an "ethnic duality" from the forty-five years of partition: that will not long survive the "national duality" which ended in 1990. There is substantial linguistic unity. "Command education" (*Kommandopädagogik*) has failed as a medium of ideological indoctrination, because the "ways of life" have not diverged much (thanks to mutual visits of West and East Germans and to the majority of East Germans being able to receive West German television). Yet, the brief period since the opening of the Berlin Wall in 1989 has provided evidence of "socialist" customs, values and expectations which have survived the collapse of their ideological "superstructure." Therefore we may posit the continued existence of "cultural" peculiarities in East Germany, similar as differentiating criteria to social class and educational standard but not to ethnicity. The viability and duration of these peculiarities cannot be predicted.

The "ethnic" specification multiculturalism is soon likely to expand. The implementation of the Single Market (from January 1, 1993) will result in growing mobility inside the European Community and soon incorporate further countries (both Western and Eastern). In the end this development might absorb the "migrants' issue" by the superordinate "Europeanisation" of multiculturalism in its proper meaning. As in other European countries, the education system in the reunified Germany must then be prepared to cope with "multicultural schools" on a large scale. Social scientists predict this trend, and a consequent immigration from Germany's Eastern neighbour countries. Above all, migration from the Soviet Union will result from its economic crisis as well as its already initiated transition to liberalising exit permits.

The conclusion to be drawn from these new perspectives for multicultural education in Germany is that multicultural education must be related to integration, which may be distinguished from assimilation. Assimilation-- the opposite of segregation--advocates one-sided adjustment; an ethnic minority conforms to the cultural norms of the majority and thereby renounces its own ethnic identity. Integration emphasises the merger and unification of two or several groups whose social position is considered as equivalent. The outcome of such integration is not assimilation of the minority in the majority, but the emergence of a new culture (Mitter 1984).

In the past such processes have often lasted for generations or even for centuries, with the various stages characterised by great variety. Therefore "integration" must be conceived and practised as an aim to be realized by openness and tolerance, above all by the readiness of all groups concerned to solve their problems and conflicts peacefully. The success of such policies depends on the good will of the immigrants (in the widest sense of this term). However, the German hosts are confronted with greater responsibility concerning legislation, administration and social communication, which can be generalised to all host nations in similar situations. German history can provide lessons both from negative *and* positive experience.

This chapter has concentrated on the inter-personal and social aspects of multiculturalism and multicultural education. However, multicultural education influences the personal development of the young (and adult) people. It is a process caused by the intra-personal coexistence of two (or several) cultures. Therefore, all solutions on the political level must provide for the individuals' freedom to choose their personal cultural identity--including the right to define it "above" historical experience and convention. For example young Germans and Turks may want to establish their identity above these ethnic and national distinctions as Europeans or global citizens. Education has to help the individual to make his/her decision, whereby the "price" resulting from every decision must not be concealed. Consequently, multiculturalism and multicultural education are likely to develop into a constituent component of pluralism to be conceived as a social *and* intra-personal phenomenon.

The education issue depends on the overarching socioeconomic and political issues of the whole social system.

Education alone cannot solve the problems. However, the education of all children and youngsters belonging to "minorities" in Germany indicates how education can contribute to the solution of the overall and particular problems.

References

Cropley, A. J. 1982. *Erziehung von Gastarbeiterkindern. Kinder zwischen zwei Welten* (Education of Migrant Workers' Children: Children between Two Worlds). 2nd ed. München: Ehrenwirth.

Mahler/Steindl, M. 1983. *Zweitsprache Deutsch für Ausländerkinder. Bildungspolitische Schwerpunkte, didaktische Grundlagen* (German as Second Language for Foreigners' Children. Foci of Educational Policy, Didactic Foundations). Donauwoerth: Ludwig Auer.

McLauglin/Graf, P. 1985. Bilingual Education in West Germany: Recent Developments. *Comparative Education* 21(3): 241-255.

McRae, V. 1981. *Die Gastarbeiter. Daten, Fakten, Probleme* (The Migrant Workers: Data, Facts, Problems). München: C. H. Beck.

Mitter, W. 1984. *Education for All.* International Bureau of Education: International Yearbook of Education, vol. 36. Paris: UNESCO.

_____. 1986. Policy issues in the education of minorities in the Federal Republic of Germany. *Education and Urban Society* 18(4): 437-448. Extended version in: *Journal of International and Comparative Education* 1(3): 721-750.

Reich H. H. 1986. *Deutsch und Daenisch in den Schulen der daenischen Minderheit in Sued-Schleswig* (German and Danish in the schools of the Danish minority in South Schleswig). *Diskussion Deutsch* 17: 343-349.

Rist, R. C. 1978. *Guestworkers in Germany. The Prospects for Pluralism.* New York: Praeger.

Smolicz, J. J. 1990. The mono-ethnic tradition and the education of minority youth in West Germany from an Australian multicultural perspective. *Comparative Education* 26(1): 27–43.

Spaich, H. 1981. *Fremde in Deutschland: unbequeme Kapitel unserer Geschichte* (Foreigners in Germany: Some Troublesome Chapters from Our History). Weinheim: Beltz.

Urban, R. 1980. *Die sorbische Volksgruppe in der Lausitz 1949–1977. Ein dokumentarischer Bericht* (The Sorbian Ethnic Group in the Lausitz Region. A Documentary Report). Marburg: Johann Gottfried Herder Institut.

INTEGRATION OF IMMIGRANTS AND REFUGEES IN UNITED STATES EDUCATION

Letha A. (Lee) See

Although the United States government has recently reformulated national immigration policies (Taft, North, and Ford 1979, Devecchi 1983, Jaegar 1983) comparatively little effort has gone into formulating a systematic policy for educating foreign-born immigrants and refugees (See 1986). Research specifying appropriate educational experiences for newcomers constituting a significant part of America's labor force is hardly adequate for the growing need.

The American educational system, long subject to external criticism and internal disagreements over multiethnic expectations and cross-cultural competency (Banks 1988), has yet to deal with conflicting notions about assimilation, pluralism, nationalism, bilingualism, and multiculturalism in the socialization of newcomers. The educational process for the foreign-born seems to create a conflict of values and ideologies with a consequent resistance to, or compliance with, the dominant culture's social mores and ideologies. The result is generally further alienation of newcomers or isolation from their original culture (Banks 1988).

Of an estimated fourteen million non-naturalized immigrants beyond the age of compulsory public schooling during the 1920s (Seller 1978), less than two percent attended night school regularly, despite intensive advertising and campaigning to attract them. Later research suggests that the problem may have been inadequate procedures to engage the foreign-born in the educational process rather than their lack of motivation. Cross-cultural thinkers realize that education of the

451

foreign-born is a desirable goal for acculturation and assimilation (Miller 1916, Hartman 1948, Korman 1967, Carlson 1975) but responsibility for the success of such education is shared by the foreign born and the educational system for adults in the United States.

In order to understand the challenge of educating the foreign-born near the end of the twentieth century and consequently integrating them into mainstream America, one needs to see a demographic profile of the new foreign-born populations and examine the cross-cultural issues involved in their education. A review of the early Settlement House Movement and its modifications serves as a model for planning new educational programs. The goal is to close educational gaps and provide excellent instruction for millions of new arrivals entering the United States from all over the world.

Although the words seem to conjure up similar images, *immigrant* and *refugee* are different. An immigrant deliberately settles in another country but retains the option of returning home, while a refugee is forced to leave his homeland and cannot return. *Foreign-born* is an umbrella term to include all persons born outside the United States. Though they can never become president, the foreign-born nevertheless receive certain rights and privileges from the government (U.S. Constitution, Article II, Sec. I, # 5) and they may have great economic and/or social success in the United States.

For purposes of the present study, the words immigrants and refugees refer to all foreign-born arrivals in the United States. Recent groups include Cubans, Asians, Haitians, and Afghans, as well as the 1.3 million legal and illegal aliens already residing in the United States (North 1988).

Psychological Effects of Migration

One must appreciate the emotional trauma experienced by people who leave their home country and come to the new world (See 1986). The individual is separated from his/her past life, while the decision to remain in the new country signals an end to one life and the beginning of another.

Lindsay (1983) notes that some individuals migrate in search of a better lifestyle, some with encouragement of their home governments, national business firms, or multinational organizations. Her commentary points out that mass migration can stimulate national development and open undeveloped areas for settlement.

But not all migrants leave their home countries willingly. Many escape adverse conditions of life-threatening situations. Swift and convulsive changes, human rights violations, violence, political upheavals, withdrawal of colonial authority and breakups of empires, economic depression, famine, and religious persecution have brought--and still bring--millions of foreign-born individuals to America in waves of migration (Myrdal 1944, Taft, North, and Ford 1979, See 1987, Ogden 1984).

Regardless of the reasons that bring the foreign-born to America, educators, government officials, and law-makers have both the responsibility and the opportunity to provide educational experiences for cross-cultural competency in a sophisticated society from which everybody can benefit. They may be integrated for many classes.

Profile of the Foreign-Born

Historically, America is a nation of immigrants; but the present study examines only two groups. The first, or "older" bulge of twenty-one million eastern and southern Europeans, including Polish, Hungarians, Lithuanians, Jews, Ukrainians, Czechs, Slovaks, Croats, Serbs, Italians, Macedonians, and Greeks, came to America beginning around 1880. The second bulge, including Filipinos, Koreans, Chinese, Mexicans, and Cubans, began coming about 1960 and continue to arrive. There were fourteen million foreign born in the 1980 Census. During the preceding twenty years, over one million from southeast Asia, including Vietnamese, Laotians, and Kampucheans (Cambodians), came as refugees. One hundred thousand Jews and other ethnics from the Soviet Union, twenty-nine thousand from Cuba and the Latin American countries, and smaller numbers from underdeveloped countries in Africa also arrived during those later years (Momeni 1984, Gardner et al. 1985, U.S. Bureau of Census 1985).

The birth rate of many new immigrants outpaces the birth rate of the Caucasian population, a factor significantly affecting demographics of the entire North American continent (Banks 1988). Variations exist between and among the two groups, but enough common characteristics exist to warrant further study and explanation. Many newcomers, in addition to being dark in complexion, differ in manner, religion, and medical practices, among other things. Additionally, their distinctive music, dance, and graphic and plastic arts, together with their general non-adaptive behavior, pose obstacles for many Americans. Some come from nomadic regions with tribal customs of geographical clustering and communalism, which differ considerably from American notions of rugged individualism. Others practice close kinship and maintain extended family traditions that often collide with the American idea of nuclear family. Many have non-Western metaphysical views and a highly evolved but "non-American" system of spiritual thought (Mbiti 1970, Akbar 1980, Noble 1980, See 1989).

To compound the problem for American integration, the most recent Asian, African, Caribbean, and Hispanic migrants speak over 105 different languages. Largely agrarian and unaccustomed to urban life, these Third and Fourth World groups possess few survival skills for a post-industrial society. They appear lost in a society of high technology and complex communication systems. Their group mores and old-world ideologies often collide with traditional American beliefs and practices (See 1986) and call into question Western scientific thought (Kuhn 1970, Capra 1982, See 1986). As Zelinsky (1973) puts it, "A mechanistic world is a quantifiable one, so that it is hardly surprising to find everything numbered and counted, or to note the ardent accumulation of statistics by a people who dote on digits" (p. 60). Seeing the Western world as Zelinsky describes it, newcomers are propelling a significant shift in the Western scientific paradigm.

A clash in cultural values, while not necessarily intentional, occasionally results in economic and class issues. Although such conflicts hardly threaten institutional structure of social equilibrium, they nevertheless destabilize the American social system of which education is a part. Some individuals cannot accommodate the powerful cross-currents (Loomis 1920, Jencks and Lauck 1926, Hartman 1948, Solomon 1956, Jones 1960, See 1986).

Plans for educating the foreign-born, which only a short time back seemed an elementary task, have now grown complex. Educators and social scientists, more directly than other vocations, are called upon to train other professionals and devise curricula for untangling complex social problems.

Consider the recent entry of thousands of Asians and Hispanics--especially Mexicans--and other groups seeking sanctuary. Like the Europeans arriving at Ellis Island during the former era of migration, the newcomers felt helpless when reaching Florida and Texas borders. Physically uprooted and daring to start over in a strange land, some suffered serious neurotic disorders stemming from disruption and dislocation (Blumenthal 1975, Westermeyer and Vang 1983, Kinzie 1988). What is worse, many unknowingly entered a new and strange environment that does not welcome groups intent on establishing colonies among their compatriots and refusing to learn the language of the host country. Their flight to the United States can be seen as a desperate act by individuals fleeing poverty and disorder, only to be insulated in an unfriendly, culturally isolated ghetto (See 1986).

In spite of these events, the significant problem facing educators is how to maintain continuity of Western values and mainstream American culture while acknowledging and respecting the cultural pluralism of the foreign-born.

Cross-Cultural Issues in Educating the Foreign-Born

Education has a responsibility for teaching all individuals to cope with new problems, adapt to their new environments, and develop survival and relationship-building skills. Its major role in cross-cultural issues is the acculturation of the foreign-born. Related issues are the complex processes of teaching and learning across cultures. Those involved in educating the foreign-born will need an understanding of, and appreciation for, cultural diversity. And this takes time.

To be effective, educators must be sensitive to the characteristics, abilities, and methods that have enabled the foreign-born to cope with exploitation, a hostile environment, and depersonalization. Such awareness provides a professional knowledge base for education aimed at making newcomers into productive members of society.

Education for Social Adjustment

A number of experiences aim at equipping the foreign-born for social adjustment in a technological society. Social adjustment services--education, counselling, and supporting functions for dealing with daily life--can provide instruction for integrating newcomers into American society through community, religious, and family resources.

Education for social adjustment acquaints newcomers with the host culture on a variety of levels, familiarizing them with social, physical, and institutional forces. Initially, social adjustment services may overlap with general orientation provided by settlement agencies: learning to use the transportation systems, operate elevators, and read traffic signals. While such tasks seem comparatively minor, the foreign-born from rural backgrounds usually feel frustrated in American urban centers and cannot function in them without training. In such cases immediate survival skills become paramount.

Once geographical navigation and life adjustment skills are mastered, the foreign-born are ready for formal educational and institutional systems. But first they must become familiar with educational situations and learn appropriate behavior.

Adult Education

During the nineteenth and early twentieth centuries, thousands of immigrants and refugees jolted federal officials into recognizing the importance of adult education and making the government responsible for providing it. Adult education, whether formal or vocational, enabled newcomers to use English in communicating with others and to master simple mathematics for job skills. Educated newcomers with adequate skills were expected to help teach their fellows and encourage them to attend night school where better education could lead to economic advancement (Smith 1969).

More than five decades since the first wave of immigration reached America, approximately thirty million adults experience difficulties in the work place and cannot participate effectively as citizens because they are functionally illiterate. By the year 2000, as the present work force reaches retirement age, fewer manual-labor jobs will exist. Since jobs of the future will largely require post-secondary education and computer literacy, educators must concentrate on teaching newcomers to survive in the new century.

Since poor and minority groups, including African-Americans, will be joined by uneducated aliens, such as Hispanics, and others from the Caribbean nations, there is potential for conflict until educators and social scientists find a way to defuse the danger (See 1986). With the assistance of purposefully formed groups, like the Progressives of the early twentieth century, perhaps the best solution for minimizing tension lies in stamping out illiteracy.

Cross-Cultural Teaching and Learning

Having established the priority for educating an ever-increasing number of foreign-born newcomers, educators search for appropriate ways to teach them. Highly significant integrative research for adult learning has been done by Knowles (1970, 1972, 1975, 1980) whose model reflects the views of Kidd (1973) and White (1989) in maintaining that adult learners shun environments where the atmosphere is strained and where little opportunity exists to express oneself and take personal responsibility for education.

In his characterization of adult learners, Knowles (1975, 1978) employs a comparative approach, assuming that adult expectations and learning styles are significantly different from those of children. He contends that there should be independence and self-directed learning. This quest for independence dates back to the 1920s when a foreign-born university founder tired of being taught like a child wrote:

> Some Americans think . . . that we immigrants can comprehend only such thoughts as "I see a cat; the cat is black"--as the teachers in the evening schools make grown men repeat. But the minds of most immigrants are not so feeble as that. For the poor man, America is all work-work-work. We believe in work, all right, but we want thought and education to go along with it. So we took up questions about the beginning of things -the creation of the world, the theory of evolution, primitive man, and development of language. (Seller 1978, 90)

Although Knowles' work has been well received in educational circles throughout the western hemisphere, it has certain limitations when applied to Third and Fourth World population groups. In fact, his work is too broad to provide much insight into how social milieux affect education and training or influence the rate of learning, and particularly the most effective approach to be used for diverse populations. But he has introduced some valuable concepts, even though they may be speculative when applied across fields and cultures.

Currently, the most respected cross-cultural theoretical work on adult literacy is that of Brazilian educator Freire (1979, 1972, 1973, 1978), much of it written in exile. Freire relates adult learning to class and race, and he maintains that the setting for an oppressive system is inherent in its educational process. Freire illustrates his theory by contrasting two views of education. One is the "banking concept," where teachers are in control of knowledge and students become depositories of the teacher's knowledge. The second is the "dialogical educational system," where students and teachers become "critical coinvestigators." Since many American educators are sensitive to differences in cultures and world views, the "dialogical model" would seem to have wide potential and thus help arrest external differences, racial superficialities, and artificial problems. In brief, it seems that Freire's relaxed environment where dialogue can be exchanged would help any newcomer.

In some Third and Fourth World countries, educators are considered very important persons who are honored, respected, and revered for their age, knowledge, and accomplishments. On the whole they are accorded politeness, are expected to direct learning using authoritative methods, and are not to be challenged in the classroom, even by adult learners. A challenge to a professor is considered rude, tasteless, and inappropriate. From this world view, and from a cultural perspective, the most that could be expected from newcoming students would be Freire's notion of the educator as "co-investigator."

How the Foreign-Born Learn

A related cross-cultural issue examines how the foreign-born learn. Handlin (1959) notes that since migration does not wipe away the earlier experiences of the foreign-born, understanding their views of learning, education, and authority will help to ease adjustment.

Two traditional educators, Tyler (1969) and Reynolds (1976), contend that various methods must be employed in constructing a curriculum and in helping learners master the information at hand. Tyler believes that a failure to understand certain cultural nuances is a major deterrent to cross-cultural adult learning. Similarly, Korman (1967) asserts that understanding the newcomers, respecting their religion, ideology, and politics, and accepting them as persons worthy of respect, will promote a sense of worth and a suitable environment for learning. Failure to acknowledge these variables may result in initial reluctance to become totally involved in the educational process.

Settlement House Movement: Model for
Educating the Foreign-Born

Caught up in the expansive tide of the nineteenth century Progressive Movement in America, immigrants received excellent educational service and support from predominantly middle-class reformers who lived among them in settlement houses in eastern and midwestern cities. The Progressives, a group of liberal-thinking, prudent, concerned young educators, scholars, and agents of change, voluntarily assumed legal and moral obligation for settling newcomers. They worked closely with bilingual, bi-cultural personnel who also assisted new arrivals. From the beginning they determined to meet the needs of immigrants.

The Progressives wanted to create a benevolent society that abhorred social Darwinism, excessive competition, and materialistic values. Some Progressives feared that political machines, large corporations, and widespread scandal threatened democratic institutions and would corrupt newcomers before they could join mainstream America. They aspired to bridge the gap between the classes and hoped immigrants would infuse American society with simple peasant values (Lubove 1965).

While some historians argue that the Settlement House Movement intended to create an important link between the new immigrant and the American-born, others contend that many middle--and upper--class Americans felt guilty about the plight of the immigrants and wanted to accept them into the social system. Middle-class Americans realized they were recipients of the newcomers' labor, but their guilt soon disappeared and the initial patronization behavior returned (Hofstadter 1955, Davis 1967, Ehrenreich 1985, White 1986).

Some African-American social work educators have claimed that the young white women volunteers at Hull House and other settlement houses had motives that transcended their commitment to benevolent deeds. Darlington (1989), Rhone (1989), Ward (1989), and See (1989) argue that the women Progressives, mostly graduates from the nation's most prestigious women's colleges (Barnard, Bryn Mawr, Mount Holyoke, Radcliffe, Sarah Lawrence, Smith, and Vassar), were frustrated that their own education had not been put to good use nor properly appreciated by the society in which they believed. Settlement houses represented an opportunity to put their education and energy to work in teaching immigrant families. The African-Americans concede that whether the Settlement House workers were motivated out of political or personal concerns, their ultimate goal was social change, and toward that end they embraced and implemented John Dewey's (1897) thesis that education is the fundamental method of social progress and reform.

Against this historical backdrop of pioneering educational and social reform, the immigrants in major American cities gravitated to settlement houses in significant, but never overwhelming, numbers. The most impressive feature of Hull House, the best known settlement house, was its location in a ghetto, or "ethnic enclave." Because Hull House was easily accessible to immigrants, they could attend a myriad of social and educational activities which included men's and women's social clubs, adult education classes, daycare services, musical and craft activities, debates, conferences, recreational activities and strategy sessions. Most historians agree that Hull House was tremendously successful.

Founders of the Settlement House Movement, such as Jane Addams, adopted a holistic approach toward settling immigrants. While idealistic in their goals, in practice they used education to address the concrete realities of virtually every aspect of the immigrant's experience. They recognized that to integrate into American society as fully participating citizens, immigrants would have to adjust to new cultural surroundings and obtain assistance with housing, employment, social relationships and support systems, and adequate education.

These innovators perceived education as a means of fostering cooperation among immigrants and cohesion with the host society. They believed effective education must speak to the realities of everyday life, not just to academic subjects. Aware that public school systems and night school could not meet the multiple and complex educational requirements of newcomers, settlement house workers brought school to the local communities and provided programs for children and adults alike. By living and working among immigrants, Progressive educators derived a better understanding of their needs and interests and could address concerns more directly and successfully, both within and without the settlement community. They believed the whole of society would benefit from empowering immigrants and therefore designed educational activities to include linguistic, cultural, and civic experiences. They taught American citizenship to adult immigrants along with English, and they encouraged learners to explore difficulties of language and government from their own experiences.

Settlement house workers affirmed that education should be a reciprocal process--dialectical, not merely didactic--in an atmosphere of tolerance and mutual respect in which active involvement of immigrants was not only encouraged but required. They discovered that assimilation was most successful if the foreign-born were allowed to maintain important aspects of cultural heritage while preparing to join mainstream America. Rather than imposing rigid values on newcomers or attempting to extinguish ethnicity, workers acted as intercultural interpreters, mediators, and facilitators among immigrants, and between immigrants and society as a whole. By listening to and learning from the individuals they taught, Settlement House workers not only developed a profound personal appreciation for cultural diversity but also came to recognize unique positive contributions the foreign-born could make to society.

A New Progressive Initiative for Educating the Foreign-Born

The Settlement House experiment offers to educators of today valuable ideas for making life easier for newcomers facing cultural transformation. The example of early Progressives suggests that contemporary education should go to poor areas where the foreign-born usually reside. The experiment also suggests that students, volunteers, and medical interns may obtain broad experience by servicing the foreign-born in the environment where they live.

In an effort to eliminate illiteracy, retired teachers could form a domestic teaching corps and conduct classes in ethnic neighborhoods where the greatest amount of social disintegration has occurred. Professionals could offer personal attention and extend multiple services. Their mobilized effort could result in significant change for newcomers.

In addition to educational initiatives, the foreign-born could also receive improved health care in much the same way. With proper training America's youth could serve as indigenous professionals to care for foreign-born patients, serving as "street doctors" comparable to the "barefoot doctors" on medical teams in China (See 1989).

Aside from the services mentioned, time and energy could be devoted to helping the older foreign-born refine gardening skills and become "urban farmers." With ample manpower and small plots of urban land, the production of fresh fruits and vegetables could improve diet and foster group interaction.

Conclusion

For the second time in history, non-Europeans are dominating migration to the United States. And from all indications, these newcomers will be a significant part of the American population in the twenty-first century. As newcomers continue to arrive in large numbers, education offers the best hope for resolving intergroup problems. Since people do not forget their culture when they come to a new country, vestiges of old world culture will remain part of the fabric of new America. This cultural diversity could be welcomed as a means of broadening everybody's educational experience.

Specialists should collect and analyze a fusion of ideas from professional and indigenous groups in trying to initiate educational programs for the foreign-born. Innovative measures should include non-traditional methods for locating classes where the foreign-born reside, selecting educators, constructing curricula, recruiting and training teachers, using volunteers, and encouraging the foreign-born to help each other. The effort of educators must focus on the future.

Education of the foreign-born involves not so much creating new resources as new relationships and utilizing and reapplying untapped existing potentials. The current challenge calls for creativity, collaboration, and cooperation among individuals who can offer unique and essential contributions from a variety of disciplines and experiences. At the same time it encourages new relationships between immigrants and hosts as well as among the American-born who are separated from them by background, profession, or age.

Whenever diverse individuals, cultures, and world views collide, conflict may be inevitable. But when they come together with unity of purpose, as advocated in this study, the possibility exists for peaceful and progressive achievement through education, exchange of ideas, and the combination of energies.

Positive effects of educating the foreign-born could begin by adapting principles employed by the Settlement House Movement within the local community. But the possibilities for successful achievement are limitless: they extend outward, embracing and transcending individual, political, and cultural boundaries at the global level. Ultimately concerted effort could strengthen the community and create a better world.

References

Akbar, N. 1980. *The Evolution of Human Psychology for African Americans.* Published manuscript presented to SREB Student Conference. Atlanta, GA.

Banks, J. A. 1988. *Multiethnic Education: Theory and Practice.* 2nd ed. Boston: Allyn and Bacon.

Blumenthal, M. D. 1975. Measuring depressive symptomalogy in a general population. *Archives of General Psychiatry* 32: 971-978.

Capra, F. 1982. *The Turning Point: Science, Society and the Rising Culture.* New York: Simon & Schuster.

Carlson, R. 1975. *The Quest for Conformity: Americanization Through Education.* New York: John Wiley and Sons.

Darlington, M. 1989. Interview with Dr. Mamie Darlington, Dean (March 6), Atlanta University School of Social Work. Atlanta, GA.

Davis, A. 1967. *Spearheads for Reform: The Social Settlements and the Progressive Movement, 1980-1914.* New York: Oxford University Press.

DeVecchi, R. P. 1983. Determining refugee status: Towards a coherent policy. *World Refugee Survey.* U.S. Committee for Refugees, 25th Anniversary Issue. New York.

Dewey, J. 1897. *My Pedagogical Creed.* New York: Atheneum.

Ehrenreich, J. 1985. *The Altruistic Imagination: A History of Social Work and Social Policy in the United States.* Ithaca, NY: Cornell University Press.

Freire, P. 1970. *Pedagogy of the Oppressed.* New York: Oxford University Press.

_____. 1972. *Cultural Action for Freedom.* New York: Seabury Press.

_____. 1973. *Education for Critical Consciousness.* New York: Continuum.

_____. 1978. *Pedagogy in Process.* New York: Continuum.

Gardner, R. W., B. Robey, and P. C. Smith. 1985. *Asian Americans: Growth, Change, and Diversity.* Washington, D.C.: Population Reference Bureau.

Handlin, O. 1959. *The Uprooted.* New York: Grossett & Dunlap.

Hartman, E. G. 1948. *The Movement to Americanize the Immigrant.* New York: Columbia University Press.

Hofstadter, R. 1955. *Age of Reform: From Bryan to FDR.* New York: Knopf.

Jencks, J. W., and W. J. Lauck. 1926. *The Immigration Problem.* New York: Funk & Wagnall.

Jones, M. A. 1960. *American Immigration.* Chicago: University of Chicago Press.

Kidd, J. R. 1973. *How Adults Learn.* Chicago: Association Press/Follett.

Kinzie, J. D. 1988. Psychiatric clinical programs for refugees: Development, staffing, structure, and training. *National Institute of Mental Health.* University of Minnesota: Technical Assistance Center.

Knowles, M. 1970. *The Modern Practice of Adult Education.* New York: Association Press.

_____. 1972. Innovations in teaching styles and approaches based upon adult learning. *Journal of Education for Social Work* 8(2): 32-39.

_____. 1975. *Self-directed Learning: A Guide for Learners and Teachers.* Chicago: Association Press/Follett.

_____. 1978. *The Adult Learner: A Neglected Species.* 2nd ed. Houston: Gulf.

_____. 1980. *The Modern Practice of Adult Education: From Pedagogy to Andragogy.* Chicago: Association Press/Follett.

Korman, G. 1967. *Industrialization, Immigrants, and Americanizers: The View from Milwaukee.* Madison: The State Historical Society of Wisconsin.

Kuhn, T. S. 1970. *Structure of Scientific Revolutions.* 2nd ed. Chicago: University of Chicago Press.

Lindsay, B. 1983, March. *Migration and Education in Africa.* Paper delivered at the 27th annual conference of the Comparative and International Education Society. Atlanta, GA.

Loomis, F. D. 1920. *Americanization in Chicago.* Chicago: The Chicago Community Trust.

Lubove, R. J. 1965. *The Professional Altruist.* Cambridge, MA: Harvard University Press.

Mbiti, J. 1970. *African Religion and Philosophy.* Garden City, NY: Anchor Books.

Miller, H. A. 1916. *School and the Immigrant.* Cleveland: Cleveland Educational Survey, Cleveland Foundation.

Momemi, J. A. 1984. *Demography of Racial and Ethnic Minorities in the United States: An Annotated Bibliography with a Review Essay.* Westport, CT: Greenwood Press.

Myrdal, G. 1944. *An American Dilemma.* Vol. 2. New York: Harper.

Nobles, W. W. 1980. African philosophy: Foundations for black psychology. In R. L. Jones, ed. *Black Psychology.* New York: Harper and Row.

North, D. 1988. *The Foreign-Born in Atlanta: Study of Refugee Resettlement Patterns.* Washington, D.C.: Government Printing Office.

Ogden, P. E. 1984. *Migration and Geographic Change.* New York: Cambridge University Press.

Reynolds, B. 1976. *Learning and Teaching in the Profession of Social Work.* New York: Rinehart and Co.

Rhone, J. V. 1989. Interview with Dr. Joanne V. Rhone, Associate Professor of Social Work. Atlanta: Atlanta University.

See, L. A. 1986. *Tensions and Tangles Between Afro-Americans and Southeast Asian Refugees: A Study of the Conflict.* Atlanta: Wright.

_____. 1987. Emerging conflict between Afro-Americans and Southeast Asian refugees. *Social Development Issues* 2(3): 34-47.

_____. 1989. Folk medicine, folk healing and voodoo in rural health care. Paper presented at the Medical College of Georgia, Augusta.

Seller, M. S. 1978. Success and failure in adult education: The immigrant experience 1914-1924. *Adult Education* 28(2): 83-99.

Smith, T. 1969. Immigrant social aspirations and American education 1880-1930. *American Quarterly* 21(3):523-543.

Solomon, B. M. 1956. *Ancestors and Immigrants*. Cambridge: Harvard University Press.

Taft, J. V., D. S. North, and D. A. Ford. 1979. *Refugee Resettlement in the United States: Time for a New Focus*. Washington, D.C.: New Trans-Century Foundation.

Tyler, R. 1969. *Basic Principles of Curriculum and Instruction*. Chicago: University of Chicago Press.

U. S. Bureau of the Census. 1985. *Statistical Abstracts of the United States*. Washington, DC: U.S. Government Printing Office.

U. S. Constitution, Article II, Sec. 1, No. 5.

Ward, N. 1989. Interview with Professor Naomi Ward, Associate Professor Atlanta University, Georgia.

Westermeyer, J., T. F. Vang, and J. Neider. 1983. Refugees who do and do not seek psychiatric care: An analysis of premigratory and postmigratory characteristics. *Journal of Nervous Mental Disorders* 171: 86-91.

Zelinsky, W. 1973. *The Cultural Geography of the United States*. New York: Prentice Hall.

MULTICULTURAL EDUCATION IN CANADA: POLICIES AND PRACTICES[1]

Claude Lessard and Manuel Crespo

The purpose of this chapter is to describe and analyze Canadian policies and practices concerning the education of recent immigrants, i.e. those who are foreign born. Since Canada is decentralized, with education a provincial responsibility, our treatment will take into account this decentralization.

Immigration to Canada: History, Policies, and Trends

From 1945 to 1967, immigration increased considerably and was characterized by better educated immigrants, settling mainly in Toronto and (less) in Montreal. Immigrants from Southern Europe (Italians, Greeks, Portuguese) came from the "underdeveloped" regions of these countries and often formed ethnic ghettos. The percentage of "other ethnic groups" constituted twenty-six percent of the 1961 Canadian population.

    Canada began to attract a much more diverse immigrant population in terms of education, occupation and ethnic origin than previously. In 1950, only three categories of people were accepted as desirable immigrants: 1) those coming from UK,

---

[1] There exists a longer version of this paper which provides a province by province treatment. It is available upon request from the author.

471

Australia, New Zealand, USA, Eire, France; 2) relatives of individuals already resident in Canada, and 3) citizens of "non-Asiatic" countries entering Canada with "assured employment" as agriculturists, miners or lumbermen. Changes in the 1960s abolished discrimination based on country of origin and gave more weight to the occupational qualifications of the immigrant (Hawkins 1972). These changes diversified the Canadian population racially, linguistically, and religiously. From 1961 to 1981, the Asian population in Canada more than tripled and Third World countries now form the majority of the main ten contributors to Canadian immigration. The 1966 regulations selected immigrants on educational background, skills, training and need for the potential contribution of the immigrant to the Canadian marketplace rather than on race, ethnicity or country of origin.

More than 4.4 million immigrants came to Canada from 1951 to 1981. As Table 1 indicates, between 1945 and 1970, Europe was the source of seven out of every ten immigrants. Between 1981 and 1985, Asia was the principal source of new immigrants to Canada. European immigration by 1985 dropped to 22.5 percent of the total immigration. Since 1945, Canada has witnessed a dramatic increase in the number of immigrants from Asia, Central and South America, the Caribbean and Africa. In 1956, the percentages of the immigration to Canada from these regions totalled 4.3; by 1977, over 50; and by 1985, 68.4. In 1986, the percentage of immigrants living in Canada were: European, 62; Asian, 18; American, 7; Caribbean, 5; South and Central American, 4; and African and Oceanian, 5 (Secretary of State 1988). By 1986, almost nine and a half million Canadians reported non-British, non-French ethnic origin.

There is considerable provincial variation in the distribution of "other" Canadians (i.e. non-English, non-French population) and immigrants (people born outside Canada) (see Table 2). 11.3 percent of Canadians report being of non-English, non-French mother tongue (when asked about their home language, the percentage drops to 5.9). 15.4 percent were born outside Canada; among these, 30.5 percent were born in a non-European country (excluding the U.S.). The Maritime provinces have relatively few "other" Canadians and immigrants. Ontario has, in total numbers and percentage, the largest

Table 1. Immigration by Last Country of Permanent Residence (percentage)

Country	1956	1961	1966	1971	1977	1982	1985
United Kingdom	30.6	16.5	32.5	12.7	15.7	13.6	5.3
France	2.3	3.3	4.0	2.4	2.4	1.9	1.7
Italy	16.9	19.7	16.2	4.7	3.0	1.2	0.8
Germany	15.8	8.7	4.8	1.9	2.0	3.7	1.9
Other (Europe)	22.7	24.5	18.7	21.0	12.4	17.6	12.8
Total (Europe)	88.3	72.7	76.2	42.7	35.5	38.0	22.5
Africa	0.4	1.5	1.9	2.3	5.5	3.7	4.2
India	0.2	0.8	1.1	4.4	4.8	6.4	4.8
Other (Asia)	1.9	3.0	6.0	13.8	22.5	27.9	41.0
Total (Asia)	2.1	3.8	7.1	18.2	27.3	34.3	45.8
Australia	1.2	2.0	2.1	2.4	1.3	0.7	0.6
United States	5.9	16.1	9.0	20.0	11.2	7.7	7.9
Central & S.Amer.	1.0	2.0	1.4	4.6	8.0	7.5	11.6
Caribbean	0.8	1.8	2.1	9.0	10.4	6.7	6.8
Other	0.3	0.1	0.2	0.8	0.8	1.1	0.7
Total	100%	100%	100%	100%	100%	100%	100%

Source: *Annuaire du Canada* 1988, 2.35, Bathnagar 1981, 75.

Table 2. **Distribution of Allophone Canadians (neither French nor English): Canada & Provinces, 1986 Census**

Provinces		Nationally Born Mother Tongue	Home Language	Immigrants European	* Non European
Nfld.	N	3765	1765	8920	1745
	%	0.7	0.3	1.6	18.9
P.E.I.	N	1340	370	4320	595
	%	1.1	0.3	3.4	13.6
N.S.	N	15890	8125	40465	7650
	%	1.8	0.9	4.6	19.4
N.B.	N	7885	3590	26960	3305
	%	1.1	0.5	3.8	12.2
Quebec	N	393725	274640	527145	194415
	%	6.0	4.3	8.1	36.8
Ontario	N	1354610	723475	2081195	587670
	%	14.9	8.0	22.9	28.2
Manitoba	N	197195	83755	142220	44505
	%	18.6	7.9	13.4	31.3
Sask.	N	132750	40295	71980	15830
	%	13.1	4.0	7.1	22.0
Alberta	N	314200	128870	368750	122910
	%	13.3	5.5	15.6	33.3
B.C.	N	416335	187310	630670	211205
	%	14.4	6.6	21.9	33.5
Canada	N	2860570	1468325	3908160	1191040
	%	11.3	5.9	15.4	30.5

*(Not USA)
Percentages calculated over total population
Source: Statistics Canada 1987

immigrant population. British Columbia and Quebec follow in total numbers, British Columbia, Alberta and Manitoba in percentage, but the volume of immigration to Western Canada is considerably smaller than that of Ontario. In Central and Western Canada, non-European immigrants (excluding those from the U.S.) form between a fourth and a third or more of the immigrant population. Quebec has the highest percentage of non-European immigrants, with British Columbia, Alberta and Manitoba close behind, while Ontario, with over half a million, has the highest number of this category of immigrants. Almost 50 percent of all immigrants who lived in Canada in 1986 came in the period 1967-1986. Since 1967 close to two million immigrants have settled in Canada--and more than half of these in Ontario. Three quarters of a million immigrants (18.6 percent of the total) have entered Canada since 1978.

Immigration since World War Two has accelerated *urbanization*. Toronto, Montreal, and Vancouver absorbed most of the new immigrants. By 1971, in Toronto, close to half of the household heads were born outside Canada, another fifth had at least one foreign-born parent (Secretary of State 1988). In 1986, more than 1.4 million Toronto citizens reported ethnic origins other than French or English; 600,000 Montrealers and 450,000 Vancouverites did the same. Italian was the major ethnic origin in both Toronto and Montreal. Chinese was first in Vancouver and was second in Toronto. Vancouver (over 20 percent), followed by Toronto (over 15 percent), have the highest percentages of visible minority (racially distinguishable) Canadians in their population. Calgary, Edmonton, and Winnipeg also have 10 percent or more of visible minority Canadians. Halifax, Montreal, Ottawa-Hull, Kitchener, Windsor, Regina, Saskatoon and Victoria have between 5 percent and 10 percent of visible minority Canadians (Secretary of State 1988).

To synthesize, Driedger's (1979) characterization of Canada's six linguistic and cultural regions provides an overall view of the Canadian mosaic: 1) *The Northlands*--multicultural and multilingual; 2) *the West*--essentially anglophone and multicultural; 3) *Upper Canada*--anglophone and increasingly multicultural; 4) *Lower Canada*--francophone and multicultural;

5) *New Brunswick*--officially bilingual and bicultural; 6) *The Maritimes*, anglophone and Anglocultural.

The Measurement of Canadian Diversity

Methodological difficulties exist for the precise measurement of Canadian diversity. What variable do we use: mother tongue, language used at home, ethnicity--defined as feeling of belonging to a particular group or as the group of one's ancestors--or the country of origin for self or one's ancestors? The choice produces different results and consequences. Table 3 presents the distribution of the Canadian population by mother tongue and home language, for Canada and for its ten provinces. This table uses 1986 Census data to provide information for both official languages (French and English), and for over forty non-official languages regrouped in the "other category." The 1986 Census also has data on "multiple responses," i.e. those respondents who indicated having two or more mother and/or home languages, including French and English. When one moves from mother tongue to home language: the French language "loses" a percentage point; the English language "gains" close to 6 percent, and the "other" linguistic category drops from 11.3 percent to 5.9 percent. Multiple responses contain 3.8 percent (mother tongue) or 4.6 percent (home language). This data stresses the overall dominance of English as a mother tongue and home language, identifies the Quebec francophone block and de-emphasizes the "other" category, especially in terms of home language. But is the picture so simple?

Let us look at the variable *ethnicity*. Jean Burnet (1984) states:

> . . . the exact ethnic composition of Canadian society is not known. An ethnic group is made up of those who share a feeling of peoplehood . . . It is not definable in objective terms; there is always some self-selection involved. Further, it is now recognized that ethnic

Table 3. Canadian Population by Mother Tongue and Home Language, 1986 Census

Provin.		French		English		Other		Mult.	Resp.	Eng.*	Fr.*	Total**	
		MT	HL	MT	HL	MT	HL	MT	HL	MT	HL	MT	HL
Nfld	N	2005	1570	560363	550060	3765	1765	2220	2615	1120	1155	568350	564005
	%	0.3	0.2	98.6	98.9	0.6	0.3	0.4	0.4	50.4	44.2	100	100
PEI	N	5155	2895	118490	120065	1340	370	1650	1760	1340	1260	126645	125090
	%	4.1	2.3	93.6	95.9	1.1	0.3	1.3	1.4	81.2	71.5	100	100
N.S.	N	30865	21030	814135	823270	15890	8125	12295	11725	8490	7270	873175	864150
	%	3.5	2.4	93.2	95.3	1.8	0.9	1.4	1.3	69.0	62.0	100	100
N.B.	N	225090	208545	450970	464985	7885	3590	25005	24735	23050	22355	709440	701855
	%	31.7	29.7	63.6	66.3	1.1	0.5	3.5	3.5	92.2	90.4	100	100
Que.	N	5316925	5223370	580030	676050	393725	274640	241785	280425	150730	160580	6532465	6454490
	%	81.4	80.9	8.9	10.5	6.0	4.3	3.7	4.3	62.3	58.7	100	100
Ont.	N	424720	281615	6941930	7492440	1354610	723475	380435	503645	104150	111320	9101690	9001645
	%	4.7	3.1	76.3	83.2	14.9	8.0	4.2	5.6	27.4	22.1	100	100
Man.	N	45600	23840	758305	874625	197195	83755	61915	67100	10910	11485	1063015	1049320
	%	4.3	2.3	71.3	83.3	18.6	7.9	5.8	6.4	17.6	17.1	100	100
Sask	N	20725	6670	815090	910770	132750	40295	41055	38960	5190	5505	1009610	996700
	%	2.1	0.7	80.7	91.4	13.1	4.0	4.1	3.9	12.6	14.1	100	100
Alta	N	48070	17640	1914450	2093080	314200	128870	89105	100675	14150	14100	2365825	2340265
	%	2.0	0.8	80.9	89.4	13.3	5.5	3.8	4.3	15.9	14.1	100	100
B.C.	N	38240	10525	2331595	2528010	416335	187310	97200	123740	12685	12405	2883365	2849585
	%	1.3	0.4	80.9	88.6	14.4	6.6	3.3	4.3	13.1	10.0	100	100
CAN	N	6159740	5798470	15334085	16595535	2860570	1468325	954940	1159670	332610	351900	25309330	25022005
	%	24.3	23.2	60.5	66.3	11.3	5.9	3.8	4.6	34.8	30.3	100	100

*As percentage of multiple responses. ** Mother tongues calculated from 100% data; Home language from 20% data. Totals for home language are under-estimated.

Source: Statistics Canada 1987

identity is not as fixed as it once was or once was thought to be; intermarriage is only one of the factors creating possibilities for choice. (p. 24)

If *origin* is used from the 1986 census, the proportion of the Canadian population that is not British, French or Native in origin is 28.6 percent (calculated from single responses data). The "third force" is less than a third of the population-- especially if we consider home language, since English in 1986 was the home language of 66 percent of the population, and the mother tongue of 60 percent. The issue is further complicated by the multiple responses which vary considerably from province to province and are in some cases numerically important.

Table 4 reveals that, while the "other" population is scarce in the Maritimes, and totals only 10.4 percent in Quebec, it is important in Ontario and Western Canada, where it forms over forty percent of the single response population.

Nonofficial language groups are not all alike. Some retain their mother tongue as a home language much more than others. There are also differences in group structuring and mobilization towards the maintenance and promotion of linguistic and cultural traits. Also, the relative distances from the dominant Anglo-Canadian and French-Canadian cultures vary. Lumping ethno-cultural groups for statistical purposes (e.g. Black Haitians of Montreal and Japanese living in Western Canada) can hide significant differences.

The Census question on ethnicity has been rephrased for 1986 to replace *arrival in North America* with the respondent's subjective sense of belonging to a particular ethnic group or the objective reality of ancestral country of origin. This change in the question complicates inter-census comparisons. It also confuses the objective and subjective aspects of the question. Multiple responses also complicate inter-census comparisons. Previously "corrected" answers are now taken as given.

Porter (1975) disagreed with the prevalent Canadian practice of grouping Canadian and foreign-born in the same ethnic origin categories and not allowing "Canadian" as an ethnic or cultural group, therefore forcing everyone to have a non-

Table 4. Distribution of Canadian Population by Ethnic Origin, 1986 Census

Ethnicity	Canada	Nfld	PEI	N.S.	N.B.	Que	Ont	Man	Sask	Alta	BC
British	35.1	95.6	79.9	77.9	49.8	5.3	48.9	32.9	36.7	42.6	49.5
French	33.7	2.4	15.0	9.9	46.1	83.5	8.9	8.2	5.5	5.6	3.9
Aborig.	2.1	0.8	0.5	1.1	0.8	0.8	0.9	8.1	9.2	3.7	3.5
Black	0.9	0.0	0.1	1.5	0.0	0.6	1.9	0.6	0.2	0.6	0.3
German	4.6	0.3	0.7	3.9	0.7	0.4	4.8	14.1	21.3	13.2	8.4
Italian	3.9	0.0	0.1	0.4	0.2	2.7	7.8	1.2	0.3	1.7	2.7
Ukrainian	2.3	0.0	0.0	0.3	0.0	0.2	1.8	11.7	10.0	7.7	2.7
Chinese	2.0	0.1	0.1	0.3	0.2	0.4	2.6	1.3	1.2	3.5	6.4
Dutch	2.0	0.0	1.7	1.7	0.6	0.1	2.9	4.1	2.2	4.0	3.6
S. Asia	1.5	0.1	0.3	0.4	0.1	0.3	2.3	1.1	0.6	2.2	3.9
Jewish	1.4	0.0	0.0	0.3	0.1	1.4	2.1	2.0	0.2	0.6	0.7
Polish	1.2	0.0	0.1	0.3	0.0	0.3	2.0	3.2	2.2	2.0	1.1
Other	8.8	0.3	1.0	1.9	1.0	4.0	13.1	11.4	10.4	12.6	13.3
Total single (millions)	18	0.47	.074	.536	.504	6.01	5.95	.681	.605	1.34	1.09
Total % Multiple	27.9	16.6	40.8	38.0	28.1	6.9	33.9	35.0	38.7	40.6	38.2

Source: Statistics Canada 1987, Selected Characteristics for Federal Electoral Districts (20% sample data)

Canadian ethnic origin. Porter argued against the over-emphasis on ethnicity, noting that what might be strong for first generation Canadian would often be less so for others born in Canada of Canadian-born parents.

Multicultural Education: Policies and Practices

We now present multicultural education, for the federal government and the largest provinces of each of five regions. Provincial policies related to multicultural education are formulated against a backdrop of the federal government's policy of multiculturalism, which essentially legitimizes multicultural educational programs and sustains group demands in this area.

In 1963, the *Royal Commission on Bilingualism and Biculturalism* began its work, leading to the 1969 *Official Languages Act* and the formulation of a *Policy of Multiculturalism within a Bilingual Framework* on October 8, 1971. The latter policy statement on multiculturalism was made by Prime Minister Trudeau in the House of Commons, and all parties subscribed to it. At the time, it was felt unnecessary to pass legislation on this matter.

Five principles were advanced:

1) the basic principle of equality of status: "although there are two official languages, there is no official culture, nor does any ethnic group take precedence over any other";

2) pluralism as the "very essence of Canadian identity";

3) the principle of sharing the Canadian culture, including of non-British and non-French in Canadian institutions;

4) free choice of life-styles and cultural traits;

5) the concern for and protection of civil rights and human rights.

From a Canadian/federal point of view, multiculturalism is a national policy that attempts to enhance among minority groups feelings of belonging to Canada, conceived as a multicultural society, equalitarian and tolerant (McAndrew

1987). Multiculturalism thus seeks to contribute to national unity--something at the heart of the federal government legitimacy and mandate--by recognizing diversity beyond the "two solitudes" (English and French). The policy also aims to depoliticize ethnicity and to emphasize the cultural contributions of non-dominant ethnic groups.

Since education is a provincial jurisdiction, the Federal government's involvement in the area of multiculturalism has been limited to non-formal education and research oriented towards linguistic and cultural maintenance of minority groups and a better understanding and appreciation of the "Canadian mosaic." As Jean Burnet (1978) notes:

> The Multiculturalism Directorate has carried on liaison activities with ethnic communities and with the ethnic press; initiated and developed studies and research, including a series of histories on ethnic groups; assisted the Canadian Ethnic Studies' Association to develop as a full-fledged learned society with two regular publications; sponsored activities in the performing and the visual arts; assisted in programmes aimed at retention of non-official languages. (p. 107)

In 1983, it subsidized 693 ethnic schools enroling 104,419 students (40 percent in Ontario and 20 percent in Quebec), granted $4.5 million (1985-86) for in-service training of teachers and the production of curriculum material for these classes (McAndrew 1987). A further $4 million went to supplementary and community organized schools across Canada, mostly for 863 schools to teach fifty-eight different heritage languages to 127,920 students in 73,739 classes. $452,000--12 percent of the total funding--went to develop instructional material and for professional development of the teachers (Canadian Ethnocultural Council 1988).

Multiculturalism, once merely a policy statement, was enshrined in the 1982 *Constitution Act*. In July 1988, the House of Commons passed Bill C-93, the Canadian *Multiculturalism Act*. A Department of Multiculturalism is being set up within the Secretary of State.

Education and Multiculturalism

The diversity in multicultural education implies that programs, activities, and orientations should be organized into a typology. For example, Wilson (1984) identifies four categories of multicultural activities and programs:

1) English-as-second language (ESL) (in Quebec, FSL) programs or remedial official language programmes for New Canadian children;

2) Non-official language instruction for one ethnic, religious, or linguistic group, intended for cultural maintenance and preservation;

3) programs designed to stem or eradicate prejudice, discrimination or racism; and

4) curricular content to be dispensed in the social studies only, rather than incorporated into art, music, home economics, English, and other subjects, or a separate course called multicultural studies.

For Mcleod (1984), there are three approaches to multicultural education:

1) an ethnic-specific approach, which seeks to counteract assimilative forces, extend family socialisation, or generally broaden the child's or adult's knowledge of, involvement in, or acquaintance with the ethnic heritage (ethnic schools, ethnocultural programs, and language courses are oriented toward such goals).

2) a problem-oriented approach, developed to answer perceived needs or demands associated with schooling and the assimilation or integration of people of diverse backgrounds (good examples are ESL/D [English as a second language/dialect] courses, compensatory programs for the "disadvantaged," and anti-discrimination programs).

3) a cultural/intercultural approach, which focuses on developing capabilities that will enable people to live in a pluralistic society, producing individuals who will be capable of transcending the boundaries of their own ethnic cultures.

Multiculturalism in Schools of Selected Provinces

Nova Scotia is the most populous of the Atlantic provinces. Although its population is almost totally anglophone, an official policy on multicultural education is emerging after the recent appointment of a multicultural education consultant. It regularly evaluates learning materials for bias, stereotyping and prejudice. It is rewriting curriculum guidelines to include a more obvious multicultural focus and is developing/supporting/listing materials with specific ethnic (e.g. Black, Micmac, Acadian, Lebanese, Scots) or multicultural focus. It is also developing senior high level courses with a global studies focus.

English as a second language is given in classes by resource or itinerant teachers, especially in the Halifax-Darmouth metropolitan area. ESL classes have financial support from the Government of Canada. Heritage languages are usually taught by the specific ethnic groups and receive financial support from the Secretary of State.

In 1979 the Nova Scotia Teachers' Union (NSTU) established a committee to examine multiculturalism in that province and to recommend a policy. The policy established by the Teachers' Union was a broad cultural/intercultural thrust, based upon ethnocultural awareness, equality of opportunity and equality of access, teacher sensitivity, curriculum reform, and the development of support services, programs, materials, and resources (McLeod 1984).

The Department of Education has conducted a special teacher training program for Native people at the Nova Scotia Teachers' College. Dalhousie University offers a Transition Year Program for Black and Native students. The Department of Education also co-sponsors the Joint Committee of Human Rights and Education. It works closely with the Black Educators' Association, Multicultural Association of Nova Scotia, the International Education Centre, and various native organizations, and in collaboration with The Canadian Human Rights Foundation.

In terms of francophone education, Nova Scotia has, or is involved in, the following:
1) specific policy on French education;

2) schools in three districts designed as Acadian where some subjects are taught in French, others in English;

3) three schools designated as Acadian;

4) two francophone schools in which all subjects, except English, are taught in French;

5) nine district school boards offer French immersion schools or classes. There are ten immersion schools in Halifax;

6) a francophone section within the Curriculum section of the Department of Education;

7) a proposal for establishing a new francophone school and cultural centre in the Halifax-Dartmouth area;

8) a proposed establishment of a francophone community college;

9) a francophone university (Université Sainte-Anne, with thirty-one professors and 222 full time students in 1987).

Quebec is the second largest province in population. It is home of the francophone minority: 81.4 percent of its population of 6,631,500 have French as a mother tongue, and 80.9 percent speak French at home. An important anglophone minority is present in the province: 8.9 percent have English as their mother tongue, and 10.5 percent speak it at home. The category "others" regroups 6 percent of the population and 8.1 percent (over half a million people) are immigrants.

Since Confederation there has been a constitutionally protected minority school system for Protestants (which traditionally included most of the anglophones). The original protection under Article 93 of *The British North American Act* has now been extended under *The Canadian Constitution Act 1982.*

Although Quebec has resisted committing itself to an official policy on multicultural education, it provides many services to immigrants and to the ethnocultural communities.

In 1977, the Parti Québécois government passed Bill 101, which made French the official language of the province and which sought to make it the language of work for all and the language of instruction for immigrants. A 1978 White Paper on Cultural Development showed an increased awareness of the cultural diversity of the province. It did not lead to a multicultural education policy, but to the provision of programs and services. Also in 1978, Heritage language programs were introduced in Quebec schools, from 1981 as part of the *Plan d'action à l'intention des communautés culturelles.*

A ministerial committee published the Chancy report: *L'école Québécoise et les communautés culturelles* in 1985. The priorities among its over 60 recommendations were:

1) a policy of intercultural education and the preparation of a plan of action;

2) action against racial and ethnic discrimination;

3) in-service training of teachers working in multicultural schools;

4) establishment of a multicultural education resource centre;

5) coordination between the Education Ministry and the Immigration Ministry with regard to Heritage Language programs;

6) education of underschooled or illiterate youth;

7) programs for parents in ethnocultural communities.

The Ministry has not committed itself to a multicultural education policy (the first recommendation of the Chancy report), but a provincial coordinator was named in 1986 to see that the other Chancy recommendations were implemented by all departments, as well as by the school boards, especially those in the Montreal Metropolitan area where 95 percent of the immigrant population is concentrated.

In 1988, this coordinator produced the Latif Report, which has twelve recommendations. The main ones are:

1) the extension of PELO programs to all interested;

2) full-time French kindergarten classes for non-French children who are not admissible to the English schools;

3) experimentation of educational services for illiterate or under-schooled youth from ethnocultural communities;

4) hiring of teachers of ethnocultural background;

5) inclusion in pre-service teacher programs intercultural education and multi-ethnic practicum;

6) extension of in-service teacher activities related to intercultural education;

7) more research, but less based on attitudinal and perceptual data, and more on "hard" data of educational achievement of ethnocultural communities.

It is worth mentioning that Quebec governmental reports (Comité Chancy 1985 and Latif 1988) use "intercultural education," instead of "multicultural" to avoid endorsing, even implicitly, the federal multicultural policy. This federal policy is perceived by many francophones as the negation of the *two founding peoples* theory, thereby undermining bilingualism in the long run (Rocher 1976).

The Island of Montreal School Council has published material on the city's ethnocultural communities and researched the integration within schools of children from various ethnocultural backgrounds (Laperrière 1983) and on parent-school relationships. This research is still in progress.

In September 1988, the Protestant School Board of Greater Montreal (PSBGM) adopted a policy on multicultural/multiracial education. It is the only Quebec school system with a policy ideologically congruent with that of the federal government's multicultural policy.

Ontario is the most populous province of Canada, with over nine million inhabitants. Its population is mostly anglophone (76.3 percent mother tongue, and 83.2 percent home language); its French minority is proportionately small (4.7 percent mother tongue, and 3.1 percent home language), but numerically important: between 424,720 and 281,615. Ontario has 22.9 percent of its population (more than two million) foreign born. 15 percent declared that their mother tongue was neither French nor English.

Ontario has a policy on multicultural education, grounded in the principle of equal opportunity for all students to develop as completely as possible their abilities and interests, and to meet each student's special needs. "This overriding policy forms the basis upon which immigrant students are incorporated into the Ontario education system" (Letter from H. Noble, Director, Policy Analysis and Research Branch, OME).

In curricular development:

1) school boards are encouraged to develop programs that promote an understanding of people from different cultures and build self-confidence among children of varying origins;

2) discriminatory materials are kept out of the school system, and resource materials are selected to reflect the diversity of Ontario society;

3) Ministry guidelines promote equality for all students in core curriculum areas and

4) specific race relations curriculum documents are presently being developed.

In 1984, a provincial advisory committee on race relations was set up, its mandate being to formulate a race relations policy for use by school boards in Ontario. In September 1987, the committee recommended an equity policy in the following nine areas: leadership, school and community relations, research, curriculum, personnel policies and practices, staff development, assessment and placement, support services in guidance, and racial harassment. Public responses to the policy statement have been analyzed and a reaction to them and the report will be the basis for further action by the Ministry of Education. The Ministry has appointed a Special Advisor on Race Relations and a core group of advisory resource personnel in the regional offices to work with schools and community agencies to improve race relations.

Ontario has developed a variety of programs and services to facilitate the adaptation of students of ethnocultural background and to foster multicultural education. Some of the most important are: English as a Second Language or Dialect (ESL/D) for which new curriculum guidelines have been formulated by the Ministry in 1988; self-contained programs for those who have serious language deficiencies, which allow students to receive more individualized instruction in all subject areas; programs to upgrade basic skills of children with uneven or limited instruction; translation services for students and their parents; services of non-teaching support staff including social workers, counsellors, paraprofessionals and first language tutors; education referrals to social services providers; professional development for teachers in the area of race relations and ethnocultural equity; and heritage language programs.

Heritage language programs (HLP) were introduced in 1977. Under the continuing education program, HLP classes may be offered after school, on non-school days, or where numbers justify during an extension of the required school day. HLP is seen by many as a compromise: it recognizes and financially supports teaching of nonofficial languages, but it does not include these languages in the regular curriculum of the public schools. From the outset, there has been a positive response: forty-two boards were involved in 1968 when classes were opened for thirty languages and 52,713 students. In 1984-85, the corresponding figures were: seventy-five school boards, 4,197 classes, fifty-six languages and 91,757 students. HLP is now mandatory where requested by twenty-five families in any board. To assist school boards in delivering HL classes, the Ontario Ministry of Education provides a resource guide and funds to encourage the training of Heritage Languages instructors, the development of student learning materials, and to support research. Finally, Mallea (1984) reports experiments in bilingual schooling in the nonofficial languages.

In 1977 Ontario inaugurated a history course (Canada's Multicultural Heritage), for secondary schools, additional qualifications for teachers of multicultural education, encouragement for teachers to use a multicultural basis for early elementary education, and guidelines for publishers and authors to promote bias-free texts and curriculum materials.

The Ontario Ministry of Education (1979) adopted a policy statement *Special Populations in Education* which

> . . . recognized that the responsibility for preparing all Ontario students to live in Canada's multicultural society has significant implications in terms of general approaches to education, as well as in provision for special populations. In meeting the common needs of all students, publicly provided education has the task of encouraging general system sensitivity, while ensuring that individual and group needs are met in a way that will facilitate full participation by all students in the educational opportunities of the system. (p. 23)

Although Native people are indigenous to Canada, Ontario does not make specific reference to them in discussing multicultural matters. This recognizes the special nature of their claims. Instead, Ontario has provided for special membership of Native people on local boards of education, developed curriculum resources regarding Native people for schools, and appointed a ministry official to be responsible for the province's involvement in Native Education.

In 1968, the Ontario legislature passed a law guaranteeing education in French to the francophone minority and educational services for them have since expanded. For other children, French is a school subject for all elementary students from grade four and there are numerous immersion programs where most of the schooling is in French.

In 1989 an extensive public consultation on religious education in public elementary schools began, recognizing that the 1944 regulation took no account of either a multicultural society nor recent constitutional changes. In consultation with the many interest groups involved the review responds to the *Canadian Charter of Rights and Freedoms*, its interpretation by the courts, and a 1968 resolution by the legislature to consider for Ontario schools a multi-grade, multi-faith religious education curriculum.

Finally, the Ontario Ministry of Education has published important material in the area of multicultural education, including: *Multiculturalism in action: suggestions for teachers* (1977); *Race, religion, and culture in Ontario school materials: suggestions for authors and publishers* (1981); *People of native ancestry: curriculum guidelines for the senior division* (1982); *Black studies: a resource guide for teachers, intermediate division* (1983); and *The development of a Policy on Race and Ethnocultural Equity* (1987).

Ontario, in brief, may be seen as having both a policy of multicultural education and a set of programs and services geared to the objectives of the policy.

Alberta is the largest and richest population in the prairie regions. Its linguistic characteristics are typical for the West: it is anglophone (80.9 percent mother tongue, 89.4 percent home language) with a significant "other" category (13.3 percent mother tongue, 5.5 percent home language), and a small French minority (2.0 percent mother tongue, 0.8 percent home language).

Alberta has no multicultural education policy but has a strong record of support for and encouragement of multiculturalism. It supports "educational initiatives which promote tolerance, understanding, and acceptance of all peoples," which indicates multiculturalism to be important in the regular school program. Various government documents reinforce this view, for example Alberta Cultural Heritage Branch (1984):

> Alberta's people possess a diversity of cultural backgrounds from which they have nurtured the best of traditions. This rich inheritance has become a profound feature of our lives that strengthens the identity of our people. The Government of Alberta reaffirms its commitment to the Cultural Heritage of Albertans. (p. 3)

Since 1970 boards of education may authorize the use of any nonofficial language as the language of instruction in all or any of its schools. In 1974, pilot programs used Ukrainian as a language of instruction at the primary level for up to 50 percent of the school day. The Edmonton public and separate school boards sponsor bilingual programs in twenty-six schools: six Ukrainian, one Hebrew, two Mandarin, two Arabic, four German, and one Polish. In the Ukrainian/English bilingual schools, arithmetic, English language arts, and science are taught in English; social studies, physical education, Ukrainian language arts, art and music are taught in Ukrainian, with Ukrainian culture and language receiving equal emphasis.

"Saturday Schools" in "other" languages are numerous. These programs are administered by the Alberta Cultural Heritage Branch. 143 community sponsored language schools in 41 different languages and with 11,552 students have been counted. The Government of Canada has committed itself to the establishment in Edmonton of a Heritage Language Institute.

Alberta language education policy seeks to:

1) ensure that all Alberta students have the opportunity to achieve a high level of proficiency in the English language;

2) develop and make available programs to fulfill rights of francophone Albertans who qualify under section 23 of the *Canadian Charter of Rights and Freedoms* to have their children educated in French;

3) provide opportunities for English-speaking students to learn French;

4) provide opportunities for students to learn a range of languages in addition to English or French; and

5) provide opportunities for all students whose first language is not English and who require assistance to learn English.

British Columbia has the third largest population among the Canadian provinces, and its linguistic/ethnic mix differs in important respects. It is anglophone (80.9 percent mother tongue, 88.6 percent home language), has a significant "other" category (14.4 percent mother tongue, 6.6 percent home language) and a small French minority (1.3 percent mother tongue, 0.4 percent home language).

There is no policy of multicultural education, but the Education Ministry Modern Languages and Multicultural Programs Branch is presently drafting one. For the francophone minority, the *Programme Cadre de Français* confirmed the policy of parental choice of either official language as the language of instruction for their children. Efforts are also directed toward ESL programs and the teaching of nonofficial languages. In 1986, a two-volume Resource Book of ESL was published by the Ministry and widely distributed in the province. An English Second Language coordinator is developing curriculum and providing advisory/ consultative services to the province.

A project called *Alternatives to Racism* has been launched by the Ministry in cooperation with school boards. In the early 1980s, the Vancouver School Board established a policy on race relations. In 1982-83, it asked its schools to submit a plan of action on multicultural education. Eighty percent of schools organized consultative committees to foster parental participation in the planning and implementation of the policy. The main activities were professional development of teachers, curricular units on multiculturalism, special days, and thematic weeks. "Alternatives to Racism" (a non-profit Vancouver organisation) published a guide entitled *A Handbook for enhancing the multicultural climate of the school*. It has also created a program called "New Friends" for grade two students.

There is a Native Indian teacher education program at the University of British Columbia. Greater Victoria has adopted a program of affirmative action for the hiring of native teachers (Kehoe 1984).

The Educational Attainment of Ethnic Groups

One of the objectives for policies, programs, and services of education departments in Canada is to equalize educational opportunity for all Canadians, of any ethnic origin or mother tongue. This section will address the educational achievement of ethnic groups, especially at the post-secondary level.

The 1982 study (Porter, Porter, and Blishen) of Ontario students' educational aspirations, examined the influence of ethnicity by identifying three categories of parents: both parents foreign-born, one foreign-born, and both parents Canadian-born. The authors write: "If we look at the educational aspirations of the children of each of the three categories of parents, it is quite clear that in general immigrant children were at no disadvantage, particularly if they were boys" (p. 81). The evidence suggests that many immigrant parents transmit their own (high) aspirations to their children. The authors raise the question of what constitutes the norm of group educational attainment.

Porter's Ontario study on secondary school students' educational aspirations is supported by data on post-secondary achievement of many (but not all) ethnic groups. This seems to have been the case for some time. Indeed, according to Shamai and Corrigan (1987), the 1931 Census revealed that:

1) for the total Canadian school age population among Canadian born, 93.03 percent were at school;

2) Jews had the highest proportion (97.4 percent) at school;

3) Jews also had the highest proportion of pupils attending class for the largest number of days (seven to nine months) reported in the Census table (96.44 percent compared to 89.51 percent of the total Canadian born population);

4) the group doing the worst in both categories was the "Indian and Eskimo," of whom 65 percent attended school and only 56.7 percent attended for seven to nine months.

Fifty years later, Shamai and Corrigan (1987) found that the Jews are still leading, with the Asian groups following close behind. 39.71 percent of the Jews have attained university level education compared to 15.32 percent for the total Canadian population. The percentage of British is 16.88, that of French is 10.73. The Native people have the lowest representation: 4.76 percent.

Shamai and Corrigan (1987) thus conclude that the trend for fifty years is of dominance in educational attainment by the Jewish and Asian groups. These results are also consistent with the Toronto Board of Education's *Every Student Survey* (1980).

Anisef et al. (1985) report that between 1971 and 1981 many groups in Ontario whose mother language was not English (Italians, Polish, Ukrainians) raised their rate of participation in postsecondary education (full-time and part-time). This was more true for women than for men. Although from 1971 to 1981 the native people lost ground in their relative participation in postsecondary education, by 1981, most other groups with a mother language other than English had surpassed the English group in terms of participation in postsecondary non-university education.

Data from the Secretary of State of Canada (1987) support Shamai and Corrigan's analysis. Table 5 indicates higher than average participation rates in both university and total higher education for boys of visible minorities--except for Native Canadians. Except for the black girls and Native Canadians, all girls of visible minorities are over the average.

Table 5. Post-Secondary Participation Rates (per cent) by Ethnic Background, University and All-Postsecondary

Ethnicity	All Post-Secondary		University	
	Male	Female	Male	Female
British	7.8	8.9	4.7	5.5
French	7.7	7.9	2.3	2.8
Native	1.1	1.3	0.2	0.5
German	8.8	9.6	5.8	6.2
Dutch	5.9	6.7	3.1	4.1
Jewish	8.0	8.7	6.5	5.4
Italian	9.1	12.2	3.9	6.1
Chinese	14.3	14.8	11.3	10.7
Black	8.3	7.6	5.8	3.7
Indo-Pakistani	9.8	9.5	7.9	5.6
Other	10.5	11.6	6.5	8.5
All	8.3	9.1	4.3	4.1

Source: Secretary of State of Canada, 1987.

It should be noted that these rates are approximations calculated from the estimated student population of less than twenty-four years of age and the 1981 census population between fifteen and twenty-four. We must be cautious with these statistics, both because they are approximate and because there may be a "lag" between the reality they describe and the present one, which can be hypothesized to reflect recent immigration to Canada, with "refugees" coming from Haiti, Central America, South-East Asia, etc. Some of these groups may have more adaptive problems than previous immigrant groups.

We need recent "hard" data on the educational achievement of Canada's ethnic groups. Cummins (1984) writes:

> Contrary to our American neighbors who have very detailed data on school achievement of minority children, we can rely only on a small data base. We have sufficient proof of the existence of a problem, but not enough data from which we could devise solutions. (p. 62, author's translation)

The problems he points to are those of Caribbean and Portuguese students in Toronto who are often oriented toward technical-vocational programs, and those of Italian and Greek students who are obtaining mediocre results in English. Latif (1988) has also insisted on the necessity of doing research on the educational achievement of Quebec's ethnocultural communities, arguing that there are too many perceptual studies, and not enough "hard" data to identify and circumscribe problems. The only data available is from the ASOPE research project (see Sylvain, Laforce, and Trottier 1985) and it dates back to the early 1970s (Lessard 1987).

Ethnocultural Diversity and Educational Policy:
A Contingency Formulation

Although there are numerous initiatives, projects and innovations across the country, we know very little about their diffusion throughout the respective provincial educational systems, nor about their impact on school personnel, students, and school-community relations. We also do not know systematically how they have come about. In what follows, we systematize the evolving Canadian situation for multicultural education policies and practices, from the analytic framework of Contingency Theory (Lawrence and Lorsch 1967).

Contingency Theory states that the organizational environment *determines* the structural and functional arrangements of organizations. Effectiveness has to do with the match between environmental constraints and organizational adjustments. Contingency theory is employed here to organize, analyze and interpret the data presented in previous sections of this chapter. For example, educational policies with regard to recent immigrants' ethnic diversity are thus viewed as adaptive responses to a set of environmental constraints. These constraints and their articulation with the educational systems' responses are discussed.

It is necessary to identify the environmental variables and their indicators, i.e. a particular type of educational system's adaptation to diversity. The important variables we suggest to be the following:

1) the presence and relative importance of "other" groups: for example the number and percentage of people with a non-official mother language;

2) the presence and relative importance of an official language minority: the number and percentage of people with an official language mother language, as well as appraisal of group structuring and mobilization;

3) the presence and relative importance of immigrants: the number and percentage of foreign-born in the province;

4) the presence and relative importance of non-European immigration: the number and percentage of people foreign-born and non-European;

5) the degree of urban concentration of immigrants: the number and percentage of foreign-born in large urban areas;

6) the period of immigration: 1967-1986 and 1978-1986;

7) the ideological-political congruence with the federal multicultural policy.

The argument can be made in the following manner:

1) where there is a significant presence of "other" groups, pressure develops for educational services (e.g. ESL and/or HLP), modification of existing practices (e.g. changes in curriculum and material), or introduction of new ones (e.g. Human Rights Education);

2) the pressure for educational adaptations to diversity may be enhanced by the presence of a French minority of sufficient size and mobilization to demand and obtain French educational services. ("All minorities should be treated as equal; what they have, we should have also," is another way of stating this idea, which seems to be the case in Ontario and Western Canada and may operate in the future in some Atlantic province if immigration rises);

3) urban concentration of immigrants both renders imperative and facilitates the provision of services (true of Quebec, Ontario, and British Columbia, and perhaps in Nova Scotia for the Halifax-Dartmouth area);

4) the increase in non-European immigration (in this case in urban concentration) is conducive to the development of a multicultural education policy with a broad cultural/intercultural orientation. Ontario and British Columbia exemplify this tendency, and it would be applicable to Quebec also, were it not for the ideological-political variable;

5) the non-acceptance of federal multicultural policy may block or retard multicultural education policy, but not necessarily the provision of services: Quebec's situation can be analyzed in these terms.

Bourhis (1984), interprets Quebec's attitude toward multiculturalism to be

> a relationship between the indirect measures of trust and tolerance vis-a-vis multiculturalism and associated programs. Indeed, the more the Anglo-Celts and the French Canadians feel culturally and materially secure, the more they have a favorable attitude towards the consequences of multiculturalism. There also exists a positive correlation between, on the one hand, feelings of security regarding one's own group and, on the other hand, acceptance of the multicultural ideology, favorable attitudes towards multicultural programs and eventual behaviors related to multiculturalism . . . . It must be noted that the French Canadians feel less culturally and materially secure than the Anglo-Celts, so they are on the whole less tolerant to multiculturalism and related programs. (p. 35, author's translation)

The following typology of provincial Education Department's responses to diversity combines the variables, 1) multicultural education police (its existence or non-existence), 2) the services provided, and 3) the linguistic/cultural-intercultural orientation of both policies and services. We have identified four types of provincial adaptation to diversity:

1) No official policy on multicultural education, with few services (linguistic orientation).

2) No official policy on multicultural education and services with linguistic orientation.

3) No official policy on multicultural education and services with cultural/intercultural orientation.

4) Official policy on multicultural education and services with cultural/intercultural orientation.

Although not treated here, Newfoundland and Prince Edward Island correspond to type 1: there are no multicultural policies and very few services in these provinces, because their highly ethnically homogeneous and anglophone population does not seem to need them. We considered in the early phases of our analysis that Alberta fit the second type because it had ESL policy, many of the services offered have a linguistic orientation, but not a policy on multicultural education. However, after a closer look and provision of more information, we concluded that Alberta has a clear and strong multicultural outlook; the distinction between language and culture is thus to be used carefully. Nova Scotia, Quebec, Alberta and British Columbia (as well as New Brunswick, Manitoba and Saskatchewan, none of which are treated here), correspond to type 3. Ontario is a good example of type 4. It must be underlined that types 3 and 4 include eight out of ten provinces, containing more than 95 percent of the Canadian population, which indicates that the cultural/intercultural orientation is the dominant one. It seems a question of time before these patterns generalize and are accepted in all parts of the country.

Conclusion: The Ambiguities of Multiculturalism and the Pluralist Dilemma in Education

Although Canadian practices indicate that one does not need a clear and articulate policy statement to act and adapt the practices of educational systems to new realities of ethno-cultural diversity, a multicultural policy has considerable value. Such a policy defines goals and priorities, commands means, provides a framework for replacing inarticulated and piecemeal action, allows concentration of resources on explicit goals and gives clear direction for action. Such a policy is functional for evaluation purposes; uses time as a resource for change, and orders priorities. It legitimises existing practices which can thus be extended as well as innovations which can be tried and tested. It has a symbolic value which can mobilize all actors toward goal-attainment strategies. Finally, a multicultural education policy gives legitimate arguments to those claiming entitlement to the services. For all these reasons, the formulation and adoption of a multicultural education policy in the respective Canadian provinces is significant, both symbolically and politically. The data analyzed in this paper indicates that most provinces have a policy on multicultural education or are formulating one.

However, the policies and the concept of multiculturalism are ambiguous and difficult. As Bathnagar (1981, 91) reflects:

> Multiculturalism . . . is an exciting theoretical concept. It has never been seriously tried in a modern industrial state. Can it work? It depends upon the interpretation that is put upon the concept of language and culture maintenance. If it implies wholesale importation of cultures from all parts of the globe and an attempt to preserve them in an undiluted form, it is bound to fail. If, on the other hand, it means resisting total rejection of the old culture in favour of an uncritical acceptance of the new, if it means integration of the old with new values, if it means not just being an Italian, or a Canadian, but an Italian-Canadian, it might succeed.

Perceived by some observers as "a policy of cultural democracy as opposed to a policy of cultural imperialism" (Bathnagar 1981), multiculturalism is associated with rejection by racial and ethnic minorities of assimilation--even of soft assimilation (Kehoe 1984). It reflects minorities' determination to be recognized as equal to the British and the French in all spheres of Canadian life. Other observers contend it to be a dangerous policy for Quebec (Rocher 1976), because it puts all ethnic groups on the same footing and rejects the two-societies and the two founding fathers' theory. It is also seen as questioning in the long run the existence of bilingualism, for there is no clear reason for it in a multicultural (as opposed to a bicultural) state.

Still others suggest that the multicultural ideology may disguise the maintenance of inequalities. Indeed, John Porter (1975) argued that cultural differences are exaggerated by English-Canadians in order to use them as an excuse for preventing minority groups from climbing the social ladder. For him, the myth of cultural differences is the major obstacle to equality of opportunity in Canada. Since multiculturalism implies maintenance of cultural differences, it will greatly help the cause of continuing English-Canadian monopoly over elite positions in Canadian society. Porter believes that too much emphasis on ethnic differentiation almost invariably leads to the consolidation of ethnic hierarchies. Jean Burnett (1984) adds that the present federal policy "takes insufficient regard of the special problems and interests of those members of ethnic groups who are new arrivals in Canada" (p. 22). There exists also the fear of balkanization of Canada (Dorotich 1981).

Schools are expected to respond to cultural diversity and to contribute at the same time to the promotion of social cohesion and national integration. The appropriate balance between the educational needs of ethnic minority groups and those of the larger society issues of ethnicity and class can be "exacerbated by the absence of any clearly formulated concept of educational policy set in the framework of broader national policies" (Mallea 1984, 92). As noted by the Council of Ministers of Education (Mallea 1984), the absence of any clearly articulated sense of Canadian society, its values, and its needs is problematic here.

Bathnagar (1981) provides a useful distinction between a multi-ethnic pluralist society and an institutionally pluralist society: the first is committed to cultural pluralism, the second to equality of opportunity for all, including the various ethnic groups, and concerns itself with equal participation in and control of institutions. Two set of problems are thus distinguished--but in some ways interrelated: heritage language programs and participation in both areas for postsecondary education. This chapter indicates that in recent decades, there have been significant developments in Canadian educational policies and practices. On the second set of problems, we need more hard data, more differentiated research on targeted "problem" groups. We must also be wary of the danger of stereotyping particular groups.

Finally, an analogy with policies and practices oriented toward the education of inner-city underprivileged youth may be suggested. These policies and practices did not discriminate inner-city school population underprivileged students from the others. Moreover, at least in Quebec (Houle et al. 1985), there has been considerable political pressure, to extend to all students what was perceived to be good educational services for the underprivileged. The scenario may repeat itself with programs specifically designed for the ethno-cultural students.

Methodological Note

In order to secure up-to-date information on educational policies and practices related to the diversification of the Canadian school population associated with immigration, we have written to all provincial deputy ministers of Education, with the exception of Quebec's deputy minister, because all relevant information was already available to the authors for description and analysis of the situation prevalent in that province. Their response as well as the documentation made available have been most useful for the elaboration of this chapter. In some cases, follow-up phone communications with officials of the respective Education Department helped clarify the multicultural policies and practices of their educational system. A draft copy of the paper was sent to our respondents in the provincial Education Departments; all of them gave feedback and thus helped make the final version up-to-date and accurate. We wish to thank them for their collaboration. It was also necessary to contact The Department of the Secretary of State, Multiculturalism Branch, for information, statistics and documentation on federal involvement in this area. Statistics Canada, as well as Quebec's Ministry of Cultural Communities and Immigration were also consulted for up-to-date demographic information.

References

Alberta Cultural Heritage Branch. 1984. *Alberta's Cultural Heritage-Building on Tradition.* Edmonton.

Alternatives to Racism. (n.d.). *A Handbook for Enhancing the Multicultural Climate of the School.* Vancouver.

Anisef, P., M. A. Bertrand, U. Hortian, and C. E. James. 1985. *L'Accessibilité à l'Enseignement Postsecondaire au Canada, Recension des Ouvrages.* Ottawa: Direction Générale de l'Aide à l'Éducation, Secrétariat d'Etat.

Annuaire du Canada. 1988. Ottawa: Ministère de l'Emploi et de l'Immigration, Division des Affaires Publiques.

Bathnagar, J. 1981. Multiculturalism and the education of immigrants in Canada. In J. Bathnagar, ed. *Educating Immigrants.* N.Y.: St. Martin's Press.

Bourhis, R. Y. 1984. La recherche en psychologie sociale et en langues ancestrales au Canada: Examen rétrospectif et orientations futures. In J. Cummins, ed. *Les Langues Ancestrales au Canada: Perspectives de Recherche.* Rapport de la conférence, convoqueé par le Programme du Multiculturalisme. Ottawa: Secrétariat d'Etat.

Burnet, J. 1978. The policy of multiculturalism within a bilingual framework. *Canadian Ethnic Studies* 10 (2): 107-113.

_____. 1981. Minorities I have belonged to. *Canadian Ethnic Studies* 13(1): 24-36.

_____. 1984. Myths and multiculturalism. In R. J. Samuda, J. W. Berry, and M. Laferrière, eds. *Multiculturalism in Canada. Social and Educational Perspectives.* Toronto: Allyn & Bacon.

Canadian Ethnocultural Council. 1988. *The Other Canadian Languages: A Report on the Status of Heritage Languages across Canada.* Ottawa: CEC.

Comité Chancy. 1985. *L'École Québécoise et les Communautés Culturelles.* Rapport du comite. Québec.

Cummins, J. 1984. La pédagolinguistique et son contexte sociologique dans les recherches en langues ancestrales. In J. Cummins, ed. *Les Langues Ancestrales au Canada: Perspectives de Recherche.* Rapport de la conférence convoquée par le Programme du Multiculturalisme. Ottawa: Secrétariat d'Etat.

Dorotich, D., ed. 1981. *Quo vadis*, multicultural Canada? An editorial comment. *Education and Canadian Multiculturalism: Some Problems and Some Solutions.* Saskatoon: Canadian Society for the Study of Education, University of Saskatchewan.

Driedger, L., ed. 1979. *The Canadian Ethnic Mosaic: A Quest for Identity.* Toronto: Mclelland & Steward.

Hawkins, F. 1972. *Canada and Immigration Public Policy and Public Concerns.* Montreal: McGill-Queen's Univertsity Press.

Houle, R., C. Montmarquette, M. Crespo, and S. Mahseredjian. 1985. L'impact des interventions éducatives en milieu économiquement faibles: le programme de l'Opération renouveau. In M. Crespo and C. Lessard, eds. *Éducation en Milieu Urbain.* Montreal: les Presses de l'Université de Montréal.

House of Commons. 1988. *Bill C-93. The Canadian Multicultural Act* (July 12). Ottawa.

Kehoe, J. 1984. La scène canadienne--conséquences pour l'éducation. *Le Système Scolaire Face au Multiculturalisme et au Racisme.* Toronto: Association Canadienne d'Éducation.

Laperrière, A. 1983. *L'Intégration Socio-scolaire des Enfants Immigrants dans les Écoles de Milieux Socio-économiques Faibles: Une Recherche Exploratoire.* Montréal: Conseil Scolaire de l'Ile de Montréal.

Lawrence, P. R., and J. W. Lorsch. 1967. *Organization and Environment.* Cambridge, Mass.: Harvard Graduate School of Business Administration.

Latif, G. 1988. *L'École Québécoise et les Communautés Culturelles.* Rapport déposé au bureau du sous-ministre, Gouvernement du Québec: Ministère d'Éducation du Québec.

Lessard, C. 1987. Equality and inequality in Canadian Education. In R. Ghosh and D. Ray, eds. *Social Change and Education in Canada.* Toronto: Harcourt Brace Jovanovich.

Mallea, J. R. 1984. Cultural diversity in Canadian Education: A review of contemporary developments. In Samuda, Berry, and Laferrière, eds. *Multiculturalism in Canada, Social and Educational Perspectives.* Toronto: Allyn & Bacon.

McAndrew, M. 1987. Relations inter-ethniques et implication du système scolaire public dans l'enseignement des langues d'origine: Une analyse comparative du "Heritage Languages Program" en Ontario et du programme d'Enseignement des langues d'origine au Québec. Ph.D. thèse, Faculté des Etudes Supérieures, Université de Montréal.

McLeod, K. A. 1984. Multiculturalism and multicultural education: Policy and practice. In Samuda, Berry, and Laferrière, eds. *Multiculturalism in Canada. Social and Educational Perspectives.* Toronto: Allyn & Bacon.

Ontario Ministry of Education. 1979. *Special Populations in Education.* Toronto: OME.

Noble, H. (n.d.). Letter. Policy Analysis and Research Branch, Ontario Ministry of Education.

Porter, J. 1975. Ethnic pluralism in Canadian perspective. In N. Glazer, and D. P. Moynihan, eds. *Ethnicity, Theory and Experience.* Cambridge, Mass.: Harvard University Press.

Porter, J., M. Porter, and B. Blishen. 1982. *Stations and Callings: Making It Through the School System.* Toronto: Methuen.

Rocher, G. 1976. *Le Multiculturalisme Comme Politique d'Etat.* Rapport de la Conférence-Deuxième. Conférence Canadienne sur le Multiculturalisme, Approvisionnements et Services Canada.

Secretary of State of Canada. 1987. *Rapport sur la Participation de Divers Groupes Ethniques à l'Enseignement Postsecondaire.* Ottawa.

_____. 1988. *Multiculturalism . . . Being Canadian.* Ottawa: Minister of Supply and Services Canada.

Shamai, S., and P. D. Corrigan. 1987. Social facts, moral regulation and statistical jurisdiction: a critical evaluation of Canadian census figures on Education. *The Canadian Journal of Higher Education* 12(2): 37-58.

Statistics Canada. 1987. *1986 Census.* Ottawa: Minister of Supply and Services.

Sylvain, L., L. Laforce, and C. Trottier. 1985. *Les Chemisements Scolaires des Francophones, des Anglophones et des Allophones du Québec au Cours des Années 70.* Québec: Dossier 24 du Congres de la Langue Française.

Toronto Board of Education. 1980. *Every Student Survey.*

Wilson, J. D. 1984. Multicultural programs in Canadian Education. In Samuda, Berry, and Laferrière, eds. *Multiculturalism in Canada. Social and Educational Perspectives.* Toronto: Allyn & Bacon.

EDUCATIONAL INTEGRATION OF
IMMIGRANTS IN ISRAEL

Yaacov Iram

Migration is an international phenomenon that has been examined extensively by historians and social scientists. It has changed ethnic, racial, and social compositions and altered political and economic structures in many countries. Large scale immigration was responsible for the creation of nation states like the United States, Canada, and Australia (Eisenstadt 1954). Israel continues to encourage Jewish immigration and depends on it for its future development and well-being. The "in-gathering of the exiles" and the restoration of the political independence of the Jewish people in their ancient homeland was and remains the *raison d'etre* of the State of Israel (Halpern 1961, Laquer 1972).

Attitudes of host societies toward immigrants vary from rejection through passive tolerance to encouragement and support, and even to active invitation. Israel's ideology and official policy represent the positive pole of this spectrum. Indeed, the "in-gathering of the exiles" (*kibbutz Galuyot*) was expressed in 1950 in one of Israel's constitutional laws: *the Law of Return* (Eisenstadt 1967, Elazar 1985).

Israel experienced very rapid growth of its Jewish population. Immigration accounted for more than half of the increase between 1948-1977. Indeed, Israel's ethnic composition, religious and cultural character, and its socio-economic structure, were affected profoundly by the various waves of immigration both before and after the establishment of the state in 1948.

509

This chapter outlines the characteristics of immigration to Israel since 1948, the interaction of immigrants with the social and ideological milieu of their host country, and the modes of their integration into the Israel society. It also evaluates the responses of the educational system as it attempted to provide universal, free, and equal education for immigrant children from diverse countries and cultural backgrounds and to integrate them into the host society.

The integration of four groups of immigrants will be discussed here: 1) from Europe before state-hood and during the first three years of Israel's establishment, 2) from the Middle East and North Africa during the 1950s and early 1960s, 3) from the Soviet Union following the Six Day War of 1967 through the 1970s and 1980s, and 4) from Ethiopia during the 1980s.

Five earlier waves of immigration to Israel (Palestine before 1948) had specific characteristics (Bein 1952) but they shared common features. About 90 percent hailed from Europe and were usually young, educated, unmarried, and unaccompanied by parents (who frequently opposed their immigration). Their motivation was ideological: rebellion against Jewish life in the Diaspora and strong Zionist and Socialist aspirations to establish a Jewish homeland and new Jewish society (Eisenstadt 1954). More Jewish immigration from Europe came from 1948 to 1951--mainly survivors of the Nazi Holocaust, displaced persons from the camps throughout Europe, or illegal immigrants who had been banished to transit camps in Cyprus by the British Mandate in Palestine. Although their motivation was not primarily ideological, they shared with their veteran hosts many elements of Jewish-European values, culture, and religious customs and practices. Therefore they were spared most of the cultural shock experienced by other immigrants. Their unity was strengthened when the State of Israel was recognized by the United Nations in 1948.

Mass immigration to the State of Israel differed from the pre-State immigration in its size, the socio-cultural and ethnic (country of origin) composition, and immigrants' motivation. Between May 1948 and the end of 1984 more than 1,750,000 immigrants came to Israel, compared with less than 500,000 to Palestine between 1882 (the first wave of Zionist immigration) and 1948. Immigration peaked from May 1948 to the end of 1951, more than doubling the Jewish population. This influx of immigrants placed the veterans in a minority. Ethnic diversity grew. Immigration to Israel was no longer of selective groups who detached themselves from their native communities out of socialist-Zionist or religious-Zionist ideology, but rather a kind of population displacement of entire Jewish communities.

Oriental Migration and Integration

The large waves of immigrants to Israel during the first decade of its statehood changed the ethnic fabric of Israeli society. Whereas almost 90 percent of the 443,000 Jewish immigrants to Palestine before 1948 hailed from Europe (*Askenazim*) (Bein 1952) more than half of the 1,209,273 arriving between 1948 and 1964 came from underdeveloped, semi-feudal, traditional societies in the Middle East and Northern Africa (*Sephardim*). Through 1967, 50,000 Jews came from Aden and Yemen, about 120,000 from Iraq and more than 350,000 from North Africa. Between 1948 and 1967, the proportion of immigrants from Asian and African nations was 54 to 76 percent, changing the Jewish population of Israel from preponderantly European before 1948 to Oriental by the early 1960s. This "orientalization" became crucial. Having been founded by immigrants from Europe, despite her Middle Eastern geographical location, Israel has always been oriented towards the modern Western civilization with its characteristic elements of rationality, planning, future-mindedness, technological and scientific progress (Kleinberger 1969, Iram 1987).

The immigrants from the Middle-Eastern and North-African countries were of large families, poor, many with no formal education or productive occupation. Unprepared for a modern industrially oriented economy, many became disadvantaged socially, politically, and economically within modern Israeli society. The *Sephardim* faced a growing socio-economic gap, mainly in material well-being, occupational distribution, political power, and education (Smooha and Peres 1980, Smooha 1978).

Some aspects of this evolving gap were not an inevitable result of the immigration process and socio-economic or cultural background of the newcomers, but rather an outcome of unrealistic goals and misguided policies of *Mizug-galuyot* (fusion and integration of exiles) which implied rapid modernization and westernization of the Asian-African immigrants (Halper 1985). These policies were supported by the bureaucratic organization and authoritarian procedures of the process of *Klitat Aliyah* (absorption of immigrants) discussed by Eisenstadt (1954, 135-38, 172-81). Indeed, the adoption of the melting pot approach required Oriental immigrants to abandon their "primitive" ethnic cultures in favour of an *Askenazi--* based Israeli culture. This was not just a failure to appreciate the cultural variety of the Oriental immigrants but also ignored the adaptive role that culture plays in the process of immigrant integration. Furthermore, the policy of "population dispersal" (settling of immigrants in development towns in remote areas or housing them in urban homogeneous housing projects) led to geographical and community divisions between immigrants and veterans and created inequalities in educational, occupational, cultural and housing opportunities (Cohen 1970, Klaff 1980).

The ideological principles that guided Israel's policy toward immigrants were based on two sets of values drawn from political Zionism: Jewish nationalism and modern, scientific, technological, and democratic civilization. Absorption and integration of immigrants was not regarded as a formal or technical procedure of occupational and civic adjustment. It was conceived as an ideological process involving simultaneously both *de-socialization* (detachment from previous role sets, status and value systems) and *re-socialization* (adopting a new identity to become a new man/woman) (Bar-Yosef 1980, Cohen 1985). Indeed,

> The oriental immigrants were asked to adopt European culture, their own ethnic cultural heritage was denigrated as contemptible products of diaspora life, or as retrograde superstitions, unworthy of the new modern

Israeli. Veteran Israelis frequently denied that Oriental immigrant groups, such as the Moroccans, even possessed any culture at all. (Cohen 1985, 325)

The pace of absorption and integration varied. European immigrants generally identified with Western cultural, nationalistic and democratic premises, and integrated more quickly and successfully than those from the Middle Eastern and North African countries. Thus, ideological and structural factors combined with the immigrants' cultural backgrounds to produce social, economic, political and cultural inequalities: the opposite of what was intended (Halper 1985).

Israeli society was committed officially to bridge, narrow, and even close the socio-economic gap. It was argued that education should be the main tool for social, cultural, and political integration and for the forging of a unified society out of the diversified ethnic groups. Massive welfare improved the socio-economic status of the oriental immigrants, but did not overcome the continuous correlation between oriental origin, poverty and educational underachievement (Adler 1974, 1984).

Educational Integration and Orientals

Large scale immigration in the 1950s, particularly from North Africa and the Middle East, led to the issue of *disadvantaged* or *culturally deprived* children. The school performance of the disadvantaged was characterized by slow learning, underachievement, and high drop-out rate (Minkovich, Davis and Bashi 1977, Chen, Lewy and Adler 1978). The gap in school achievement between orientals and westerns persisted in the primary school. In the 1976 school year, the gap was about six months to two years (Lewy and Chen 1977). The Ministry of Education and Culture tried four major policies between 1948 and 1988 to cope with the evolving educational gap (Iram 1987). The various measures represent four distinct phases.

From 1948 to 1957, the *formal equality phase* provided free education to a student population which grew by more than 250 percent. The Compulsory Education Law of 1949 provided free education for all children of ages five to fourteen (K-8) and for those aged fourteen to seventeen who lacked elementary education. The State Education Law of 1953 established a uniform curriculum for all (Stanner 1963). It was assumed that formal equality through universal schooling and a uniform, obligatory curriculum for all would facilitate the integration of the new immigrants. This educational policy was consistent with the melting pot absorption policy (Dinur 1958). The persistent scholastic gap between Westerns and Orientals was reflected in the 1956-57 school year when the 55 percent of the school population that was Oriental produced only 13 percent of the secondary academic schools and 18 percent of the vocational schools enrolments (Bentwich 1965, Kleinberger 1969).

Failure to narrow the academic gap in education led to the *compensatory phase* (1958-1968). The low performance of Oriental students was attributed to their "cognitive deprivation" and stimulation deficiencies in their immediate environment. Consequently, compensatory programs introduced cognitive development activities at the kindergartens, grouping and streaming in the elementary school, remedial teaching, prolonged school day and school year for the disadvantaged, and boarding schools for gifted Oriental students. Although these strategies and programs displayed a greater flexibility of the educational system, their overall goal was to change or adapt Oriental students to the existing structure of an elitist educational system that remained largely responsible for the failure of many Oriental students (Smilansky and Smilansky 1967, Kleinberger 1969). By the mid-1960s the educational gap was not closing; the median years of schooling completed for Israelis aged fourteen and over was 5.9 years for Orientals, compared to 9.1 for students of European-American origin (Israel 1963).

To cope with this educational gap, a structural reform was introduced in 1968 that changed the philosophy of the educational system from its uniform procedures and academic content (Adler 1974, Kashti 1978). *The School Reform Act* changed the structure of the educational ladder from 8+4 to 6+3+3. The stated aims of the reform were raising the academic achievement of all students, closing the educational gap between ethnic groups, and encouraging social integration between students of all ethnic origins (Rimalt 1971, Amir et al. 1984). These aims were translated into practice by zoning intermediate schools and busing students in order to achieve ethnic integration; extending free compulsory schooling (K-10); eliminating screening and selection between the primary and intermediate schools; introducing comprehensive schools; extending vocational education; strengthening teacher training; and improving the curriculum of intermediate schools.

The success of the school reform is educationally and socially inconclusive (Amir et al. 1984, Minkovich et al. 1977, Iram 1987). Nevertheless, *Education In Israel in the Eighties* (1976) pointed out that despite progress in academic achievements and social integration, the goal of *equality* in these two areas was not achieved. In 1975, 47 percent of the students in primary schools were defined as "in need of care" (underprivileged) and 95 percent of these were of Asian-African origin. This may be attributed to the high correlation between achievements in school and ethnic origin, which in turn supports the high correlation between socio-economic status and ethnic origin.

Renewed social tension and ethnic protests which deteriorated into street riots in the early 1970s (Shama and Iris 1977, Cohen 1980) marked the emergence of the "new ethnicity" (Cohen 1985). Oriental Jews demanded on their own terms equal status within the emerging Jewish society of Israel. They required recognition of Oriental Jewish culture as *distinct* but *equal* to the Western dominant culture. The shift was from ethnocentrism and monoculturalism toward cultural pluralism in all spheres of society, and particularly in education.

These growing demands for cultural pluralism mark the initiation of the fourth phase in educational policy, the *Educational Welfare Program*. This phase was characterized by intense intervention at all levels of education, the family, and the community including a "Renovation of Neighborhood" program aimed at improved housing conditions and enriched socio-cultural activities for distressed areas (Israel 1976). One of the distinctive features of this phase was the revision of school curricula to include major elements of Oriental Jews' culture, literature, and history.

This most recent phase marks an explicit departure from the "melting pot" concept of *Mizug Galuyot* (integration of the exiles) dominated by Western ethnoculturalism toward cultural diversity and group particularity (Iram 1987, Masemann and Iram 1987).

At this stage of educational policy *vis-à-vis* multiculturalism, two new and distinctive groups of immigrants arrived in Israel: Jews from the USSR in the 1970s and Ethiopia in the 1980s. The immigration of these two unanticipated groups provided a stiff test of Israel's immigration policy.

Soviet Jews: Migration and Integration

Between 1968 and 1985, about 165,000 Jews from the USSR arrived in Israel. The majority of them arrived in two waves: some 82,000 in 1972-74 and about 37,000 during 1978-80 (Gitelman 1982). They came from diverse parts of the Soviet Union, and from different Soviet and Jewish subcultures. They differ in their Jewish religious traditions and commitment to its practice, in culture, educational level, occupations, and family size (Gitelman 1982, Horowitz 1986). Those from the Soviet heartland (mainly from Moscow and Leningrad) were more acculturated to the dominant Russian culture and generally occupied higher status in Soviet society. As a result of their Sovietization, they forfeited most of their Jewish identity (like the Yiddish language) and only the older members cared about Jewish traditions in their daily life. The second group came from the Baltic States, Moldavia, Western Ukraine (Galicia), and Byelorussia, which together with Poland, Romania and Slovakia, were centers of Jewish religious, cultural, political and social life from 1919-39. Since Baltic Russia, Galicia, and Moldavia were absorbed into the Soviet Union after 1939, their Jews have a higher level of Jewish knowledge and consciousness, including Yiddish, than those of Russia proper (Iram 1985). The third group came from the non-Western and less developed areas of the Soviet Union: Georgia, the Caucasus, and Central Asia, where the Jewish traditions and religion have survived more than in the European parts of the Soviet Union.

Emigration from the Soviet Union stemmed from a combination of "negative" and "positive" motives. Jews felt rejected, discriminated against, or limited in their civil rights, and they were attracted by ideology, national, or religious motives to Israel (Gitelman 1982). The process of adjustment of the immigrants and their final absorption into Israeli society are affected both by their origins and by their motives for migrating to Israel (Horowitz 1986).

Successful absorption is a multidimensional process which depends on various adjustments--economic, social, political, cultural, and educational. The Soviet immigrants from Europe and those from the Caucasus and Central Asia were successfully absorbed into Israel's economic system. Their value system of motivated workers and their professional skills, both integral components in the process of socialization in the Soviet Union, account for their adaptability to Israel's technological society (Israel 1982).

The social integration of the Soviet immigrants appears to be more problematic. About one-fourth of the Soviet immigrants were *"Bukharan"* Jews, from Georgia, Uzbekistan, Tadzhikistan and Kazakhstan. The Georgian immigrants insisted on living among other Georgians and close to members of their extended families, which prolonged their linguistic and social isolation from the Israeli society. However, after five years of residence in Israel, about two-thirds of all immigrants from the Soviet Union were satisfied with their social life in Israel. However, when asked to compare it with their satisfaction with their previous social life, 60 percent of those from the European USSR and 75 percent of the non-European Soviets claimed their previous social life was better (Israel 1982).

Another area of difficulty in adjustment is the political sphere which includes direct participation in the political process and attitudes toward political authority. The problems in political integration stem from the differences between the Soviet and Israeli political systems. Being socialized in the Soviet Union, it is difficult for most of the immigrants to appreciate the plurality of the Israeli system (Gitelman 1982). Also, they are confused in dealing with the authorities and absorption bureaucracy--repeating the difficulties of Oriental immigrants in the 1950s. Georgian immigrants felt particularly discriminated against by the absorption authorities.

Cultural absorption is determined by the degree of the immigrants' linguistic acculturation, satisfaction with their lives in their new environment, and identification with the absorbing society. Although 90 percent of the immigrants declare that they are attached to Israel, only 50 percent *feel* Israeli. Compared to earlier waves of immigration of Oriental Jews, the Soviet immigrants' economic, social and cultural absorption was successful, although their social and cultural integration was somewhat delayed (Israel 1982).

Educational Absorption of Soviet Immigrants

The educational absorption of immigrant children from the Soviet Union into the Israeli school system is the most important reflection of their demographic and geographic heterogeneity, as well as their degree of modernization and Sovietization. Students from European regions or republics of the USSR have not encountered major academic difficulties at school, and in the natural and physical sciences they sometimes had an advantage over their veteran peers. After a short adjustment most of them perform well, not only in the scientific subjects but also in the humanities (Horowitz and Frenkel 1976). Thus it is rather the social and cultural environment which presents problems of adjustment to the students and not the school itself. The differences in the social context in which the Soviet and Israeli school systems operate presents most of the difficulties for the Soviet immigrant students (Bronfenbrenner 1970). As a result of Soviet socialization, the immigrant students face social and psychological problems: conflicts between loyalty to their family that rejected the system and allegiance to the Soviet society created by socialization at school. In addition to this identity conflict, they face a contrast between the collectivist orientation of the school and society in the USSR and the individualistic orientation and personal responsibility which dominate Israeli schools. These differences are expressed in dissonances and confusions in their interactions with teachers, peers, and parents.

The adjustment difficulties of immigrant children from the southern and central Asian republics, Georgia, the Caucasus, and Bukhara are different. They have not experienced an intense communist socialization. Their difficulties arise mainly from the transition from a rather traditional, family-oriented environment into an open, modern society. Thus their social, cultural, and educational problems are similar in many respects to those of the Oriental immigrants in the 1950s: low social and occupational status and a lack of self-esteem. All these traits, when coupled with low levels of motivation, result in low achievements in school (Izikovich and Adam 1981). Researchers assume that the failure of the educational system to cope with immigrant youngsters from these three Soviet communities may be explained by its neglect of their unique cultural characteristics. Awareness of the differences among the immigrants from the various republics and regions of the Soviet Union would lead to an understanding of how different cultural backgrounds affect abilities to cope scholastically and socially with school and its environment (Hanegbi 1984, Lieblich, Ben-Schachar, and Raz 1979). Thus differentiated curricula and methods of instruction which are relevant to the background of these students should be designed and employed to enhance their social and educational integration.

Ethiopian Migration and Integration

Ethiopian Jews (sometimes called *Falasha*, which in the *Geuze* language means foreigner, outlaw, or exiled and therefore has a derogatory connotation) arrived in Israel in small groups during the 1960s. Because of their isolation from mainstream Judaism they have never received the Talmud: namely the religious law of normative Judaism (Kessler 1982, Messing 1982, Rapoport 1983). They celebrate those holidays that are mentioned in the Torah but not others like Hanukka. Indeed there were doubts among the religious authorities about whether they were to be considered Jews. It was only in 1973 that the chief Sephardic Rabbi of Israel decreed that they are indeed Jews. This recognition was formalized by the State by declaring Ethiopians Jews eligible to immigrate to Israel under the Law of Return. Between 1980 and 1985, some 14,000 immigrants from Ethiopia arrived in Israel. More than half of them arrived during "Operation Moses" from November 1984 through February 1985, when press disclosure halted the operation that had been conducted in secrecy[1].

Israel's experience with integrating immigrants from various backgrounds into the fabric of the emerging Israeli society showed that various waves of immigrants experienced difficulties. However, the Ethiopian immigrants differ from the Israeli society more than most other immigrant groups of the first forty years of Statehood. The most obvious differences between the Ethiopian immigrants and their host society was in their appearance (black skin), religious concepts and practices of Judaism (Abbink 1985), and the cultural and social gap between their society of origin--tribal-rural-traditional, underdeveloped (economically and occupationally)--and the urban-modern-industrialized Israeli society. Another difference is in the political culture--a military dictatorship with a marxist orientation in Ethiopia contrasted with Israel's western democracy. All these contribute to a "cultural shock" which many Ethiopian immigrants experienced. Indeed the absorption process of the Ethiopians is more complex (Newman 1985). It was agreed that absorption of the Ethiopians must not repeat the mistakes of the 1950s (the misguided absorption policies practised during the mass oriental immigration from Middle Eastern and North African countries) (Ashkenazi 1985). Thus the stated policy is "guarding the status and dignity of the elders of the community, encouraging traditional art, and helping the people to preserve their culture" (Donyo 1983, 7).

---

[1] The collapse of the Ethiopian regime in 1991 led to Israel rescuing the remaining Falashas.

Consequently, the absorption process of the Ethiopian immigrants provided both social and educational services from preschool through adult education, extending over a two-year period. Upon arrival, immigrants are taken to "absorption centres" with a protected orientation environment where the immigrants rest from the hardships of their travels from Ethiopia. During their one-year stay in the "absorption centre" they are assisted in securing information about relatives from whom they may have been separated, receive initial medical evaluation and treatment, and acquire gradually information about life in Israel. At the Centre they learn Hebrew and basic essential skills necessary for living in a modern society: how to run a household, shop, practice health hygiene, use appliances, and care for infants. The second year is devoted to gradual integration of the immigrants into the community. During this year they are moved to permanent housing. They are still followed by an absorption team of social workers and educators who are responsible for preparing both the immigrants and the absorbing community. During this period, immigrants are trained in vocational courses and meet with potential employers (Iram and Bernstein-Tarrow 1986).

Ethiopian Educational Absorption

The educational absorption of the Ethiopian children differs dramatically from that of the past. A substantial number of children, arriving without both or one of their parents, were placed in Youth-Aliyah boarding houses. They live and study in youth villages until completion of secondary schooling. In 1985 there were about 2,000 such youngsters (Gordon 1985). Most of the Ethiopian immigrant students were illiterates or semi-literate. Though they had a high learning potential and high motivation, they lacked learning habits and had difficulties in space and time orientation because of their peasant background. Some had never attended school, others had learned only in groups by recitation and memorization. High motivation and ambition to succeed at school sometimes resulted in stress. New approaches were needed to educate Ethiopian children-- reflecting sensitivity to their special needs during the different stages of their social and educational absorption, so all of them have been directed to the religious track of the state schools for their first year in the country. After this year, they are free to transfer. This decision was reached in consultation with the *Kessim*, the religious leaders of the Ethiopians, in the hope that the children might fill the gap in their knowledge of normative Judaism and minimize the difficulties of transition from a traditional religious society to a modern secular environment. Another policy was to integrate pre-school and kindergarten children into regular classrooms, but place primary school students into *kitot kelet* (absorption classes) for at least one year, or until they have acquired basic knowledge of Hebrew. Mainstreaming these students was left to the individual principal.

Some curricular units and materials were designed specifically for Ethiopian students. Efforts were made to produce some basic textbooks and teachers' guides to relate Jewish Ethiopian traditions and lifestyles to all students in the educational system, and particularly in schools where these students attended (Israel 1985). An attempt was also made to prepare teachers for these classes. Half of the teachers of "absorption classes" attended special in-service training, but only 10 percent of those who taught Ethiopian students in regular classes had such a training. Attempts were also made to involve Ethiopian parents in school and the community through adopt-a-family projects (Golan, Horowitz, and Shefatya 1987).

The Ministry of Education and Culture realized that educational absorption of immigrant students is a multi-dimensional process: linguistic, cultural, social, and school adjustment. In the case of the immigration from Ethiopia more than in previous occasions, it tried to adopt this comprehensive and "total" approach, with a certain degree of success (Friedman 1986). However, some of the problems stem from the Ethiopian Jews' relationship with normative Judaism represented in Israel by the chief Rabbinate. These relations are sometimes very problematic and even painful because of the demand that the immigrants undergo a ritual ceremony, with symbolic conversion (interpreted by the religious establishment as a symbolic reestablishment of long severed links between Ethiopian and other Jews). This demand is viewed by some

Ethiopians as casting doubt on their Judaism--a difference which was eventually resolved by the rabbis' mitigation of their demand to merely a ritual immersion. There is also a sense of disappointment that (despite declared policies) very little has been done to preserve and retain traditional Ethiopian elements of culture, folklore, and religious ceremonies in daily life and education except the celebration of the *SEGED* which is a religious celebration of "Return to Zion" (Abbink 1983).

Conclusion

The changing nature of immigration to Israel since 1948 has made it imperative to change strategies of absorption and also to modify educational policies. The educational absorption of immigrants requires a combination of quality and equality of educational opportunities for all, and especially for "underprivileged" groups of immigrant children (Orientals in the 1950s and 1960s, Georgians in the 1970s and Ethiopians in the 1980s). The continuous flow of students from extremely different backgrounds posed a challenge to the integrity of the educational system, stimulating ideological, conceptual, administrative, pedagogical, and curricular changes and sometimes even radical transformation. The Ethiopian phase of educational absorption raised anew the issue of the proper balance between the need to preserve unique lifestyles and religious practices, which are different from those of Oriental and Western Jews, in order to facilitate the adjustment of the Ethiopian immigrants to Israeli society. This brought to light the need to find suitable ways to strengthen the principle of cultural pluralism, which will enable fruitful coexistence between the uniqueness of various groups and the common elements and characteristics of the emerging Israeli society.

The adoption of flexible and imaginative strategies in the process of socioeconomic, cultural, and educational absorption of immigrants might be crucial to the success of Israeli society in dealing with new immigrants in the 1990s from Ethiopia and potential mass immigration from the Soviet Union.

References

Abbink, J. 1983. Seged celebration in Ethiopia and Israel: Continuity and change of a Falasha religious holiday. *Anthropos* 78: 789-810.

_____. 1985. An Ethiopian Jewish "Missionary" as cultural broker. *Israel Social Science Research* 3: 1-2, 21-32.

Adler, C. 1974. Social Stratification and Education in Israel, *Comparative Education Review* 18(February): 10-23.

_____. 1984. School integration in the context of the development of Israel's educational system. In Amir, Sheran, and Ben-Ari, eds. *School Desegregation--Cross Cultural Perspectives*. Hillsdale, New Jersey: Lawrence Erlbaum Associates.

Amir, Y., S. Sheran, and R. Ben-Ari, eds. 1984. *School Desegregation--Cross Cultural Perspectives*. Hillsdale, New Jersey: Lawrence Erlbaum Associates.

Ashkenazi, M. 1985. Studying the students. *Israel Social Science Research* 3: 1-2, 85-96.

Bar-Yosef, R. 1980. Desocialization and resocialization: The adjustment process of immigrants. In E. Krausz, ed. *Migration, Ethnicity and Community*. New Brunswick, New Jersey: Transaction Books.

Bein, A. 1952. *Return to the Soil--History of Jewish Settlement in Israel*. Jerusalem: Zionist Organization.

Bentwich, J. 1965. *Education in Israel*. London: Routledge and Kegan Paul.

Bronnbrenner, U. 1970. *Two Worlds of Childhood, U.S. and U.S.S.R.* New York: Russell Sage Foundation.

Che, M., A. Lewy, and C. Adler. 1978. *Process and Outcomes in Education: Evaluating the Contribution of the Middle School to the Educational System.* Tel-Aviv University and the Hebrew University (Hebrew).

Cohen, E. 1970. Development towns: The social dynamics of "planted" urban communities in Israel. In S. N. Eisenstadt, R. Bar-Yosef, and C. Adler, eds. *Integration and Development in Israel.* Jerusalem Universities Press.

_____. 1980. The black panthers and Israeli society. In E. Krausz, ed. *Migration, Ethnicity and Community.* New Brunswick, N.J.: Transaction Books.

_____. 1985. Ethnicity and legitimation in contemporary Israel. In E. Krausz, ed. *Politics and Society in Israel.* New Jersey: Transaction Books.

Dinur, B. 1958. *Values and Ways.* Tel-Aviv: Urim (Hebrew).

Donyo, O. 1983. *Considerations in Determining the Absorption Policy of Ethiopian Immigrants.* Alim (Hebrew).

Eisenstadt, S. N. 1954. *The Absorption of Immigrants.* London: Routledge and Kegan Paul.

_____. 1967. *Israeli Society: Background, Development and Problems.* London: Weidenfeld and Nicolson.

Elazar, D. J. 1985. Israel's compound policy. In E. Krausz, ed. *Politics and Society in Israel.* New Jersey: Transaction Books.

Friedman, I. 1986. Social and educational aspects in the absorption of Ethiopian immigrants. *Ethiopian Jews and Their Absorption in Israel: Findings, Lessons, Bibliography and Abstracts.* 2d ed. Jerusalem: Henrietta Szold Institute.

Gitelman, Z. 1982. *Becoming Israelis: Political Resocialization of Soviet and American Immigrants.* New York: Praeger.

Golan, P., T. Horowitz, and L. Shefatya. 1987. *The Adjustment of Student Immigrants from Ethiopia to the School System (Report 230).* Jerusalem: The Henrietta Szold Institute and the Hebrew University (Hebrew).

Gordon, U. 1985. The Ethiopian Era. *Youth Aliyah Bulletin* (June): 3-5. Jerusalem.

Halper, J. 1985. The absorption of Ethiopian immigrants: A return to the fifties. *Israel Social Science Research* 3: 1-2, 112-136.

Halpern, B. 1961. *The Idea of the Jewish State.* Cambridge, MA: Harvard University Press.

Hanegbi, R. 1984. The immigrant youngster from the Caucasus: Coping with his new environment, *Integration of Immigrant Adolescent.* Jerusalem: Youth Aliya.

Horowitz, T. R., ed. 1986. *Between Two Worlds: Children from the Soviet Union in Israel.* Lanham, MD: University Press of America.

Horowitz, T. R., and E. Frenkel. 1976. *Adjustment of Immigrant Children to the School System in Israel.* Jerusalem: The Henrietta Szold Institute (Hebrew).

Iram, Y. 1985. The persistence of Jewish ethnic identity in interwar Poland and Lithuania, 1919-1939. *History of Education* 14(4): 273-282.

_____. 1987. Changing patterns of immigrant absorption in Israel: Educational implications. *Canadian and International Education* 16(2): 55-72.

Iram, Y., and N. Bernstein-Tarrow. 1986. Differing models of immigration absorption and acculturation: North America, the Middle East and Africa. Paper presented at the 30th Annual Conference of the Comparative and International Education Society, 13-16 March, Toronto.

Israel, Central Bureau of Statistics. 1963. *Language, Literacy and Educational Attainment.* Jerusalem: Government Printer.

_____. 1982. *Survey on Absorption of Immigrants, Five Years after Immigration.* Ministry of Immigration Absorption Jerusalem: Government Printer (Hebrew).

Israel, Ministry of Education of Education and Culture. 1976. *Education in Israel in the Eighties.* Jerusalem (Hebrew).

_____. 1985. *Yachad Shivtei Israel* (Uniting the Tribes of Israel). Jerusalem (Hebrew).

Izikovich, R., and V. Adam. 1981. The social absorption in school of immigrant youngsters from the Caucasus. *Iyunim Behinuch* (Studies in Education). Vol. 39 (Hebrew).

Kashti, Y. 1978. Stagnation and change in Israeli education. *Comparative Education* 14(June): 151-161.

Kessler, D. 1982. *The Falashas: The Forgotten Jews of Ethiopia.* London: George Allen and Unwin.

Klaff, V. Z. 1980. Residence and integration in Israel: A mosaic of segregated peoples. In E. Krausz, ed. *Migration, Ethnicity and Community.* New Jersey: Transaction Books.

Kleinberger, A. F. 1969. *Society, Schools and Progress in Israel.* Oxford: Pergamon.

Laquer, W. 1972. *A History of Zionism.* New York: Holt, Rinehart and Winston.

Lewy, A., and M. Chen. 1977. Differences in achievements: A comparison over time of ethnic group achievements in Israeli elementary school. *Evaluation in Education* 1: 1.

Lieblich, A., N. Ben-Schachar, and N. Raz. 1986. Learning and adaptation problems of children from the Caucasus mountains in Israel. In Horowitz, ed. *Between Two Worlds: Children from the Soviet Union in Israel.* Lanham, MD: University Press of America.

Masemann, V., and Y. Iram. 1987. The right to education for multicultural development: Canada and Israel. In N. Bernstein- Tarrow, ed. *Human Rights and Education.* Oxford: Pergamon.

Messing, S. 1982. *The Story of the Fallashas.* New York: Balshon.

Minkovich, A., D. Davis, and Y. Bashi. 1977. *Evaluation of the Educational Achievements of the Elementary School in Israel.* Jerusalem: The Hebrew University.

Newman, S. 1985. Ethiopian Jewish absorption and the Israeli response: A two way process. *Israel Social Science Research* 3(1-2): 104-111.

Peres, Y. 1976. *Ethnic Relations in Israel.* Tel-Aviv: Sifriat-Hapoalim and Tel-Aviv University (Hebrew).

Rapoport, L. 1983. *The Lost Jews: Last of the Ethiopian Falashas.* New York: Stein and Day.

Rimalt, E., ed. 1971. *The structure of the elementary and secondary education in Israel.* Report of the Parliamentary Committee on the Structure of Education in Israel. Jerusalem: The Knesset (Hebrew).

Shama, A., and M. Iris. 1977. *Immigration Without Integration: Third World Jews in Israel.* Cambridge: Schenkman Publishing Company.

Smilansky, M., and S. Smilansky. 1967. Intellectual advancement of culturally disadvantaged children: An Israeli approach for research and action. *International Review of Education* 13: 410-431.

Šmooha, S. 1978. *Israel: Pluralism and Conflict.* London: Routledge and Kegan Paul.

Smooha, S., and Y. Peres. 1980. The dynamics of ethnic inequalities: The case of Israel. In Krausz, ed. *Migration, Ethnicity and Community.* New Jersey: Transaction Books.

Stanner, R. 1963. *The Legal Basryis of Education in Israel.* Jerusalem: Ministry of Education and Culture.

SECTION V

CONCLUSION: SCHOOLING

AND TEACHER EDUCATION

AN ASSESSMENT, IMPLICATIONS FOR SCHOOLING AND TEACHER EDUCATION

Douglas Ray and Deo H. Poonwassie

The Social Context: A Summary and Evaluation

Inequality is more likely than not, both in society and education. It arises from many agencies that are more or less immune to the activities of the school: the family, the workplace, the media, the neighborhood acquaintances, casual conversations . . . These influences of society cannot be overcome by an agency of the state, nor by a particular non-governmental organization like a religious group, nor by an independent community or business operation. On the other hand, limitations on the effectiveness of education are not an excuse for doing nothing. The schools can do more than most agencies.

The educational questions and educational disadvantages of minorities deal with five relationships.

1) What schooling is appropriate for minorities to preserve their identity but not isolate them from the majority populations of their nation?

2) How can the minority populations interact successfully with the host populations--especially if the latter are blind to minority interests and rights?

3) What must be learned about minorities and their rights by all children as part of their basic education concerning their civic responsibilities?

4) What steps can be taken in school policy, the curriculum, teacher education, and evaluation to support the required level of autonomy?

5) Who must take these steps, in addition to seeking the necessary resources?

Various nations provide some partial answers and suggest methods that can be pursued by education. These suggestions are drawn from a range of conditions, various political and religious perspectives, and a mixture of research and practical experience by men and women in widely differing societies.

These varied perspectives are presented as suggestions for educational policy, particularly in schooling and teacher education. The conclusions here are stated boldly as a means of stimulating further analysis. They are keyed to one or more chapters that explore the theme in depth.

Unity is Often Unrealistic

Many nations want to reduce diversity. The attitudes of Israel to its "exiles" illustrate well the conflicting concerns: the desire to reunite all of the Diaspora and the need to retain social cohesion in Israel. This cultural conditioning regards particular groups of migrants as "difficult to assimilate," and some Israeli governments (and some educators) have not accepted the right of certain Jews to reject assimilation on imposed terms. Israel demonstrates the dilemma more easily because of the enormous significance of migration to the present and future composition of that nation. As in other nations, the local "tradition" is usually defended and imposed for all--even although the tradition has taken its present form during the last two generations and continues to change.

In other nations similar patterns exist. If current tendencies for assimilation persist, the outcome for some *peoples*[1] that exist only or mainly as minorities in other nations

---

[1] *Peoples* are cultural or ethnic groups that exist in law as separate and unique societies, perhaps with transborder territories or despite dispersion from various causes. A people does not cease to exist because their schools are closed by an unsympathetic government.

will be cultural genocide. Where many of the minorities begin as refugees (as in Sudan and several nations that are not part of this collection) there may be a very slow integration until the future location of such minorities can be established.

Other minority populations will not succeed in achieving guaranteed futures in states that seek to integrate them. Britain, Germany, the USSR, Sudan and India illustrate some of the problems, even where the populations have lived in that region for generations, often independently from migration.

Aboriginal Education is a Special Case

The ideas about what is desired by the current majority of a nation may not persuade the Aboriginal population, and they are a people with a special right. Their choices for education do not necessarily render them inferior. Indices of quality introduced for the rest of society may not properly apply in the Aboriginal sector.

Svennson notes that the Sámi have successfully pressed for more control of their children's education but not confined this to a single system. However, as the choice of Sámi schools is gradually expanded, every part of these new systems protects the ancient traditions without freezing the Sámi community into reindeer herding and similar pastimes. The costs for educating the Sámi in these circumstances are not detailed, but the relatively prosperous Scandinavians believe that there is an obligation for society to permit their oldest separate peoples to evolve while maintaining the part of their traditions that they still value.

The theme of parental choice is echoed by Smith in his account of recent changes for New Zealand Maori and is suggested by Jordan in her account of social, political, economic, and educational conditions for the Australian Aborigine.

Language Influences Educational Opportunity

Smith and Svennson indicate that early reinforcement of traditional language seems to be the major factor in reinforcing cultural identify. If the mother tongue is secure from childhood,

536 Schooling and Teacher Education

if the family is free to use it whenever convenient, the cultural pride of identity enables the child to learn a great deal about other societies, their languages and their techniques of science and government--concepts that presumably undermine some of the traditional means by which their people manipulated their resources and ordered their societies.

The impact of language on the curriculum and expectations of education are discussed further in the cases of Canada, China, Sudan, Germany, and the Spanish Basques. In these situations the size of the language community makes an important difference as to how completely and how long the separate instruction will be proffered. As Jordan notes for Australia, there may be dozens of Aboriginal languages over a huge area and some compromises must be made. Again, unity is unrealistic.

Religion May Be the Key to Cultural Identity

In some cases religious differences are more important than language or ethnicity and race. India reflects these differences well. Here there is a splendid mixture of indicators that have resulted from centuries of intermarriage and migration, and for most families the most valued and permanent indicator is likely to be religion. The Sudan indicates a similar reliance upon religion, with people regarding language as a tool rather than an instrument of permanent identification.

Of course, despite unity of religion, there may be important groups that may or may not correspond with national boundaries. Divisions within the Christian (German), Islamic (Bahrain), and Buddhist (China) traditions show this capacity.

Efficiency Must Be Maintained

Separate educational communities are only affordable and educationally viable if there is some means of collecting children to achieve a critical mass. Smith indicates that the size of educational "nests" can be very small, but their existence at the inception of formal socialization and education is critical. Svennson traces a system of education culminating with small Sami colleges--some of them boarding where youth form the bonds of the next generation. Poonwassie shows how a combination of itinerant teachers and modern technology can achieve the desired efficiency with widely scattered populations. Binda shows how tiny states can hardly meet this challenge.

Mutual Respect is Prerequisite to Success

Jordan argues that mutual respect is possible between Aborigine and the newcomers now dominating the institutions of Australia. Aborigine welcome knowledge about the other society once it is clear that there will be no more attempts to eliminate them. Ghosh and Talbani indicate that colonial institutions and ideas were more acceptable to an independent nation than could have been foreseen in the days of the Raj. See contrasts the perception by typical U.S. institutions of Americans of different visible minorities. Japanese Americans are secure; African-Americans are not. The widespread expectation of deference (not just difference) maintains grievances.

Minority Leadership Influences Success

All the authors of Aboriginal thinking and programs (Section II) argue that a large measure of decision making should and perhaps must come from the aboriginal community themselves. For example, The Maori, Sámi, Pueblo Navaho (and also the Spanish Basques) have decided independently that a degree of separation is necessary for their cultural survival, and that the transformation of the educational system for the majority is beyond their capacity. Ulster has been hampered because control lies beyond the control of the minority community (Catholics). The *Gastarbeiter* (guest workers) in Germany also must accept what the *Laender* (provinces) provides the system unless an exception is negotiated by a more distant authority: the government of the country that they left, or the European parliament or courts.

The initial steps to survival seem to be the creation of separate schools, with separate curricula, taught by a significant number of minority leaders. Usually majority concepts of evaluation are rejected because they condemn minorities to cope with majority objectives. Astute minorities realize that some such systems are not in their interest and should therefore be resisted. With some reservations and adaptation, these forceful arguments suit local situations which vary widely within several of the nations concerned.

The British experience with open decision making[2] presents problems to minorities, in the opinion of Gundara and Jones. A similar perspective emerged during the 1980s in the United States, with its worst effects being born by the African-American minority.

Traditional Stigmas are Hard to Overcome

Not all stigmatized populations are aboriginal, nor of a different race, religion, language, or ethnic group. All or some of these variables may signal their disadvantage. Franco notes that rural children in Colombia (who are not otherwise distinguishable by race, language, or religion) are systematically disadvantaged in securing education and jobs which depend upon education. They are therefore virtually consigned to a life as peasants, or if they migrate to the cities, as laborers or domestic workers.

Ibrahim describes a similar situation for the Sudan, but notes the congruence of several disadvantaging factors: isolation, minority language or religion, ethnicity, amount and form of income. These factors are less telling than the condition of the parents: their education, income, residence, associates. Even though the state system of the Sudan cannot afford to provide for all, the families with the right ideas and connections ensure that their children attend religious or other independent schools.

---

[2] Actually some centralization of decisions has been introduced in the name of safeguarding children against social promotion, and has made it difficult for minorities to achieve the curricula that would be best for their children. Other educational decisions have not been centralized, enabling bigoted parents or educational authorities to deny equal rights to minority children.

These unequal practices are the modern equivalent of traditions that extend back for generations, and current policies of the government to extend equal opportunity are hampered by lack of resources and the political pressure of the favored citizens to improve the national system qualitatively instead of expanding the numbers served by its lower levels of schools.

Ghosh and Talbani identify the same situation in India, where history records two thousand years of unbroken systematic stigmatization. Religious and cultural traditions are the reason, for ancient families arrogated advantages unto themselves and Hindu society institutionalized the structure as castes. The required social, political, legal, and educational changes have become policy, but are frustrated by the political power of those who would lose advantages if the reforms were completed. Successive governments have tried and failed to institutionalize the changes. In consequence, children of the lower castes, rural and village children, and especially girls, are likely to be deprived of schooling or face an abbreviated and impoverished school experience. Meanwhile, India has some of the world's best schools and universities available to the children of well born and well connected families--the modern version of being Brahmins or (a legacy of the colonial period) Europeans. The society may embrace the principle of equality, but those with the current advantages want their privileges preserved, and education can only whet the appetite of those who are not favored.

See discusses another classic example of systematic disadvantage. Nearly all African-Americans are descended from slaves, who from the time of their "immigration" in chains have known no other nation. For the first century after emancipation, they struggled with inferior segregated schools and virtually no access to higher education. Since 1954, this pattern has been legally forbidden but practised by subterfuge. The current disadvantages of African-Americans are clearly documented: 1) they have about 50 percent of the average income and far higher rates of unemployment; 2) their homes are smaller, more crowded and more costly; 3) their health problems are more numerous and serious--they face inadequate health services, malnutrition arising from poverty, and more drug addictions, all of which lead to shorter life spans; and 4) legal systems typically arrest more African-Americans and sentence them more harshly for crimes committed.

The school systems reflect similar biases. Many communities are *de facto* segregated on the basis of residence, leading to racial differentiation in all related institutions, including schools. African-Americans with significantly better qualifications do not secure equal chances--and this discrimination occurs in schooling for both pupils and teachers.

Differences Become Disadvantages

Differences appear to be objective, however, advantages or disadvantages are partly subjective. Streaming into "inferior" programs is widespread, and the label is usually imposed by the dominant group and accepted as fact by the minority. Drop-out rates by minorities reflect discontent with their facilities, programs, and teachers. Drop-outs are perceived by society as deserving third-rate jobs and structural unemployment. Schools are not a sufficient answer, and recognizing the limitations on what they can accomplish, some minority children have given up.

The choice may be between the general system (state controlled in most cases) or the independent sector. Leadership of the African-American community has come to a critical collective choice: either to join the contest within mainstream America and abandon their cousin African-Americans or to sacrifice personal prospects in a bid to improve the collective situation. Evidently, they will not receive much support from the American majority.

France has a long tradition of providing "opportunities" for the disadvantaged communities of the nation, and recently this practice was extended to (French) settlers throughout the Empire, and then to citizens of the French overseas departments. As these became independent nations, their populations were accorded the right to migrate to France, there to live as citizens. Proud people that they are, some of them refused to become French in all matters, for they believed in the preservation of elements of their own cultures. They distinguished between acquiring the techniques required for life in France and becoming truly French. They recognized that acceptance by the French would be won gradually if at all.

This resistance was met in part by an *ad hoc* modification of the French system of teacher education, responding to local needs and ideas that had not yet been fully explored. A great deal of evaluation of the several programs was necessary, and for the first time the Ministry of Education agreed to this bottom-up form of educational adjustments. There is some doubt that parity of esteem will immediately result.

Two other nations have long standing differences among their populations, but aboriginal status does not fit precisely: even longevity of occupation of particular lands and historical documentation of cultural distinctiveness may not establish an undisputed claim. Both China and the Soviet Union have taken steps to reduce the tensions among their minority populations, where the distinctiveness is likely to be ethnic or linguistic and may be religious as well. During the imperial periods of both China and Russia, there were periodic military expeditions, and recent history has been a mixture of firm limits and encouragement to participate in the national affairs.

Alternatives Become Advantages

A "different" program that is devised by leaders of the minority to serve their ends will have a kinder appraisal, especially by the minority group. These different programs shine in all the aboriginal cases, and also in the Spanish Basques. It may still be labeled "inferior" by those in power, but its effects will not be imposed and may be positive. For example, there is a prospect that "their" program will inspire children to work harder and longer for their educational advancement, and because they feel close to their teachers and share the objectives of schooling, they may participate more actively in the improvement of the system.

Northern Ireland and the Basques of Spain reflect traditions of separate development in the population that have been noted for centuries, and both have educational reforms that have recently become quite positive.

Tarrow notes that the Basques in Spain are no longer politically oppressed and have become economically advantaged. Recently, they have assumed control over much of their educational system and transformed it. The long-run success of their venture depends upon their work, their citizenship contributions, and the consequent attitudes of others.

Hughes deals with the Catholic-Protestant fissure of Ulster. Both groups have important allies abroad to bolster their aspirations and expectations. The relative poverty of Northern Ireland results from low wages and few jobs, burdens which have been foisted disproportionately upon the Catholic sector. Hughes notes that educational justifications for this disadvantage are more fable that reality but there are still some important differences: variations what is typically studied by youth in these two groups; in the drop-out age; and the proportions of youth studying vocational programs. Hughes describes Ulster as a typical poor nation, coping with insufficient numbers of jobs and a British government that is unwilling to relieve the pinch. He dismisses as exaggeration the dangers of life in Belfast.

The educational solutions have included improving the technical quality of the schools for both Catholics and Protestants, and socializing each into a better awareness of the prospects of a shared and humane future. These efforts, Hughes notes, are among the better examples of their types.

Social Programs Beyond Schooling

The work of the schools is often insufficient to reduce discrimination and disadvantage. Some nations (including the United States, Britain and Germany) focus upon the economic advantages that must be provided. Others assume that jobs will be found for all, that incomes will differ in many cases, but that wealth does not equate with well-being.

In some of the early Soviet democratization of culture, systems of writing were devised to preserve the languages that would eventually have perished if all had been required to learn and use Russian. This cultural preservation gave some prominence to the arts and cultural contributions of the minorities, but simultaneously schools were expanded in the scattered populations, became compulsory, and children learned Russian along with their mother tongue. As a result of these efforts, the Soviet Union has one of the highest literacy rates in Asia and Soviet minorities are usually better educated than their counterparts across any particular border. The means by which this was accomplished have been discussed for two generations, and current efforts attempt equal status for minorities.[3]

Chinese current policies are similar. They supplement Chinese studies with minority cultural programs intended to preserve the ethnic minority language and culture. Since few of these regions approach the high levels of attendance and low drop-outs that are usual for Soviet minorities, it is likely that most Chinese minority school leavers are functionally illiterate or shortly lapse into that condition. Unable to compete in the job market of modern Chinese metropolitan society, they are essentially consigned to life in their original province.

Welcoming Newcomers May Be a Good Investment

Some societies have concluded that badly divided societies use their human resources ineffectively, and the costs of suppression and under-utilization far outweigh those of compromise and assistance. During the last few decades Germany developed industrially by adding millions of foreign workers to its domestic population. This enabled the rising demand for industrial and domestic workers to be met despite the division of Germany and the decline in birthrate. The Gastarbeiter came from various Eastern and Southern European and nearby Asian nations. They never acquired German citizenship and were originally expected to retire to their nations of birth, and education of their children continued to maintain this fiction, even for those born in Germany. This education of millions of aliens for continued underclass status

---

[3] Russian minorities must learn not only their own language and culture but also that of Russians if they hope to compete successfully. Meanwhile, the Russian majority is free to learn foreign languages, cultures, and the techniques that enable them to compete for the prized international and official jobs.

in the wealthiest society of Europe creates ideological and theoretical problems, for it denies elements of the democracy and international reputation that Germany has fostered since 1945. The problem has been compounded since 1989, when the Berlin Wall came down. It was accelerated by German reunification in October 1990.

How can education contribute to the solution of this problem? It must heal the rift developed within a society that Gastarbeiters cannot fully enter as a citizen, nor can their children. A related problem concerns the conferring of German rights to work and education for all arriving from the reunified Eastern Provinces, and perhaps those of German heritage who have lived for years or generations in Eastern Europe. Obviously there are problems of a potential selection among foreign born, foreign status, and perhaps domestic workers who want the same jobs. If the educational/political problem is well handled, it will likely promote a flood of further German immigrants from Eastern Europe. Bahrain shows that some of the same problems exist among the prosperous OPEC of Asia.

The United States offers a contrasting position, for there the long established African-American community receives no preference. All compete for available jobs whether at the low or the high-end of the qualifications scale. Resentment by the displaced African-Americans is understandable but American governments and businesses see the decisions about who to hire (and for that matter, who to admit to citizenship) as matters of seeking the best rather than the first, i.e. previous migrants or native born have no priority over the most recent arrivals-- provided the latter are willing and able to do the work. There is also the long tradition of American acceptance of migrants and provision of some economic opportunities for them.

The American position is theoretically consistent with U.S. treatment of aborigine. Until recently the argument that certain rights accrued from long occupation of the lands was scoffed, and property rights depended upon title deeds and payment of taxes. It is also consistent with international decisions concerning human rights of refugees, but not all the migrants to the United States are refugees. The difficulties of the U.S. position are: 1) economic and humanitarian arguments favor different kinds of migrants/refugees; 2) government services are inadequate for the numbers of persons involved, and 3) governments do not really control the matter for many recent immigrants are illegal, existing if they can in the private sector or in the fringe exchange economy.

The educational programs available in both Germany and the United States vary substantially among states and communities. See discusses some revivals of classical programs which were devised by well-to-do, highly skilled and motivated but unappreciated establishment females of a former era. There are counterpart persons in current society, and the charitable-educational contributions are socially applauded and personally rewarding. See indicates that despite the efforts of today's philanthropists, there is little evidence that these institutions are the best that America could do. Mitter notes that different Laender have programs, each reflecting their local political traditions, so the rational or legal solutions are interpreted in various ways.

Welcoming Migrants is Doing the Right Thing

Are Israeli or Canadian positions really different from those of Germany, Britain, the United States?

Lessard and Crespo examine a complex of research models that suggest that Canada allows newcomers to retain aspects of their cultures; provides limited government funds for this purpose, curbs overt discrimination that might limit opportunities, and affirms the importance of all cultures to the Canadian mosaic. These general principles are given provincial interpretations which perhaps reflect the wealth of that region: the richer provinces rely upon migration. Maybe it pays.

Two recent transformations have come: provinces increasingly select migrants and create the environment for their welcome, and the source of migrants has switched progressively from Europe to Asia, the Caribbean, and Africa. Racism has been adapted to the new situation. Instead of being a measure by which the boundaries were defended against unsuitable immigrants, it has become a tension in the social relations of most cities and some rural communities, particularly where the visibly different newcomers are resented and perhaps feared.

The educational implications of these changes in Canadian society are similarly felt differently by regions. However, the obligation of Canada and by implication of its citizens to avoid discriminatory treatment of any citizen has resulted in periodic legal or human rights tribunals defending the disadvantaged, and racism or religious bigotry is officially reprimanded and forbidden in government policy. Teacher education is strongly affected. Teachers are selected without regard to their ethnic or religious status unless a case can be made for affirmative action, in which case the qualified candidates from the selected category move to the front of the line. Courses include instruction on the non-discrimination policies that must be adhered to, and professors or teachers who fail to maintain these standards face discipline or dismissal.

Iram does not discuss migration as an economic imperative but as a political and religious duty. Once the migrants arrive, the programs of Israel and Canada have similar goals and methods, with education (including schooling) playing an important role.

Implications for Schooling and Teacher Education

The cardinal objective of schooling is to do its best with the available resources. More would always be desirable. Sometimes this maxim prevents the extension of schooling to all members of society, so equality would then suggest that the well-to-do should provide for their own children and that some fair system should determine which poor children go to school. Gender, race, religion, and probably language should be excluded from the selection. Some of the best prepared and therefore most likely to succeed for a given educational investment will not be preferred, but the message conveyed to the rest of society will be one of social justice. This system would fulfill the minimal ideal of equal opportunity.

The second objective of schooling should be to ensure that all children attending have equal prospects of gaining from the education that is offered. Identical programs might turn into very unequal ones, for some of the children might be induced or required to study things which their parents or their culture disapprove. Under these circumstances, the learning may be resisted by the most intelligent children, who will suffer the consequences during evaluation. The solution is to ensure that *equivalent* education is provided where possible, for example with suitable adjustments made on the basis of language, ethnicity, religion and perhaps gender. This system may cost more than a single track schooling, but its effectiveness for children of minorities will be substantially more, and the consequences for society will be a subliminal message of great importance: differences are accepted and met with suitable adjustments *as a right.*

The third objective of schooling is that children should secure equal benefits as a result of their education. That implies that extraneous factors will not be permitted to disadvantage them in the work place, in securing services in society, in seeking leadership roles, nor in the penalties that they might suffer from having inadequate training or preparation. These principles are very difficult and expensive to implement, and most of the required decisions are made by persons who are not necessarily employees of the state so legal action would be required to enforce the policy. Many nations have no mechanism for doing this. Where they exist, such systems are used sporadically, and the rest of society is intended to be instructed by the decision and follow its principle without coercion. Practice evidently lags some distance behind theory in these matters.

Teacher education is important to these notions of equity in education. The teacher is a role model, personally and immediately responsible for both teaching and evaluation, for keeping order among the pupils, and identifying the ideals that children should pursue. This implies that teachers are (or should be) continually assessed for their performance, before they are selected for teacher education, during their pre-service program, as apprentice teachers, and as experienced and emulated teachers in the field.

In-service education is the only solution for another important factor in teaching: changes continue in society, and knowledge that was mastered during the initial professional education is gradually forgotten or outdated. The means by which the in-service education is accomplished may (and probably should) vary with the age of the learner, the technology available, the significance of the changes that have occurred, and the standards that can be mounted. Only with constant and relatively successful attempts to remain current and competent in their work is it appropriate for teachers to be assured of tenure and regular increases in income. If they cannot display this successful and continuing interest in maintaining or improving their own qualifications, they reduce the loyalty of society and their students to them, and without that continuing support, the profession loses standing.

NOTES ON CONTRIBUTORS

NOTES ON CONTRIBUTORS

Aman Attieh was born in Lebanon and studied at the American University of Beirut, and then at the University of Texas. She has taught in Saudi Arabia and at the University of Texas and has consulted for educational planning in North Yemen and Alaska. She has taught, developed and administered language programs in the United States. Her publications include social analyses of Saudi Arabia and interpretations of Arabic literature for English audiences.

Jeannine Bardonnet-Ditte is "*agrégé* in philosophy (a successful candidate at the competitive examination conducted by the State to appoint faculty for colleges and universities). She was Director of the *Ecole Normale* (teachers college) of Paris for ten years, and was in charge of the formation of both national education inspectors and college teachers. She is now the President of the Civic Education Committee in charge of proposing new teaching programs to the National Teaching Programs Council and to the Ministry of Education.

K. P. Binda was born in Trinidad and educated in the Caribbean and Canada. He now teaches at Brandon University, with special responsibility for education in Northern Manitoba. His publications focus on education for development, both in the Canadian North and the Caribbean.

Manuel Crespo was born in Cuba and studied in several universities. He now teaches comparative education and sociology at Université de Montréal, and writes extensively about Latin America and policy issues, centering upon political and sociological questions.

551

Beatriz Franco is Colombian, educated in Bogotá and Canada. She has taught in Colombia and Canada, and is presently a research associate at the University of Western Ontario. Her publications deal with Latin America and cultural diversity.

Ratna Ghosh was born in India and educated there and at the University of Calgary. She is a Professor in the Department of Administration and Policy Studies at McGill University where she teaches sociology and comparative education. She consults extensively on international projects, and is involved in intercultural studies and international administration. She has been President of the Shastri Indo-Canadian Institute. Her publications focus on minority education, women, human rights and education and development.

Jagdish Gundara was born in India and educated in Canada and Britain. He directs the Multicultural Education Unit and teaches at the University of London, with special interest in international education. His publications deal with policy and practice in cultural diversity and human rights, both in Britain and abroad.

Andrew S. Hughes was born in Northern Ireland, and educated there and in Canada. He has taught and administered teacher educational programs in Canada. His publications deal with curriculum and policy issues.

Azza Ibrahim is Sudanese, and was educated at the universities of Khartoum and London. She was an executive in the administration of programs for Sudanese higher education. Her writing has been in policy, especially equity in student finance in higher education.

Yaacov Iram is Israeli, with an international education and extensive travel and research experience. He is Deputy Director of Education at Bar-Ilan University, and Chairman of its Department of Educational Studies. He has been a Post-Doctoral Scholar at the University of Pennsylvania, a Fulbright Scholar-in-Residence at Tufts University, and Visiting Scholar at

Stanford University. His extensive publications deal with higher education and educational policy in their international and comparative perspectives.

Crispin Jones is a lecturer at the University of London, Institute of Education, where his interests are in multicultural education and comparative education.

Deirdre Jordan was educated in Australia and London and is now Chancellor of Flinders University of South Australia. Her extensive writing on minority education centers on the Aboriginal identity and social interaction.

Jacques Lamontagne was born in Montreal and teaches sociology and comparative education at the University of Montreal. He is a gifted linguist, with extensive experience in Chinese education and culture. His publications deal with minority educational policies and the evaluation of programs.

Claude Lessard was born in Quebec and teaches comparative education and sociology of Education at Université de Montréal. He is currently Dean of Education there. A gifted sociologist and linguist, he has documented the educational opportunities of several minorities in Canada.

Linda Lippitt is Director of the Learning Approaches Research Center at the Santa Fe Indian School in Santa Fe, New Mexico. Dr. Lippitt works with teachers and students in language acquisition, learning styles, and curriculum development. Prior to coming to Santa Fe, she developed language acquisition and curriculum programs for Hispanic migrant students in California.

Wolfgang Mitter is Director of the German Institute for International Pedagogical Research in Frankfurt. He is president of the World Council for Comparative Education Societies. His research focusses on European education, notably Eastern Europe, and includes important international studies.

Deo H. Poonwassie was born in Trinidad and educated in the West Indies and Canada. He has taught, researched, and administered programs within Manitoba (Canada), associated with adult education, Native persons in Canada, and teacher education for the Caribbean. His writing has been associated with these interests. He now teaches at the University of Manitoba.

Douglas Ray was born in Canada and educated at Alberta and London. He has taught, researched and developed curricula internationally, with a special interest in cultural differences and human rights in education. He teaches social foundations, multiculturalism, and comparative education at the University of Western Ontario.

Mary Romero is Director of the Gifted and Talented Research Project at Santa Fe Indian School in Santa Fe, New Mexico. The Project is attempting to identify giftedness from a Pueblo community's perspective and to investigate the assessment instruments used in the identification of gifted children. Mary has taught Special Education for seven years and is a Certified Educational Diagnostician. She is a member of Cochiti Pueblo, one of the seven Keresan Pueblos of New Mexico.

Letha A. (Lee) See was born in Oklahoma and was educated at several American universities including Bryn Mawr College. She has lectured nationally and internationally. She now teaches social work at the University of Georgia. Dr. See has a special interest in refugee resettlement and designing international remedial programs through education and social service intervention. Her publications include work on immigration and injustice in the United States.

Graham H. Smith teaches at the University of Auckland. His extensive publications emphasize the education of the Maori. He was a member of the New Zealand government commission on Maori education.

Tom G. Svensson teaches at the Ethnographic Museum of the University of Oslo. He has travelled widely and is an excellent linguist with special interest in aboriginal education worldwide. His publications have been selected for international publications.

Abdulaziz Talbani was born in Pakistan and educated there and in Canada. His research concerns racism and education, and education for development. He is a Ph.D student at McGill.

Norma Tarrow was born in the United States and studied in New York. She has travelled extensively, becoming a good linguist while conducting research in Israel, China, Latin America and Spain. She is an authority on human rights in education. She teaches social foundations and comparative education at the California State University, Long Beach.

INDEX

INDEX